Advances in Software Startups

Nirnaya Tripathi • Henry Edison • Xiaofeng Wang
Editors

Advances in Software Startups

Generative AI, Product Engineering and Business Development

Springer

Editors
Nirnaya Tripathi
M3S Research Unit
University of Oulu
Oulu, Finland

Henry Edison
Blekinge Institute of Technology
Karlskrona, Sweden

Xiaofeng Wang
Free University of Bolzano
Bolzano, Italy

ISBN 978-3-032-04293-4 ISBN 978-3-032-04294-1 (eBook)
https://doi.org/10.1007/978-3-032-04294-1

This Springer imprint is published by the registered company Springer Nature Switzerland AG
The registered company address is: Gewerbestrasse 11, 6330 Cham, Switzerland

Preface

Software startups are one of the most dynamic and influential parts of the global innovation landscape. In recent years, this sector has undergone significant changes due to rapid technological advancements, particularly in areas such as artificial intelligence, data-driven decision-making, low-code/no-code development tools, and automated engineering environments. These developments have created both opportunities and challenges for new ventures seeking to build competitive, scalable, and resilient software products.

What sets today's startups apart from those of the past is their close relationship with cycles of technical innovation. Tools that were once only available to large tech companies are now accessible to small teams with limited resources. The potential of Generative AI (GenAI) to inspire and speed up innovation is widely recognized. In the context of software startups, GenAI can assist during the early stages of the innovation process, from ideation to solution validation. This enables founders with little or no programming experience to brainstorm, prototype, and test new applications in days instead of months. This democratization of innovation has opened doors for a broader range of entrepreneurs, but it has also introduced new challenges in product validation, market fit, and organizational capability.

The field of software engineering research has evolved significantly in its examination of startups. Researchers are focusing on common challenges related to team dynamics, architectural decisions, agility, and customer engagement. Both academia and industry are now interested in understanding the factors that contribute to the success or failure of software startups, as well as how these startups can leverage technological advancements to maintain growth.

This book aims to document, analyze, and share the latest developments at the intersection of engineering, business, and startup strategy. It provides a comprehensive synthesis by combining empirical research, practical experience, and educational approaches to support both academic inquiry and practical application. Rather than being a static collection of knowledge, it serves as an evolving platform for discussion and exploration.

Target Audience This book is designed for a diverse yet interconnected group of readers who are engaged with or affected by software startups:

- Entrepreneurs and startup founders seeking evidence-based strategies, innovative tools, and case studies to support their ventures
- Startup team members, such as developers, product managers, marketers, and designers, seeking to better understand how current trends affect their roles
- Investors and venture capitalists interested in understanding the emerging frontiers that shape startup viability and scalability
- Mentors, advisors, and consultants who play guiding roles in startup accelerators, incubators, or corporate innovation labs
- Educators and academic leaders aiming to develop or refine curricula on entrepreneurship and innovation in a world shaped by rapid digital transformation

Potential Benefits The book provides a comprehensive overview of advances in the software startups topic through academic research, educational practices, and practitioner experiences. Readers will benefit from:

- Up-to-date Insights: Through curated chapters on AI for product innovation, product engineering in startups, business development and growth, and educational innovation, readers will gain access to the latest information on how software startups are evolving.
- Actionable Knowledge: Case studies and experience reports illustrate real-world applications, providing practical frameworks and strategies that can be implemented in a startup context.
- Educational Value: Chapters contributed by educators illustrate how startup-related knowledge is taught, facilitating its transfer to classrooms, workshops, and training programs.
- Cross-disciplinary Perspectives: The book bridges domains of technology, business, education, and social impact, equipping readers with a multidimensional understanding.

As a comprehensive resource, this book is designed not only to inform but also to inspire, enabling readers to engage meaningfully with the challenges and opportunities in the modern software startup landscape. The book consists of the following three themes, each highlighting various aspects of advancements in software startups.

Theme I: Generative AI for Startups GenAI offers substantial potential for startups by transforming essential activities such as ideation, prototyping, and pitching. The chapters in this section present scientific evidence and practical experiences that illustrate how GenAI can be applied in startup operations. They discuss the benefits that have been realized, as well as the challenges that startups may face when adopting GenAI.

Theme II: Product Engineering The challenges of product engineering for new products and services are dynamic and change rapidly as startups grow. Unfortunately, the current state of product engineering in startups is often limited. The chapters included in this theme highlight advanced engineering processes for developing new products and services. This encompasses hypothesis engineering and experimentation for early-stage startups, the role of product management, and the adoption of agile methodologies in the startup context.

Theme III: Business Development and Growth This theme addresses challenges related to business and growth. The chapters within this theme contribute to aspects such as structured decision-making in pricing strategies, entrepreneurial opportunities created by emerging technologies, and the growth of startups supported by ecosystems. Additionally, it examines the internal dynamics of startups during their scale-up phase and highlights educational strategies for nurturing future entrepreneurs for business development.

Prerequisites To effectively engage with the chapters organized by themes in this book, readers are encouraged to have foundational knowledge relevant to each theme's focus areas. For the first theme, GenAI for Startups, readers should have a basic understanding of GenAI technologies, including large language models and prompt engineering, as well as familiarity with startup development processes. In the second theme, Product Engineering, a solid background in software engineering principles is essential. This includes knowledge of system architecture, development practices, and agile methodologies. Familiarity with product management and hypothesis-driven development is also beneficial. In the context of the Business Development and Growth theme, it is essential to understand startup business models, ecosystem support structures, the Lean Startup methodology, pricing strategies, and customer segmentation. A foundational understanding of pedagogical methods, like experiential and project-based learning, is particularly relevant for those interested in entrepreneurial educational strategies.

Acknowledgment We would like to express our sincere gratitude to the ICSOB 2024 Organizing Committee for their invaluable support in hosting the 2nd International Workshop on Advances in Software-Intensive Startups, which took place alongside ICSOB 2024. This workshop served as a catalyst for generating and shaping several foundational ideas for this book. We extend special thanks to Slinger Roijackers (Jansen) and the entire organizing committee for making this event possible. The brainstorming sessions held during the workshop were instrumental in identifying emerging and impactful topics for the book chapters. We also appreciate the enthusiastic contributions of all workshop participants: Asad Ali, Sarra Ben Ltaief, Veronica Dell'Aera, Siamak Farshidi, Marco Mondini, Gijs Oliemans, Frédéric Pattyn, Alex Polyakov, Usman Rafiq, Sergio Rico, Andrey Saltan, Mario Simaremare, Casper Van Schothorst, Triando, and Yueqiang Xu, who participated both in person and online. Thank you all for your valuable insights!

We would like to express our gratitude to the XP 2024 community and the Software Startup Research Network (SSRN) for their continuous inspiration and intellectual engagement. Their influence significantly enhances our understanding of the dynamic landscape of software startups. This indirect yet impactful support has fostered the collaborative and interdisciplinary spirit that is reflected in this book.

Oulu, Finland — Nirnaya Tripathi
Karlskrona, Sweden — Henry Edison
Bolzano, Italy — Xiaofeng Wang

Contents

About the Editors

Nirnaya Tripathi is a senior lecturer and adjunct professor associated with the University of Oulu, specializing in the fields of software startups, entrepreneurship, and innovation management. His research focuses on understanding the dynamics of startups, particularly in the context of software and technology-driven businesses. His work often explores themes such as product development and ecosystem roles within startups, aiming to provide actionable insights that can help new ventures succeed in competitive and rapidly evolving markets.

Henry Edison is a senior lecturer/docent in software engineering at the Blekinge Institute of Technology, Sweden. He has been an ELLIIT recruited faculty member since 2022. His research interests include empirical software engineering in the area of software product innovation, software startups, agility, and AI for software product innovation. His research examines current and future practices and trends of software development processes and tailors them to suit different contexts, from startups and new emerging to large and established organizations. He is actively publishing in leading journals and conferences in the software engineering field.

Xiaofeng Wang is an associate professor at the Faculty of Engineering, Free University of Bozen-Bolzano. She has many years of experience in the research areas of agile and lean software development, software startups, and human aspects in software engineering. She has collaborated with industry, including several multiple-international corporates, in various national and European projects. She is actively publishing in both software engineering and information systems venues. She is also active in serving various conferences related to software development and business.

Chapter 1
Advances in Software Startups: Engineering, Business, and Beyond —Overview

Nirnaya Tripathi, Henry Edison, and Xiaofeng Wang

Abstract Software startups operate in fast-paced and uncertain environments, often facing constraints related to limited resources and experience. This introductory chapter provides an overview of the upcoming chapters of the book that reflect diverse challenges and emerging opportunities that software startups encounter today. This chapter outlines the book's three core themes (Generative AI for startups, product engineering, and business development and growth). Through its 16 chapters, the themes emphasize the importance of Generative AI in startup development, hypothesis-driven development, ecosystem support for startup growth, innovative business models, pricing strategies, and entrepreneurial education. This comprehensive advanced startup knowledge offers researchers and practitioners valuable insights into how engineering, business, and other areas intersect in the evolving landscape of software startups.

Keywords Software startups · Generative AI · Product engineering · Business development · Growth

1.1 Introduction

Software startups are startups in which software plays a central role in the innovations they are working on, typically as the product or service under development [5, 12]. The key characteristics of software startups are limited resources, a lack

N. Tripathi (✉)
M3S Research Unit, University of Oulu, Oulu, Finland
e-mail: Nirnaya.Tripathi@oulu.fi

H. Edison
Blekinge Institute of Technology, Karlskrona, Sweden
e-mail: henry.edison@bth.se

X. Wang
Free University of Bolzano, Bolzano, Italy
e-mail: xiaofeng.wang@unibz.it

N. Tripathi et al. (eds.), *Advances in Software Startups*,
https://doi.org/10.1007/978-3-032-04294-1_1

of experience, and a strong reliance on cutting-edge technologies. [15]. Research indicates that creating viable solutions during the early stages of a software startup is particularly challenging [6, 19]. For example, Giardino et al. [6] examine the most common obstacles faced by early-stage software startups during their initial period. These challenges include technological issues, customer acquisition, securing funding, team development, defining a minimum viable product (MVP), and achieving product-market fit.

Generative AI (GenAI) is the most recent force that is disrupting the landscape of software startups. GenAI refers to artificial intelligence technologies that can create new content [3], including text, images, audio, and video. These technologies utilize advanced machine learning techniques and neural networks to process vast amounts of information and generate original outputs that mimic human-generated content [3]. An increasing number of software companies are utilizing GenAI to streamline their development processes through various forms of task automation, including code generation, test case generation, debugging, deployment, expert replacement, and documentation [8, 9, 14]. Studies also indicate that GenAI has significant potential to foster and accelerate innovations [1, 4]. It can assist companies in the early stages of their innovation initiatives, from ideation to the solution validation phase [4, 16].

However, it is also cautioned that GenAI has various challenges. These include issues such as bias, hallucinations, and the potential for inaccurate responses [8, 9, 14]. Furthermore, privacy violations can occur for various reasons, such as unauthorized use of sensitive information, identity theft, and data leakage. Additionally, AI models are trained on existing data, which often include publicly available materials from the Internet. This raises concerns when GenAI outputs contain copyrighted material, as it remains unclear where the boundaries for fair use lie and when copyright infringement begins. There are also uncertainties surrounding the concept of joint authorship between the user and the AI [7]. The chapters collectively explore how GenAI transforms software startups by enabling task automation in Chap. 2, offering diverse benefits and use cases in Chap. 3, enhancing prototyping and early innovation in Chap. 4, supporting content creation for startup pitching in Chap. 5, and proposing adaptive frameworks for GenAI integration in Chap. 6. At the same time, they acknowledge the challenges of bias, privacy, and ethical concerns that must be addressed to ensure responsible adoption.

Product Engineering The importance of software startups as the main source of innovative software products and services that contribute to global economic growth and competitiveness has been widely acknowledged [18]. However, the challenges of product engineering are highly dynamic and tend to shift rapidly as startups grow and become mature [2]. Unfortunately, the current engineering methodologies provide limited guidance for adapting to these changing conditions or for identifying the most appropriate practices to adopt [10]. Poor choices in selecting engineering practices can result in either over- or under-engineering the product, which in turn may lead to inefficient use of resources and missed opportunities in the marketplace. Within this theme, we have six chapters that investigate the engineering process of new products and services. Chapters 6 and 7 discuss how the experimentation approach can help software startups in tackling uncertainties continuously and systematically. Chapters 8 and 9 reported product management activities in the startup context, including feature prioritization. Chapters 10 and 11 showcase how startups can adopt and adapt agile methodologies to improve the development of new products and services.

Business Development and Growth One of the most important factors for a software startup is having a business development strategy that supports continuous growth and the potential to reach the Unicorn stage. Business development and growth are highly dynamic processes that may involve rapid innovation, various pricing strategies (such as freemium models, dynamic pricing, and pay-per-use), market experimentation, resource management, and the evolution of business models [11, 13]. As software startups often operate in resource-constrained and highly uncertain environments, they often struggle to adapt to shifting customer requirements, evolving technology scenarios, and limited access to investment and skills. As startups develop, they face various challenges, including developing effective pricing strategies, entering new markets, addressing internal organizational challenges, and evolving within their ecosystems [17].

To deepen the understanding of business advancements in software startups, the final theme explores several key aspects of business development and growth through five chapters. It begins with the introduction of a structured pricing canvas in Chap. 13. Chapter 14 focuses on strategic adaptation, demonstrating how existing social business models can be reshaped to transform the traditional education industry. Chapter 15 extends the analysis to the role of ecosystems, examining how external environmental factors influence startup development. Chapter 16 addresses the organizational challenges startups face during scaling. Finally, Chap. 17 highlights the integration of startup-oriented teaching methods into higher education.

In the next section, we will outline the book's structure and provide a detailed overview of its chapters.

1.2 Summary of the Chapters

The book is organized into three main themes and consists of seventeen chapters. The first chapter serves as an introduction to the remaining sixteen chapters. The first theme, GenAI for Startups, contains five chapters (Chaps. 2–6). The second theme, Product Engineering in Startups, contains six chapters (Chaps. 7–12). The final theme focuses on business development and growth in startups, which contains five chapters (Chaps. 13–17).

Chapter 1: Advances in Software Startups: Engineering, Business, and Beyond—Overview
The first chapter, which is this one, provides an outline of the book's chapters and key concepts, such as software startups, GenAI, product engineering, and business development.

Generative AI for Startups

Chapter 2: Generative AI for Startups—A Systematic Mapping Study
The rapid advancement of GenAI technologies has created both opportunities and challenges across various industries. This literature review chapter presents a mapping study designed to provide a structured overview of the current research landscape regarding GenAI in startups. Following established methodological guidelines, the authors identified 21 relevant studies from an initial sample of 236 publications retrieved from four major academic databases. The chapter offers a consolidated view of how GenAI is currently integrated within the startup. The authors aim to inform both scholars and practitioners who seek to understand the strategic and operational implications of adopting GenAI in startup environments.

Chapter 3: The Promise of Generative AI for Software Startups—Potential Benefits and Use Cases
Despite the growing interest in GenAI, its application in software engineering (SE) remains in the early stages. Organizations are still in the process of identifying viable use cases, new tools are constantly emerging, and widely accepted practices have yet to be established. This chapter aims to provide insights from existing research on software startups and recent advancements in GenAI for SE. The authors argue that software startups may be better positioned to adopt GenAI, as some of the typical challenges associated with its adoption are less pronounced in startup environments. Additionally, the chapter outlines current industry use cases based on recent studies and discusses practical considerations for integrating GenAI into startup workflows.

Chapter 4: From Idea to Code—The Evolution of Prototyping in AI-Driven Startups
Drawing from personal experience as both a founder and an advisor to startups, the author of this chapter emphasizes that demonstrating a clear vision, often through a minimum viable prototype, has always been crucial for transitioning from concept to credibility. Traditionally, this process has required technical skills that many business-focused founding teams do not possess. The chapter argues that GenAI could significantly lower the barriers to early validation by enabling non-technical founders to effectively articulate and prototype their ideas. Through this reflective account, the chapter provides insights into how GenAI might transform the early stages of startup development by broadening access to prototyping and changing how technology is utilized during ideation and validation.

Chapter 5: Patterns for Startup Pitch Video Creation with Generative AI Support
Pitch videos are essential for startup founders to effectively communicate their business ideas to external audiences. However, creating high-quality pitch videos can be particularly challenging for early-stage ventures, which often face constraints in time, budget, and creative expertise. This chapter explores the potential of GenAI tools to help overcome these challenges. The authors discuss how the accessibility and efficiency of GenAI technologies can assist startup teams in producing pitch videos more effectively. Additionally, the chapter provides a framework for integrating GenAI into startup communication workflows, aiming to enhance the clarity and impact of pitch videos.

Chapter 6: daBML—An Extension on the "Build Measure Learn" Loop for Generative AI Process Adoption
Startups that wish to adopt GenAI often encounter challenges that existing frameworks, which are typically designed for larger enterprises, do not adequately address. This chapter introduces the daBML framework, an adaptation of the well-known Build-Measure-Learn (BML) loop. The authors demonstrate how to implement the daBML framework through four internal use cases from a later-stage software startup. These examples illustrate the framework's potential to help teams structure their GenAI initiatives, manage associated risks, and evaluate outcomes through iterative and resource-efficient processes.

Product Engineering

Chapter 7: Hypothesis Engineering in Software Startups—From Business to Architecture
Among the many reasons for software startup failure, the lack of a structured development process is a key determinant. A structured process, such as experimentation, enables startups to continuously identify critical product assumptions, prioritize, and test them in a scientific manner. However, research shows that the adoption of experimentation by software startups is limited due to over-emphasis on technical needs without considering the real customer needs. In this chapter, the authors proposed HyMap and ArchHypo, techniques based on hypothesis engineering that translate uncertainties in requirement elicitation and software architecture into hypotheses. The use of HyMap and ArchHypo can help practitioners implement a holistic hypothesis-driven development process and improve their ability to adapt, experiment, and align technical efforts with business goals.

Chapter 8: Experimentation Practices in Indie Game Startups
Experimentation is essential for successful software product and business development, particularly in game startups. These startups require standout qualities that set them apart from competitors. Therefore, it's crucial for them to continuously experiment in order to identify these qualities before running out of time and resources. In this chapter, the authors provide insights and recommendations on how to perform experimentation and game testing in the pre-release stage of game

development. The insights and recommendations are also valuable for startups with value propositions centered around an interactive and satisfying user experience.

Chapter 9: Getting Started with Product Management in Software Startups
The role of product management is well recognized in established and large companies. Product management takes full responsibility for a product's success, from defining product vision and strategy and managing the product development, including its performance once it is released in the market. However, such a role in software startups is not well understood. This chapter shows that the need for a product management function in software startups is evident, such as to avoid a bad product-market fit and adverse responses from early users after the first release. The authors also highlight the most required product management activities in software startups.

Chapter 10: How Does Product Feature Prioritization Work at Software Startups?
Software startups operate with high speed, adaptability, and rapid iterations. In such a dynamic environment, managing and prioritizing the product features becomes more critical. However, existing requirement prioritization techniques are formal and data heavy, which may not align with the fast decision cycles in startups. In this chapter, the authors identify the common requirement prioritization criteria in the startup context. The chapter shows that cost, time-to-market, return on investment, and expected revenue are considered the main criteria for prioritization in startups. Practitioners could reflect on and consider the financial aspects in their prioritization processes.

Chapter 11: AI-Powered Toolchain Framework for Agile Software Development in Startups
Agile principles and values on collaboration, adaptability, and iterative development are considered suitable for startups. These principles allow startups to respond quickly to feedback, deliver incremental improvements, and manage the limited resources effectively. At the same time, the emergence of GenAI enables the automation of repetitive tasks, analyzes data, and supports decision-making. In this chapter, the authors report the investigation of integrating GenAI tools such as GitHub Copilot, ChatGPT, Fireflies, etc., to support agile software development projects. Practitioners are provided with the empirical evidence of GenAI tools in agile projects in the startup context.

Chapter 12: Do Agile Practices Inhibit Innovation?
Agile has been the de facto most adopted development method in software startups. Its adoption usually happens gradually from ad hoc to a more structured, and is not strictly bound to a particular method (e.g. Scrum, Kanban or XP). Based on interviews with startup practitioners in Europe and Asia, the authors investigate how agile methods (i.e., practices, ceremonies, and rituals) leverage software startups' innovation. Practitioners are now provided with evidence that core agile

practices, such as iterative feedback loop, daily standups, and retrospectives, enable startup teams to innovate continuously. On the other hand, overemphasis on sprint completion and switching between sprints hinder innovation. The chapter also provides recommendations on how to adopt agile methods in startup teams.

Business Development and Growth

Chapter 13: Designing an SaaS Pricing Strategy Canvas—Guiding Startups Toward Structured Decision-Making
One of the most complex and strategically significant challenges that startups face is pricing. Many startups struggle to identify and implement effective pricing strategies due to limited resources and inherent market uncertainties. This chapter contributes significantly to the book's overall theme by proposing a scientifically grounded pricing strategy canvas specifically designed for SaaS startups using literature review, expert interviews, and validation workshops. This canvas enables entrepreneurs to make iterative and data-driven pricing decisions. It incorporates elements from established business modeling tools and has been validated through feedback from practitioners, allowing startup founders to systematically evaluate pricing options. By integrating essential business considerations, this canvas provides entrepreneurs with a practical tool to navigate the complexities of pricing decisions.

Chapter 14: From Classrooms to Social Commerce—How 5G Is Turning Educators into Software Entrepreneurs
Traditional perspectives highlight the importance of founders having solid engineering backgrounds. However, this chapter disputes that notion by showing that non-technical founders can thrive in software entrepreneurship. They can achieve this by utilizing their industry knowledge, influence-based business strategies, and new technologies like 5G and AI. The chapter using a SierEDU also demonstrates how educators have adopted 5G technology and the economics of influencers to develop an innovative social commerce platform, transforming their roles from educators to software entrepreneurs. This chapter motivates people from various backgrounds to explore and participate in the software industry today, rather than feeling restricted by a lack of technical skills. The authors stress that while technical skills can provide a significant competitive advantage in some new software ventures, they are increasingly less vital for others, especially in the current era of accessible technology.

Chapter 15: Digital Health Entrepreneurship—A Founder's Perspective on Ecosystem-Supported Growth
Digital health solutions show great potential in enhancing traditional healthcare. However, software startups in this domain often encounter significant challenges, such as intense competition, limited resources, and the necessity for strong support from their ecosystem. This chapter examines and evaluates the key elements of the ecosystem that influence the development and market success of digital health products. These elements include entrepreneurship, market dynamics, finance,

technology, human capital, and supporting factors. The study emphasizes that ecosystem support is vital at every stage of development and provides practical recommendations for professionals in the field.

Chapter 16: Internal Organization of Software Startups During the Scale-Up Process
Many startups are launched, but only a few manage to grow effectively and achieve significant exits. This chapter highlights the importance of understanding the scaling process in this context. By examining three venture-backed software startups that successfully went public with billion-dollar valuations, the chapter uses the Lean Startup framework to explore the scale-up process. It focuses on the internal organization and resource allocation across key functions of software startups during the scaling phase. The chapter reveals trends in revenue growth, job creation, and the essential roles that marketing and sales play in achieving successful scale-up outcomes.

Chapter 17: Shaping the Next Generation of Entrepreneurs—Educational Strategies for Startup Business Development
In the current fast-evolving digital economy, the growth of startups in emerging industries necessitates strong problem-solving abilities, critical thinking skills, effective leadership, and the ability to work collaboratively across disciplines. Approaches like Education 4.0 underscore the importance of digital responsibility and lifelong learning to equip individuals for the unpredictable nature of entrepreneurial careers. This chapter examines how entrepreneurial-focused teaching strategies can be incorporated into higher education to foster entrepreneurial mindsets. It showcases case studies from educational institutions, emphasizing active learning methods, especially Project-Based Learning (PBL) and Challenge-Based Learning (CBL). Furthermore, the chapter provides actionable suggestions for educators and practitioners, highlighting the need for ongoing feedback loops and the development of partnerships with industry.

References

1. Bilgram, V., Laarmann, F.: Accelerating innovation with generative AI: AI-augmented digital prototyping and innovation methods. IEEE Eng. Manage. Rev. **51**(2), 18–25 (2023)
2. Crowne, M.: Why software product startups fail and what to do about it. In: Proceedings of IEEE International Engineering Management Conference, pp. 338–343 (2002)
3. Ebert, C., Louridas, P.: Generative AI for software practitioners. IEEE Softw. **40**(4), 30–38 (2023)
4. Füller, J., Hutter, K., Wahl, J., Bilgram, V., Tekic, Z.: How AI revolutionizes innovation management – perceptions and implementation preferences of AI-based innovators. Technol. Forecast. Soc. Chang. **178**, 121598 (2022)
5. Giardino, C., Wang, X., Abrahamsson, P.: Why early-stage software startups fail: a behavioral framework. In: Proceedings of 5th International Conference on Software Business, pp. 27–41 (2014)

6. Giardino, C., Bajwa, S.S., Wang, X., Abrahamsson, P.: Key challenges in early-stage software startups. In: Lassenius, C., Dingsøyr, T., Paasivaara, M. (eds.) Agile Processes in Software Engineering and Extreme Programming, pp. 52–63. Springer, Berlin (2015)
7. Golda, A., Mekonen, K., Pandey, A., Singh, A., Hassija, V., Chamola, V., Sikdar, B.: Privacy and security concerns in generative AI: a comprehensive survey. IEEE Access **12**, 48126–48144 (2024)
8. Haji, S., Sheehy, W.: Exploring the Impact of AI Tools on Swedish Startups - A Qualitative Analysis of Operations Optimization and Alignment with the Lean Startup Development. Ph.D. thesis, Uppsala University (2023)
9. Hou, X., Zhao, Y., Liu, Y., Yang, Z., Wang, K., Li, L., Luo, X., Lo, D., Grundy, J., Wang, H.: Large language models for software engineering: a systematic literature review (2024). https://doi.org/10.48550/arXiv.2308.10620
10. Klotins, E., Unterkalmsteiner, M., Chatzipetrou, P., Gorschek, T., Prikladnicki, R., Tripathi, N., Pompermaier, L.B.: A progression model of software engineering goals, challenges, and practices in start-ups. IEEE Trans. Softw. Eng. **47**(3), 498–521 (2019)
11. McDonald, R.M., Eisenhardt, K.M.: Parallel play: startups, nascent markets, and effective business-model design. Adm. Sci. Q. **65**(2), 483–523 (2020)
12. Melegati, J., Edison, H., Wang, X.: Xpro: A model to explain the limited adoption and implementation of experimentation in software startups. IEEE Trans. Softw. Eng. **48**(6), 1929–1946 (2022)
13. Saputra, D.I.S., Indartono, K., Handani, S.W.: Business models based on technology for startup. J. Innov. Bus. Econ. **3**(02), 91–98 (2019)
14. Simaremare, M., Edison, H.: The state of generative ai adoption from software practitioners' perspective: an empirical study. In: The 2024 50th Euromicro Conference on SEAA, pp. 106–113. IEEE, Piscataway (2024)
15. Sutton, S.M.: The role of process in software start-up. IEEE Softw. **17**(4), 33–39 (2000)
16. Triando, Simaremare, M., Wang, X., Prasad, A.S.R.: The use of generative AI tools in the inception stage of software startups. In: Proceedings of 15th International Conference on Software Business, pp. 439–453 (2024)
17. Tripathi, N., Oivo, M., Liukkunen, K., Markkula, J.: Startup ecosystem effect on minimum viable product development in software startups. Inf. Softw. Technol. **114**, 77–91 (2019)
18. Unterkalmsteiner, M., Abrahamsson, P., Wang, X., Nguyen-Duc, A., Shah, S., Bajwa, S.S., Baltes, G.H., Conboy, K., Cullina, E., Dennehy, D., Edison, H., Fernandez-Sanchez, C., Garbajosa, J., Gorschek, T., Klotins, E., Hokkanen, L., Kon, F., Lunesu, I., Marchesi, M., Morgan, L., Oivo, M., Selig, C., Seppänen, P., Sweetman, R., Tyrväinen, P., Ungerer, C., Yagüe, A.: Software startups - a research agenda. e-Informatica Softw. Eng. J. **10**, 89–123 (2016)
19. Wang, X., Edison, H., Bajwa, S.S., Giardino, C., Abrahamsson, P.: Key challenges in software startups across life cycle stages. In: Sharp, H., Hall, T. (eds.) Agile Processes, in Software Engineering, and Extreme Programming, pp. 169–182. Springer, Berlin (2016)

Theme I: GenAI for Startups

Chapter 2
Generative Artificial Intelligence in Startups: A Systematic Mapping Study

Usman Rafiq, Marlene Klotz, Frédéric Pattyn, Triando, Matteo Biasi, Xiaofeng Wang, and Christoph Stöckmann

Abstract The recent advancements in generative artificial intelligence (GenAI) technologies have created new opportunities and challenges across various industries. In response, companies of all sizes and sectors have been exploring, adopting, and utilizing these technologies. Startups, in particular, stand out to benefit significantly from revolutionary GenAI technologies due to their focus on innovation, operating within limited resources and uncertainty, and short runways. Although research on GenAI has received significant attention, it remains fragmented across disciplines and underexplored. To address this gap, the current chapter aims to provide a comprehensive view of current research trends, opportunities, challenges, tools, and technologies of GenAI in startups. Following established protocol and guidelines, we conducted a systematic mapping study and identified 21 relevant studies from an initial pool of 236 studies, collected from four academic databases. Our findings reveal trends in research on GenAI for startups, GenAI opportunities, GenAI challenges, and GenAI tools used in startups. These findings provide an overview of GenAI's capacity for startup practitioners to leverage its full potential while highlighting challenges that can amplify startup risks. Furthermore, we established a linkage between the startup stages and areas where GenAI presents the most significant opportunities and challenges. Finally, we suggest several practical implications based on these insights.

U. Rafiq (✉) · M. Klotz · Triando · X. Wang · C. Stöckmann
Free University of Bozen-Bolzano, Bolzano, Italy
e-mail: usman.rafiq@unibz.it; marlene.klotz@unibz.it; dtriando@unibz.it; xiaofeng.wang@unibz.it; christoph.stoeckmann@unibz.it

F. Pattyn
Department of Business Informatics and Operations Management, Ghent University, Ghent, Belgium
e-mail: frederic.pattyn@ugent.be

M. Biasi
MetaEsse S.R.L, Bolzano, Italy
e-mail: matteobiasi@metaesse.com

N. Tripathi et al. (eds.), *Advances in Software Startups*,
https://doi.org/10.1007/978-3-032-04294-1_2

Keywords GenAI · Entrepreneurship · Innovation · Artificial intelligence · Startup · Early-stage companies · Technology adoption · Literature review

2.1 Introduction

The proliferation of generative artificial intelligence (GenAI), particularly large language models (LLMs), in recent times is significantly changing the way individuals and organizations work. Based on their training data, these tools can learn patterns, retain contextual information, and generate novel content [4, 8]. This has led organizations to pay increasing attention to these technologies to support a variety of tasks, such as brainstorming ideas, making decisions, approaching innovation, developing software, creating media and marketing, and compiling reports [7]. According to a recent poll by Gartner [2], organizations across numerous domains are increasingly leveraging GenAI in customer experience and retention, revenue growth, cost optimization, and business continuity. Industries such as media, marketing, film, IT, and healthcare are widely embracing, deploying, and leveraging GenAI in its full capacity [8]. In addition to its utility in established organizations, GenAI is also reshaping entrepreneurial processes, eventually becoming a unique resource for startups [7].

Startups are organizations known for driving innovation and the economy. However, more than 90% of startups fail.[1] The existing literature identifies a number of reasons for this alarmingly high failure rate. Among the most cited reasons, scarcity of resources, lack of knowledge, and experience in startups are often mentioned [21]. For some authors [1], moving from idea to market and developing an effective business model remain a challenging endeavor. Other commonly identified issues include problems with product development, cash flow management, premature scaling, poor allocation of available resources, and insufficient market research [11]. Considering these distinguished challenges, startup organizations stand out to benefit from revolutionary GenAI technologies [7].

While there has been an ever-growing increase in the scientific literature exploring the potential of GenAI for particular industries, existing research on GenAI for startups is fragmented and spans across several disciplines. Thus, the literature still does not provide a comprehensive view of trends, opportunities that GenAI holds for startups, and challenges they face in adopting or using these technologies [8]. Therefore, how GenAI can be effectively used in the entrepreneurial process in startups is still not fully known [7]. To address this gap, we present a systematic mapping study (SMS) that aims to identify, classify, and analyze existing literature on GenAI for startups. In particular, our objective is to have a comprehensive view of current research trends and provide a description of what has been reported in the literature for startups and GenAI. We followed the guidelines proposed by Petersen

[1] https://explodingtopics.com/blog/startup-failure-stats

et al. [13] to conduct this study. Through a systematic searching and screening process, we identified 21 empirical studies, which are found relevant and within the scope of this book chapter.

Our results are interesting to both startup researchers and practitioners. For researchers, we provide an overview of fragmented research on GenAI for startups, facilitating the identification of gaps, trends, and unexplored subtopics. On the other hand, for startup practitioners, we present practical insights. Practitioners can learn how startup teams in the real world have utilized GenAI in various startup activities. In addition, this chapter also explores what sorts of challenges startups might have to face when using GenAI. Therefore, the main contribution of this chapter is to provide a clear, empirically backed understanding of GenAI opportunities, common pitfalls, mapping of these to startup stages, known GenAI tools, and practical recommendations for using GenAI effectively.

2.2 Background and Related Work

2.2.1 Overview of Generative AI and Large Language Models

GenAI is an overarching term to represent a series of approaches to generate new content, such as text, images, audio, or code [18]. GenAI uses deep generative models to generate new content from existing data using deep learning approaches. GenAI-generated content resembles human-created content and is often indistinguishable [18]. Likewise, GenAI uses LLMs to generate content, understand inputs, provide context, and refine outputs [19]. A few examples of LLMs include GPT-4, Gemini, LLama, and Claude. Since their inception in late 2022, GenAI technologies have gained tremendous recognition and acceptance. The continuous and rapid progress in GenAI technologies and their conversational interfaces has led to a wide recognition and acceptance across several domains [17]. Companies and businesses are getting attracted toward GenAI because of its potential benefits to accelerate productivity, improve efficiency, and automate tasks originally performed by humans [17]. Therefore, more and more companies are turning toward GenAI to leverage its full potential.

Despite the tremendous benefits of using GenAI, the existing literature also sheds light on several limitations. Commonly cited limitations include dependency on the training data, unknown data sources, accuracy of data, and growing risk of diminishing human cognitive skills [19].

2.2.2 Startup Characteristics and Key Challenges

Startups are defined as human institutions defined to offer innovative products or services under extreme conditions of uncertainty [16]. These organizations strive to develop their product and business models simultaneously. Innovation and market-driven contexts are often associated with these companies [9]. The existing body of knowledge on startups is growing, and it often characterizes startups as software startups [20]. According to [20], software startups are companies focused on offering innovative products or services, where software exists as a core element of the startup.

Several studies tried to look at the distinguishing characteristics of startups. For example, in their foundational SMS on startups, Paternoster et al. [10] coined six distinguishing traits of startups: lack of resources, high reactivity, focus on innovation, uncertainty, rapid evolution, and time pressure. Therefore, we summarize and define startups as innovative, highly reactive, and rapidly evolving companies, working under extreme conditions of uncertainty and inadequate resources.

Startups face numerous challenges while moving from ideation to market [7]. Giardino et al. [3] identified key challenges that startups face, particularly at early stages. These challenges were categorized into four dimensions, that is, team-related, product-related, market-related, and, finally, financial challenges. To better understand and mitigate some of these challenges, existing literature on startups proposed various life-cycle models for startups [15]. One notable example is the model proposed by Klotins et al. [5]. Klotins et al. [5] proposed four stages of startup, that is, inception, stabilization, growth, and maturity. The inception and stabilization stages are referred to as early stages, while growth and maturity represent the late stages of startup development. During this journey, startups either adopt a "learning by doing" or a "learning by thinking" approach to define and validate their business models [7]. However, the "learning by doing" method is well known among startup founders and often labeled as a lean startup methodology. On the contrary, "learning by thinking" is the method that is taught in entrepreneurship education in universities and centers around planning and defining actions beforehand [7]. Despite the existence of these two methods, there remains a need for a toolkit to effectively design and validate the business models in startups.

2.3 Research Methodology

We conducted a systematic mapping study (SMS) to synthesize the existing knowledge on GenAI in startups. To do so, we followed the guidelines of Petersen et al. [13]. After defining four research questions (GenAI trends, GenAI opportunities, GenAI challenges, GenAI tools and frameworks), we searched established scientific databases for the relevant literature. We searched Scopus, IEEE Xplore, ACM Digital Library, and Web of Science using a core search string. The string was customized according to each database, and the search was performed on March 14, 2025. In general, we obtained a collection of 236 studies from our search results. Subsequently, we conducted a two-stage screening of this initial pool. First, we applied inclusion/exclusion criteria based on the study title and abstract. This step yielded 34 potentially relevant studies. Second, we applied the criteria to the full text of these studies according to our criteria and considered 18 studies that addressed our RQs. We added three more studies using the backward snowball technique, resulting in 21 primary studies in total.

To extract the data from these 21 studies, we defined and applied a structured template. We analyzed the data to address research questions (2-3) using thematic analysis. In parallel, we performed quantitative mapping to address research questions 1 and 4. To ensure transparency, we provided a comprehensive description of our SMS protocol as well as a sorted list of included studies of this book chapter in an online repository [14].

2.4 Results

In this section, we present our findings according to each RQ and understand how GenAI is being adopted and used in the startup context.

2.4.1 RQ1: What Is the Current State of Research on GenAI Applications in Startups?

We analyzed the data from several perspectives to understand the state of research on GenAI and startups. In particular, we tried to understand how the field is evolving. We did this by classifying the studies based on:

(a) **Publication trends:** The included studies were classified according to their publication years, from 2023 to 2025. Figure 2.1 shows the publication trends over the years. We found only four studies in 2023, marking the initial research phase since the launch of ChatGPT in late November 2024. The trend in the figure shows a sharp increase in 2024. This spike reflects a growing interest in the topic. This could be due to the wider accessibility of these tools and a surge in the adoption of GenAI by startups.

(b) **Research methods used:** We classified the studies further based on their main research methodology. We found that most of the studies utilized a survey as a research method to showcase the GenAI adoption and usage for startups. In particular, eight studies have utilized a survey. This makes sense as the field is emerging, and a survey could help in the gathering of broad insights about the topic. This was followed by case studies and action research. Likewise, there was only one study that utilized descriptive research and one that relied on the authors' expert opinion. Figure 2.2 shows the common methods used in the studies.

(c) **Type of research reported:** We also classified studies based on the type of research reported. Figure 2.3 shows how many studies appear in journals, conference proceedings, workshop papers, or as a book chapter. We found

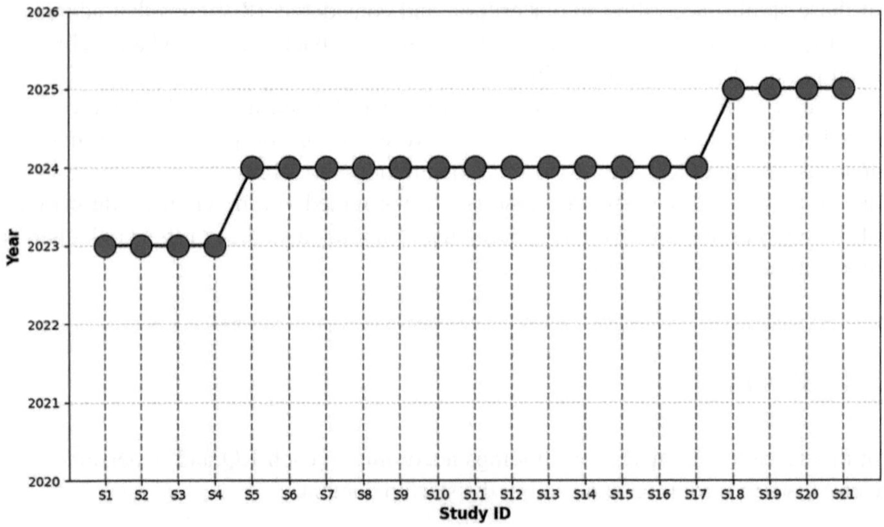

Fig. 2.1 Distribution of studies over the years

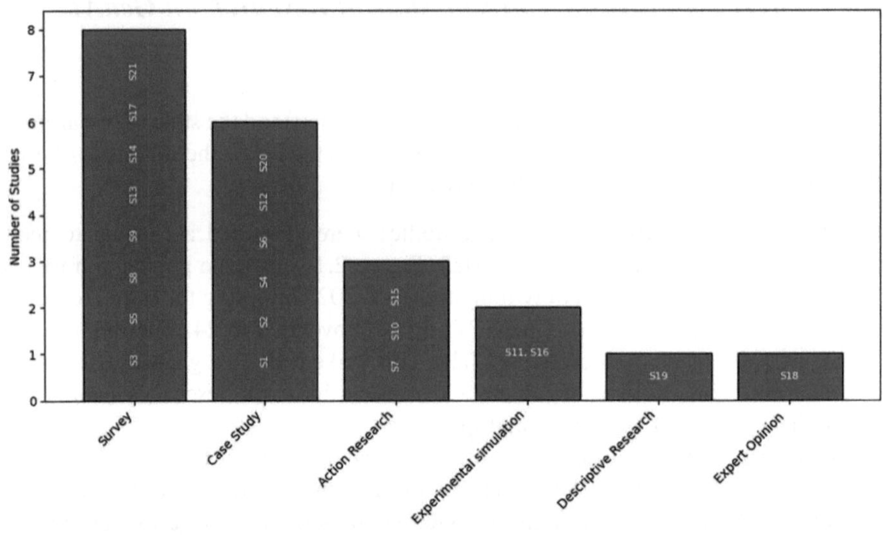

Fig. 2.2 Research methods used in selected studies

that most of the studies (S1, S2, S6, S7, S10, S11, S12, and S14) are peer-reviewed journal articles. This trend shows a growing maturity on the topic under discussion. Followed by this, 38% of the studies are published in the conference proceedings. Among other types of publications, we found two workshop papers (S16, S19) and one book chapter (S9).

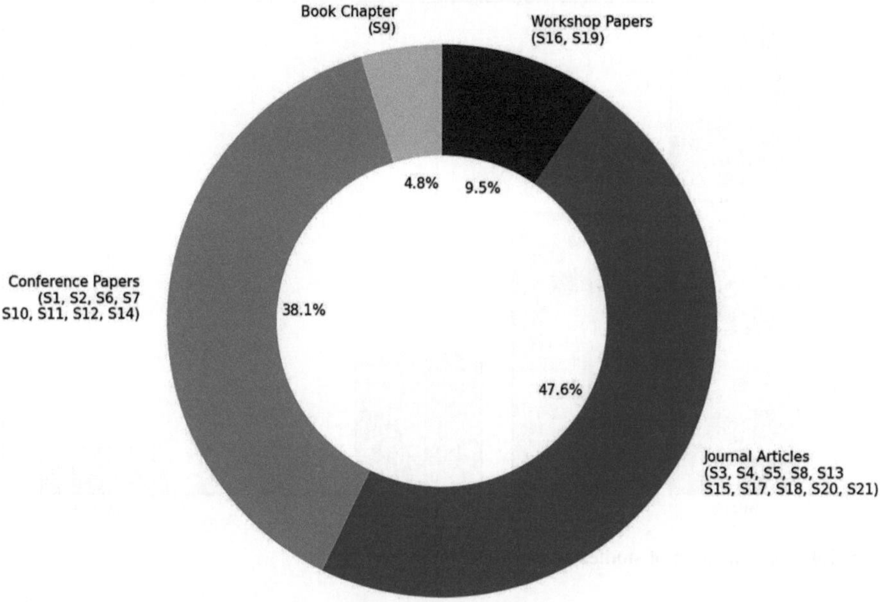

Fig. 2.3 Classification of studies according to publication types

The most frequently occurring venue for the publications was the European Conference on Innovation and Entrepreneurship. It was followed by the International Conference on Agile Software Development, which remained the second most frequent venue for our included studies.

(d) **Contributions made:** We also created a classification of studies based on the contributions made. The categorization of contributions is taken from the SMS guidelines provided by Petersen et al. [12]. We found that most of the contributions made in the literature are in the form of a process. Ten studies have contributed in terms of the process. It means that these studies have either proposed some sort of practices, provided guidelines, or defined some activity for the startups regarding GenAI. We found that this trend, in terms of contributions made, shows a strong emphasis on methodological improvement in the startup ecosystem. It means that the evolving literature on GenAI for startups has proposed new practices for carrying out various types of startup-related tasks in the context of GenAI. Furthermore, six studies have presented a model. Three studies have designed and introduced a tool (e.g., for pitch development and evaluation), reflecting a practical implementation of GenAI usage for startups. Lastly, one study has offered conceptual contributions, while one study provided a framework for GenAI adoption. Figure 2.4 shows the categorization of contributions made by the selected studies.

(e) **Research facets used:** There are six types of research facets introduced and discussed in [12]. These are validation research, evaluation research, solution

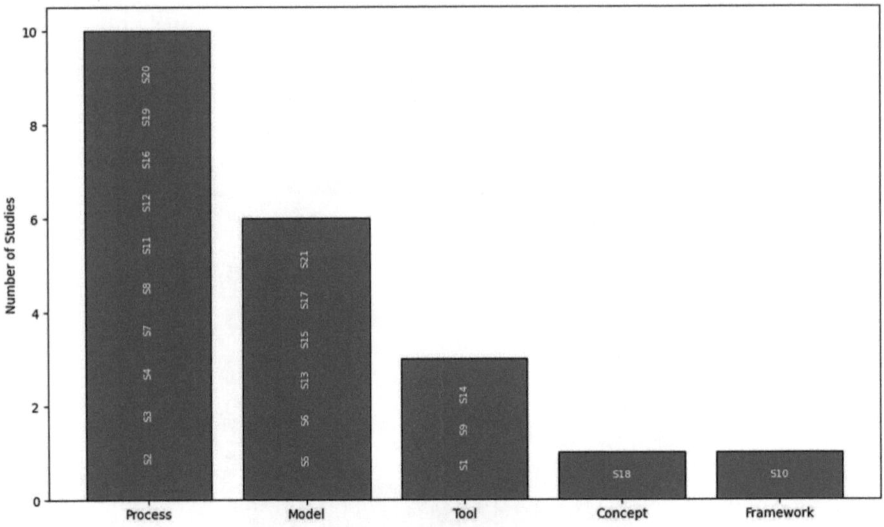

Fig. 2.4 Classification of studies according to publication types

proposal, philosophical papers, opinion papers, and, lastly, experience papers. Among our selected studies, we observed that 14 of the studies fall under the evaluation research category. It means that the techniques are implemented in practice within the real-world context and evaluations are also made. The next most common facet we found is the solution proposal. A solution proposal is the facet where a solution-novel or significant extension is proposed for a problem [12]. This is followed by validation research where techniques are investigated in controlled environments and without real-world context. Notably, only one study is based on the experience of authors, which shows a limited presence of startup practitioner-driven insights in the existing literature. Figure 2.5 shows the distribution of studies according to the research type facets. Overall, this classification demonstrates a strong presence of empirical studies and a growing focus on practical evaluation of the proposed practices, tools, and solutions for startups.

Lastly, we made an effort to distribute studies on GenAI for startups across the context of the studies, contributions made, and research facets used. Figure 2.6 shows the studies according to three key dimensions, i.e., the context facet (vertical axis), the contribution facet (horizontal axis), and the research facet (right side). This visualization illustrates a mapping of the current research trends in GenAI for startups. The bubbles present in Fig. 2.6 show the frequency of studies in each intersection. The size of the bubble depends on the number of studies in the pair of categories in the corresponding coordinates. The percentage written below the bubbles shows the relative proportion of studies. Moreover, the context facet demonstrates the context or topics discussed in the included studies. In our data, this

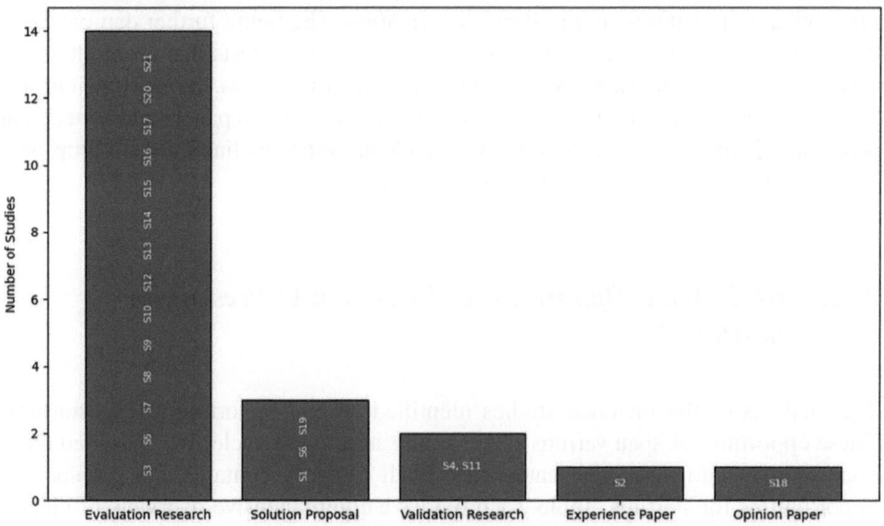

Fig. 2.5 Classification of studies according to publication types

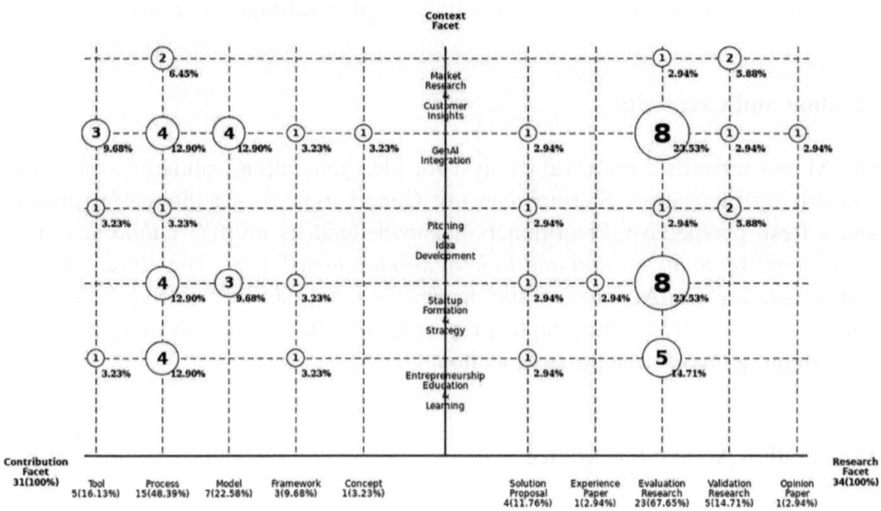

Fig. 2.6 Systematic map of GenAI for startups

includes topics related to entrepreneurship education and learning, startup formation and strategy, pitching and idea development, GenAI integration, and, lastly, market research and customer insights.

The results illustrated on the map in Fig. 2.6 show that most of the existing literature in GenAI for startups is evaluation research. There are more than 67% of the studies that are focused on GenAI Integration and startup formation and strategy. It also shows that the existing research is distributed across the startup journey, from ideation and market research to strategy formation. The figure further demonstrates that process contributions are in highest focus, which suggests that researchers are mainly studying how startups can implement GenAI across the startup journey. Lastly, we identified a minimal coverage of studies in opinion papers and conceptual proposals. It indicates that the research trends are more inclined toward empirical studies rather than developing theoretical foundations.

2.4.2 *RQ2: What Opportunities Does GenAI Present for Startups?*

The analysis of the included studies identified several opportunities for startups. These opportunities span various stages of the startup life cycle. We classified these opportunities into nine main categories. Each category contains a set of specific opportunities for startups. Table 2.1 provides a comprehensive overview of GenAI opportunities for startups, demonstrating the main category of GenAI opportunities, the corresponding subcategories, and the studies in which these are discussed. In the following paragraphs, we narrate these opportunities through a use-case narrative.

Ideation and Creativity

GenAI can serve as a powerful catalyst for idea generation, validation, reflection, and driving innovation. Startups can use GenAI tools to get thoughtful insights and a fresh perspective. Practitioners acknowledged its utility: "*I think it is very good to get some inspiration and to help develop ideas*" [S3]. Therefore, adopting and integrating GenAI into the startup development can help startups accelerate innovation through visionary inputs, replacing traditional brainstorming activities. This might not have been possible without GenAI.

Information Access and Advice

GenAI greatly improves the speed and scope of information access. This can facilitate startups, particularly early-stage startups, in acquiring expert advice and actionable insights. This opportunity is illustrated in the following excerpts: "*You are able to gather information extremely fast from multiple sources*" [S3]. "*Entrepreneurs use it [GenAI] to identify individuals, organizations, and resources to help achieve their goals.* " [S15].

Fast access to information and advice can speed up startup activities. Consequently, GenAI can enable quicker and informed decisions. Overall, this opportunity can accelerate startups' growth and agility.

Table 2.1 GenAI opportunities reported in selected studies

Main category	Subcategory	Relevant studies
Ideation and Creativity	Idea Generation	S3, S8, S14, S16, S18, S20
	Idea Validation	S14, S15
	Drive Innovation	S3, S5, S10, S16, S17, S18, S21
	Startup Reflections	S9
Information Access and Advice	Access to Information	S3, S7, S10, S15, S16, S17, S19, S20
	Seeking Advice	S3
	Digital Mentoring	S14, S15, S16
Productivity and Efficiency	Improved Efficiency/Workflows/Cost	S3, S6, S10, S12, S13, S17, S18, S20, S21
	Improved Productivity	S3, S12, S20
	Informed Decisions	S13, S20, S21
Content and Communication	Pitch Development	S2, S4
	Pitch Evaluation	S1
	Pitch Simulation	S1
	Content Creation	S2, S4, S18, S19, S20, S21
	Persona Creation	S7, S11, S21
	Effective Communication Strategies	S17, S19
Business Model and Strategy Development	Business Model Development	S1, S3, S5, S11
	Customer Engagement	S21
	Tailored Offerings	S20, S21
Entrepreneurial Support	Opportunity Exploration	S8, S15, S17
	Success Enhancement	S20, S13
Team Communication and Collaboration	Improved Team Collaboration	S12, S13
	Team Formation	S8
	Team Cohesion	S10
	Cross-Team Communication	S17, S19
	Cross-Cultural Collaboration	S7
Market Research	Customer Development	S11, S20
	Market Analysis	S3, S6
	Competitive Analysis	S5, S13, S17
Product Development	Accelerated Product Development	S5, S19
	Enhanced User Experience	S19, S21

Productivity and Efficiency

GenAI also improves startups' operational productivity and efficiency. This is usually done in terms of automating routine tasks and streamlining workflows. Consequently, scarce resources of startups can be better utilized in other essential activities. Various startups reported and acknowledged extraordinary improvements in productivity and efficiency. For example: "*The capacity of ChatGPT to synthesize contextual information and provide clarity reduces the cognitive load on entrepreneurs and enhances their ability to make informed decisions*"[S21]. The reduced load on startup founders can facilitate them focusing on other strategic and creative tasks. Expressing the same opinion, another startup highlighted the support of GenAI in decision-making and efficiency improvements: "*GenAI can provide data-based decision-making aids, which help the team make better decisions for the overall well-being of the team and to improve efficiency*" [S10].

Content and Communication

GenAI enables startups to generate content of various types, ranging from pitch decks to marketing content and visual aids. The following quote clearly articulates such opportunities: "*[The] team decided to generate its own images using DALL-E and Microsoft Bing. These technologies allowed the team to not only save time but also be very specific with its demands*" [S2]. Likewise, another startup acknowledged the content creation through GenAI and customizing the content for different audiences and purposes: "*For different stakeholders, i.e., elevator pitch, crowdfunding, twitter, stroy telling*" [S4]. Content creation and communication capabilities through GenAI can enable the startups to save time and human resources and promote effective interactions with customers, investors, team, and partners.

Business Model and Strategy Development

Defining and evaluating business models can be a time-consuming and subjective activity in startups. GenAI can assist startups in developing and refining business model strategies. Customer engagement and tailored offerings to customers are also facilitated. Therefore, through these opportunities, startups can reduce uncertainty and accelerate business and strategic development. The opportunity is acknowledged by one of the participants in this excerpt: "*It can be used to create an example of an already existing business model*" [S3].

Alongside, customer engagement can be improved in startups by integrating conversational support of GenAI tools. It can be done to improve onboarding engagement, enhance retention, and analyze customer feedback. The opportunity is highlighted in the following quote: "*ChatGPT serves as a versatile conversational agent, empowering entrepreneurs to redefine customer engagement*" [S21].

Entrepreneurial Support

GenAI offers startups complete entrepreneurial support. Ranging from opportunity exploration agents and digital mentoring to increasing chances of a startup's success, GenAI can be integrated into all sorts of startup activities. It is experienced and quoted by one of the startups: "*Now, we feel more confident about starting a business, knowing how to use tools like ChatGPT and what kind of support we can expect from it*" [S8].

While explaining the relationship between the use of GenAI tools and startup success, an empirical study found a positive relation between these factors: "*The more generative AI tools are used, the greater their perceived benefit to business performance*" [S20].

Team Communication and Collaboration

Team dynamics can also be improved with GenAI tools. Startups can use conversational assistance and multilingual support of these tools to empower team communication and collaboration. This is particularly helpful for remote or cross-cultural teams/startups. The opportunity is reported in the following words: "*GenAI can support cross-team communication, such as automatic time zone tracking with multi-lingual translation, generating and managing communication artifacts (e.g., emails), visualizing data and ideas, creating presentations, transcribing, and summarizing discussion*" [S19].

Market Research and Customer Discovery

Customer development and market research are essential activities carried out by startups and are often resource-consuming. GenAI empowers startups to simulate customer conversations, test hypotheses, and conduct market research. Through GenAI, startups can reduce uncertainty and do it much faster than the traditional way of doing it. As quoted by one study: " *LLMs may be used as simulators of prospective consumers to perform customer discovery tasks*" [S11].

Product Development

GenAI offers substantial support for prototyping, minimum viable product development, coding, and debugging of the software product. It not only contributes to the development but also significantly enhances the speed of the development. Studies also noted its role in enhancing user experience. Thus, GenAI can be used by startups as a tool to move fast from concept to offering a minimum viable product. For example, one study acknowledged it in the following words: "*This technology [GenAI] can also help software startup entrepreneurs in their programming tasks, including, for instance, generating or debugging the software codes in response to the entrepreneur's prompts*" [S5].

Overall, GenAI offers various opportunities for startups throughout the lifecycle, ranging from brainstorming and idea generation to accelerating product development, enabling speedy access to information and expert advice, and providing tools for informed decision-making. Taken together, these capabilities can empower startups to operate efficiently within limited resources, reduce uncertainty, and innovate faster, ultimately enhancing the odds of success.

2.4.3 RQ3: What Are the Key Challenges Faced by Startups in Leveraging GenAI?

Our data shows that startup companies are enthusiastically leveraging GenAI across various activities. We also explored and discussed the opportunities that it promises to startups in our previous section. However, there exist some challenges as well in the implementation and usage of GenAI, and startups might find it challenging to deal with these challenges. Such challenges can strain the limited resources of startups and amplify their risks. We report 16 studies that noted and highlighted such challenges in the context of startups. We categorized these challenges into three distinct categories. These main categories are trust and reliability challenges, technical and operational challenges, and ethical and social challenges. Table 2.2 provides an overview of GenAI challenges for startups, subcategories, and the studies where these challenges are indicated.

Table 2.2 GenAI challenges reported in studies for startups

Main category	Subcategory	Studies
Trust and Reliability	Trustworthiness	S2, S3, S10, S20
	Lack of transparency	S3
	Lack of quality control	S20
	Inaccurate information	S12
	Lack of creativity	S3
	Algorithmic bias	S20
	Hallucination	S7, S15
	Personal/customer data breach	S20
Technical and Operational	Prompt engineering dependency	S2–3, S5–7, S9–10, S12, S16
	Tool capability mismatch	S12
	Lack of specific and real-time data	S3
	GenAI adoption dilemma	S12
	Co-evolution with GenAI	S10
Ethical and Social	Ethical challenges	S11, S16, S20
	Privacy and legal issues	S11, S16, S20
	Socioeconomic inequality	S20

Trust and Reliability Challenges

Several startups reported hesitation in fully trusting GenAI and raised their voices over blind reliance on its outputs. As one founder highlighted: "*You don't know where GPT pulls its information from, so you don't truly know if it's credible or not. It could be giving you information from the easiest and most abundant sources like Wikipedia*" [S3].

This lack of trust and reliability deteriorates the confidence of the startup founders who are looking for complete entrepreneurial support from GenAI. To address such challenges, we noted that startup teams find themselves revisiting GenAI outputs and running manual controls to make sure that the output is usable. While we found that GenAI tools are replacing the traditional brainstorming process for idea creation and validation in startups, startups are still required to manually check and adjust the outputs. For example, the feedback given in the following quote clearly articulates that GenAI is still not a substitute for cognitive human efforts and thus cannot (yet) provide trustworthy results: "*Certain key words and phrases are overused. You still have to go in and fine tune the business model to sound less robotic*" [S3].

Technical and Operational Challenges

Startups face various technical and operational challenges when they start adopting and implementing GenAI. Our data shows various challenges in this category. One of the most highlighted is prompt engineering dependency. The effectiveness of GenAI heavily depends on the way startup teams input and engage with GenAI tools. Various studies reported prompt engineering as a bottleneck, limiting the technical and operational efficiency of startups. As one study emphasized: "*Prompt engineering skills are vital for fully leveraging LLMs, but they do not come naturally and need to be learned*" [S16].

Therefore, knowing how to design and frame inputs is a skill that needs time to learn. On the other hand, startups, especially at early stages, are in short supply of time and resources. Therefore, learning this skill could be costly. Consequently, the dependency on prompt engineering and learning this skill can undermine the potential benefits of GenAI.

Another significant challenge in this category is the tool capability mismatch. It means that not all GenAI tools are suitable for all sorts of tasks. Relying on one can jeopardize the anticipated benefits of GenAI. To address this challenge, startups must understand and learn which tools are good for a particular task. It is recommended in the following words: "*Users should learn which kind of tools have what kind of capabilities*" [S12].

In conclusion, the technical and operational challenges are not trivial, especially when we consider early-stage startups. These companies may spend more time experimenting with GenAI rather than executing and completing their tasks. Similarly, relying on multiple tools for different jobs can add a burden to limited resources. To address these challenges, startups must undergo additional training and cognitive load, which might be overwhelming for them.

Ethical and Social Challenges

Ethical and social challenges are highlighted by startups as well; however, not a majority of studies talk about them. This category contains ethical challenges, privacy and legal challenges, and, finally, the challenge of socioeconomic inequality.

Ethical challenges can create risks for startups as there remains an uncertainty that how GenAI outputs are produced. The outputs can reflect societal biases and stereotypes embedded in the data used to train GenAI models. This could generate inaccurate information, for instance, when a startup uses GenAI to create customer personas or create promotional content for customers. Thus, the output could exclude marginalized groups from potential customers. This challenge is highlighted in the following words: "*Ethics must be considered for this use case of GAIs [GenAI]. Potential biases and misrepresentation due to societal stereotypes and boundaries found on the internet, including the exclusion of minorities, may yield inaccurate information*" [S11].

So far, we have understood that the GenAI's output is dependent on the prompt that startups input to it. However, when providing prompt, teams could add sensitive or personal information to third-party tools. At the same time, it is essential to add such information to generate customized responses. However, this could lead to legal liabilities or damage to the reputation of startups, especially when there are no data anonymization protocols. The absence of such frameworks is something that we can expect from early-stage startups. The challenge is highlighted in the following quote: "*Privacy and legal issues, particularly regarding data privacy laws, may also arise when providing real-world customer data prompt the LLM for expanded customer analysis and discovery*" [S11].

Beyond these risks, there is a general risk of inequality in the adoption and usage of GenAI. The distinguished characteristics of GenAI make them stand out to benefit the most from GenAI. However, such companies also face the greatest challenges and barriers to adopting and utilizing GenAI. This creates a huge barrier in the adoption of GenAI by startups because of limited time, resources, and skills. One study noted this challenge while stating: "*Those who are in biggest need of AI productivity effects have the least resources and higher constraints to adopt it*" [S12].

GenAI has substantial benefits for startups. However, startups are required to thoughtfully integrate it to maximize the potential benefits. Startups that address these challenges proactively will be in a better position to increase the odds of success. This can be done by developing prompt engineering skills, designing an ethical and privacy framework, and delivering constant human attention to the outputs.

2.4.4 *RQ4: What Specific GenAI Tools, Frameworks, and Technologies Are Being Adopted by Startups?*

Our data reveals a list of 16 GenAI tools, frameworks, and technologies being used for various purposes in startup activities. The list includes Canva, ChatGPT, Claude, Copilot, DALL-E, Firefly, Gemini, Grok, LangChain, Llama, Microsoft Bing, Midjourney, Pi, Synthesia, Wenxin Yiyan, and, finally, Xunfei Xinghuo. As one might expect, the most commonly referenced and studied GenAI technologies in our data are from the OpenAI family, that is, GPT-3.5 and GPT-4. Its use is mentioned more than 20 times. Mostly, startups are using LLMs like GPT-4 and in some cases both GPT-4 and GPT-3.5. Other commonly found tools include Google's Gemini and Microsoft's Copilot. Going in the same vein, one instance (S19) did not describe any GenAI tool, although it is intensively describing use-cases for product development in startups. Figure 2.7 describes the frequency of tools, frameworks, and technologies referenced in our data.

Among this list, there are some general-purpose GenAI tools and technologies, while others are domain or purpose specific. We noted that the general-purpose tools, frameworks, and technologies are ChatGPT, Claude, Gemini, Bing, Grok, Pi, and LangChain for general purposes. However, tools such as Canva, DALL-E, Firefly, Midjourney, Synthesia, Wenxin Yiyan, and Xunfei Xinghuo are domain specific. We found that the core objectives of using these tools were image generation, video creation, and speech recognition. However, some startups, indicated in S1, S6, and S9, have used the LangChain framework to develop chatbots. It included its use in pitch evaluation, startup assistance, and as an advisory tool.

Our analysis also revealed that GenAI tools and technologies were utilized for various purposes. It includes idea generation, refinement and validation, business model development and evaluations, entrepreneurial support, team formation and collaboration, customer, and market research.

2.5 Summary and Practical Implications

Our findings present a wide range of opportunities that startups have realized or experienced. Nevertheless, these companies are also facing challenges that amplify existing risks. Based on the startup life-cycle stages [6], we mapped both opportunities and challenges associated with the adoption and utility of GenAI during each phase of a startup. Therefore, Table 2.3 provides an overview of where and how GenAI can add better value or increase risks in the startup journey.

Drawing on the collective findings of the chapter, we offer several practical implications for startups and practitioners, intended to leverage the potential of GenAI.

- **Adopt GenAI Earlier:** Startups, particularly at the early stages, should adopt and integrate GenAI tools early to generate business ideas, explore problems,

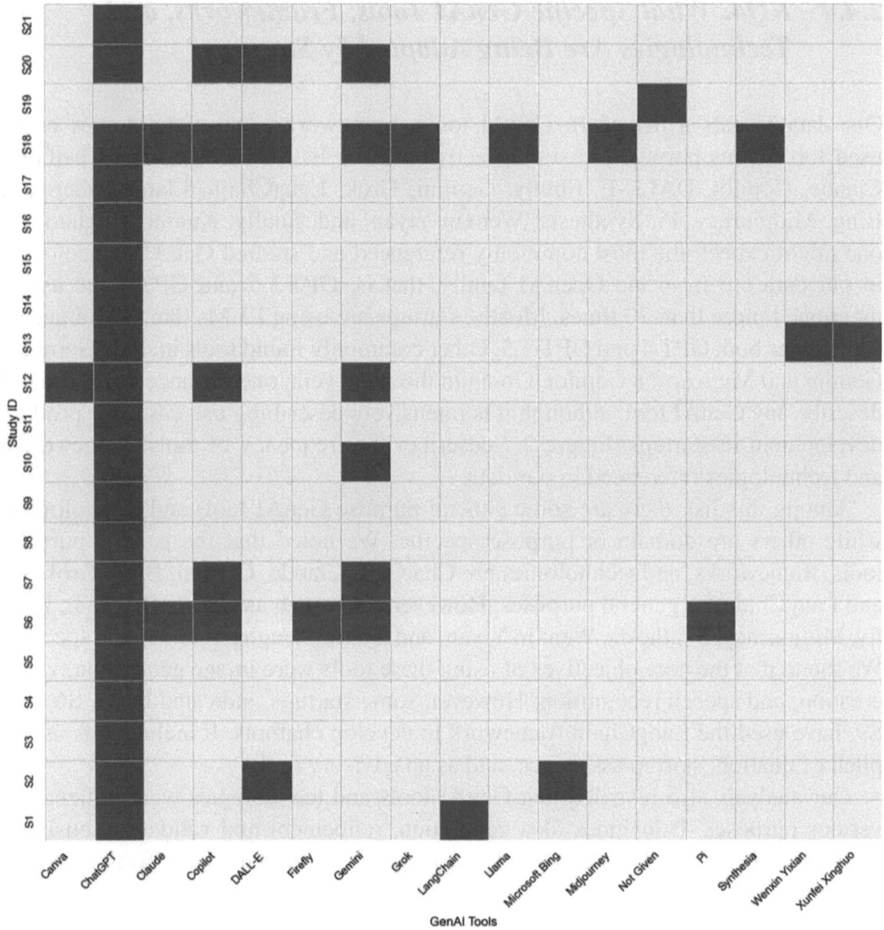

Fig. 2.7 Overview of Generative AI tools and technologies reported in selected studies

and find opportunities. GenAI can show hidden angles and strengthen the early phases of startup creation by acting as a co-founder.

– **Foster Human-GenAI Collaboration:** While GenAI holds and shows promising benefits for startups, its most critical challenge is the lack of trust and reliability in GenAI output. This is pertinent for startups, especially early-stage startups, who work under extreme uncertainty and limited resources. In such environments, any incorrect assumption or poor decision can shorten the runway for the startup. Therefore, startup teams must develop and integrate human-GenAI collaboration. It means that all the outputs shall be cross-checked and teams shall act as evaluators and co-creators. Startup teams shall also develop their mindset that GenAI is not yet a silver bullet but it can still be enormously helpful for a variety of startup specific activities. The GenAI outputs shall be

Table 2.3 Generative AI opportunities and challenges across startup lifecycle stages

Startup stage	GenAI opportunities	GenAI challenges
Inception	– Ideation and Creativity	– Prompt engineering dependency
	– Information Access and Advice	– Lack of transparency
	– Entrepreneurial Support	– Trustworthiness issues (hallucination, inaccurate info)
	– Market Research	– Lack of specific and real-time data
	– Content and Communication	– Socioeconomic inequality
	– Business Model and Strategy Development	
	– Accelerated Product Development	
Stabilization	– Content and Communication	– Prompt engineering dependency
	– Productivity and Efficiency	– Lack of quality control
	– Entrepreneurial Support	– Tool capability mismatch
	– Market Research	– Personal/customer data breach risks
	– Accelerated Product Development	– Lack of specific and real-time data
		– Trustworthiness issues (hallucination, inaccurate info)
Growth	– Team Communication and Collaboration	– Prompt engineering dependency
	– Market Research	– Lack of specific and real-time data
	– Productivity and Efficiency	– Ethical challenges and privacy/legal issues
	– Entrepreneurial Support	– Trustworthiness issues (hallucination, inaccurate info)
Maturity	– Productivity and Efficiency	– Co-evolution with GenAI
	– Entrepreneurial Support	– Ethical challenges and privacy/legal issues
	– Team Communication and Collaboration	– Trustworthiness issues (hallucination, inaccurate info)

complemented and contextualized with the domain expertise, when making a strategic decision.

- **Accelerate Product Development:** Startups can adopt several GenAI tools (e.g., ChatGPT, Copilot) to write code or build mock-ups or minimum viable products. By accelerating product development, startups can reduce development time and the need for technical expertise.
- **Streamline Content Creation:** Startups can use GenAI to produce customized content. For example, content can be produced through GenAI for investor pitch decks, social media posts, or Web site content.
- **Select GenAI Tools Carefully:** Our data revealed startup teams using a number of tools for a variety of purposes. Startups should understand which tools are

good for them according to their needs and goals. In this way, startups can avoid wasted resources and inefficiency.

- **Define Data Privacy and Protection Framework:** Oftentimes, startups need to add customer and business data with their prompts. Therefore, teams should ensure compliance with laws and devise data protection and anonymity practices before feeding these data to third-party GenAI tools. In addition, outputs must also be evaluated by teams from a fairness and inclusion perspective.
- **Develop Prompt Engineering Skills:** GenAI output is heavily influenced by the way a prompt is crafted. Therefore, founders should invest time in learning prompt engineering skills, providing training to their teams, and sharing best practices. This is particularly recommended for late-stage startups.

While our chapter highlights GenAI research trends, opportunities, challenges, and tools, there is still a need to investigate further. Future research should explore and develop tools and methodologies that simplify GenAI integration for startups. Moreover, another future avenue could be to investigate the effects of GenAI adoption over time, exploring how opportunities and challenges evolve throughout the lifecycle of the startup.

Acknowledgments This research was supported by the European Regional Development Fund (ERDF) for the project *GENESIS* under Grant No. EFRE1067.

References

1. Contigiani, A., Levinthal, D.A.: Situating the construct of lean start-up: adjacent conversations and possible future directions. Ind. Corp. Change **28**(3), 551–564 (2019)
2. Gartner: Beyond ChatGPT: The future of generative AI for enterprises, https://www.gartner.com/en/topics/generative-ai. Accessed: 6 April 2025
3. Giardino, C., Bajwa, S.S., Wang, X., Abrahamsson, P.: Key challenges in early-stage software startups. Lect. Not. Bus. Inf. Process. **212**, 52–63 (2015). https://doi.org/10.1007/978-3-319-18612-2_5
4. Goel, R.K., Nelson, M.A.: Awareness of artificial intelligence: diffusion of ai versus chatgpt information with implications for entrepreneurship. J. Technol. Transf. **50**, 1–18 (2024)
5. Klotins, E., Unterkalmsteiner, M., Gorschek, T.: Software engineering knowledge areas in startup companies: A mapping study. In: Software Business: 6th International Conference, ICSOB 2015, p. 6. Springer (2015)
6. Klotins, E., Unterkalmsteiner, M., Chatzipetrou, P., Gorschek, T., Prikladnicki, R., Tripathi, N., Pompermaier, L.B.: A progression model of software engineering goals, challenges, and practices in start-ups. IEEE Trans. Softw. Eng. **47**(3), 498–521 (2019)
7. Kostis, A., Lidstrom, J., Nair, S., Holmstrom, J.: Too much ai hype, too little emphasis on learning? Entrepreneurs designing business models through learning-by-conversing with generative ai. IEEE Trans. Eng. Manag. **71**, 15278–15291 (2024). https://doi.org/10.1109/TEM.2024.3484750
8. Mariani, M., Dwivedi, Y.K.: Generative artificial intelligence in innovation management: a preview of future research developments. J. Bus. Res. **175**, 114542 (2024)
9. Melegati, J., Chanin, R., Sales, A., Prikladnicki, R.: Towards specific software engineering practices for early-stage startups. In: International Conference on Agile Software Development, pp. 18–22. Springer International Publishing, Cham (2020)

10. Paternoster, N., Giardino, C., Unterkalmsteiner, M., Gorschek, T., Abrahamsson, P.: Software development in startup companies: a systematic mapping study. Inf. Softw. Technol. **56**(10), 1200–1218 (2014)
11. Pattyn, F., Rafiq, U.: Smart scaling for software startups through financial requirements prioritization criteria. In: International Conference on Software Business, pp. 454–460. Springer (2024)
12. Petersen, K., Feldt, R., Mujtaba, S., Mattsson, M.: Systematic mapping studies in software engineering. In: 12th International Conference on Evaluation and Assessment in Software Engineering (EASE). BCS Learning & Development (2008)
13. Petersen, K., Vakkalanka, S., Kuzniarz, L.: Guidelines for conducting systematic mapping studies in software engineering: an update. Inf. Softw. Technol. **64**, 1–18 (2015)
14. Rafiq, U., Klotz, M., Pattyn, F., Biasi, M., Wang, X., Stöckmann, C.: Supplementary Material for A Systematic Mapping Study on GenAI in Startups (2025). https://doi.org/10.6084/m9.figshare.29433128.v1. https://figshare.com/articles/dataset/Supplementary_Material_for_A_Systematic_Mapping_Study_on_GenAI_in_Startups/29433128
15. Rafiq, U., Wang, X., Guerra, E.: Data analytics in software startups: understanding key concepts and critical challenges. Inf. Softw. Technol. **180**, 107652 (2025)
16. Ries, E.: The Lean Startup: How Today's Entrepreneurs Use Continuous Innovation to Create Radically Successful Businesses. Crown Currency, New York (2011)
17. Ruokonen, M., Ritala, P.: How to succeed with an ai-first strategy? J. Bus. Strat. **45**, 396–404 (2023). https://doi.org/10.1108/JBS-08-2023-0178
18. Strobel, G., Banh, L., Möller, F., Schoormann, T.: Exploring generative artificial intelligence: A taxonomy and types (2024). https://scholarspace.manoa.hawaii.edu/items/2323c064-ba02-4fc5-826b-2ff3364bdfd9
19. Thanasi-Boçe, M., Hoxha, J.: From ideas to ventures: building entrepreneurship knowledge with LLM, prompt engineering, and conversational agents. Educ. Inf. Technol. **29**, 24309–24365 (2024). https://doi.org/10.1007/s10639-024-12775-z
20. Unterkalmsteiner, M., Abrahamsson, P., Wang, X., Nguyen-Duc, A., Shah, S., Bajwa, S., Baltes, G., Conboy, K., Cullina, E., Dennehy, D., Edison, H., Fernandez-Sanchez, C., Garbajosa, J., Gorschek, T., Klotins, E., Hokkanen, L., Kon, F., Lunesu, I., Marchesi, M., Morgan, L., Oivo, M., Selig, C., Seppänen, P., Sweetman, R., Tyrväinen, P., Ungerer, C., Yagüe, A.: Software startups - a research agenda. e-Informatica Softw. Eng. J. **10**(1), 89–123 (2016). https://doi.org/10.5277/e-Inf160105
21. Wang, X., Attal, M.I., Rafiq, U., Hubner-Benz, S.: Turning large language models into ai assistants for startups using prompt patterns. In: Lecture Notes in Business Information Processing. vol. 489 LNBIP, pp. 192–200. Springer Science and Business Media Deutschland GmbH (2024). https://doi.org/10.1007/978-3-031-48550-3_19

Chapter 3
The Promise of Generative AI for Software Startups: Potential Benefits and Use Cases

Kai-Kristian Kemell and Henry Edison

Abstract Generative AI (GenAI) is at the center of global hype and has been argued to transform knowledge work, including software engineering (SE). However, the field is still nascent. Companies are still exploring use cases, new tools are constantly emerging, and good practices are still missing. Although much research on the topic has recently been published, the practical applications of GenAI as a research area are still emerging, and research focusing on software startups is currently lacking. In this chapter, we use existing research on software startups and recent research on GenAI for SE to discuss the promise of GenAI for software startups. By highlighting and synthesizing findings of existing research from these two fields, we (a) argue why the problems currently associated with GenAI adoption and use are not as relevant for software startups, resulting in startups being in an advantageous position; (b) argue why, based on startup literature, GenAI is particularly useful for software startups; and (c) list current industry use cases based on existing research and discuss practical considerations related to GenAI adoption.

Keywords Generative AI · Startups · Software startups · Benefits · Use cases

3.1 Introduction

Generative AI (GenAI) has been argued to transform software engineering (SE), among various other fields of work. Currently, there is notable hype surrounding technology and related tools. However, practical impacts are still emerging, and the benefits of tools for industrial use are unclear. A 2024 JetBrains survey [19] reports

K.-K. Kemell
Faculty of Information Technology and Communication Sciences, Tampere University, Tampere, Finland
e-mail: kai-kristian.kemell@tuni.fi

H. Edison (✉)
Blekinge Institute of Technology, Karlskrona, Sweden
e-mail: henry.edison@bth.se

N. Tripathi et al. (eds.), *Advances in Software Startups*,
https://doi.org/10.1007/978-3-032-04294-1_3

that 73% of developers, based on self-reporting, currently save only 0 to 4 hours per week thanks to AI, pointing to any larger impacts still being underway. Indeed, existing studies using empirical data from industry discuss various problems related to the adoption and use of GenAI in real-world industry SE contexts [9, 23, 37, 42, 44].

However, as startup researchers, we have noticed that many of these challenges seem related to situations less commonly faced in startup contexts. Startups differ from more mature software organizations in various ways, leading to a unique context in terms of SE [14, 34, 45]. We argue that, by drawing on existing research on software startups, as well as recent research on GenAI for SE, we can highlight how startups can make use of GenAI while avoiding some of the challenges currently associated with it. Thus, we also argue that software startups can potentially find GenAI more useful than more established organizations.

This chapter examines existing research on software startups and GenAI for SE. By highlighting and synthesizing the findings of existing research from these two fields, we encourage early-stage startups to explore GenAI. Specifically, we (a) argue why the problems currently associated with GenAI adoption and use are not as relevant for software startups and (b) argue why, based on startup literature, GenAI is particularly useful for software startups. As a further, practice-oriented contribution, we list current industry use cases based on existing research and discuss practical considerations related to GenAI adoption.

To conclude this introduction, we provide a succinct overview of the chapter and its contents as follows:

- **Who is this chapter for?** This chapter is intended for early-stage startups and aspiring startup practitioners, although our discussion may also be of interest to academic audiences. The contents may also be relevant for startups further along in the startup life cycle, such as those already scaling up. However, early-stage startups are the focus of this chapter.
- **What is the purpose of this chapter?** This chapter is intended to motivate and encourage the exploration of GenAI tools in software startup contexts by highlighting how and why they can be useful specifically for software startups. This is done by highlighting and synthesizing the results of existing research. We also provide current industrial use cases found in existing research and discuss some practical examples based on existing research.
- **What is NOT the purpose of this chapter?** This chapter is not a list of tools and toolchains for the use cases currently proposed. In a field as fast-moving as GenAI currently, any specific toolchains we propose would likely be outdated by the time this chapter is published. Although we discuss some general considerations related to tool selection, we do not recommend or list any specific tools.

The remainder of this chapter is structured as follows. In Sect. 3.2, we provide the key characteristics of software startups and the state of the GenAI practices for

SE. Then, we discuss the advantages of Gen AI for software startups in Sect. 3.3. In Sect. 3.4, we present scenarios and use cases of how GenAI supports early-stage software startups. The chapter concludes with a discussion and conclusion in Sect. 3.5.

3.2 Background

This section discusses the unique challenges of software startups and the current state of industrial practices of GenAI use for SE.

Key Concepts

Generative AI (GenAI) Ebert and Louridas [12] summarize that GenAI "can synthesize— or generate-the answers to the questions you pose." It is a broad concept that encompasses different types of machine learning (ML) models used to generate (hence the name) a variety of content, including text, audio, images, and video. Thus, the concept in practice is more about the outputs of the models rather than the technical details of how the outputs are achieved. As far as technical details are concerned, various types of ML models fit under the umbrella of GenAI, as the concept is used in both practitioner and academic literature today. For example, many of today's GenAI models for text generation are based on transformer architecture [12], while image and video generation models are often diffusion models [7].

Large Language Models (LLMs) LLMs belong under the umbrella of GenAI. They focus on natural language processing and can generate a wide variety of content [12, 32]. What constitutes a "large" language model is hardly universally agreed upon however. Much of the recent hype related to GenAI is focused on LLMs specifically, as LLMs are versatile tools capable of various types of tasks that can generate textual content ranging from poems to program code.

Early-Stage Startups As this chapter is primarily aimed at early-stage startups, it is prudent also to define what exactly this refers to. Here, we refer to the software startup lifecycle model presented by Wang et al. [47]. They split the startup life cycle into six phases: (1) concept, (2) in development, (3) working prototype, (4) functional product with limited users, (5) functional product with high growth, and (6) mature product. By "early-stage startup," we refer to software startups in phases between 1 and 3.

3.2.1 Software Startups: Characterization and Challenges

To understand why and how GenAI could be particularly beneficial for startups, we need to determine factors that might contribute to this being the case. Thus, we discuss earlier literature in light of how startups have been characterized. In other words, what is a software startup, past a concise definition for one? Additionally, we will discuss the challenges that earlier literature argues startups face. This is done so that, later in this chapter, we may discuss what makes GenAI particularly useful for startups, either as a result of their unique characteristics compared to more mature organizations or because it may help them tackle some of the challenges they face.

Existing literature on software startups includes a lot of discussion on what *is* a software startup. Past providing a concise definition for one, this discussion has approached the notion by (a) providing common characteristics for software startups and (b) trying to understand how software startups differ from more mature organizations. In terms of characteristics, existing research associates the following characteristics with software startups: (1) highly reactive, (2) innovation, (3) uncertainty, (4) rapidly evolving, (5) time pressure, (6) third-party dependency, (7) small team, (8) one product, (9) low-experienced team, (10) new company, (11) flat organization, (12) highly risky, (13) not self-sustained, (14) lack of resources, and (15) little working history [34]. According to Wang and Nandhakumar [46], startups are overall characterized by disadvantages, which may stem from the aforementioned characteristics.

In terms of software engineering specifically, startups also differ from other types of organizations. Startups seldom use traditional agile methodologies [34], and their suitability for startups has been questioned [6]. Nonetheless, startups do use individual agile practices [31], largely in an ad hoc fashion [13]. Overall, software development in startups is characterized by a severe lack of resources [14], with the startup team being the key resource [21, 39, 40]. Quality has low priority [26], and speed is often prioritized, resulting in technical debt [33].

3.2.2 Generative AI and Large Language Model Use: Challenges and Current State of Industrial Practice

Various benefits have been associated with the use of GenAI in SE. These include increased productivity and time-saving through the elimination of menial tasks, faster or easier information retrieval, and learning aids [9, 23]. Overall, the tools are perceived as being useful, and companies are showing growing interest toward GenAI for SE [15, 19]. However, in real-world SE settings, the adoption and use of GenAI are nonetheless marked by various challenges at present.

On the organizational level, companies are struggling to make use of GenAI due to data privacy and regulatory issues [23, 42, 44]. Organizational bureaucracy hinders organizational adoption, and the fast-moving field poses challenges to organizations trying to decide which tools and licenses to commit to [23]. In some cases, no clear or suitable use cases are perceived [42]. The difficulty of quantifying the benefits of GenAI [15, 23], or their being unclear overall [42], may also act as a challenge by making it harder to justify the adoption costs. Later in this chapter, we argue that these are less problematic for startups, especially early-stage ones.

In addition, there are various challenges related to the adoption and use of GenAI at the individual user level. Challenges related to the outputs of GenAI tools, and particularly LLMs, are widely discussed, such as inaccurate outputs, low-quality outputs, generic outputs, hallucinations [23, 42], and bias—even in the context of SE, such as assumptions related to organizational structure [44]. In terms of outputs, cutoffs in training data are also one challenge [44], as a model may not have an up-to-date understanding of, e.g., some libraries. The quality of individual prompts can be difficult to evaluate for users [23], making it harder to understand one's performance in relation to the tools. As with any tool, there are also tool-specific usability challenges to consider [23].

However, the potential usefulness of GenAI tools is arguably shown by individual users' interest in them. While organizations may be slower to adopt these tools and provide licenses for them actively, individual developers are often using the tools on their own, according to surveys from GitHub [15] and JetBrains [19]. Shadow IT—the use of software services outside those officially sanctioned by the organization [17]—also seems potentially common for GenAI tools [23].

The prevalence of shadow IT also highlights their current primary use mode: as personal assistants for individual employees. Few organizations have been using GenAI in a specific process and used it with some degree of automation [23]. Various current industry use cases for GenAI for SE are discussed in the literature, i.e., [23, 42]. We outline these in detail later in this chapter.

3.3 How Do Startups in Particular Benefit from the Rise of GenAI?

While the use of GenAI in real-world SE contexts is a nascent area of both research and practice, existing research and practitioner surveys have outlined current issues related to GenAI adoption and use. We have given a summative overview of these in Sect. 3.2. Now, we discuss them in more detail in relation to startups specifically and why we argue that many of the currently perceived problems are not necessarily so impactful for early-stage startups.

Problem 1 Data privacy issues and related regulations make it more difficult to utilize GenAI in industry SE contexts [23, 42, 44]. Problems may arise from (a) customer code, (b) being protective of own proprietary code, and (c) data privacy issues related to some parts of the code or some data.

What does this mean for early-stage startups? While one still has to be careful when it comes to data-related legislation, code-wise startups may find these issues less relevant. While developing your own initial product, you will seldom face project-specific issues arising from customer-imposed restrictions, and for most startups, your early code is hardly anything to be protective of.

Problem 2 Due to the bureaucracy [23], larger organizations tend to approach GenAI in a tool-focused manner, weighing their options on which tools to adopt and which licenses to purchase. This poses challenges in a fast-moving field like GenAI currently, where new, better models constantly surface and long-term investments are difficult to gauge.

What does this mean for early-stage startups? An early-stage startup can rely on personal licenses to quickly test and adopt new tools instead of having to rely on slow organizational bureaucracy to acquire enterprise licenses.

Problem 3 Lack of clear or viable use cases [42]. One problem both individual users and organizations face in relation to GenAI is a perceived lack of good use cases in some cases.

What does this mean for early-stage startups? Based on the literature, a perceived lack of use cases can boil down to various factors, such as an individual user being unable to use suitable tools. Alternatively, this can simply be a problem of GenAI performance overall, still lacking for specific use cases. However, startups may find this less of a hurdle through experimentation with different state-of-the-art tools and being able to utilize GenAI more widely and freely within the organization.

Problem 4 Quantifying the benefits of GenAI is difficult [15, 23, 42]. Companies are currently finding it difficult to put a number on the positive impacts of GenAI. This can hinder adoption in larger organizations where license purchases may need to be justified with numeric estimates of their value.

What does this mean for early-stage startups? While you may still be curious about quantifying the benefits of the tools you use, this is unlikely to present a notable obstacle.

Problem 5 (LLMs Struggle with Large, Complex Code Bases) LLMs struggle with a global understanding of codebases [16]. They struggle to understand complex relationships in code and struggle with high algorithmic complexity [23]. Studies indicate, for example, that LLMs generate syntactically correct and functional code for simpler numerical tasks but encounter substantial difficulties with more complex, parallelized, or distributed computations [10]. Moreover, given their limited context window, they can only "see" so much code at a time. These limitations are compounded in large code bases, as proprietary company code bases routinely comprise millions (or even billions) of lines of code [16].

What does this mean for early-stage startups? An early-stage startup working on the initial version of its product is unlikely to have a large or complex codebase yet in many cases. Moreover, if much of the code is AI generated, it is likely that AI will also be able to handle it better. However, any startup developing highly complex software as its product may still find itself facing such issues.

Problem 6 (LLM Performance Varies Between Programming Languages) LLMs, and particularly LLMs intended for coding, perform well with languages that are represented well in the training datasets but may struggle with "low-resource" languages that are not [8].

What does this mean for early-stage startups? Consider using commonly used programming languages in order to ensure that GenAI tools work better. This also applies to libraries and other tools or assets you may use in your work. Where possible, consider popular options to make it more likely that the AI is well versed in them in terms of its training data.

To summarize, while GenAI arguably presents various potential for software companies of all kinds, startups can be argued to be in a particularly advantageous position in terms of GenAI adoption and use. Existing research has highlighted different *problems* that software organizations currently face while adopting GenAI tools, and we have argued why these problems are not so problematic for software startups, on the other hand.

GenAI tools are particularly helpful for accelerating prototyping and thus reducing time to market, particularly benefitting startups. Startups are also far less hindered by bureaucracy in terms of technology adoption [5]. Similarly, startups seldom have legacy systems to be concerned about and are less hindered by integration constraints in terms of existing processes [5]. Furthermore, the key challenge startups face is perceived to be a severe lack of resources [14]. By using GenAI tools, and possibly agents, to automate tasks where possible, eliminate menial tasks for employees where possible, and speed up work where possible, GenAI can be used to alleviate what is often perceived to be the biggest challenge faced by startups. By comparison, while larger enterprises can certainly also reap the same benefits from GenAI, the adoption process of these tools is likely to take far more effort and planning.

3.4 How Can Early-Stage Software Startups Leverage GenAI?

We discussed previously that many of the current challenges associated with GenAI use in industry SE contexts may not be relevant to early-stage startups. In this section, we discuss how GenAI can be useful for startups, specifically in light of existing literature on software startups. In terms of methodology, this chapter is an essay that summarizes and synthesizes relevant existing research and, on occasion, grey literature; this is not an empirical study or a *systematic* literature review or mapping study.

Among the 17 key challenges for software startups [47], the most common key challenge for startups is building the product. Other challenges related to this are building the team and being over capacity/having too much to do. While "building the product" is a wide problem that encompasses various types of more atomic problems, we argue that GenAI nonetheless has notable potential here, especially for early-stage startups. We also consider idea validation, and especially product validation, closely related to building the product. However, we discuss them separately next.

In terms of **building the product**, GenAI has the potential to help in the early-stage startup context as follows:

- GenAI tools can help eliminate menial tasks [9]. For startups, this can mean getting more done with a smaller team. In one case study, a startup remarked that GenAI let them "punch above their weight class" [23]. By eliminating menial tasks, a small team can better focus their efforts on important ones.
- GenAI is useful for learning new things and speeding up information retrieval [23, 37, 42]. This is particularly useful, especially for novice startup entrepreneurs. Early-stage startup work also involves various tasks that do not directly contribute to product development, such as setting up a company in the legal sense.
- LLMs especially are particularly versatile tools capable of various tasks, from code generation to marketing [23, 42]. This can help early-stage startups make up for missing capabilities in their team, tackling product development issues stemming from missing team capabilities. A business-oriented team may utilize GenAI to produce early MVPs of the idea fast in order to better communicate their vision to potential new team members. Similarly, a more tech-oriented team may leverage GenAI to help with other aspects, such as planning pitches. While LLMs may not be able to automate tasks fully, and their performance varies based on various factors, they can still help save resources, helping startups that commonly struggle with resources.
- It has been argued that GenAI (LLMs) may help improve code quality [12, 37]. Startups often struggle with technical debt [14, 24]. Thus, GenAI has the potential to help through either refactoring of existing code or by helping to write better code to begin with in terms of quality.

One of the key challenges or causes of failures for software startups is **insufficient idea or product validation**, or in more conventional software engineering terms, problems related to requirements engineering (RE) [26]. In startup contexts, RE activities are often discussed under the umbrella of so-called validation activities [22]. Many of the key challenges listed and ranked by Wang et al. [47] are also directly or indirectly related to the idea or product validation, namely, in descending order of importance (based on Wang et al.): (a) customer acquisition, (b) business model, (c) minimum viable product, (d) product market fit, and (e) problem-solution fit.

The Lean Startup [36] philosophy also stresses the importance of actively trying to *validate* one's idea and product by, for example, building Minimum Viable Products (MVPs) and utilizing different types of MVPs to gather data at different stages. Moreover, taking too long to produce an initial version of the product is a common challenge [25]. MVPs are experiments used to learn whether the underlying business hypotheses are valid or not. When the results do not prove viable, startups need to pursue new directions immediately or pivot [11]. It could prevent a startup from bankruptcy if the time between pivots is minimized.

In terms of **idea and product validation**, GenAI has the potential to help in the early-stage startup context as follows:

- While GenAI tools may struggle with large, complex code bases [16], they seem to excel at setting up new projects (scaffolding, boilerplate code) [23, 35]. This suggests they may be useful for getting early MVPs out faster in terms of programming.
- GenAI can help the experimentation with the product by providing early and meaningful feedback before testing it with the actual users [41]. This can be done by, e.g., utilizing LLMs to impersonate users for requirements engineering activities at an early stage [43].
- LLMs can be used to support qualitative data analysis in different ways [2]. While in scientific data analysis their performance may still be lacking in terms of scientific rigor, in business contexts, they may offer valuable support for going over large quantities of qualitative data. LLMs could be utilized to analyze qualitative data from popular conversation platforms (e.g., Reddit) to understand user sentiments regarding some topics in order to provide validation for ideas. Such data may be used in various ways to either develop new ideas or validate existing ones.
- LLMs can be used to create validation instruments, such as interview guides or surveys and questionnaires [43].

3.4.1 Current Industry Use Cases

Given how quickly GenAI is advancing, giving outright tool recommendations, as mentioned in the introduction, is not the purpose of this chapter, as they are likely to become outdated quickly. On the other hand, existing research has listed current industry *use cases* for generative AI in SE. These may give general ideas of what GenAI might be useful for currently and in the near future, regardless of individual tools being utilized. These may be built on by experimenting with different tools.

Based on our previous studies [23, 42], we outline 30 potential SE-related use cases, grouped into eight categories:

- Ideation and design: (1) idea generation, (2) assisting system design (e.g., high-level architecture suggestions), (3) content creation for product (e.g., concept art), (4) marketing content creation
- Requirements and planning: (5) requirements engineering (various tasks; prioritizing, tagging, refining, etc.), (6) project plan generation, (7) decision-making support, (8) CV creation for internal company use (for project resourcing; primarily for large organizations)
- Development: (9) code generation, (10) refactoring, (11) explaining or summarizing existing code, (12) debugging, (13) code migration

- Testing and quality assurance: (14) test case generation, (15) test automation, (16) test case selection, (17) setting up error handling
- Knowledge and collaboration: (18) documentation, (19) information retrieval, (20) meeting transcripts and summaries, (21) learning, coaching, and training
- Deployment, infrastructure, and maintenance: (22) deployment, (23) configuring infrastructures, (24) managing self-evolving software, (25) maintaining legacy software, (26) code migration
- Data and analytics: (27) business prediction, (28) extracting and structuring data and data analysis
- Translation and support: (29) language support and translation, (30) customer support

Additionally, Simaremare et al. [43] list GenAI use cases for startups based on a literature review. However, these are not limited to use cases found in industrial settings, whereas the above are use cases other companies are currently exploring in practice.

3.4.2 Practical Startup Examples Based on Research

Example 1 (Start-Cards) Starting in 2019, we began to develop a scientific, card-based method for early-stage startups, StartCards [22], which was published in 2023. The method consists of a deck of cards, each of which describes a startup practice based on both gray and academic literature. These practices are intended to help early-stage startups familiarize themselves with existing good practices that are argued to be helpful for early-stage startups.

Each of the cards conforms to the same three-part template. First, each card contains a motivation, which explains why the topic of the card should be paid attention to. Second, the "what to do" part of the card contains the main content of the card in the form of a brief description of the practice (the "what" and "how"). Finally, each card contains a "common mistakes" field that contains the "don'ts" to the "dos" of the "what to do" part.

Figures 3.1 and 3.2 showcase two example cards from the StartCards. The "Great Pitch" card (Fig. 3.1) gives startups a brief overview of what a pitch is and how and why one should prepare one, while the "Be Ready to Pivot" card (Fig. 3.2) explains the practice of pivoting and its importance. In this fashion, the cards present individual startup practices in a concise manner and motivate their importance to more novice startuppers.

For comparison, if one were to prompt any cloud-based LLM service using the prompt *"I am a new startup entrepreneur. Could you help me prepare a pitch for my startup by giving me an overview of what a good pitch should contain?"*, one would get highly similar content as a response. In fact, the response would contain far more information, given that the StartCards [22] were designed to be concise in order to fit on A5-sized physical cards.

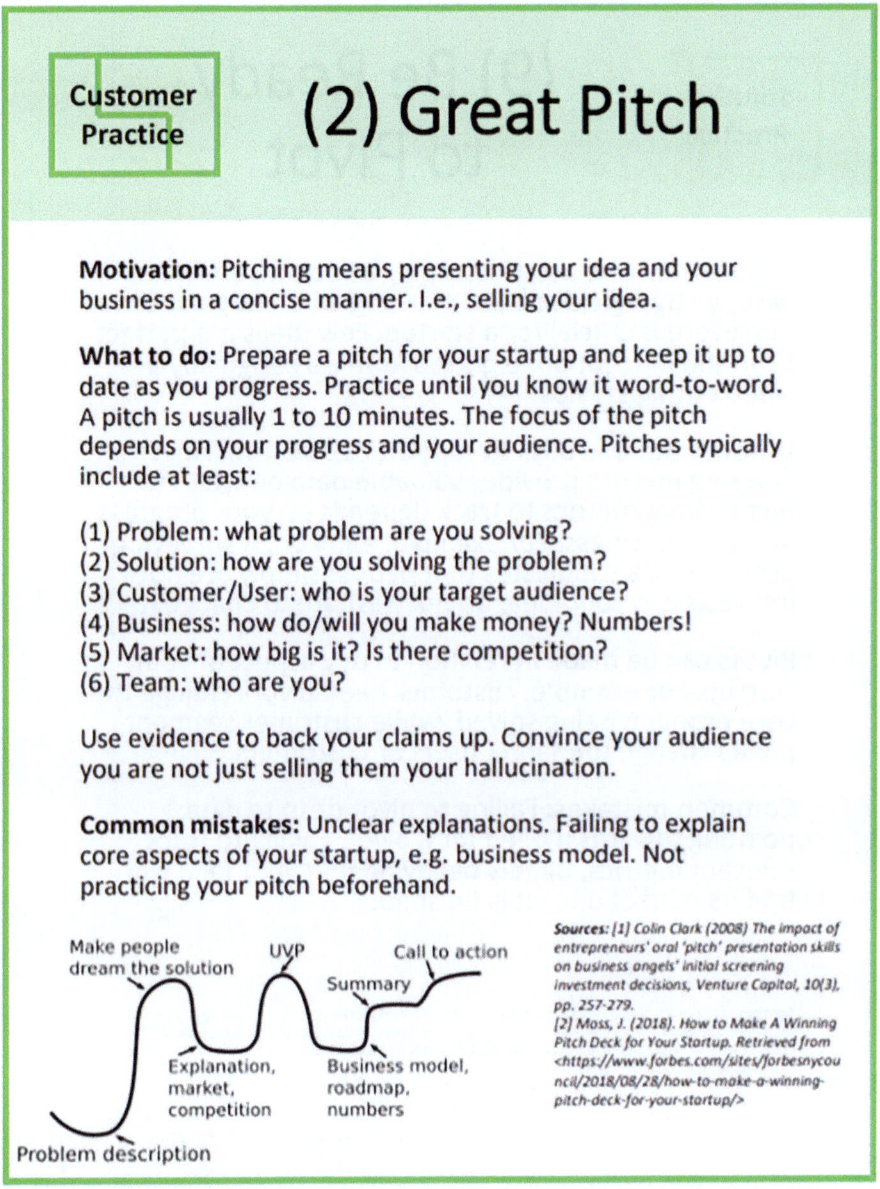

Fig. 3.1 StartCard example: Card (2) [22]

Solution Practice

(9) Be Ready to Pivot

Motivation: The act of changing direction, business-wise; a strategic decision. Knowing when to pivot or to persevere is crucial for a startup. Few ideas are perfect from their inception; e.g., YouTube was originally a video dating service.

What to do: Use data to support decision-making. Tracking metrics provides valuable data on when to pivot. What metrics to track depends on your progress and your business. For example, early on, if surveying potential users indicates that people simply are not interested in your idea, do not hesitate to change it.

Pivots can be made in relation to any aspect of your startup. For example, customer need pivots change the core problem being solved, while customer segment pivots change the target users or customers.

Common mistakes: Failing to pivot despite data pointing towards a need for a pivot. Failing to track relevant metrics. Blindly believing that your idea will find its market once it is finished.

Sources: *[1] Bajwa, S. S., Wang, X., Nguyen-Duc, A., and Abrahamsson, P. (2016). How Do Software Startups Pivot? Empirical Results from a Multiple Case Study. In: Maglyas A., Lamprecht AL. (eds) Software Business. ICSOB 2016. Lecture Notes in Business Information Processing, vol 240. Springer, Cham.*
[2] Bajwa, S., Wang, X., Nguyen-Duc, A., Chanin, R., Prikladnicki, R., Pompermaier, L., & Abrahamsson, P. (2017). Start-Ups Must Be Ready to Pivot. IEEE Software, 34, 18-22.
[3] Bajwa, S., Wang, X., Nguyen-Duc, A., & Abrahamsson, P. (2017). "Failures" to be celebrated: an analysis of major pivots of software startups. Empirical Software Engineering, 22(5).

Fig. 3.2 StartCard Example 2: Card (9) [22]

Leveraging GenAI to Use StartCards The StartCards [22] were intended to give a brief overview of each practice so that their users could then look up more information on their own as needed, possibly by using the references on each card. GenAI tools with search capabilities, meaning virtually any larger cloud-based LLM service these days, are well suited for this purpose. The StartCards can be used by novice or up-and-coming startup entrepreneurs to get an overview of potential good practices, and GenAI tools can then be used to supplement the basics found on the cards. This could also be done in relation to Agile practices, the Lean Startup [36], or any other well-known practices and methods.

Example 2 (Active Persona) User participation is critical and often endorsed as an intervention in new product development [27]. The main argument for this is that users are experts in their own lives. Thus, involving them will help development teams emphasize and gain more detailed knowledge about their specific situations: their needs, wishes, and requirements. Getting enough user participation and meaningful feedback throughout the new product development stages is still an unresolved challenge for many reasons [20]. For example, users are not always available and willing to participate in projects that require a long commitment. Access to a subset of users also provides a limited sample of the views of end users. Moreover, misunderstanding user feedback can have major consequences and lead to misguided decisions [29]. This is exacerbated in the software startup context, where a lack of user feedback wastes their limited resources and increases time to market, ultimately putting the company's survival at high risk [30].

The persona technique has been promoted as a strong tool to understand the needs of potential users. However, this technique is not widely used in the software development industry [4]. Recently, research shows that conversational agents endowed with personality have gained traction from researchers from various domains, such as mental health [1] and games [3]. Several studies have been conducted to develop personas using LLM [18, 28]. A study by Salewski et al. [38] showed that GenAI provides better feedback when it pretends to be a domain expert or persona while performing simple tasks.

To fill the gap, we envision Active Personas (AP), fictional users capable of generating contextual feedback [41]. An AP encapsulates user personas and other requirement engineering artefacts (i.e., user scenarios, user stories, concept mindmaps, etc.) as an object that shares the characteristics of a group of users. APs will be implemented using GenAI technologies to create novel humanlike generated content in various modalities, including texts, images, audio, videos, and simulations.

Figure 3.3 illustrates the role of AP in providing meaningful feedback. A startup team discovers a potential problem from an initial user reach out. The team then builds a prototype of a hypothetical solution in the form of, for example, a mockup and defines the user personas. Instead of testing the solution directly with the end users, the team can do iterative internal experimentation with AP instances

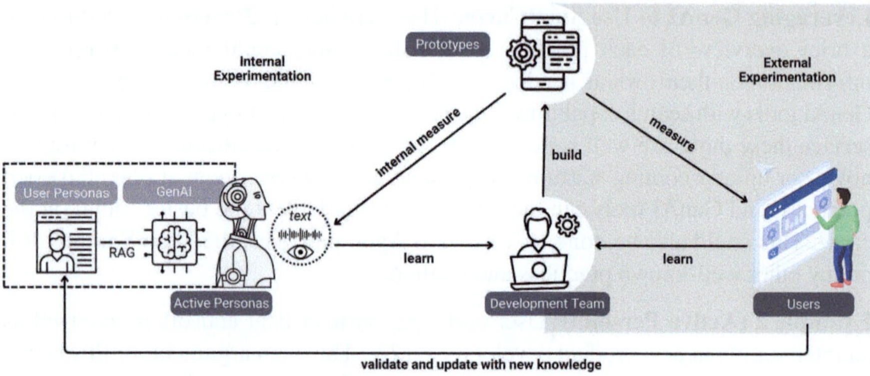

Fig. 3.3 Active Personas in the search of problem-solution fit [41]

to get immediate feedback on the prototype and make improvements (see the left side of the figure). The interaction can be in various modalities. When the team has confidence in the prototype, they can reach out to the user for external experimentation (see the right side of the figure).

3.4.3 Which Tools to Adopt and Use?

While specific tools and tool chains could provide further tangibility to the discussion in this chapter, we wanted to focus on the big picture instead of getting bogged down by individual practical applications. GenAI as a field is nascent and currently the target of global hype. With new ML models and tools based on them constantly emerging, the state of practice and state of the art are in constant motion. Therefore, any tool we now recommend may no longer be relevant in six months. Hence, we urge those interested in specific tool recommendations to instead turn to gray literature, such as blogs and video content from other practitioners. To this end, we also do not recommend specific commercial tools ourselves to remain objective. Nonetheless, there are some general considerations to take into account when selecting tools.

Generic or Specific Model? Is a generic, out-of-the-box model sufficient to achieve your goals, or is something more specific (e.g., a fine-tuned model or a Retrieval Augmented Generation (RAG) application) needed? Evaluate the planned use cases, and weigh the available options. If unsure, it can be useful to start with a generic, cloud-based model just for piloting purposes in order to understand the need and evaluate what these tools are and are not capable of.

Is Prompting Enough? Many problems can be overcome with different prompting approaches. A fine-tuned or higher-performing model is not necessarily required. In many cases, straightforward and well-defined queries are always the best. However, learning to prompt takes time and effort, and it can be difficult to gauge when the problem really is prompt and when it is the model [23]. Various prompting tips and guides are available online and in research papers as well, including the prompt pattern catalog [48].

Open Source and Local or Proprietary and Cloud Based? Data privacy and legislative concerns are big reasons for larger organizations to consider open-source alternatives [23]. There are other potential benefits to running models locally, however, such as being able to run models without guardrails and having complete control over the hosting.

Do You Need a Specific Tool? Various GenAI-based tools offered by different service providers exist that offer specific functionalities and not just a cloud-based LLM for you to prompt. Depending on the use case, it may be worth exploring available commercial tools that offer various additional functionalities for what you want to achieve with AI, if achieving your aims using generic models with no additional tool support seems unfeasible.

Agentic AI? Moving past just using LLMs as personal assistants in an organization may involve AI agents that act with more autonomy to complete tasks after receiving the initial prompt. Whereas LLMs by default are chatbots, AI agents are capable of utilizing tools and are intended to "do" things rather than just responding to user inputs [5]. AI agents can be leveraged to give AI the capability to interact with various software tools, which can be key in making LLMs more than just conversational assistants. One well-known example of a specialized AI agent is the deep research mode now available on many LLM cloud services, intended to help users find scientific research and gray literature on specific topics.

What to Do When Correct Outputs Are Critical? In some use cases, such as when AI outputs are sent to a user, it is even more important to ensure the quality of each output. Guardrails, which cloud-based LLM services typically come with by default, offer one safety net, but additional tools may be required. For example, LLMs can be used to evaluate the outputs of other LLMs before they are sent to the user.

3.5 Discussion and Conclusions

In this chapter, we have discussed why and how software startups may be in an advantageous position in relation to GenAI compared to more mature, established software organizations. We have also discussed how GenAI can be leveraged to specifically help startups by focusing the discussion on the key challenges software startups face, according to research.

This chapter is intended to be practitioner oriented, and its implications are primarily practical. The contents of this chapter may help early-stage software startups better make use of GenAI by highlighting how they, specifically, may benefit from it. We have discussed current problems associated with GenAI use for SE in real-world SE contexts and have argued why these problems are not so impactful for software startups. We have discussed how GenAI can help software startups tackle key challenges they face. We have also listed current industry use cases for GenAI in SE and discussed some practical examples rooted in research and some general considerations for individual tool selection, all of which can inform startup practitioners.

In terms of research, this chapter may also serve to inform future research by discussing recent studies on GenAI for SE that utilize industrial data. While writing this chapter, we paid attention to how little research there currently is on software startups in relation to GenAI. Overall, research on software startups builds on the idea that software startups are different from other types of software organizations [45]. It has been argued that, for example, the agile methods are not suited for software startups [6], even as they remain the industry standard today. In a similar fashion, this chapter has made a case for why startups are also different from the point of view of GenAI, based on recent studies on GenAI for SE based on industrial data. We encourage further research on the use and adoption of GenAI in the context of software startups in order to understand better how the unique startup context impacts GenAI use and adoption, as startup research has done for various other phenomena.

Key Takeaways for Practitioners

Software organizations across the globe are currently adopting and using GenAI and are facing various challenges while doing so. Yet many of these challenges are not so relevant for software startups, putting software startups in an advantageous position. We have discussed these in detail in Sect. 3.3.

GenAI can help software startups tackle key startup challenges discussed in existing research, making it particularly useful for startups. These are discussed in detail in Sect. 3.4.

Various potential use cases for GenAI for software organizations, and software startups more specifically, can be found in existing research. In Sect. 3.4.2, we have given detailed examples built on existing research, while in Sect. 3.4.3, we have listed a larger number of current industry use cases in less detail.

There are currently numerous potential GenAI tools available, and it is not always clear for practitioners which ones to adopt for which use case. We have discussed some general considerations for GenAI adoption in terms of what types of tool(s) to use in Sect. 3.4.3, though without focusing on specific tools, given the fast-moving field.

Acknowledgments This work has been supported by (1) ELLIIT, the Swedish Strategic Research Area in IT and Mobile Communications, and (2) the Research Council of Finland project 358714, SYNTHETICA (Multifaceted Ripple Effects and Limitations of AI-Human Interplay at Work, Business, and Society).

References

1. Ahmad, R., Siemon, D., Gnewuch, U., Robra-Bissantz, S.: The benefits and caveats of personality adaptive conversational agents in mental health care. In: Proceedings of Americas Conference on Information Systems (2021)
2. Bano, M., Hoda, R., Zowghi, D., Treude, C.: Large language models for qualitative research in software engineering: exploring opportunities and challenges. Autom. Softw. Eng. **31**(1), 8 (2024)
3. Barthet, M., Khalifa, A., Liapis, A., Yannakakis, G.: Generative personas that behave and experience like humans. In: Proceedings of 17th International Conference on the Foundations of Digital Games (2022)
4. Billestrup, J., Stage, J., Nielsen, L., Hansen, K.S.: Persona usage in software development: Advantages and obstacles. In: Proceedings of 7th International Conferenc on Advances in Computer-Human Interactions (2014)
5. Bornet, P., Wirtz, J., Davenport, T.H., Cremer, D.D., Evergreen, B., Fersht, P., Gohel, R., Khiyara, S.: Agentic Artificial Intelligence: Harnessing AI Agents to Reinvent Business, Work, and Life. Irreplaceable Publishing, New York (2025)
6. Bosch, J., Holmström Olsson, H., Björk, J., Ljungblad, J.: The early stage software startup development model: A framework for operationalizing lean principles in software startups. In: Fitzgerald, B., Conboy, K., Power, K., Valerdi, R., Morgan, L., Stol, K.J. (eds.) Lean Enterprise Software and Systems, pp. 1–15. Springer, Berlin, Heidelberg (2013)
7. Cao, H., Tan, C., Gao, Z., Xu, Y., Chen, G., Heng, P.A., Li, S.Z.: A survey on generative diffusion models. IEEE Trans. Knowl. Data Eng. **36**(7), 2814–2830 (2024)
8. Cassano, F., Gouwar, J., Lucchetti, F., Schlesinger, C., Freeman, A., Anderson, C.J., Feldman, M.Q., Greenberg, M., Jangda, A., Guha, A.: Knowledge transfer from high-resource to low-resource programming languages for code llms. Proc. ACM Programm. Lang. **8**(OOPSLA2), 677–708 (2024)
9. Coutinho, M., Marques, L., Santos, A., Dahia, M., França, C., de Souza Santos, R.: The role of generative ai in software development productivity: A pilot case study. In: Proceedings of the 1st ACM International Conference on AI-Powered Software, pp. 131–138 (2024)
10. Diehl, P., Moraru, M.: LLM benchmarking with llama2: Evaluating code development performance across multiple programming languages. arXiv preprint arXiv:2503.19217v1 (2025)
11. Duc, A.N., Abrahamsson, P.: Minimum viable product or multiple facet product? the role of MVP in software startups. In: Sharp, H., Hall, T. (eds.) Agile Processes, in Software Engineering, and Extreme Programming, pp. 118–130. Springer International Publishing, Cham (2016)
12. Ebert, C., Louridas, P.: Generative AI for software practitioners. IEEE Softw. **40**, 30–38 (2023)
13. Giardino, C., Unterkalmsteiner, M., Paternoster, N., Gorschek, T., Abrahamsson, P.: What do we know about software development in startups? IEEE Softw. **31**(5), 28–32 (2014)
14. Giardino, C., Paternoster, N., Unterkalmsteiner, M., Gorschek, T., Abrahamsson, P.: Software development in startup companies: the greenfield startup model. IEEE Trans. Softw. Eng. **42**(6), 585–604 (2016)
15. GitHub: Survey: The AI wave continues to grow on software development teams (2024). https://github.blog/news-insights/research/survey-ai-wave-grows/

16. Gu, A., Jain, N., Li, W.D., Shetty, M., Ellis, K., Sen, K., Solar-Lezama, A.: Tasks, challenges, and paths towards ai for software engineering. In: ICLR 2025 Third Workshop on Deep Learning for Code (2025)
17. Haag, S., Eckhardt, A.: Shadow it. Bus. Inf. Syst. Eng. **59**, 469–473 (2017)
18. Huang, Y., Kanij, T., Madugalla, A., Mahajan, S., Arora, C., Grundy, J.: Unlocking adaptive user experience with generative ai. In: Proceedings of the 19th International Conference on Evaluation of Novel Approaches to Software Engineering (2024)
19. JetBrains: State of developer ecosystem report 2024. https://www.jetbrains.com/lp/devecosystem-2024/
20. Karolita, D., McIntosh, J., Kanij, T., Grundy, J., Obie, H.O.: Use of personas in requirements engineering: a systematic mapping study. Inf. Softw. Technol. **162**, 107264 (2023)
21. Kemell, K., Elonen, A., Suoranta, M., Nguyen-Duc, A., Garbajosa, J., Chanin, R., Melegati, J., Rafiq, U., Aldaeej, A., Assyne, N., Sales, A., Hyrynsalmi, S., Risku, J., Edison, H., Abrahamsson, P.: Business model canvas should pay more attention to the software startup team. In: 2020 46th Euromicro Conference on Software Engineering and Advanced Applications (SEAA), pp. 342–345. IEEE Computer Society, Los Alamitos, CA (2020)
22. Kemell, K.K., Nguyen-Duc, A., Suoranta, M., Abrahamsson, P.: Startcards—a method for early-stage software startups. Inf. Softw. Technol. **160**, 107224 (2023)
23. Kemell, K.K., Saarikallio, M., Nguyen-Duc, A., Abrahamsson, P.: Still just personal assistants? – a multiple case study of generative ai adoption in software organizations. Inf. Softw. Technol. **186**, 107805 (2025). https://doi.org/10.1016/j.infsof.2025.107805
24. Klotins, E., Unterkalmsteiner, M., Chatzipetrou, P., Gorschek, T., Prikladnicki, R., Tripathi, N., Pompermaier, L.B.: Exploration of technical debt in start-ups. In: Proceedings of the 40th International Conference on Software Engineering: Software Engineering in Practice, pp. 75–84 (2018)
25. Klotins, E., Unterkalmsteiner, M., Gorschek, T.: Software engineering antipatterns in start-ups. IEEE Softw. **36**(2), 118–126 (2018)
26. Klotins, E., Unterkalmsteiner, M., Gorschek, T.: Software engineering in start-up companies: an analysis of 88 experience reports. Empir. Softw. Eng. **24**(1), 68–102 (2019)
27. Kujala, S., Kauppinen, M., Lehtola, L., Kojo, T.: The role of user involvement in requirements quality and project success. In: The 13th IEEE International Conference on Requirements Engineering, pp. 75–84 (2005)
28. Leão, R., Ayach, F., Lameirão, V., Fontão, A.: A prompt engineering-based process to build proto-personas during lean inception. In: Proceedings of the Brazilian Symposium on Software Engineering (2024)
29. Li, Z.S., Arony, N.N., Devathasan, K., Sihag, M., Ernst, N., Damian, D.: Unveiling the life cycle of user feedback: Best practices from software practitioners. In: Proceedings of 46th International Conference on Software Engineering (2024)
30. Melegati, J., Edison, H., Wang, X.: Xpro: A model to explain the limited adoption and implementation of experimentation in software startups. IEEE Trans. Softw. Eng. **48**(6), 1929–1946 (2020)
31. Nguyen-Duc, A., Kemell, K.K., Abrahamsson, P.: The entrepreneurial logic of startup software development: a study of 40 software startups. Empir. Softw. Eng. **26**, 91 (2021)
32. Ozkaya, I.: Application of large language models to software engineering tasks: opportunities, risks, and implications. IEEE Softw. **40**(3), 4–8 (2023)
33. Pantiuchina, J., Mondini, M., Khanna, D., Wang, X., Abrahamsson, P.: Are software startups applying agile practices? The state of the practice from a large survey. In: Proceedings of International Conference on Agile Software Development, pp. 167–183 (2017)
34. Paternoster, N., Giardino, C., Unterkalmsteiner, M., Gorschek, T., Abrahamsson, P.: Software development in startup companies: a systematic mapping study. Inf. Softw. Technol. **56**(10), 1200–1218 (2014)
35. Peng, S., Kalliamvakou, E., Cihon, P., Demirer, M.: The impact of ai on developer productivity: Evidence from github copilot. arXiv preprint arXiv:2302.06590 (2023)

36. Ries, E.: The Lean Startup: How Today's Entrepreneurs Use Continuous Innovation to Create Radically Successful Businesses. Crown Business, New York (2011)
37. Russo, D.: Navigating the complexity of generative ai adoption in software engineering. ACM Trans. Softw. Eng. Methodol. **33**(5), 1–50 (2024)
38. Salewski, L., Alaniz, S., Rio-Tirto, I., Schulz, E., Akata, Z.: In-context impersonation reveals large language models' strengths and biases. In: Proceedings of 37th International Conference on Neural Information Processing Systems (2023)
39. Seppänen, P.: Yes, We Can! Building a Capable Initial Team for a Software Startup, pp. 45–59. Springer International Publishing, Cham (2020)
40. Seppänen, P., Liukkunen, K., Oivo, M.: Little big team: Acquiring human capital in software startups. In: Proceedings of the 18th International Conference on Product-Focused Software Process Improvement, pp. 280–296 (2017)
41. Simaremare, M., Edison, H.: Accelerating new product development: A vision on active personas. In: Proceedings of International Conference on Software Business, pp. 461–466 (2024)
42. Simaremare, M., Edison, H.: The state of generative ai adoption from software practitioners' perspective: An empirical study. In: 2024 50th Euromicro Conference on Software Engineering and Advanced Applications (SEAA), pp. 106–113 (2024)
43. Simaremare, M., Triando, Rico, S.: Exploring the potential of generative AI: Use cases in software startups. In: International Conference on Agile Software Development, pp. 3–11. Springer (2024)
44. Ulfsnes, R., Moe, N.B., Stray, V., Skarpen, M.: Transforming Software Development with Generative AI: Empirical Insights on Collaboration and Workflow, pp. 219–234. Springer Nature Switzerland, Cham (2024)
45. Unterkalmsteiner, M., Abrahamsson, P., Wang, X., Nguyen-Duc, A., Shah, S., Bajwa, S., Baltes, G., Conboy, K., Cullina, E., Dennehy, D., Edison, H., Fernandez-Sanchez, C., Garbajosa, J., Gorschek, T., Klotins, E., Hokkanen, L., Kon, F., Lunesu, I., Marchesi, M., Morgan, L., Oivo, M., Selig, C., Seppänen, P., Sweetman, R., Tyrväinen, P., Ungerer, C., Yagüe, A.: Software startups - a research agenda. e-Informatica Softw. Eng. J. **10**(1), 89–123 (2016)
46. Wang, G., Nandhakumar, J.: Strategic swaying: How startups grow digital platforms. In: ICIS 2017 Proceedings (2017)
47. Wang, X., Edison, H., Bajwa, S.S., Giardino, C., Abrahamsson, P.: Key challenges in software startups across life cycle stages. In: Sharp, H., Hall, T. (eds.) Agile Processes, in Software Engineering, and Extreme Programming, pp. 169–182. Springer International Publishing, Cham (2016)
48. White, J., Fu, Q., Hays, S., Sandborn, M., Olea, C., Gilbert, H., Elnashar, A., Spencer-Smith, J., Schmidt, D.C.: A prompt pattern catalog to enhance prompt engineering with chatgpt. arXiv preprint arXiv:2302.11382 (2023)

Chapter 4
From Idea to Code: The Evolution of Prototyping in AI-Driven Startups

Matteo Biasi

Abstract This book chapter examines how AI-driven prototyping is transforming startup product development by enabling non-technical founders of startups to build functional digital products rapidly and independently. Tracing the shift from traditional coding to no-code tools and Generative AI, the chapter highlights the strategic advantages of speed and accessibility while cautioning against risks related to scalability and maintainability. Moreover, the chapter also concludes that AI reshapes, but does not replace, the role of developers, positioning them as architects of sustainable systems in a new, leaner startup model.

Keywords Prototyping · Product development · Rapid iteration · Minimum viable product

4.1 Introduction

In the evolving landscape of startup innovation, early-stage ventures have long faced a fundamental challenge: validating their ideas in a credible, tangible way. For startups operating in uncertain markets or experimenting with disruptive technologies, the need to demonstrate a working prototype often became a barrier to progress. Traditionally, this meant building a minimum viable prototype—an effort that typically required technical expertise. As a result, non-technical founding teams struggled to get their ideas off the ground, while purely technical teams often built solutions in search of a problem, lacking the market insight to position their products effectively.

The startups that managed to bridge this gap—those combining strategic business insight with a pragmatic view of technology—were often the ones that succeeded. These teams treated technology not as the core product but as a tool to deliver business value. By focusing on the underlying business proposition and using

M. Biasi (✉)
MetaEsse S.R.L, Bolzano, Italy
e-mail: matteobiasi@metaesse.com

N. Tripathi et al. (eds.), *Advances in Software Startups*,
https://doi.org/10.1007/978-3-032-04294-1_4

technology as a vehicle rather than a destination, they created solutions that resonated with markets and investors alike. This approach enabled them to validate their ideas faster and more effectively, regardless of technical complexity.

To avoid the pitfalls of misaligned teams or overengineered prototypes, startups should reframe early validation around customer needs and business value—not technical execution alone. Empowering non-technical founders with tools to prototype and test ideas quickly can prevent unnecessary dependence on technical talent in the earliest stages. Likewise, encouraging technical founders to ground their innovations in real-world problems can prevent wasted effort on solutions without demand. Ultimately, fostering cross-functional collaboration and adopting technology as a means—not the mission—is key to navigating the validation phase more successfully.

4.1.1 A Personal Retrospective on Technical Barriers

When I launched my first startup in 2013, the technological bar was hauntingly high. Developing a compelling digital product required both deep technical expertise and significant time. Even building a mobile application that functioned smoothly was a complex engineering task, consuming a disproportionate share of both budget and attention. This left little space for founders to focus on core startup fundamentals: problem-solution fit, market validation, iteration, and strategic business modeling. Many teams found themselves exhausted by technical challenges before they ever reached customer feedback loops.

Between 2015 and 2020, the situation began to shift. The rise of modern development frameworks, better IDEs, and community-driven documentation made the development process more accessible. Although the need for technical skills remained, junior developers could now assemble MVPs with less effort and time. The accessibility of online learning platforms also democratized entry into software development. Yet, coding remained an essential skill, and a technical co-founder was still perceived as a necessity.

The real disruption came between 2020 and 2023 with the emergence of no-code platforms. Tools like Bubble, Adalo, and Glide allowed business-savvy founders to build functional applications through visual editors without writing a single line of code. For the first time, I met entrepreneurs with no technical background who independently built and deployed MVPs, raised funding, and validated concepts—all without involving a technical partner at the earliest stages. These platforms, while powerful, still demanded a logical mindset and a basic understanding of product design and user flow, which remained a limiting factor for some.

4.1.2 The Post-2023 Shift: AI-First Prototyping

From 2023 onward, we have entered an unprecedented era where generative AI, particularly large language models (LLMs), has dramatically lowered the barriers to technical execution. I've witnessed a profound transformation: founders who, until recently, sought my help to build prototypes are now capable of delivering complex applications entirely on their own. Using AI tools, they simply articulate their vision in natural language—describing what they want to build—and receive functional outputs: code, UI layouts, hosted applications, and even marketing pages.

These are not just simple mockups; they are fully functional, deployable products that are often made available to real users within a matter of days. With minimal effort, even founders without technical backgrounds are now capable of generating production-ready frontend code, integrating essential backend functionalities, deploying applications to cloud environments, implementing user authentication and analytics tracking, and dynamically iterating on user experience and interface designs.

The implications of this shift are profound. The prototyping phase is no longer a luxury reserved for tech talents, teams with in-house engineers, or outsourcing budgets. Today, with tools like Lovable, Bolt, or Manus, a solo founder can ideate, build, and ship—without writing a single line of code manually.

4.1.3 A Recalibration of Startup Dynamics

The conventional startup model—typically centered around a partnership between a "business person" and a "technical co-founder"—is undergoing a fundamental transformation. Today, founders with strong business acumen can independently build and test their ideas without the delays associated with hiring technical talent or negotiating equity agreements. This shift carries important implications: it significantly shortens the time required to validate ideas, reducing it from months to mere days; it lowers the initial capital needed, as the involvement of a full-stack developer is no longer essential from the outset; it accelerates the pace of iteration by enabling faster feedback cycles and more agile pivots; and it broadens access to entrepreneurship, providing a viable pathway for individuals without formal technical training.

While technical co-founders and engineers remain essential for scaling and product stability, their role is shifting. They are becoming more valuable in post-validation stages—optimizing infrastructure, refactoring prototypes, and building long-term maintainable systems—rather than being the gatekeepers of initial experimentation.

This chapter sets the stage for the journey ahead. As we proceed, we'll dive into how past experience shaped today's shifts, explore the strategic importance of prototyping, and examine the real capabilities and limitations of AI tools for modern startup development. This is no longer just evolution—it's a reinvention of what it means to build a product from scratch in the age of artificial intelligence.

4.2 Background

To fully understand the present, we must reflect on the path that brought us here. The process of prototyping in startup ecosystems has undergone a series of evolutions driven by technological shifts, cultural changes in product development, and a redefinition of what constitutes "technical execution." This chapter retraces that path across three critical eras: the era of hardcoded engineering, the rise of rapid development frameworks, and the democratization brought by no-code platforms.

Looking back at my own journey, I realize that my entrepreneurial drive has always preceded my interest in technology. For me, as for many, programming was never the end goal—it was a means to an end, a tool that enabled me to start building and launching ventures even as a teenager, without the need for financial capital. However, that path demanded a steep intellectual investment: mastering complex technical skills before being able to execute on any business vision. Today, with the advent of AI tools that abstract away the complexities of software development, that barrier is beginning to dissolve. And I see that as a fundamentally positive shift. I can now envision a younger version of myself starting a company in this new era—free to focus entirely on market needs, user acquisition, and business model design without being slowed down by the technical implementation of a product, at least in the early stages. This evolution doesn't just lower the bar for entry; it redefines the role of the entrepreneur, allowing them to operate closer to their strategic zone of genius from day one.

4.2.1 The Era of Hardcoded Engineering (2005–2015)

In the early 2000s and into the first half of the 2010s, prototyping a digital product was often indistinguishable from building the actual product [3, 4]. Startups had to write everything from scratch: server-side logic, database integrations, front-end interfaces, and hosting infrastructure. Frameworks like Ruby on Rails (launched in 2004) and Django (2005) began to offer structure and opinionated design patterns, but even with these tools, the burden of execution remained high.

For example, implementing a user authentication flow traditionally involved several complex and time-consuming steps [11]. Developers had to manually write the SQL schema, manage sessions and encrypt cookies, design the login interface using HTML and CSS, and ensure secure data exchange while handling password hashing.

Every feature involved full-stack development. Prototypes, therefore, took weeks or even months to construct and often demanded full-time engineering teams.

Business founders without a technical co-founder had little choice but to either hire freelance developers or remain stuck in the idea phase [3].

During this era, technical execution was synonymous with company formation. I've seen many teams evaluated primarily on the basis of their technical chops. The phrase "I just need a technical co-founder" became a recurring meme among non-technical founders. This dependency significantly shaped startup team composition and investment strategies for more than a decade.

4.2.2 The Rise of Rapid Development Frameworks (2015–2020)

The second wave of change came with the maturation of full-stack JavaScript and component-based front-end frameworks. React (2013), Vue (2014), and Angular (revamped in 2016) shifted the paradigm of Web application development [6, 7]. Developers now had access to modular UI systems, reusable components, and virtual DOM performance improvements.

Simultaneously, backend-as-a-service platforms (like Firebase), cloud deployment (Heroku, Netlify), and opinionated stacks (MERN, JAMstack) enabled teams to bypass much of the low-level configuration [7]. Prototyping became faster and slightly more forgiving. A single junior developer could now build what once required a small team.

Several key shifts have contributed to this transformation. The widespread adoption of code reuse and templates, such as UI libraries and GitHub boilerplates, has significantly accelerated the scaffolding process. At the same time, DevOps has been greatly simplified—deploying an application can now be as straightforward as connecting a GitHub repository and clicking "Deploy." Additionally, the emergence of robust API ecosystems has enabled seamless integration of complex functionalities; services like Stripe, Twilio, and SendGrid offer plug-and-play solutions for payments, messaging, and email communication.

Still, while these advancements reduced the friction, you still needed to code—just more efficiently. The skill ceiling remained high enough to exclude non-technical founders from building without help. For these individuals, prototyping often involved managing outsourced teams or learning to code themselves.

I had the opportunity to experience all these changes firsthand. During this period, within my startup, we were simultaneously working on the development of our own product while also building small software tools for third parties in order to sustain ourselves financially. Although we had created our own framework to support the development of our product, using established frameworks like Vue for our clients' projects consistently proved to be much faster. In the end, all the investments we had made in building our internal framework turned out to be futile—it quickly became obsolete and too costly to explain to new team members.

4.2.3 No-Code and Low-Code Democratization (2020–2023)

A dramatic shift occurred between 2020 and 2023 with the explosion of no-code and low-code platforms [1, 9]. The promise was simple yet revolutionary: build software applications visually, using drag-and-drop interfaces and configurable logic blocks, rather than traditional programming.

Among the most influential platforms in this space were Bubble, a full-stack Web application builder offering database integration and dynamic page generation, and mobile-focused tools like Adalo and Glide, which provided native-like app development capabilities [1]. These platforms significantly reshaped the prototyping process by empowering non-technical founders to create functional minimum viable products (MVPs) without relying on engineers [9]. They also enabled more rapid iteration through visual debugging and logic editing and reduced early-stage development costs by minimizing the need for technical hires.

Nevertheless, these benefits came with certain trade-offs [1, 9]. Users often encountered limitations in performance and scalability, were constrained by rigid design frameworks that made deep customization challenging, and faced steeper learning curves than the platforms initially suggested.

More critically, users still needed to learn the tool, understand conditional logic, and manage databases visually. While no-code tools dramatically increased accessibility, they required a "builder mindset"—a blend of product thinking, logical structuring, and UX sensitivity. Many business founders struggled to bridge this cognitive gap.

Despite these limitations, no-code platforms redefined the prototyping landscape. Early adopters raised millions with products built entirely in Bubble or Glide, and agencies emerged to support no-code development full-time. This period was pivotal: it proved that you didn't need to write code to launch software—you just needed the right tool.

During this period, for the first time, founders began approaching me not to ask for help as a technical co-founder in building their products but rather to seek advice on how to use the low-code platform they had chosen.

4.2.4 The Emergence of AI-Native Tooling (Post-2023)

From 2023 onward, we observed the convergence of generative AI and software development workflows. Tools like GitHub Copilot, ChatGPT, Claude, and Replit Ghostwriter began to shift the interface of software creation from code to conversation.

AI-native tooling introduced a new possibility: natural language as the new programming language.

This shift had profound implications for the product development process. Founders were now able to simply describe a user story or workflow and receive not just mockups but actual code or even a functioning application. Artificial intelligence further amplified this capability by generating documentation, test suites, deployment scripts, and user interface layouts within seconds. Entire code repositories could be scaffolded through iterative, conversational interactions within AI-powered integrated development environments, fundamentally changing how software is conceived and built.

Moreover, tools like Replit's "Deploy" button, Vercel's Next.js integrations, and GPT function calls allowed individuals with no dev experience to deploy working Web/app prototypes with minimal guidance.

For the first time in startup history, the cost of prototyping approached zero. What once took easily more than $20k and three months could now be done for free over a weekend.

In fact, on several occasions, I encountered founders who had already developed their product entirely on their own. The most striking case was that of an accountant who spent a year building and launching an online platform to support business analysis. Working alone, and relying solely on ChatGPT, he was able to download the necessary software, configure hosting services, and write the entire application by himself. I was truly impressed when I saw the result. As we will later discover, the product was not ready for commercial release since it is not technically maintainable, yet it served as an excellent tool for validating the idea and attracting investment.

But there is still a downside. Even though AI tools have dramatically lowered the technical barriers to entry in product development, they still demand a baseline of digital competence—such as navigating interfaces, using prompt-based logic, and integrating third-party services. This requirement tends to favor younger generations, who have grown up immersed in digital environments. In contrast, older founders, particularly those without prior exposure to software workflows, face a significant disadvantage. Their limited familiarity with these tools may prevent them from fully capitalizing on the speed and autonomy that AI now enables, creating a widening gap in the entrepreneurial landscape (Table 4.1).

Table 4.1 A quick summary of the prototyping eras

Period	Main methodology to build an MVP	Required technical skills	Development speed
2005–2015	Manually coding	Deep coding experience, design (UI/UX), Web infrastructure setup and maintenance	Slow, months
2020–2023	Visual builders or mockups	Basic coding experience, basic design (UI/UX)	Medium, a month
2023 and after	Vibe coding (AI based development)	Basic design (UI/UX)	Fast, a week

4.2.5 *The Changing Role of Developers*

The democratization of prototyping has not rendered developers obsolete; instead, it has redefined their role within the development process. In this evolving landscape, developers act more as curators and validators than as traditional builders. Their expertise is increasingly focused on reviewing, refactoring, and optimizing code generated by AI tools. Rather than constructing initial versions of products, they are now responsible for architecting systems that are scalable and robust. Moreover, developers play a critical role in embedding AI into the core logic of applications, enabling products to become more context-aware and adaptive to user needs.

Just as designers evolved from pixel-pushers to UX strategists with the rise of Figma and design systems, developers are now moving up the stack—away from line-by-line implementation and toward system-level thinking and AI orchestration.

In my experience, this emerging scenario is making junior developer roles increasingly less sought after, in favor of more experienced developers who are better equipped to understand and advise on architectural decisions. I anticipate that, in the coming years, there will be growing discussion around how challenging it will become to attract and train the next generation of developers.

This historical grounding prepares us for the chapters ahead. In the next section, we'll examine the strategic function of prototyping, not just as a technical act but as a core business process that drives learning, funding, and product-market fit in AI-first environments.

4.3 The Strategic Value of Prototyping

Prototyping is often misunderstood as a technical or design task—something confined to engineers and UX teams. In reality, especially within startups, prototyping is a core strategic function. It sits at the intersection of product validation, user discovery, investor signaling, and internal learning. The way a startup approaches prototyping can determine the speed at which it learns, the quality of its pivots, and ultimately its trajectory toward product-market fit.

4.3.1 *Prototypes as Learning Engines*

In traditional engineering, prototypes are proof-of-concept artifacts—functional mockups that test viability. In startups, their role is broader: they are experiments wrapped in UX. A good prototype doesn't just show what a product could look like—it generates insight.

There are four key questions a prototype can help answer [8]:

- Desirability: Do users actually want this?
- Feasibility: Can we build this with the resources we have?
- Usability: Can users understand and navigate the solution intuitively?
- Viability: Will this work as a business?

Prototypes are the primary tool through which early-stage teams validate assumptions across these four dimensions. The faster a team can test and iterate, the more it learns. In startups of the AI era—where the space is ambiguous and user expectations evolve rapidly—learning velocity becomes an even more fundamental competitive advantage.

4.3.2 *From Mockups to Working Interactions*

It is important to distinguish between mockups and functional prototypes. While mockups are static representations that convey visual direction, branding, and layout, functional prototypes are dynamic and interactive, often simulating real user flows even if they rely on placeholder data or simplified logic.

In the era of AI-driven development, static mockups have become less valuable. Stakeholders—whether they are users, investors, or internal team members—increasingly expect to engage with working software, even if it is still fragile or incomplete. This shift means that early-stage prototypes must now offer tangible interactions, such as a chatbot capable of basic dialogue, a dashboard that displays real or simulated data, or a user flow that convincingly mimics the onboarding or sign-up process.

These don't need to scale or even be secure—they just need to work enough to test a core assumption. A functional prototype is a lens: it lets everyone involved see what the world could look like if the product succeeded. That imaginative leap is often what gets investors to fund, users to care, and teams to commit (Table 4.2).

Table 4.2 Understand when building software is necessary

Is building software necessary?	Explanation
Understand if there's a real problem worth solving	No, conduct interviews or surveys with potential users
You need to understand if potential customers are interested in your concept	No, simply pitch your idea
You need to understand if your idea is clear to your potential customers	No, simply develop some mockups
You need to validate a regular user experience	No, simply develop some mockups
Explore how users behave in a new conceptual environment	Yes, interactive software may be required to observe real user behavior
Determine which features are essential versus nice to have	No, use card sorting or fake-door testing
You need to build a first MVP	Yes, you can use AI to build it

To illustrate how investor expectations are shifting, about two years ago I collaborated with a startup by supporting the creation of prototyped mockups for their product concept. It was not a technically complex project; for their business model, the product itself was more of a commodity. I assumed that a visual preview of the concept would be sufficient for investors, with the understanding that the actual product would be built after securing funding. That assumption turned out to be entirely wrong. Most investors rejected the project simply because there was no MVP yet, asking the team to return once it was ready. However, this effectively prevented the startup from moving forward, as the investment was needed precisely to develop the MVP. Had this happened today, with the possibility of building an AI-powered MVP from the outset, the startup's story might have unfolded quite differently.

4.3.3 Prototypes as Communication Devices

Early-stage startups often face alignment challenges. Founders see one version of the product, designers another, and engineers a third. The prototype becomes a shared object of focus—a tangible artifact that crystallizes ambiguity into something the team can discuss, critique, and improve.

In this context, prototyping serves not only as a development tool but also as a vital form of internal communication. It helps clarify the fundamental questions of what problem the team is addressing, how the user navigates through the proposed solution, and which features are essential versus those that are optional. By making these aspects explicit, prototypes align the team's understanding and guide decision-making throughout the product development process.

With the advent of AI-powered tools, the ability to prototype is no longer limited to multidisciplinary teams. Today, individual founders—particularly those with strong business acumen but limited technical skills—can autonomously develop functional prototypes. This shift dramatically lowers the threshold for transforming abstract ideas into testable artifacts, enabling a single person to drive early-stage product exploration and validation. As a result, prototyping becomes not only a communication tool within teams but also a personal tool for entrepreneurial experimentation and iteration.

For investors, a well-designed prototype also serves as a signal of execution capability. A founder who can produce a compelling demo—even if AI-generated or no-code—demonstrates momentum, clarity, and agency. It creates FOMO.

4.3.4 Prototypes as Fundraising Catalysts

In an environment where funding is limited and competition is fierce, the ability to rapidly develop prototypes often becomes a critical advantage. Delivering a timely and well-designed prototype can open doors to valuable opportunities such as securing pre-seed investments from angel investors or accelerators, obtaining pilot project commitments from early enterprise clients, and establishing partnerships with academic or institutional stakeholders. This emphasis on speed and quality in prototyping can significantly influence a startup's trajectory and access to resources.

The psychology is simple: people don't invest in ideas—they invest in evidence of execution. And today, with AI tooling, that evidence can be generated in days. A working GPT-based agent, an auto-tagging pipeline, or a synthetic data dashboard—all built in Lovable, Bolt, or Manus—can unlock conversations that would otherwise require months of development.

The most effective founders use prototyping not only to validate product concepts but also to refine their pitch narratives. A single prototype can be presented in multiple ways depending on the audience or purpose—for example, as a novel interface for data exploration, a tool designed to automate workflows, or the backend architecture supporting intelligent assistants. This versatility allows founders to tailor their message and demonstrate value from different perspectives, enhancing their ability to engage stakeholders and secure support.

Each version can be tailored to a different audience—product buyers, investors, or tech reviewers. Prototypes allow to shape perception.

4.3.5 The Strategic Role of Prototyping

In the fast-paced environment of AI-driven startups, prototyping is no longer just a development tactic—it is a strategic function. Understanding when and how to prototype can offer disproportionate leverage, enabling founders to move quickly, reduce risk, and maintain alignment across teams and stakeholders.

There are several key moments when prototyping becomes especially valuable. Immediately after ideation, a prototype can validate a concept with real or proxy users, helping confirm that the problem and proposed solution are well aligned. Prior to fundraising, a functioning prototype can demonstrate traction or signal potential, offering tangible proof to investors. During a pivot, it allows a team to explore new directions with minimal cost and commitment. Before hiring, a prototype can align candidates around a shared product vision and execution strategy. And after receiving customer feedback, a rapid iteration helps show that the team is learning and adapting—critical signals for both users and stakeholders.

Crucially, the objective of a prototype is not to be perfect but to enable progress. A good prototype is fast enough to generate learning yet credible enough to inspire confidence.

This requires a strategic mindset. Many founders make the mistake of over-building too early, seeking correctness rather than insight. But effective prototyping reframes the process—not as an engineering task but as a tool for focused experimentation and validation. The right mindset starts by asking: What is the minimum needed to test this assumption? Who are we trying to convince—users, investors, or ourselves? How quickly can we generate meaningful feedback, and what decisions will we make based on it?

In the context of AI startups, where the landscape shifts weekly and new tools or APIs continuously unlock new possibilities, adopting this mindset is not optional—it is essential. Prototyping, when used strategically and taking leverage of AI-based tools to build it, becomes a core lever for clarity, speed, and adaptability.

In the next section, we will drive deeper into the illusions and opportunities that AI-driven prototyping presents. We will examine both the potential risks and the transformative advantages this technology brings to the product development process, especially for startups navigating the challenges of rapid innovation and validation.

4.4 From Idea to Code: The Illusions and Opportunities of AI-Prototyping

Over the last few years, the notion that software development requires technical expertise has been fundamentally challenged. With the advent of no-code platforms and generative AI, individuals without a background in programming can now create functional digital products—sometimes in a matter of hours. This is not a theoretical shift; it is already happening and fast. But like any disruptive change, it comes with both unprecedented opportunities and critical risks.

4.4.1 The Illusion of Mastery

One of the most overlooked risks in this new paradigm lies in a subtle form of overconfidence [10]. Many non-technical entrepreneurs, having acquired a surface-level understanding of digital tools, now believe they possess sufficient knowledge to build scalable products. While AI can indeed generate usable software, most of these tools are still best suited for disposable prototypes, not long-term solutions. Applications built entirely via AI or no-code platforms tend to lack structural robustness, scalability, and maintainability—qualities that are crucial for software intended to endure beyond the initial stages of validation [10].

In practice, AI-generated software often lacks the architectural coherence required for future iterations or integrations. Without foundational design patterns, version control, or standardized documentation, such systems are at risk of becoming unmanageable if pushed into production. Therefore, while AI enables access, it does not replace the principles of sound software engineering.

This shift calls for a high degree of caution. I have, unfortunately, witnessed numerous cases where founders, impressed by the speed of AI-assisted tools, made problematic assumptions—saying things like "I built this in a day with Lovable,

Table 4.3 Comparison of AI-based development tools vs traditional software development in a scale of 0–10

	AI-based development	Traditional software development
Speed of development	10	6
Ease of use	7	1
Working software	7	7
Customizable software	8	10
Maintainable codebase	2	7
Secure software	2	7
Performing software	3	7
Scalable software	1	7

why would it take a month to develop properly?" or even claiming "Now I know how to code too." Such statements reflect a dangerous tendency to underestimate the complexity of software development.

This underestimation can be especially harmful when the product itself is central to the startup's success. In these cases, relying too heavily on quick AI-generated solutions often leads to the accumulation of significant technical debt and a lack of long-term product stewardship. Over time, this approach can result in critical scalability issues and, ultimately, the failure of the startup.

Moreover, this mindset has a damaging effect on technical teams. Developers may begin to feel undervalued or unnecessary, despite the fact that their expertise remains essential for building scalable, secure, and maintainable systems. Founders who fail to grasp these dynamics place both their technical team's morale and their startup's long-term sustainability at serious risk (Table 4.3).

4.4.2 Speed as a Strategic Asset

Yet, within these limitations lies a powerful opportunity: speed. Entrepreneurs can now move from idea to functional prototype at a pace that was previously unimaginable. Features that once took weeks to build can now be implemented in a day. In the time it used to take to explain requirements to a development team, an early-stage founder can build, test, and release a product—complete with analytics and user tracking.

This capability fundamentally changes the way we approach product validation. Rather than relying on static mockups or pitch decks, founders can:

- Present a working version of their concept
- Gather real user feedback
- Extract behavioral data from actual usage

This shift reduces the ambiguity typically associated with early-stage feedback and makes validation faster, more concrete, and more actionable.

This approach proved to be particularly valuable in a startup where a situation had emerged in which the tech team, overwhelmed by technical debt and operating understaffed, was unable to deliver—even at the MVP level—certain features that were in high demand from clients.

As a result, the sales and customer support teams took the initiative. Using AI tools—specifically Lovable—they began creating a series of mini-MVPs to showcase to clients during sales conversations or developed add-ons that could be used alongside existing features to compensate for missing functionality in the main product.

Being able to leverage this speed of development was critical for maintaining business continuity during a period when the tech team was under pressure. In fact, the company eventually decided to formally integrate this rapid development capability into the core product, creating an internal app dashboard. This move allowed them to offer clients a greater sense of consistency and continuity with features that might otherwise have been developed manually in months.

4.4.3 A New Role for Non-technical Teams

What's particularly transformative is the way AI empowers non-technical stakeholders—especially those involved in product, sales, or marketing [2]. These individuals, often closest to customer pain points, can now participate directly in prototyping and testing new product features.

For instance, in a startup environment I've been involved with for several years, we've seen commercial and sales teams independently build and test AI-generated features based on client feedback. Without writing a single line of code, these teams can create fully functioning MVPs (Minimum Viable Products) that simulate the intended user experience. If a feature proves valuable and gains traction, it is only then handed off to the engineering team for full-scale development (Table 4.4).

This not only accelerates the iteration loop but also ensures that the engineering team works on features that have already demonstrated real-world value. The result is a more resource-efficient and user-driven development pipeline.

4.4.4 From Validation to Refinement

But the benefits extend beyond validation. AI-generated prototypes allow stakeholders to refine both the functionality and interface of a product before any code is committed. In traditional workflows, even validated features often undergo extensive modifications after release, as real users reveal edge cases or usability issues. Implementing these changes post-development often incurs technical debt, reducing the maintainability of the software.

Table 4.4 Which approach and when

For what?	Mockups	Vibe coding (AI based)	Traditional software development
Validate the idea of a product	Yes	No	No
Validate the concept of a product	No	Yes	No
Build the core of a product	No	No	Yes
Validate a new feature of an existing product	Yes, if complex	Yes, if simple	No
Integrate a new feature in an existing product	No	Yes, if simple and separated from the core flow	Yes, if it's strictly integrated in the core flow
Integrate scalable and validated features	No	No	Yes

With AI-assisted prototyping, these refinements can happen upstream. Stakeholders and users engage with near-final versions of features early in the process, surfacing critical insights at a point where changes are less costly. This reduces the risk of major rework and increases the chances of building sustainable, scalable software architectures later on.

4.4.5 *Toward Modular, Hybrid Product Architectures*

Another emerging pattern I'm seeing is the use of AI-generated micro-features that operate in parallel with the core product. Startups are beginning to experiment with modular architectures, where features created with no-code or AI tools are embedded into the main product temporarily for testing [5]. If the experiment succeeds, the feature is then rebuilt and integrated into the main codebase with proper engineering standards.

This modular approach allows startups to explore adjacent opportunities without compromising the integrity of their core product. It represents a flexible, low-risk pathway to innovation.

4.4.6 *Implications for Design and UX*

Finally, these changes have significant implications for UI/UX professionals. Designers must now consider a broader spectrum of implementation strategies, including the potential for features to be rapidly prototyped or delivered by non-technical users. Rather than focusing solely on what a technical team can build, designers should explore hybrid user interfaces—ones that accommodate and integrate AI-driven functionalities built outside the traditional development lifecycle.

This shift calls for a new design mindset: one that is more iterative, modular, and inclusive of rapid, AI-assisted prototyping cycles. It challenges designers to think not just in terms of fidelity and feasibility but also in terms of real-time validation and adaptability.

In the next chapter, we will summarize how AI-driven prototyping is fundamentally transforming the landscape of startup product prototyping and how new approaches enable smaller teams and even solo founders to rapidly and cost-effectively validate product ideas, reshaping team dynamics and accelerating growth with greater agility and efficiency.

4.5 Conclusions: Rethinking Startup Structures in the AI Prototyping Era

The transformative impact of AI on product prototyping is not limited to technology—it is reshaping the very structure, cost, and dynamics of how startups are conceived and scaled. As artificial intelligence lowers the barrier to building and validating digital products, new organizational models are emerging, characterized by leaner teams, faster iterations, and more fluid technical roles.

4.5.1 Fixing the Problem: AI as a Bridge Between Business Vision and Product Execution

Historically, early-stage startup success depended heavily on the presence of a technical co-founder or engineering team. AI is now decoupling this dependency by providing business-minded individuals with tools to independently materialize and test their ideas.

The implications of this shift are substantial. Business-oriented founders, even those without coding experience, now have the ability to create functional prototypes that extend well beyond traditional mockups or presentation slides. This capability allows them to become investor-ready by demonstrating convincing minimum viable products (MVPs) through working software rather than relying solely on pitch decks. Furthermore, the rise of AI tools has facilitated the emergence of the one-person company, where a single founder can independently ideate, build, test, and even market a product—often achieving early traction without the need for a larger team.

AI democratizes product creation, shifting power toward business founders by removing their reliance on early technical teams.

4.5.2 A Faster Approach: AI as a Validation Engine in Scale-Up Organizations

Even for startups beyond the initial MVP phase, AI introduces a new validation paradigm. Mature teams can use AI tools to test ideas without disturbing the core product roadmap or engineering pipeline.

In growth-stage startups, the role of prototyping expands across the organization, enabling parallel validation tracks. Non-engineering teams such as product marketing and customer success can independently build and test prototypes alongside the core development process. This capability accelerates iteration cycles, allowing new features or user flows to be prototyped, tested with users, and refined within a matter of days. As a result, product planning becomes more informed and efficient, with only validated, and tested, features being handed over to engineering—thereby minimizing rework and reducing the accumulation of technical debt.

Now, when a scale-up's go-to-market team identifies a new user need, within a week, it can build a stand-alone prototype, test it with real users, and collect data to justify full development. This cycle happens with minimal involvement from the engineering team.

AI-powered prototyping enhances organizational agility, accelerating innovation without increasing engineering workload.

4.5.3 Changing the Culture: A Shift in Early-Stage Startup Composition

As AI reduces the need for early technical capacity, the composition of founding teams is changing. The traditional "business + tech" duo is being replaced—at least temporarily—by business-only teams supported by external expertise.

Emerging trends I see in the startup ecosystem reflect a shift toward business-led early teams, where founders with backgrounds in product management, marketing, or operations are increasingly driving initial development. Technical hiring is often deferred until after a clear product-market fit has been established, allowing startups to remain lean in their early stages. This approach supports modular scaling strategies: minimum viable products are first built and validated using no-code or AI-driven tools, with full technical implementation reserved for the point at which the product's value has been clearly demonstrated.

In the near future, early-stage startups will be smaller, leaner, and more business oriented. Technical teams will become essential only during scaling and infrastructure phases.

4.5.4 The Rise of External Technical Advisors

In this new paradigm, technical expertise is not eliminated—it is repositioned. Founders and early-stage teams increasingly rely on freelance engineers and AI consultants to provide strategic guidance rather than implementation.

The role of technical freelancers is also evolving in response to these changes. Rather than focusing solely on hands-on development, many are now acting as strategic advisors. They assist non-technical founders in selecting the most suitable combination of no-code and AI tools for their specific use cases. Additionally, they play a crucial role in identifying potential risks and limitations of AI-generated prototypes, such as concerns related to data security, performance, and scalability. Importantly, they also serve as a bridge to full-scale development, facilitating the transition from AI-built MVPs to robust, production-grade software architectures when the product is ready to scale.

For these reasons, I see the demand for part-time technical advisors continuing to grow. These experts play a critical role in helping business founders navigate early choices and avoid costly missteps.

4.5.5 Summary and Key Takeaways

AI is fundamentally altering how digital ventures are launched and grown. It enables faster prototyping, broader participation in product development, and leaner operational structures. But it also demands new frameworks for validation, technical planning, and cross-functional collaboration.

That leads to the following implications for the future of startups:

- AI-first prototyping lowers entry barriers: Founders no longer need to be coders; business professionals can now launch software products without technical co-founders.
- One-person companies are viable: Founders can ideate, validate, and fundraise independently.
- The role of the technical co-founder is changing: Less about bootstrapping the MVP, more about building the post-validation infrastructure.
- AI accelerates development but does not replace software engineering; it serves for rapid prototyping rather than building sustainable, long-term systems.
- Growth-stage startups gain agility: AI enables feature validation managed directly by sales and customer success teams, speeding up product evolution.
- Technical hiring becomes strategic: Developers are no longer gatekeepers to prototyping but enablers of scalability and productization.
- UI/UX designers face a new challenge and opportunity with AI-driven prototyping: they must create hybrid interfaces that seamlessly integrate long-term functionalities developed by the technical team while simultaneously enabling interaction with prototype features created independently by non-technical users.

Table 4.5 Modern tools used by a startup for each kind of activity

Activity	Tool used
Validate product ideas	Figma, Canva, or Penpot for mockups; Typeform or Maze for quick user feedback
Validate working product concepts (light interactivity)	Figma, Canva, or Penpot for mockups
Test early user behavior and engagement with a functional prototype	Vibe code with tools like Lovable, Manus
Build the first stable version of the product	Modern frameworks like Next.js, Nuxt.js, Node.js, Supabase, or Firebase
Validate additional features to integrate into the product	Use feature flags (LaunchDarkly, Split.io) + integrate micro features built with Vibe code tools
Integrate new validated features into the core of the product, making it scalable	Full-stack frameworks like Next.js, Nuxt.js, Node.js, Supabase, or Firebase

– Freelance tech advisors become essential: Early-stage guidance ensures that AI usage aligns with long-term scalability (Table 4.5).

The convergence of AI and product prototyping marks the beginning of a new entrepreneurial era. Startups are no longer constrained by headcount, technical skills, or engineering bandwidth. What matters most now is clarity of vision, speed of execution, and discipline in validation. AI provides the tools—what remains is for founders to use them wisely.

References

1. Council, F.T.: How will the no-code market grow in 2023? Forbes (2023). https://www.forbes.com/councils/forbestechcouncil/2023/04/04/how-will-the-no-code-market-grow-in-2023. Accessed: 30 Jun 2025
2. Fischer, M., Lanquillon, C.: Evaluation of generative ai-assisted software design and engineering: A user-centered approach. In: International Conference on Human-Computer Interaction, pp. 31–47. Springer (2024)
3. Galli, M.S.: The history of web developers tied to browser development (2023). https://hackernoon.com/the-history-of-web-developers-tied-to-browser-development. Accessed: 30 Jun 2025
4. HTML Goodies: State of the web in 2010: Css3, html5, jquery use growing (2010). https://www.htmlgoodies.com/news/state-of-the-web-in-2010-css3-html5-jquery-use-growing/. Accessed: 30 Jun 2025
5. Kumar, R.: Generative ai in software architecture: Transforming design and development processes (2023). Available at: https://www.researchgate.net/publication/391570354_Generative_AI_in_Software_Architecture_Transforming_Design_and_Development_Processes
6. Myllärniemi, V., Kujala, S., Raatikainen, M., Sevońn, P.: Development as a journey: factors supporting the adoption and use of software frameworks. J. Softw. Eng. Res. Develop. **6**, 1–22 (2018)

7. Rahman, M.S.I., Islam, M.R., Hassan, M.M., Hasan, K.T.: Evolving web application development frameworks: A survey of ruby on rails, python, and cloud-based architectures. ResearchGate (2023). https://www.researchgate.net/publication/387893067_Evolving_Web_Application_Development_Frameworks_A_Survey_of_Ruby_on_Rails_Python_and_Cloud-Based_Architectures. Accessed: 30 Jun 2025
8. Ries, E.: The Lean Startup: How Today's Entrepreneurs Use Continuous Innovation to Create Radically Successful Businesses. Crown Currency, New York (2011)
9. Staff, C.: Low-code development platforms to grow 25% in 2023. Computerworld (2023). https://www.computerworld.com/article/1616390. Accessed: 30 Jun 2025
10. Truss, M., Schmitt, M.: Human-centered ai product prototyping with no-code automl: conceptual framework, potentials and limitations. Int. J. Human–Comput. Interact. **41**, 1–16 (2024)
11. Tutorialzine: Making a Cool Login System with PHP, MySQL & jQuery (2009). https://tutorialzine.com/2009/10/cool-login-system-php-jquery. Accessed: 30 Jun 2025

Chapter 5
Patterns for Startup Pitch Video Creation with Generative AI Support

Marko Nakov, Xiaofeng Wang, and Eduardo Guerra

Abstract Pitch videos are visual tools that assist startup founders in effectively communicating their business ideas. It is commonly used for crowdfunding campaigns, accelerator applications, and marketing purposes. Despite its crucial importance, startups might find the production of their own pitch video highly challenging, given the potential lack of time and expertise in the artistic field. Generative AI (GenAI) tools, with their widespread accessibility and time-saving characteristics, can be promising supporting tools for startup teams to create pitch videos. Given the nascent nature of GenAI technology, there is a scarcity of literature on the usage of GenAI to support startups in general and pitch video creation in particular. This book chapter aims to define GenAI-powered solutions to common challenges that startups might face when developing a pitch video with traditional methods. The focus of the study revolves around defining and proposing a set of patterns, emphasizing the underlying structure and the methodological processes behind GenAI-based solutions. The patterns were evaluated in a workshop and follow-up interviews with workshop participants to gain a better understanding of their application. These patterns will assist the integration of generative AI into effective startup pitch video creation and eventually facilitate the effective communication of startup ideas.

Keywords Artificial intelligence · Startups · Pitch videos · Generative AI · GenAI · Patterns

5.1 Introduction

Startup teams need to communicate their business ideas to various startup ecosystem players, such as mentors and investors, on various occasions, e.g., fundraising events and pitch competitions. Pitch video is a powerful tool for a startup team to communicate their vision, demonstrate their product, and attract potential investors.

M. Nakov (✉) · X. Wang · E. Guerra
Free University of Bolzano-Bozen, Bolzano, BZ, Italy
e-mail: xiaofeng.wang@unibz.it; eduardo.guerra@unibz.it

N. Tripathi et al. (eds.), *Advances in Software Startups*,
https://doi.org/10.1007/978-3-032-04294-1_5

An effective pitch video can significantly increase a startup's chances of securing funding, attracting talent, and engaging early customers.

Traditionally, creating high-quality pitch videos required substantial resources, including specialized skills in scriptwriting, videography, editing, and graphic design. This resource requirement creates a barrier for many early-stage startups operating with limited budgets and small teams. Startup teams often find themselves faced with an unappealing choice: allocate scarce resources to professional video production or produce lower-quality videos that may undermine their message.

Generative artificial intelligence (GenAI) technologies present a promising solution to this dilemma. The rapid advancement of large language models (LLMs), text-to-video generators, and AI-powered editing tools has created new possibilities for automating and enhancing various aspects of pitch video creation. These technologies can potentially democratize access to high-quality video production capabilities, allowing startup founders to focus on refining their core message while leveraging AI to handle technical aspects of production.

Despite this potential, startup teams lack clear guidance regarding the effective integration of GenAI tools into the pitch video creation process. Questions persist about the quality, authenticity, and effectiveness of AI-assisted pitch videos compared to traditionally produced alternatives. Furthermore, the rapidly evolving nature of GenAI technologies makes it challenging for startup teams to identify the most suitable tools and approaches for their specific needs.

The study presented in this chapter aims to provide support to startups to effectively apply generative AI for pitch video creation. However, focusing on some specific AI tools that are currently in use would not be a wise choice, as this field is in constant development. New AI models are being released with a very high frequency, and current ones might become obsolete in the near future. Instead, focusing on more generic application patterns of GenAI tools might be more future proof. Therefore, the goal of our study is to adopt a pattern-based approach to provide guidelines and illustrate practical AI-based solutions for problems that may arise during the creation of pitch videos for startups.

5.2 Startups, Pitch Videos, and GenAI

Startups are not small companies, distinguished by their ability to grow and, oftentimes, their brilliant ideas [16]. Figure 5.1 depicts a common life-cycle representation of startups.

The failure rate in this field is relatively high: less than one-third of the total number of startups become a stable company. This success rate is due to several challenges that founders have to face across all stages. Financial challenges are prevalent among all startups, as finance is fundamental for the startup's life-cycle [18]. It is easier to collect funds if the idea is valid and the startup is trustworthy in the eyes of investors.

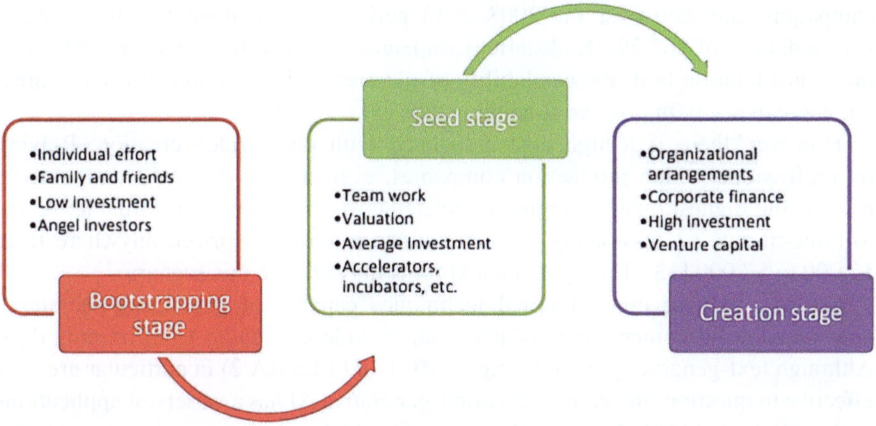

Fig. 5.1 Life-cycle of startups [18]

What has been proven to help during funding periods is the availability of a pitch video [15], which can be defined as a short video, usually between two and five minutes, giving an overview of the product or service to the target audience. The pitch video should address some critical points, such as the issues in the current situation, the solution proposed by the startup, and its characteristics.

A pitch video is a way to express visually the characteristics, current problems, and solutions that a particular startup is trying to address with its service or product. A successful pitch video aims to speak to what motivates the target audience: A focus on market opportunity will be more suitable if the pitch video aspires to reach a venture capitalist, whereas a non-profit organization will likely be motivated by a video revolving around large social impact. Therefore, the initial step will be to focus on the people who may have an interest in the startup idea and what their needs are [19].

In its initial part, a pitch video should grab the viewer's attention by clearly introducing the product or service and by showing its advantages. The video length should not exceed four minutes so people can make it to the end and remain engaged. A call-to-action clip, where viewers are directly asked to do something, is a valid possibility to end a pitch video. Lastly, another role should be that of being a potential backer answer to customers' and investors' common questions, such as *What is your product/service? How does it make my life better? Do I trust the startup?*

Several studies demonstrate that pitch videos bring value to startups. For example, Kolbe et al. analyzed the existing literature at that time on how effective pitch videos were in the context of a crowdfunding phase [15]. Using a dataset of 48,526 US-based crowdfunding campaigns from 2009 until 2012, Mollick found a positive correlation between the availability of a video pitch and funding success [17]. A direct correspondence between a project's funding success and the presence of a pitch video was also discovered in a study that analyzed a sample of 47,139 campaigns launched over the 2008–2013 period on Indiegogo [5]. In a similar way, a dataset of 267,295 Kickstarter campaigns launched from 2009 to 2015 took into consideration both the availability of pictures and video and showed a direct correspondence with positive funding results [4].

However, there is a high cost associated with pitch video creation. Relying on professional video production companies, even though they will undoubtedly provide the highest quality output, the related costs are often not affordable: A two to three-minute professionally produced video is typically priced anywhere from $2,000 to $7,000 [13]. Emerging GenAI tools may change this scenario.

GenAI refers to computational techniques capable of generating seemingly new, meaningful content such as text, images, video, or audio from training data. Although text-generating models (e.g., GPT-4 and LLaMA 2) in particular are very effective in question-answering scenarios, generative AI has a variety of applications in the artistic field [8]. At first sight, generative AIs are often seen as a threat to the art economy, as they seem to automate artistic production completely. However, behind, for example, an AI-generated image, there are numerous steps and choices that the single user should take into consideration: choice of the AI model, selection of an input image or typing a prompt from scratch, experimenting with many parameters settings that are often made available, and the iteration of the process until a satisfactory output has been obtained. AI-based artworks are therefore the result of time and effort from human artists, starting from the concept, through all the adjustments up to the final output [12].

In recent history, numerous advances in the artistic field were initially predicted to indicate the "end of art" and revealed instead a recasting of the practices and roles of creators. For some artists of the nineteenth century, the arrival of photography was seen as a threat to painting. Although portrait photography largely replaced portrait painting and yielded a short-term job loss for this category of artists, it eventually gave rise to Impressionism and the Modern Art movement. A similar fate was also observed with the advent of music production digitization through sound synthesis and digital sampling. Rather than leading to "the end of music," it introduced an unusual way of producing and listening to music, ultimately providing a route for new genres [7]. In the same way, GenAI can be positively seen not as the most dramatic "end of art" that has ever taken place but more as an opportunity, likewise in the past, to generate new forms of expression. To make an analogy, in which all that can be considered "art" is represented by a castle and artists are its residents, GenAI will probably close a couple of doors strictly and make those rooms almost inaccessible, but at the same time, it will open and create dozens of new spaces, most of them being unknown still today.

5.3 Pattern Creation Process

This study was initiated around June 2024, some months after OpenAI's video generation model Sora was first announced. Since then, a large number of companies have developed their generative model for video generation, encouraging healthy competition and expanding the possibilities for users. Moreover, the numerous videos shared across the Web depicting the capabilities of AI models made generative AI a very trending topic during the summer of 2024. Most AI tools that claim to be "AI video generators" could be classified into one of three major categories:

- AI video editors/assemblers. It consists of all those AI tools that utilize existing clips and, based on a prompt, merge a selected number of short videos into a longer one. Some AI tools that fall into this category are Fliki, Invideo, Veed.io, and Movavi.
- AI avatars, ideal for online courses and presentations. Some examples are Synthesia, HourOne, and Colossyan.
- AI tools that, given a text prompt, could generate brand-new video content. Some of the most famous and commonly used tools are Sora by OpenAI, Gen-3 by Runway, Veo 2 by Google, Hunyuan Video, and Kling 1.6.

The last category was the one this study was focused on. Several possible candidate AI models were reviewed, and the quality of each of them was assessed. Some tools were not accessible due to geographical restrictions. All the AI tools that have been tested out work based on credits: each video generation costs a specific amount of credits based on factors such as video length, the model used, and extra features (e.g., lip sync, effects). The free plan usually provides a small number of monthly credits and allows the user to utilize an older version of the model. A premium plan should be purchased to access fully customizable features and the latest AI model.

After trying different AI video generation tools with their free version, we decided to investigate further with Kling AI and Gen-3 by Runway by upgrading to their premium version. The features provided by Kling AI were only related to AI images and AI video (text-to-video, image-to-video, and lip sync), whereas Gen-3 had, apart from the ones just mentioned, a surprisingly big set of other AI tools, such as "Expand Image," "Video to Video," "Super-Slow Motion," "Blur Faces," "Clean Audio," and many more. We did not have the opportunity to try all of them during the models' assessment for pitch video generation. Although both have their own documentation guide for the prompting technique, only one model was outputting quality video content with stable consistency. Despite still being a bit far from completely realistic results, Kling AI has been, overall, the AI tool that managed to generate videos with the most convincing physics and motion. A high frequency of videos with distortions and strange movement was the main factor that made Gen-3 by Runway be excluded.

In November 2024, an interaction was initiated with several teams of university master students taking part in the course "Entrepreneurial Software Engineering." A part of the course required students to develop a startup idea and generate a pitch video. Since some teams had already started working on their pitch video with different approaches, it was a great occasion to gather different points of view and offer support for their video creation process. Eventually, the student members of a startup idea called "Whopika" were interested in collaborating to create their pitch video. Their idea revolved around a mobile app that helps users meet new people by creating or attending nearby events. The pitch video is intended to depict the monotonous life routine that a worker might experience, the discovery of the Whopika app with a focus on its features, and, at the end, a clip of the same worker enjoying an event found inside the app.

The AI tools we used for this project were Midjourney for the images and Kling AI for transforming these images into visual clips. Despite Kling AI allowing the generation of videos with only a text prompt, we found that using an input image led to more realistic results. Instead of using the selected image as the first frame of the generated video, it is also possible to choose the last frame: in that way, the AI model will try to accomplish the requested prompt by placing the input image at the end of the created clip. After reading the documentation of the AI tools we used and having tried numerous prompts with several customization parameters (over 100 total prompts across Midjourney and Kling AI), we achieved a satisfying result. However, the pitch video was not ready yet, as a part of the video required recording a particular shot traditionally with a camera. Lastly, the editing task also had to be done without AI's support. It included tasks such as putting the clips together, inserting static slide images during the video, and adding background music.

During the whole study process, we kept tracking new promising AI models and the new releases of existing ones. In such a dynamic situation, it was clear that focusing on the correct way of using a couple of AI tools could have become outdated in a very short period of time. Therefore, building on practical experiences with specific AI tools, the study aimed to share the learnings and define methodological patterns that could still be relevant when newer AI models replace the current ones.

5.4 Patterns for Startup Pitch Video Creation

The structure of the patterns adopted in this study is borrowed from software design patterns, as defined in [9]. Their definition is particularly well suited for our case study, as it requires each pattern to address a frequently occurring problem in a predefined environment. Moreover, the core solution should be reusable, though its implementation may vary across instances. The adopted structure and the components, specific to this study, are as below:

- **Context**: The startup context in which the problem arise
- **Problem**: Issues associated with current approaches used by startups
- **Solution**: AI-driven solution and its implementation details
- **Applicability**: In which scenarios the pattern is appropriate
- **Advantages**: Key factors supporting the proposed AI solution
- **Challenges**: Potential difficulties and feasible solutions, if present
- **Related patterns**: How this pattern is related to the others

5.4.1 Pattern 1: Image Generation

"Instant Graphics, No Sweat: AI to the Rescue!"

Context Although videos generally require active motion, images can still have a strong relevance in pitches. Illustrations that might appear throughout the video, such as logos, banners, or graphics, are all images developed by graphic designers. There will probably be numerous shots of the startup's product or service from different points of view, for which a professional photographer and possibly a recording studio are needed. If the pitch video idea requires interactions with the service or product, then the cost of actors should be added to the final price. Considering that these are only basic requirements and that each startup might have specific needs, it is clear that the issues that team members will face are both organizational and economic.

Problem How to generate meaningful images for the pitch video in an economical way?

Solution Use generative AI to generate the target image, by specifying in the prompt elements, such as the light, the angle, and the color tone.

Generative AI is a valid choice for creating not only images of the same persona or object in various contexts but also complementary elements such as logos, landscapes, or background illustrations. This can be achieved with text prompting through text-to-image or image-to-image models.

Quality pictures are based on several aspects, each of which significantly impacts the emotional tone and severity that an image evokes. Some important elements should be clearly defined when writing the prompt text in the AI model of choice. The first is lighting: it has a crucial impact on the representation of an image's characters, colors, and mood. A frontal lighting source highlights every aspect and exudes complete clarity, whereas a lateral or even backlight is generally associated with a quite mysterious and dark mood. Camera position and angle determine the primary focus and how it will be perceived: a low-angle shot creates a more authoritative look, a POV (point of view) shot helps the viewer empathize, and a high-angle shot produces a sense of vulnerability. Emotional tone plays a crucial role in images; therefore, another important factor that should be mentioned inside the prompt text is the color tone(e.g., cool-warm color spectrum, high-low contrast). These elements affect the effectiveness and accuracy of an AI-based image.

Once the AI model of choice has generated an image, the best practice would be to analyze the output, detect possible issues and mismatches between the prompt and the image, and rerun the generation with the text prompt changed accordingly. This process should be repeated until the output image aligns with the artistic goals. Figure 5.2 reveals, through a practical example, the value behind effective prompting techniques and how the terminology just discussed can be used to empower the message and mood that the image wants to deliver.

Prompt: Generate an image of a man walking inside a park. In the background, a group of people is playing basketball.

Output image:

Prompt: Generate an image of a man walking on a quiet street at dusk, heading toward a basketball court illuminated by warm streetlamp lights. In the distance, a group of people can be seen playing basketball and laughing together. The man wears a basketball jersey and white shorts. The mood is dark and melancholy.

Output image:

Fig. 5.2 Prompt comparison with DALLE 3

Applicability Despite image generation models being under continuous development, they have already become very efficient in representing objects, landscapes, and personas. This makes AI-based images a suitable solution in numerous scenarios. In the marketing and advertising fields, for example, AI models could generate product visualizations in different contexts. Also, in a period in which social networks are a crucial tool used by companies to deliver ideas and engage the public, prompts could be used to create captivating banners and logos. Within the limits of pitch videos, AI images can be used as input in image-to-video models to create the clips that will compose the final video.

Advantages The strongest point of text-to-image AI models for image generation is that they offer customization and freedom of expression in such an easy and accessible manner that replicating the same artwork in the real world would be way more expensive and challenging. For startups or companies in general, AI tools can be used to create unique and brand-oriented images for marketing purposes, without the need to create and prepare the environment for real photo shooting. Another key factor of AI models for image generation is their cost-effective and time-saving characteristics: the cost for AI tools such as DALLE 3 or Midjourney is very affordable, and with all the rising models that are being developed, soon the fees can be expected to be even lower. Image-generation AI tools can be utilized not only for generating new images from scratch but also for editing existing ones, the so-called image-to-image models. Lastly, some models contain a crucial feature that allows users to reuse some characteristics of images that were generated before. Midjourney allows for maintaining the facial and physical traits of another image with the "Character Reference" setting. If the aim is instead to match the look,

Fig. 5.3 Character and style references inside Midjourney

mood, and feel of a generated image, then the "Style Reference" settings should be used. Figure 5.3 depicts a practical usage of both reference features.

Lastly, what made generative AI stand out and rapidly grow in popularity in recent times is its fast accessibility and ease of use. The most common models usually provide extensive documentation with suggestions concerning specific prompting patterns and customization. Also, they generally have a dedicated section for discovering successful prompts and images made by other users. It could be used as a starting point for taking inspiration and identifying practical terms or structures. In conclusion, generative AI allows inexperienced individuals to create quality images.

Challenges Despite their benefits, AI-generated images pose issues and limitations that must be addressed. One common complication that some models (e.g., Midjourney) present is the inaccuracy in rendering areas with text or numbers, which are oftentimes replaced instead with random and unknown symbols. Although generative AI models became somewhat convincing in representing basic and simple illustrations, probably given by their high occurrence in the training datasets, they may still fail in depicting realistic motion, perspectives, and, therefore, dimensions of the represented objects. Also, there is an inherent trade-off that users must accept when utilizing AI tools for image generation: despite how well and how descriptive the prompt can be, it is hardly possible to have control over the whole generated image. The model might introduce unexpected elements, such as colors, people, or objects, that were not explicitly required by the prompt. This unpredictability reduces the overall control that users have on the final output and highlights why the manual work done by artists and designers still provides greater precision and intent in the image creation process.

To mitigate these challenges, users should focus on crafting precise and detailed prompts, experimenting with different phrasing, and iterating across multiple generations to refine their outputs. It could also be helpful to feed intermediate results back into the model to steer the generation closer to the intended outcome.

Related Patterns The images generated by AI models through this pattern are well suited for integration with the "Video Clips Creation" pattern. AI-based pictures can serve as a starting point for an animated video, reducing the need for manual content creation.

5.4.2 Pattern 2: Video Clips Creation

"Skip the Production Studio - AI Videos for Startups"

Context The requirements of a startup organizing the recording of a pitch video are influenced and can vary based on the area in which it operates. Some videos might require actors, a recording studio, technical equipment, or a professional team that will take care of everything just mentioned. Therefore, it needs a conspicuous dose of organizational and economic effort.

Problem How can startups create short clips for a pitch video without technical skills and cost-effectively with artificial intelligence?

Solution Providing quality prompts to AI video models can generate effective clips that might be merged to produce a pitch video.

AI video models provide great support in generating effective video clips. The most commonly used AI video models are usually based on two main types of input data: text-to-video and image-to-video. The former is used to generate a video clip based only on a text prompt, whereas the latter requires an image as input (a text prompt description is optional but highly recommended). Despite not being as common as the ones just mentioned, some AI tools, such as Pika Labs and Runway Gen-3, allow the creation of customized animations or styling effects with a video given as input, thanks to the so-called video-to-video models.

When searching for AI video models with the highest quality, it may be unclear how and based on which aspects to rate and categorize them. Some may excel in specific tasks or in representing particular styles, whereas others may be suitable for more general purposes. A study [14] published in 2024 proposed VBench, a benchmark designed to decompose "video generation quality" into 16 specific dimensions. Figure 5.4 depicts how several video models performed on each of these dimensions. Their project is completely open source, including all the prompts, generated videos, and evaluation methods. Regardless of the AI tool of choice, there is a set of settings and features shared across most of them. The generated video can be either in a horizontal (16:9) or vertical format (9:16). In our digital world, where

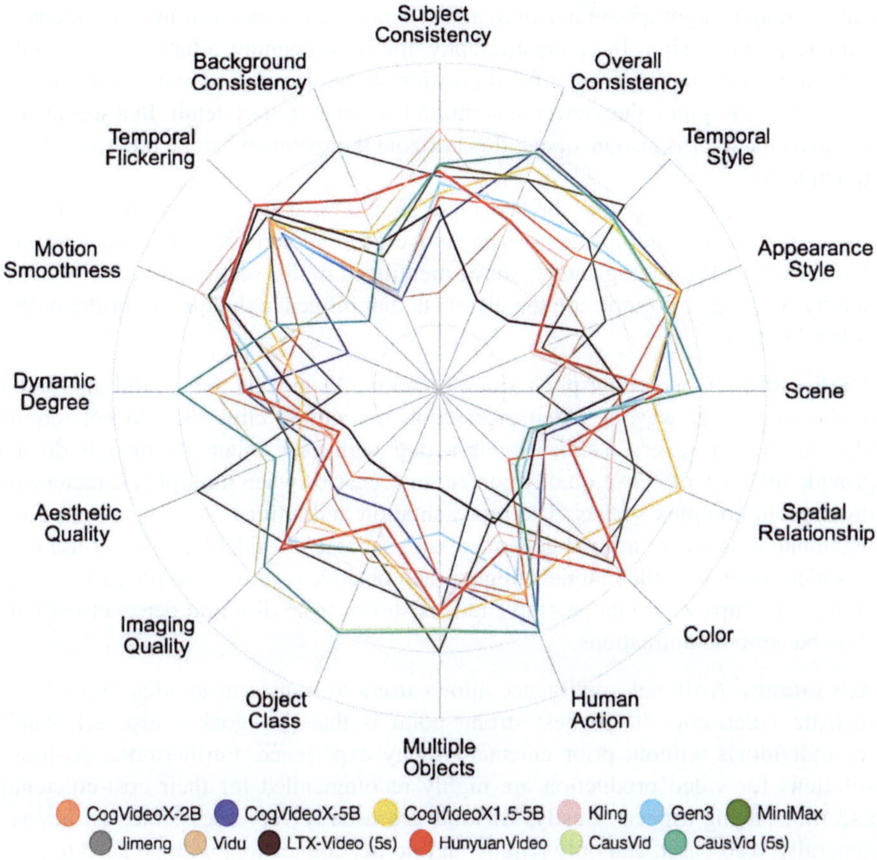

Fig. 5.4 Graphical representation of the 16 dimensions considered in VBench [14]

tons of content is delivered on mobile devices, having the possibility to create videos conceived for smartphones artificially is an important detail.

Also, the duration setting is adjustable as well. However, short clips (∼5 s) with a clear and brief text prompt should be preferred to longer videos representing several actions or movements. Also, once a clip is ready, some tools (e.g., Kling AI and Runway Gen-3) allow users to define a new prompt input and to extend the video by using the last frame of the previous clip as a starting point.

In the scenario of image-to-video generation, the input picture does not necessarily have to serve as the initial frame of the generated video. Input figures can also be intended as the ending frame of the clip. Their relative prompt text has to be, in that case, describing the whole scene that leads to that final moment, represented by the chosen input image.

An essential feature that gives a more realistic and emotional impression is the camera movement. Depending on the tool, the usage and tuning of this element may vary. Considering a close-up of an individual, a zooming-in movement of the camera may be appropriate in a dramatic or emotional scene, as it invokes intensity, intimacy, and tension. In cinematography, the term panning refers to a horizontal camera motion starting from a fixed position. It can be used to enhance a sense of discovery or to guide the viewer's attention toward a desired detail. In a scenario in which a character is also involved, this horizontal movement can be utilized to build anticipation.

As for image generation, the text input should be as detailed and descriptive as possible. However, multiple actions and movements should be avoided when writing the text input. The settings and features mentioned in this section, together with the quality of the text prompt, are the elements that influence the quality of the output video the most.

Applicability Concerning pitch video creation, AI models are a valid alternative to the traditional way of video production for simple clips that do not require high motion or several elements interacting with each other. AI models do not provide the most effective quality content in scenarios when multiple characters are involved in complex scenes. The representation and animation of landscapes and inanimate objects are instead generated with satisfactory fidelity. Another use case in which image-to-video models might reach positive results is for product concept animation: clips where the startup's idea is shown from different perspectives with slow but smooth animations.

Advantages Artificial intelligence allows users to transform an idea into a fairly realistic video clip. Its biggest strong point is that this goal is also achievable for individuals without prior cinematography experience. Furthermore, AI-based solutions for video production are highly recommended for their cost-efficiency and time-saving aspects. Lastly, AI tools are usually very accessible, as they are generally Web-based and only require an Internet connection, with no need to meet any technical requirements from the point of view of the user's device.

Challenges Although impressive advancements in generative AI video models have been made, one of their biggest challenges remains the representation of motion and physics in a realistic manner. A recent study [3] addresses these issues and proposes a novel framework that can be applied to any AI video model with minimal adaptations, not requiring modifications on the training set or scaling the model. Instead of considering motion as an implicit effect during video generation, VideoJAM unifies the learning process by using appearance and motion representation in the following way:

- During the training phase, the goal is to predict from one learned representation both the generated pixels and their motion.
- During interface (video generation), VideoJAM introduced a mechanism to enhance temporal coherence by using the model's own evolving motion prediction.

Despite the potential that this framework possesses, it still faces some limitations. VideoJAM struggles to capture motion in "zoomed-out" scenarios (e.g., a skydiver

Table 5.1 Comparison of different video generation methods across appearance and motion metrics [3]

Method	Appearance metrics				Motion metrics	
	Aesthetic quality	Image quality	Subject consistency	Background consistency	Motion smoothness	Dynamic degree
CogVideo5B	51.1	52.9	91.3	95.3	97.3	**87.5**
RunWay Gen3	55.1	55.1	90.7	95.2	98.4	84.4
Mochi	49.5	48.8	89.7	95.2	98.4	78.1
Sora	56.8	57.7	93.0	96.4	98.7	82.0
Kling 1.5	**58.5**	**60.4**	**93.9**	**96.5**	**99.2**	64.8
DiT-30B	49.2	56.8	91.3	95.5	98.8	71.1
+VideoJAM-30B	51.2	55.9	93.0	96.1	99.0	82.3

deploying their parachute) and when complex physics of object interaction is captured (e.g., a soccer player kicking a ball).

The same research study proposed a motion benchmark based on VBench. In Table 5.1, both motion smoothness (higher implies smooth motion) and dynamic degree (higher implies more motion) are represented in a comparison table with the most common video models, along with the base model Dit-30B enhanced by Video-JAM-30B. Kling 1.5 shows the lowest dynamic degree with the best motion smoothness. The VideoJAM framework applied to the based model DiT-30B obtained the most optimal balance of the two motion metrics, showing a possible implementation of VideoJAM on AI video models in the near future [3].

A final consideration of the challenges for AI-based video creation refers to the speed of the generated clips. From personal experience, Kling 1.5 reduces the velocity of the final video, creating a slow-motion effect and reducing the overall quality. However, this issue and other complications related to physical motion fidelity have been distinctly improved with Kling 1.6.

To address these limitations, users are encouraged to formulate prompts with precise descriptions of the intended motion and to incorporate light post-production editing (such as adjusting playback speed and applying basic video cuts) to enhance temporal coherence and overall video quality.

5.4.3 *Pattern 3: Script Generation*

"No Writer? No Worries! AI, Your New Scriptwriter"

Context The content of a script is fundamental as it determines the information that investors might retain after watching a pitch video. But not only that, the mood and emotional tone of the script highly influence the delivery effectiveness of a pitch video. However, developing a high-quality script is a necessary but also quite challenging task. Before the advent of AI, startup founders who found themselves in difficulties while writing a pitch video script would have needed to hire scriptwriters.

Problem Do LLMs have the potential to enhance startup members in the writing process for a pitch video script?

Solution Leverage LLMs to generate, iterate, and refine pitch video scripts by writing prompts that reflect the startup's goals.

In recent times, AI tools for enhanced script writing have been developed. These models typically accept a text input and generate a detailed and complete script document. The text prompt should be a detailed description of the startup's product/service, together with the mood and sentiment that the script should maintain.

AI tools such as ToolBaz and Simplified are capable of generating complete scripts with definitions of actors, locations, background songs, transitions, and relative timestamps. Figure 5.5 showcases a very brief script produced with ToolBaz for a startup called Whopika (presented during the study process in Sect. 5.3). The prompt used was quite short and simple: "A startup called Whopika is launching a mobile app for helping users create and join city events." Moreover, optional settings have been specified as follows:

- **Objective of Script**: "A script for a startup pitch video"
- **Length**: Too short (150–300 words)
- **Tone/Mood**: Uplifting
- **Audience Age Group**: 35+ Years

This example shows that, despite LLMs (Large Language Models) being under continuous development, they have already reached a point where scripts for pitch videos can effectively be generated from scratch.

Applicability AI tools for scriptwriting are extremely user-friendly and effective in numerous startup scenarios. They are very valuable for obtaining brand new script proposals but also for gathering inspiration on how to structure the pitch video, which actors and location to consider, and more.

Advantages In the case of image, video, or audio creation, imperfections in the generated content may lead to new generations as changes on the prompt and/or parameters have to be made. The strongest benefit when using AI tools for scriptwriting is that the generated output is text. Therefore, it can be easily copied and edited by users without the need to rerun different prompts multiple times.

Furthermore, scriptwriting with AI support is typically accessible without any costs. The reason is that these tools are usually based on LLMs that are already public and free.

Challenges A global concern that was raised among large language models is related to the overuse or dependency on AI, which may definitely negatively impact humans' curiosity and creativity in the long run.

Okay, here's a script for a startup pitch video for Whopika, designed to be uplifting and target an audience aged 35+.

Title: Whopika: Connecting Your City, One Event at a Time

(Video opens with warm, inviting shots of people enjoying local events: a farmer's market, a concert in the park, a community art show.)

(Upbeat, positive music playing in the background.)

Narrator: (Warm, friendly voice) Remember those moments when you stumbled upon something amazing happening in your city? A hidden gem, a spontaneous gathering, a memory made…

(Cut to a shot of the Whopika app interface, clean and easy to navigate.)

Narrator: But how often do those moments *really* happen? Life gets busy. We get stuck in routines. Missing out on the vibrant pulse of our communities.

(Cut back to diverse people smiling and interacting at events.)

Narrator: That's why we created Whopika. Whopika is a mobile app designed to help you discover and participate in the events that matter to *you*.

(App interface again, highlighting key features: event creation, searching by interest, map view.)

Narrator: Whether you're looking to create a neighborhood book club, join a local hiking group, or simply find the best live music in town, Whopika makes it easy to connect with your city and the people in it.

(Cut to founder/team member briefly addressing the camera with a genuine smile.)

Founder: We believe that strong communities are built on shared experiences. Whopika is our way of fostering those connections.

(Back to narrator, app interface with call to action.)

Narrator: Download Whopika today and start exploring! Reclaim your free time, discover new passions, and build lasting connections. Whopika: Your city awaits.

(Final shot: Whopika logo with website and app store links. Music fades slightly.)

Fig. 5.5 Script generation example with ToolBaz

Moreover, considering that training datasets are based on content created by individuals, AI-generated text might present gender, cultural, or racial bias. For example, training an AI on historical hiring data from a company that favors male applicants may lead to biased hiring recommendations [2].

To mitigate these risks, users should actively revise and modify the AI-generated scripts, incorporating their own critical thinking and originality to ensure the content aligns with their unique ideas, values, and target audience.

Related Patterns This pattern can be seen as a strong starting point, as it can be effectively integrated with several other patterns. A pitch video script generated using AI tools can include detailed suggestions, such as the appearance of actors, specific actions to be performed, camera movements, or the emotional tone of the soundtrack. Therefore, this pattern leads naturally to the use of other patterns such as "Image Generation," "Video Clips Creation," and "Background Music Generation," creating an interconnected workflow.

5.4.4 Pattern 4: Background Music Generation

"Your Pitch, Your Soundtrack - AI Sets the Perfect Tone"

Context Music has always played a major role in delivering an emotional tone in videos. There are numerous online platforms that provide royalty-free stock songs for a reasonable price. It is also possible, although more challenging, to find online companies that provide audio material for commercial use completely for free on the Internet. However, the search for the desired background music is, most of the time, a quite laborious and long process.

Problem Can music generated with AI be effectively used in startup pitch videos?

Solution Utilize AI-based music generation tools to create tailored soundtracks that match the emotional tone of a pitch video.

Artificial intelligence can be a medium to generate customized and unique music content. AI tools in this field usually revolve only around text inputs given by users, further enlarging the value of effective prompt writing.

It is quite common, for example, to include a specific genre (jazz, hip-hop, reggae, country, etc.) for which the model should aim. A detailed description of the expected mood is also incredibly valuable information. Should the generated instrumental be energetic, emotional, relaxed, or dark in style? Similarly, the energy that a music track delivers is highly affected by tempo, defined in BPM (beats per minute). Pop music is usually played in a range between 100 and 130 BPM, tango songs are instead between 62 and 66 BPM, and the salsa genre is typically in the range of 180–300 BPM [10]. Beyond tempo, other musical elements such as harmony and chord progressions significantly influence the emotional character of the soundtrack, with major tonalities typically evoking a more positive mood, while minor chords tend to convey a more tense emotional tone. Furthermore, it is generally possible to require the AI models to include only one or a set of instruments inside the generated soundtrack. Startups may benefit from this feature, as having a background based on a few instruments might not distract users' attention from the main aspects of a pitch video. Moreover, variations on loudness and intensity throughout the track may play a crucial role in creating expressiveness and emotional engagement. Lastly, some AI tools allow the creation of music with a defined duration that has to be explicitly written inside the input prompt.

Taking inspiration from the aspects mentioned in this section and defining a descriptive text prompt may be helpful in obtaining a high-quality and customized soundtrack.

Applicability Given the numerous online music collections that provide royalty-free content at an accessible cost, AI tools for music generation should be seen by startups as a possibility to obtain customized background songs in a short amount of time.

Advantages AI tools for music generation share some common positive aspects among most artificial intelligence tools: affordability, availability, and velocity of generation. Moreover, these tools are generally able to produce up to four songs with one prompt, giving users more freedom of choice.

Challenges A soundtrack can be considered completely effective if a certain degree of quality is ensured throughout the entire audio content. This is not always the case for AI-generated songs, as it does not always happen that AI music is created with a proper introduction and outro section. Soundtracks may immediately start with a high dynamic rhythm or end in a truncated way, without any type of fade-out effect.

An important point to be aware of is related to the repetitiveness of the melody inside a track. Some AI tools (e.g., Beatoven AI) have a tendency to reuse the base melody pattern across most of the generated content, which may not be exclusively a negative aspect in cases of pitch video, where the background music should only have a supportive role.

A factor to take into consideration for AI audio generator models is related to the licenses for commercial use. Based on the AI tool of choice, a premium version may be necessary to have legal rights for business purposes, such as pitch videos.

To address these challenges, users are advised to, if necessary, perform manual adjustments (such as modifying entry and exit volumes or making precise cuts) using dedicated audio editing software or integrated tools within video-editing programs, to ensure seamless and professional integration into the pitch video.

5.4.5 Pattern 5: Video Translations

"Let AI Do the Talking, Literally"

Context In recent times, English has become the worldwide predominant language in the working and business fields. Therefore, it has become common practice to create pitch videos in English to reach the biggest number of potential customers and investors. However, this approach creates a potential language barrier with non-English-speaking countries and a potential revenue loss as a consequence. An applicable solution would be to rely on an external professional company for a dubbing service. However, this way of working will not reach a completely realistic effect, as the actors' lip movements will be synced to the original language and not the one the video has been dubbed into. Moreover, economic aspects have to be considered, as professional dubbing services may have a price range of 15-60$ per minute [6].

Problem How to achieve quality translation for pitch videos without relying on professional dubbing companies?

Solution Artificial intelligence tools offer an accessible alternative to traditional dubbing for multilingual pitch videos, providing additional features such as lip synchronization and subtitles.

Tools such as HeyGen, BlipCut, and Vidnoz provide AI-based support for translating a video to multiple languages. Complementary features like subtitles and lip sync, used to deliver a more realistic and effective representation, are already included most of the time. These tools are usually very intuitive and straightforward to use as they only require the user to upload a video and select the original and the desired output language.

Applicability AI-powered tools for video translations may be suitable for any startup that has an interest in reaching a wider audience by targeting countries with unique and language-specific customized pitch videos.

Advantages AI video translation widens startup opportunities by creating language-based customized pitch videos. While the English version will oftentimes be the most viewed, AI-based translations are a cost-effective solution to gain a global audience. Furthermore, the value of these tools is enhanced by the additional AI-powered features (e.g., lip sync and subtitles generation) that are already included.

Challenges Artificial intelligence is still far from perfection in video translation tasks. Firstly, the AI voices used for the different languages are not based on the video's original voice actor. This effect can be mitigated in some AI tools, such as HeyGen, by uploading a local voice file, which will affect voice consistency across all languages.

Secondly, imperfections and errors during the translation process could occur. AI may particularly struggle in translating common sayings and phrasal verbs, with the risk of completely misinterpreting the original message.

One effective approach involves producing an original pitch video featuring complex syntax and constructions tailored for native English speakers, alongside a simplified version employing clearer and more straightforward language specifically designed to facilitate more accurate AI-based translations for non-English-speaking audiences, thereby minimizing the risk of misinterpretation.

5.4.6 Pattern 6: Video Editing

"Cut, Trim, Wow—AI for video editing"

Context Video-editing tools require sufficient skills and professional expertise in order to deliver effective results. A wide range of modifications may be needed, based on the aim of the project. Even in the case of minor adjustments, startups may have the need to get in touch with video-editing professionals. As for the other patterns, the biggest concerns for startups will be the lack of specific skills and the economic aspects.

Problem How can startups effectively apply minor edits on existing video clips without editing skills and in a cost-effective manner?

Solution AI-powered tools enable quick and simple video modification through text prompts, reducing the need for editing expertise.

Not as commonly as images and video generations, some AI models provide video-to-video capabilities. The most famous is Sora by OpenAI, which allows users to upload a video and type a text that describes the edits that are needed. It may be used, for example, to add or remove small objects or to revise the style of a video. Some aspects, such as the format (e.g., 16:9, 4:3, 1:1) and the duration, are bound to the original video. Compared to the other patterns, AI tools for video editing are the ones that allow less user customization: the final result will be determined mainly by the input video, the text prompt, and the remix strength (how intense the modifications should be).

Applicability This pattern may be effective with any kind of input video. However, edits on AI-generated footage should be avoided as the results may not be as convincing as in the case where real-world videos are used as input. In case of AI-generated content, the best approach would be to rewrite the prompt with the required changes, rather than using video-to-video models for the editing. In the case of pitch video creation, this pattern would ideally be used in order to perform small additions and/or removals without significantly altering the meaning of the original video.

Advantages AI video-to-video models present some strong points that are commonly shared with other patterns. It fills the lack of knowledge that startups may have in video editing, thereby reducing the entry barrier and making this professional field more accessible. Moreover, it is a cost-effective solution, as it reduces the need for startups to hire professionals for simple editing tasks, saving both money and time. Lastly, even for startup teams that have technical knowledge, AI can still be the fastest and most efficient option for small video edits. While video-to-video models are not perfect yet, AI tools will likely become a common choice for slight video editing in the near future.

Challenges Similar to video generation, video-to-video models may still struggle in representing motion and physics in a realistic manner. Also, AI-driven video-editing tools offer users less control compared to traditional and manual editing methods. This limitation can be particularly critical for projects requiring high levels of precision and customization. Nevertheless, given the continuous and rapid advancements in the AI field, the development of more controllable and effective AI-based video-editing tools appears to be promising in the near future.

5.5 The Evaluation of the Patterns

5.5.1 *The Evaluation Process*

The defined patterns were presented first as a poster in a workshop revolving around GenAI and its usage in the field of startups. The 25 participants were either from different local startups or knowledgeable in terms of GenAI and startups. Through the event presentation, we recruited four participants who were interviewed after the workshop, to provide more elaborate evaluations on the proposed patterns as well as their perspectives on using GenAI for creating pitch videos.

The interviewees are in close and frequent contact with startups, and some of them are also co-founders of one or more startups themselves. The first interviewee has an academic background in economics and business engineering. Professionally, she has working experience as a manager in sales and marketing, having worked in various companies and startups. In two of these startups, the interviewee played a key role, either as an early supporter or as part of the founding team. The second participant who took part in the interview process has an educational background in economics, entrepreneurship, and innovation. He is a founder or co-founder of two startups, one located in northern Italy and the other in western Germany. The third interviewee has a mixed academic background, having studied computer science, entrepreneurship, and innovation. In addition to experience in the IT field and other sectors, he is a co-founder of two startups and the sole founder of another. The last participant has an educational background in software engineering and has worked as a full-stack developer, project manager, and product owner. Additionally, he is the founder of two startups operating in the IT sector.

5.5.2 *The Evaluation Results*

The workshop has been a great opportunity to engage with founders and experts from diverse backgrounds. It allowed us to present the patterns to an audience and to get direct feedback from professional individuals on the current and future use of GenAI. Although none of the participants had previously used AI to create pitch videos for their startups, the discussions revealed a strong openness and positive attitude toward the potential of AI in this area. Generally, the perceived effectiveness of patterns was influenced by the individual's expertise. For instance, a musician considered the pattern about background music generation less useful while finding greater value in a pattern outside of his professional domain, such as image generation. Among all patterns, the video translation pattern generated the most interest, as it was considered the most mature and cost-effective solution.

In contrast, the four interviews with founders and experts have revealed a selective and context-dependent appreciation of the patterns. More specifically, the pattern related to image generation was often evaluated as effective. The participants recognized its potential for creating consistent visual assets, such as character representations and visual graphics, which can significantly enhance the visual coherence of pitch videos.

The proposed pattern for pitch video script writing pattern received moderate endorsement. AI-generated scripts may be valuable as a starting point from which it is possible to obtain inspiration. However, it is crucial to maintain human revision in order to have a sense of authenticity, emotional engagement, and natural flow.

A pattern that brought mixed responses was the one related to the generation of background music with AI. While its utility was acknowledged, especially for marketing or demo videos, it was not considered critical for investor-facing pitch videos, where music could sometimes be perceived as distracting or unnecessary.

The participants' perception of the pattern for video translation was positive in contexts targeting international audiences. Participants agreed that translated videos could enhance reach, especially during crowdfunding campaigns. Nevertheless, in the case of investor pitches, translations were generally considered slightly inappropriate, given the expectation of direct communication and language competence from the startup founders.

Lastly, AI-based video generation and video-editing patterns were viewed as the least mature. Participants described current AI-generated video outputs as artificial and disconnected from the authentic representations required in pitch videos. It has also been emphasized that pitch videos are among the most sensitive and intimate forms of content that startups produce and share, often serving as a direct reflection of the company and the founders themselves. For this reason, relying on AI for pitch video creation was not considered, for now, a professional or appropriate approach. While the potential of these technologies was acknowledged, their present state was considered inadequate for sensitive, high-stakes communication like pitching.

Table 5.2 summarizes the main ideas about the perceived effectiveness and the current AI tools for the six patterns. In conclusion, the validation process confirmed that patterns related to image generation, script writing, and video translation are currently offering the highest practical value. On the other side, patterns for music generation, video editing, and video generation are either secondary or still technologically immature for the context of startup pitch videos.

5.5.3 Broader Insights

Beyond the focus on pitch video creation and its patterns, the one-on-one interviews surfaced broader reflections on how startups are effectively integrating GenAI technologies in various operational areas.

Startups mentioned the use of AI for content creation in marketing and for customer communication. Generative AI is already being utilized for newsletters, generating social media posts, and automating initial outreach emails to potential clients.

Table 5.2 Summary of patterns with perceived effectiveness and representative AI tools

Pattern	Perceived effectiveness	Current AI tools
Image generation	High: Produces high-quality visuals with strong stylistic control, though sometimes limited by prompt precision	Midjourney, DALLE, Adobe Firefly
Video generation	Moderate: Visually compelling but limited by motion realism and controllability	Kling AI, Sora, Runway, Pika
Script generation	High: Enables rapid drafting and iteration with creative flexibility	ToolBaz, Simplified, Nolan AI
Background music generation	Moderate: Effective for emotional tone, though requires manual refinement	Mubert, Soundraw, Beatoven, Suno
Video translation	High: Expands reach and accessibility, with strong support for lip sync and subtitles	HeyGen, BlipCut, Vidnoz
Video editing	Low: Useful for small changes, but limited control over precise edits	Sora, Runway, Descript AI

Another valuable employment of AI that was also reported during the interviews was related to internal processes, such as knowledge management, document drafting, and the onboarding processes for new employees. A substantial time saving achieved by leveraging AI to extract information from complex documents or to generate technical documentation was highlighted by the participants.

Regarding video creation in its broader term (besides pitch videos), the participants expressed cautious optimism about the integration of AI in commercial video production, such as promotional teasers, demos, and tutorials.

Finally, there is an expectation that the current fragmented landscape of AI tools may converge into integrated platforms very soon, allowing startups to combine tasks like writing, designing, creating images, translating, and video editing within a unified environment. This would definitely enhance and incentivize startups to utilize AI tools even more.

5.6 Conclusions

This study aims to explore the applications of GenAI for pitch video creation and to define practical patterns to help startups effectively leverage AI for pitch video creation, which has become necessary due to a potential lack of time and artistic expertise among startup founders. As a result, a total of six AI-powered patterns have been defined to assist startups in their pitch video creation journey, followed by a validation process that involved several startup founders and experts.

Despite being able to define common patterns for pitch video creation, this study has several limitations. The first one refers to the number of AI models that have been tested. Veo 2 and Adobe Firefly were released recently and were not part of the AI tools taken into consideration during the study process. Furthermore, not all tools have been utilized at their full potential, as it was not feasible to unlock each of them with the premium plan. The second limitation is the lack of knowledge of the authors in the artistic field, which includes photography, graphic design, music, and video production. The technical references present inside the patterns (e.g., lighting, camera movement, music composition, etc.) are not the result of direct experience in the art domain but are based on the AI models and their documentation descriptions. Lastly, a significant limitation of this study is the absence of practical application of the proposed patterns by actual startup teams or entrepreneurs. While a systematic analysis of AI-generated content and related documentation has been applied for the patterns, they remain, at this stage, conceptual frameworks rather than tested methodologies.

As the concluding remarks, we would like to point out that this study has primarily highlighted the strong points of GenAI. Nevertheless, there are sensitive weaknesses introduced by AI that should be carefully taken into consideration, including how safely personal information is processed by AI models, potential violation of copyrights and intellectual properties, as well as potential disputes over authorship of AI-generated content [1, 11]. Given the quick development that AI has gone through in the last few years, it is understandable that most legal regulations have not been redesigned yet to align with the rapid advancements of AI. However, it should be a societal concern to regularize this field in the upcoming times.

Acknowledgments We would like to express our sincere gratitude to all participants of the workshop and, in particular, to the four founders and startup experts who generously took part in one-on-one interviews. Their insights have been extremely valuable in enriching our study and supporting the evaluation of the patterns from a startup-oriented perspective.

References

1. Al-kfairy, M., Mustafa, D., Kshetri, N., Insiew, M., Alfandi, O.: Ethical challenges and solutions of generative ai: An interdisciplinary perspective. In: Informatics, vol. 11, p. 58. Multidisciplinary Digital Publishing Institute, Basel (2024)
2. Chapman University, Bias in AI. https://www.chapman.edu/ai/bias-in-ai.aspx
3. Chefer, H., Singer, U., Zohar, A., Kirstain, Y., Polyak, A., Taigman, Y., Wolf, L., Sheynin, S.: Videojam: Joint appearance-motion representations for enhanced motion generation in video models. arXiv preprint arXiv:2502.02492 (2025)
4. Courtney, C., Dutta, S., Li, Y.: Resolving information asymmetry: signaling, endorsement, and crowdfunding success. Entrep. Theory Pract. **41**(2), 265–290 (2017)
5. Cumming, D.J., Leboeuf, G., Schwienbacher, A.: Crowdfunding cleantech. Energy Econ. **65**, 292–303 (2017)
6. Dubbing Cost Explained. https://www.voquent.com/dubbing/costs/

7. Epstein, Z., Hertzmann, A., the Investigators of Human Creativity, Akten, M., Farid, H., Fjeld, J., Frank, M.R., Groh, M., Herman, L., Leach, N., et al.: Art and the science of generative AI. Science **380**(6650), 1110–1111 (2023)
8. Feuerriegel, S., Hartmann, J., Janiesch, C., Zschech, P.: Generative AI. Bus. Inf. Syst. Eng. **66**(1), 111–126 (2024)
9. Gamma, E.: Design Patterns: Elements of Reusable Object-Oriented Software. Person Education, Upper Saddle River (1995)
10. Genres BPM explained. https://www.musical-u.com/learn/rhythm-tips-for--identifying-music-genres-by-ear
11. Golda, A., Mekonen, K., Pandey, A., Singh, A., Hassija, V., Chamola, V., Sikdar, B.: Privacy and security concerns in generative AI: a comprehensive survey. IEEE Access **12**, 48126–48144 (2024)
12. Hertzmann, A.: Can computers create art? In: Arts., vol. 7, p. 18. MDPI, Basel (2018)
13. How Much Does Video Production Cost. https://dmakproductions.com/blog/how--much-does-video-production-cost/
14. Huang, Z., He, Y., Yu, J., Zhang, F., Si, C., Jiang, Y., Zhang, Y., Wu, T., Jin, Q., Chanpaisit, N., et al.: Vbench: Comprehensive benchmark suite for video generative models. In: Proceedings of the IEEE/CVF Conference on Computer Vision and Pattern Recognition, pp. 21807–21818 (2024)
15. Kolbe, M., Mansouri, S., Momtaz, P.P.: Why do video pitches matter in crowdfunding? J. Econ. Bus. **122**, 106081 (2022)
16. Magalhães, R.P.C.: What is a startup?: a scoping review on how the literature defines startup. Master's thesis, Universidade Catolica Portuguesa (Portugal) (2019)
17. Mollick, E.: The dynamics of crowdfunding: An exploratory study. J. Bus. Ventur. **29**(1), 1–16 (2014)
18. Salamzadeh, A., Kawamorita Kesim, H.: Startup companies: Life cycle and challenges. In: 4th International Conference on Employment, Education and Entrepreneurship (EEE), Belgrade (2015)
19. The Secret to Successfully Pitching an Idea. https://www.youtube.com/watch?v=l0hVIH3EnlQ&t=1s&ab_channel=TED

Chapter 6
daBML: An Extension on the "Build-Measure-Learn" Loop for Generative AI Process Adoption

Gijs Oliemans and **Marco Mondini**

Abstract Startups adopting generative AI (GenAI) often face challenges not addressed by existing enterprise-oriented frameworks. Fast feedback cycles, resource constraints, and high uncertainty require a lightweight approach that goes beyond traditional maturity models. This chapter introduces *Define-Analyze-Build-Measure-Learn* (daBML), an extension of the Build-Measure-Learn (BML) loop, tailored to guide generative AI adoption in startup environments. By adding two upstream phases—*Define* and *Analyze*—the framework supports clearer scoping, risk awareness, and value alignment before experimentation begins. The framework is illustrated through two internal use cases from a later-stage software startup, covering domains such as software development, product design, operations, and commercial outreach. These examples demonstrate how daBML can help teams frame GenAI initiatives, identify adoption risks, and track impact through lightweight iterations. While promising in practice, the framework remains conceptual and is not yet empirically validated. Future work should explore how daBML performs across varied startup contexts and how it supports long-term integration of generative AI beyond initial pilots.

Keywords Generative AI · Toolset · Build-Measure-Learn · Technology adoption · Organizational impact

6.1 Introduction

As generative AI (GenAI) capabilities continue to develop, organizations are actively exploring how these systems can function as internal assistants to streamline

G. Oliemans (✉)
University of Amsterdam, Amsterdam, Netherlands
e-mail: gijs.oliemans@student.uva.nl

M. Mondini
Independent Researcher, Amsterdam, Netherlands
e-mail: mmondini@mondspace.com

N. Tripathi et al. (eds.), *Advances in Software Startups*,
https://doi.org/10.1007/978-3-032-04294-1_6

workflows and enhance operational efficiency [9, 40]. For startups in particular—especially those operating in software development—generative AI is increasingly viewed as a tool to support automation, boost creativity, and accelerate decision-making cycles [20, 43]. Studies have documented generative AI applications across departments such as marketing, IT, operations, risk, and human resources, showcasing its potential to reshape work practices and augment human capabilities [8, 15].

Despite this growing momentum, it remains unclear how startups can effectively adopt generative AI technologies [6, 42]. Several questions remain open: which departments and roles benefit most from generative AI? How do these tools restructure workflows or responsibilities? And what strategies can guide adoption under constraints of limited resources, technical expertise, and time [6, 43]? Compounding this uncertainty is the difficulty of determining the right timing and scale of investment to ensure measurable returns [13, 22].

In response, a growing body of research has begun to address the organizational and strategic dimensions of AI adoption. Prior work has proposed AI capability assessment models, AI maturity frameworks, and phased adoption strategies aimed at supporting structured integration [4, 7, 21, 26]. However, these models are largely tailored to enterprises and may not sufficiently reflect the dynamic, iterative, and resource-constrained realities of startup environments [2, 37]. While some studies explore the financial valuation of AI-driven businesses [33], others highlight the importance of aligning AI initiatives with business goals through structured evaluation frameworks [11, 23].

For software startups, generative AI offers opportunities for rapid prototyping, workflow automation, and cost reduction—particularly in areas like product development, recruitment, software testing, and customer engagement [43]. However, implementation is not without challenges. Startups often face high setup costs, limited generative AI literacy, and uncertainty in estimating long-term impact or return on investment [25, 35]. Moreover, issues related to intellectual property, model bias, and compliance further complicate adoption, especially in the absence of dedicated AI governance structures [29, 49].

Against this backdrop, it becomes evident that startups require more than generic AI maturity models or enterprise-oriented toolkits. What is needed is a lightweight, flexible approach that accommodates fast-paced experimentation while maintaining strategic clarity and risk awareness. Such an approach should help startups not only identify relevant generative AI opportunities but also reflect critically on feasibility, organizational readiness, and long-term value. This chapter addresses that need by exploring how structured yet adaptive frameworks can support generative AI adoption in startup environments. Building on startup-centric methodologies and informed by recent research, it introduces a process model designed to support intentional, iterative, and low-risk adoption of generative AI within software startups.

6.2 State of the Art

6.2.1 Generative AI in the Business

Generative AI has demonstrated significant potential across several key impact areas within startup environments, particularly those characterized by resource constraints and high levels of uncertainty. The most frequently cited domains include productivity, creativity, decision-making, automation, innovation, and knowledge management. These areas represent the primary vectors along which generative AI can drive tangible improvements in business performance.

In terms of productivity and automation, generative AI enables startups to reduce manual workloads by automating repetitive and time-consuming tasks [49]. This includes areas such as internal documentation, customer service automation, and content summarization, allowing employees to focus on higher-value work [8, 17, 30]. These capabilities directly contribute to increased operational efficiency and lower process overheads. Creativity and innovation are equally prominent themes in generative AI literature. Tools like large language models and image generators can augment human ideation and content production, acting as co-creators in marketing, product design, and software development workflows [8, 30, 44]. This augmentation accelerates early-stage experimentation and supports broader innovation cycles, especially relevant in startups seeking novel business models or rapid prototyping capabilities [29, 36].

In the context of decision-making, generative AI tools offer domain-specific assistance by extracting insights from large volumes of data, providing recommendations, and generating synthetic outputs that inform strategic choices [16, 27, 32]. This includes applications across engineering, HR, and operations where fast, informed decisions are critical [17, 29, 41]. Such support can enhance decision quality, reduce biases, and speed up analysis in high-stakes or time-sensitive scenarios.

Knowledge management is another area where generative AI can add value, particularly by generating onboarding documents, FAQs, meeting summaries, and contextualized internal communication [30, 41]. These applications facilitate organizational learning and internal transparency, helping startups maintain alignment as they scale.

Finally, the measurement of generative AI impact has increasingly moved beyond traditional financial metrics. Recent frameworks emphasize the importance of tracking KPIs such as efficiency gains, user adoption rates, time saved per task, and employee satisfaction to assess the real-world value of generative AI deployments [24, 31, 44]. These indicators support data-driven iteration and help align generative AI initiatives with strategic business goals.

6.2.2 Existing Adoption Frameworks and Limitations

Organizations adopting new technologies have long relied on established frameworks such as the Technology Acceptance Model (TAM) [12, 47], the Technology-Organization-Environment (TOE) framework [3, 45], Business Process Management (BPM) [14], and DMAIC from Lean Six Sigma [1]. While each contributes valuable perspectives—user intentions (TAM), organizational context (TOE), structured process improvement (DMAIC), and workflow optimization (BPM)—they share significant limitations when applied to startups experimenting with generative AI. These models are largely enterprise oriented, assume stable environments, and lack the agility needed for early-stage experimentation [28, 50].

Other frameworks, such as McKinsey's 7S [39, 48] and ADKAR [19], focus more on internal alignment or individual-level change management, offering limited value for organizations undergoing fast-paced technological transformation. Even the Build-Measure-Learn (BML) loop [38], widely embraced in startup product development, falls short when applied to complex internal adoption efforts—it prioritizes speed over analytical depth and often lacks structured guidance for risk or stakeholder alignment [10].

In contrast, a growing body of literature directly addresses the challenges of generative AI adoption. The AI Capability Assessment Model (AI-CAM) by Butler et al. [7] evaluates maturity across business, ethics, data, and governance domains. Holmström and Carroll [20] offer a strategic typology of AI innovation strategies along augmentation and automation axes, while Strobel et al. [41] introduce a taxonomy of GenAI system types and associated risks. These models are helpful in classifying innovation types and surfacing early risks but offer little in the way of a repeatable process.

Gupta et al. [18] contribute a startup-specific adoption model for prototyping technologies, incorporating factors like recyclability, ease of use, and behavioral intention. Although not exclusive to AI, it is particularly relevant for early-stage GenAI experimentation. Bettoni et al. [4] focus on SME readiness, highlighting constraints such as limited data, low technical literacy, and cost. Baek et al. [2] propose a quality evaluation model for AI-based services, grounded in user experience and feedback loops—highly aligned with startup needs. Tursunbayeva and Gan [46] contribute a holistic checklist (TOP framework), emphasizing organizational culture, trust, and workforce empowerment.

While these frameworks provide valuable insights—particularly around readiness, risks, and classifications—most remain descriptive and fragmented. Few offer a lightweight, actionable process tailored to the realities of startups: limited resourcing, fast iteration cycles, and uncertain returns. The daBML framework addresses this gap by integrating strategic scoping, feasibility reflection, and lean experimentation into a repeatable adoption process—bridging the divide between academic models and startup practice.

6.3 Research Method

In this chapter, we present a conceptual framework aimed at guiding the adoption of generative AI in later-stage startups. The approach is exploratory and design oriented, with a strong emphasis on practical relevance and applicability.

First, the *daBML* framework was constructed as a conceptual extension of the Build-Measure-Learn loop. While not the result of a formal empirical study, the framework draws conceptually on academic literature discussing the limitations of existing adoption models and the emerging characteristics of generative AI technologies. Rather than aiming to develop a new theory, the framework seeks to offer a practitioner-oriented structure that responds to recognized gaps in current practice—particularly regarding risk awareness and strategic alignment prior to experimentation.

Second, the framework is illustrated through a real-world use case involving a later-stage startup. Four real examples—based on actual organizational decisions and adoption scenarios—are used to demonstrate how the framework could be applied in practice. These examples help ground the framework in realistic startup dynamics and validate its relevance across different types of generative AI integration.

By combining conceptual development with practitioner-oriented explanation and grounded illustration, this study contributes a toolset that supports structured yet agile adoption of generative AI technologies in startup environments.

6.4 Key Findings

6.4.1 Build-Measure-Learn as the Foundation for (AI) Adoption in Startups

The Build-Measure-Learn (BML) loop, introduced by Ries in the Lean Startup methodology [38], has emerged as a widely adopted model for structuring innovation and experimentation in startup environments. Although originally developed for product validation, BML's underlying principles—rapid iteration, minimal upfront investment, and real-world feedback—make it well suited to internal innovation contexts as well.

For example, Cook [10] applies BML to educational innovation, showing how it can be used to introduce and iterate on internal processes by treating users (e.g., students or staff) as key feedback sources. This reinforces the idea that process adoption can mirror product adoption: both involve building something new, rolling it out to users, and refining based on real-world interaction and adoption behavior. In this way, BML's learning cycle becomes a practical tool for testing not only external products but also internal technology-driven changes such as generative AI use cases.

Both require rapid feedback, fast iteration, and a minimal investment approach to reduce uncertainty and validate value creation. Its core premise—rapidly building a minimal viable implementation (MVI), measuring outcomes, and iteratively learning from real-world feedback—aligns well with the fast-paced and resource-constrained reality of startups. For later-stage startups (10–50 employees), the BML approach continues to offer a pragmatic structure to navigate uncertainty, particularly when experimenting with emerging technologies like generative AI [5, 44].

Compared to more established process and technology adoption models—such as TAM, TOE, BPM, or DMAIC discussed in Sect. 6.2—BML offers significantly greater agility and responsiveness. Traditional models tend to emphasize structured planning, user acceptance, or enterprise-wide alignment, making them less suitable for fast-paced experimentation in uncertain startup environments. In contrast, BML provides a lightweight, learning-oriented cycle that prioritizes user input and rapid iteration over rigid planning or top-down implementation [34].

However, as discussed in Sect. 6.2, BML also has notable limitations when applied to the adoption of complex technologies like generative AI. It lacks structured mechanisms for framing innovation goals, assessing feasibility, or anticipating organizational risks—factors that are especially important given the broader scope, uncertainty, and potential impact of generative AI initiatives. Such technologies frequently intersect with ethical concerns, regulatory ambiguity, data governance, and workforce dynamics. In short, misaligned or premature adoption can lead to wasted resources, trust erosion, and unintended consequences at scale.

To address these challenges, we position BML not as a stand-alone solution but as a foundational component to be extended. The *daBML* framework builds on the strengths of BML while introducing two preceding phases: *Define* and *Analyze*. These additions provide startups with tools for clearer scoping, early risk reflection, and strategic alignment—before entering the experimental Build-Measure-Learn cycle. In the following sections, we present the complete framework and illustrate how these components enhance the applicability of BML in generative AI adoption contexts.

6.4.2 daBML

The growing interest in adopting generative AI within startups is met with a fragmented body of frameworks, most of which either lack the iterative speed needed for early-stage ventures or fail to provide practical guidance on how to assess and measure impact. While existing process models such as the Build-Measure-Learn (BML) loop from the Lean Startup methodology offer a strong foundation for rapid iteration, they fall short in analytical depth—particularly when applied to AI adoption contexts that require risk evaluation, capability assessment, and impact measurement. To address this gap, we introduce the daBML framework: an extension on the Build-Measure-Learn loop (Fig. 6.1). The framework consists

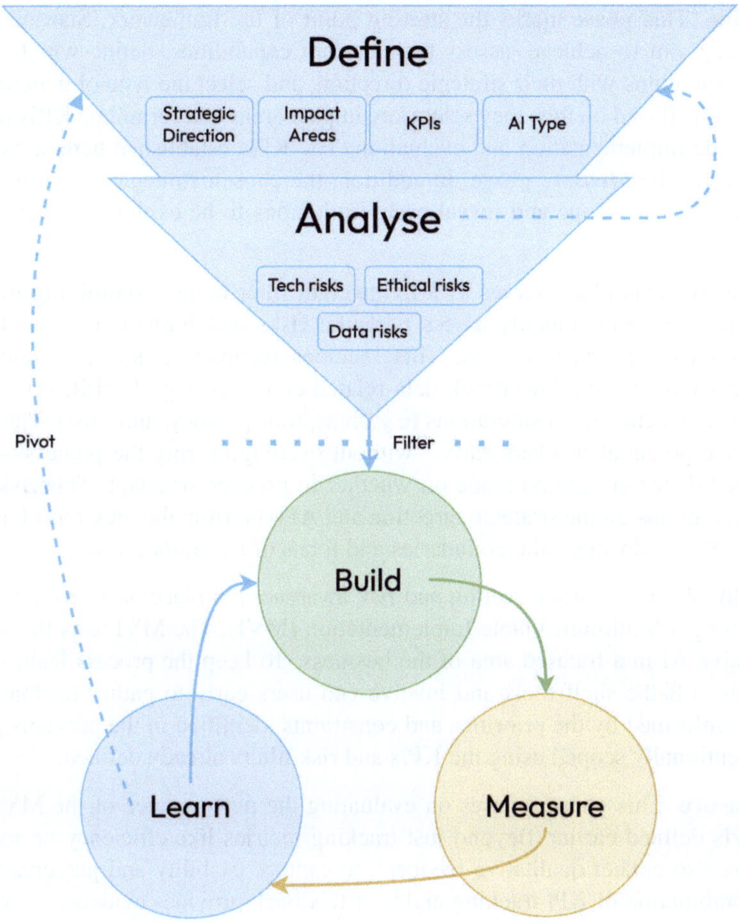

Fig. 6.1 Visual representation of the daBML framework. The process starts with two upstream phases—*Define* and *Analyze*—that guide strategic direction and assess risks before entering the iterative Build-Measure-Learn loop

of the BML logic but expands it with two preceding phases, *Define* and *Analyze*, each grounded in insights from recent literature on AI capabilities, typologies, and governance models. As presented in the framework, we see that phases *Build*, *Measure*, and *Learn* represent the three phases of the BML cycle. If needed to be classified under one of the BML components, the *Define* and *Analyze* phases would align best with the concept of learning and are hence grouped under *Learn*. When trying to align the core of the BML extension with a fitting title, we constructed *daBML*. Since the abbreviation BML is widely used for the Build-Measure-Learn loop, and this toolset is merely an extension on the framework, we add "da" to represent the new components *Define* and *Analyze*, respectively.

1. Define This phase marks the starting point of the framework. Startups clarify what they aim to achieve, assess their current capabilities, define which type of innovation aligns with their strategic direction, and select the type of generative AI technology. Based on this, they select key impact areas and formulate KPIs that will later guide implementation and evaluation. The KPIs established here serve as the baseline for the *Measure* phase. In addition, the chosen strategic direction and AI type help set the scope and reveal early limitations to be explored in the *Analyze* phase.

2. Analyze This phase serves as a lightweight filter before committing to experimentation. Startups quickly assess potential risks and limitations related to the proposed use of generative AI. This includes technical risks (e.g., integration complexity or system downtime), data-related concerns (e.g., GDPR, privacy, and security), and ethical considerations (e.g., bias, transparency, and trust). The goal is to surface potential blockers early—without overengineering the process—so that informed decisions can be made on whether to proceed or adapt. This risk-aware reflection builds on the strategic direction and AI type from the previous phase. The insights here help shape the boundaries and focus of the *Build* phase.

3. Build With a clearer direction and risk awareness in place, startups move on to developing a Minimum Viable Implementation (MVI). The MVI tests the value of generative AI in a focused area of the business. To keep the process lean, startups often use off-the-shelf tools and involve end-users early to gather feedback. The MVI is informed by the priorities and constraints identified in the previous phases. It's intentionally scoped using the KPIs and risk filters already defined.

4. Measure This phase focuses on evaluating the performance of the MVI using the KPIs defined earlier. Beyond just tracking metrics like efficiency or accuracy, startups also collect qualitative feedback to capture usability and perceived value. The combination of KPI tracking and user feedback provides evidence on whether the strategic goals from *Define* are being met in practice.

5. Learn Startups synthesize findings from both quantitative and qualitative results to determine next steps. They may choose to scale up, refine and iterate, or pivot to a new approach—depending on what they've learned. Evaluation outcomes loop back into earlier phases: feeding into a new *Define* phase (in case of a pivot) or directly informing the next *Build* phase (in case of refinement).

6.4.3 The "New" Components: What Is da?

Define: Context and Framing

The first component of the daBML framework—*Define*—serves as the foundation for any generative AI adoption effort. Its primary aim is to establish strategic clarity before engaging in technical experimentation or implementation. In this phase, startups articulate the intended purpose of the AI initiative, the organizational context in which it will be deployed, and the expected business outcomes. This includes identifying which roles, departments, or processes will be affected and clarifying the overarching goals such as improving productivity, augmenting creativity, supporting decision-making, or streamlining operations.

A core part of this step involves examining several contextual considerations: Which internal stakeholders or teams will be most impacted by the initiative? What organizational pain points or inefficiencies are currently present in the targeted process? What would success look like from both a business and end-user perspective? How will the added value of generative AI be recognized or demonstrated early, even before formal KPIs are established? And finally, what assumptions are being made—explicitly or implicitly—about the potential of generative AI in this specific context?

By setting the context early on, startups can avoid the pitfalls of vague or overly ambitious AI projects that lack strategic alignment. This framing phase is particularly crucial in resource-constrained environments, where experimentation without clear direction can lead to wasted effort or misalignment with core business needs.

Define: Applying Theoretical Models

To further ground the strategic direction, the *Define* phase incorporates conceptual models that help teams frame their generative AI use case. One such model is the quadrilateral framework proposed by Holmström and Carroll [20], which distinguishes AI innovation strategies along two dimensions: the degree of automation and the extent of augmentation of human capabilities. This model enables startups to classify potential use cases into four quadrants, helping surface underlying assumptions about the role of AI in the target process. As shown in Fig. 6.2, the quadrants include *(i)* low automation and low augmentation, where minimal AI involvement may indicate that traditional tools suffice; *(ii)* high automation and low augmentation, typically aligned with rule-based or repetitive task automation; *(iii)* low automation and high augmentation, which supports human expertise and creative output; and *(iv)* high automation and high augmentation, where AI actively contributes to decision-making or co-creation. By situating a proposed use case within this space, teams gain a clearer sense of scope, required capabilities, and the anticipated interaction between human and AI actors. This classification also initiates a critical line of questioning: Are we seeking efficiency through automation, enhancement through augmentation, or both? What level of human involvement is expected or desired? These early reflections are essential for shaping the evaluation criteria and feasibility assessments that follow in the next phase.

Following the strategic classification of objectives using the automation-augmentation space, the next step involves selecting the appropriate type of generative AI technology to support the intended business value. To this end, the typology proposed by Strobel et al. [41] offers a structured lens through which

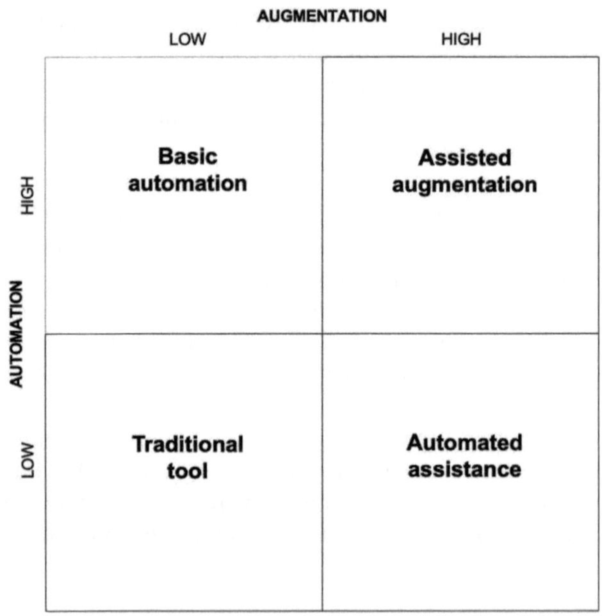

Fig. 6.2 Quadrilateral model of Holmstrom and Carroll [20] © 2024, used under CC BY 4.0 license

startups can categorize potential generative AI applications. This mapping helps translate abstract strategic aims into concrete AI functionalities, ensuring that selected tools align with the specific nature of the intended outcomes.

Strobel et al.'s framework identifies five distinct categories of generative AI systems, each suited to different types of value creation (Fig. 6.3). *Generators* are designed for novel content creation and are particularly relevant in contexts like marketing, communications, or product design, where original output such as text, imagery, or video is required. *Reimaginators* focus on transforming existing material while retaining its core intent—making them suitable for tasks such as editing, personalization, or format adaptation, often used in internal knowledge sharing or communication workflows. *Assistants* provide targeted, domain-specific support and are often deployed in environments such as engineering, legal, or customer service, where contextual understanding and operational relevance are key. *Synthesizers* are effective in generating summaries or synthetic outputs from complex data, serving use cases that demand data aggregation, reporting, or insight extraction. Finally, *Enablers* constitute the infrastructural layer of generative AI, offering capabilities for scalable deployment, integration with enterprise systems, or support for other AI services.

The process of aligning generative AI typologies with business objectives involves reflecting on the type of value the organization seeks to deliver—whether that be innovation, optimization, or enhanced support capabilities—and assessing

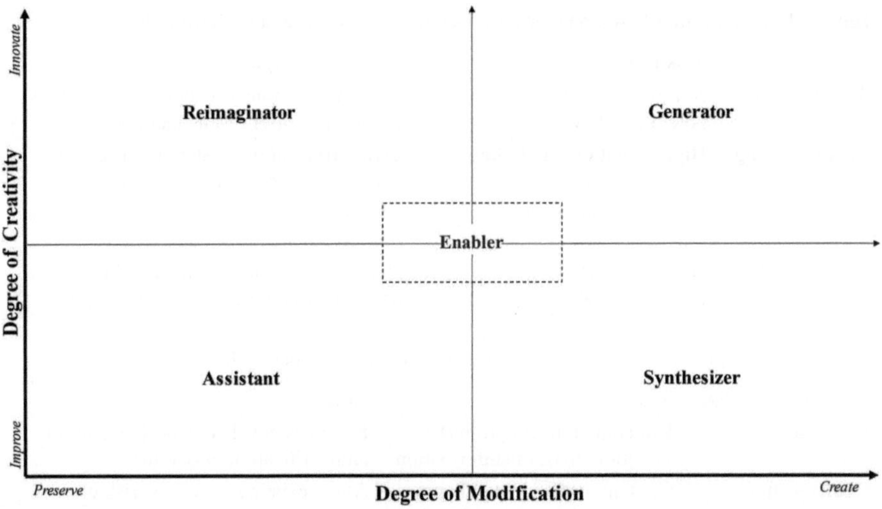

Fig. 6.3 Typology matrix of Strobel et al. [41] © 2024, used under CC BY-NC-ND 4.0 license

which generative AI type is most likely to realize those outcomes. This typological mapping complements the earlier strategic framing and helps refine the technical scope of the initiative.

Analyze

The second phase of the daBML framework, *Analyze*, serves as a conceptual filter that helps assess the viability of the proposed generative AI initiative before committing to implementation. This phase builds upon the strategic framing established in the *Define* phase—particularly the innovation strategy derived from the automation-augmentation space (Table 6.1) and, where applicable, the selected generative AI typology (Table 6.2). Its primary objective is to uncover key risks, constraints, and limitations that may otherwise go unnoticed in the rush to experiment.

By examining potential barriers related to legal compliance, data governance, ethical implications, and technical feasibility, startups gain a more complete understanding of the context in which the generative AI solution will operate. For instance, a solution classified as high automation and high augmentation—particularly when coupled with a *Generator*-type model—tends to carry elevated risk. These systems often produce novel outputs with limited human oversight, raising concerns around reliability, accountability, and safety. In such cases, additional controls or safeguards may be required before proceeding to development.

Key considerations at this phase include legal and regulatory compliance (e.g., data privacy, intellectual property, or sector-specific laws), as well as safety, interpretability, and accessibility. Startups should also reflect on feasibility—whether

Table 6.1 Risk profiles based on innovation strategy (Holmström and Carroll [20])

Quadrant	Risk profile	Typical risk types
L Aut / L Aug	Minimal innovation risk; potentially low value	Missed opportunity, underutilization of AI capabilities, user disengagement
H Aut / L Aug	High operational risk; low human oversight	Error propagation, system failure, over-automation, compliance issues
L Aut / H Aug	Human-AI interaction risks	Misguidance, trust erosion, cognitive bias reinforcement
H Aut / H Aug	Highest complexity and compound risk	Hallucinations, lack of traceability, ethical or legal violations, accountability gaps

Table 6.2 Risk profiles by generative AI application type (Strobel et al. [41])

Generative AI type	Risk types	Notes
Generator	Hallucination, copyright/IP violation, bias, misinformation	Produces novel content; low control and verification of outputs
Reimaginator	Content distortion, confusion, trust issues	Alters existing materials; risk of altering meaning or tone
Assistant	Misleading advice, automation bias, over-reliance	Guides decision-making in domain-specific tasks; critical in regulated fields
Synthesizer	Data misrepresentation, nuance loss, bias amplification	Aggregates and condenses data; may obscure detail or introduce bias
Enabler	Integration complexity, infrastructure lock-in, data exposure	Underlying infrastructure risks; often hidden early in adoption

the necessary data, infrastructure, or expertise are realistically within reach—and whether the intended solution will be equitably accessible to its intended users. These reflective questions not only help mitigate risk but also support responsible innovation by ensuring that the system's potential impact is assessed across operational, ethical, and social dimensions.

Ultimately, the *Analyze* phase helps determine whether to proceed with the proposed generative AI initiative as scoped, to revise certain assumptions or parameters, or to postpone implementation until foundational issues are addressed. It provides a lightweight yet structured opportunity to course-correct before resources are invested in building a Minimum Viable Implementation.

6.4.4 Applying the Framework: Use Cases

To illustrate how daBML supports generative AI adoption in startup environments, we highlight two internal use cases from a late-stage European software startup (±50 employees). These examples demonstrate how the framework guides adoption through strategic framing, risk reflection, rapid experimentation, and iterative learning.

Use Case 1: AI-Assisted Code Generation (Technical)

Context Developers frequently encountered repetitive coding tasks in both legacy and greenfield environments. These low-value tasks contributed to cognitive fatigue and slowed delivery.

Define and Analyze The objective was to reduce cognitive load and improve development flow. This use case aligned with a *low automation, high augmentation* strategy, using an IDE-integrated assistant combining **Generator** and **Reimaginator** functions. Risks included hallucinated suggestions, over-reliance by junior developers, and compliance with internal policies. Lightweight governance measures—peer review, IDE-only use, and developer-led control—were sufficient to mitigate these concerns.

Build-Measure-Learn A Minimum Viable Implementation (MVI) was rolled out by enabling the assistant within existing IDEs. Feedback was gathered through informal team retrospectives. Developers reported improved task efficiency, smoother flow, and reduced friction during implementation, especially for repetitive or unfamiliar code. While experienced developers integrated the tool easily, junior developers required onboarding guidance. The assistant was retained for internal tasks, and prompt design documentation was improved in response to user feedback.

Use Case 2: Generating Wireframes from Prompts (Non-technical)

Context Product managers needed to quickly explore and communicate new feature ideas but were constrained by limited design resources.

Define and Analyze The use case targeted faster visual prototyping and stakeholder alignment, following a *low-automation, high-augmentation* strategy. The tool combined **Generator** and **Reimaginator** features to produce mockups from text prompts. Risks included low fidelity, design inconsistency, and overconfidence in AI outputs. Because outputs were not externally shared, compliance and reputational risks were minimal.

Build-Measure-Learn A lightweight pilot was launched with no technical integration. Product managers used the tool in discovery sessions to quickly generate wireframes, which were reviewed by designers before further development. The tool accelerated ideation and stakeholder input, reducing design bottlenecks. It was adopted as an optional step in the early discovery phase, supported by internal documentation on prompt crafting and clear expectations about output quality.

6.4.5 Limitations

This research is conceptual and illustrative in nature. Although the framework is grounded in literature and supported by real-world examples from a later-stage startup, these examples serve as demonstrations rather than formal validation. No user studies or multi-organization testing was conducted to evaluate the framework's effectiveness across diverse startup contexts. The application of the framework was retrospective and scoped internally, meaning its utility during live adoption processes or in earlier-stage startups remains untested. Additionally, the KPIs and evaluation metrics used in the case examples were mostly qualitative and based on informal feedback, rather than standardized measurement approaches.

Another limitation concerns the foundation on which the framework builds. As noted in the key findings, the original purpose of the Build-Measure-Learn (BML) loop lies in product validation and early-stage business model testing. While it has been extended in this work to support internal AI adoption processes, such a shift requires careful consideration. The assumptions that underpin BML—fast iteration, minimal investment, and clear product-market feedback—do not always transfer seamlessly to the complexities of internal technology adoption, particularly in the case of generative AI. This recontextualization may overlook challenges around change management, governance, and organizational learning that BML was never intended to address.

These limitations suggest opportunities for future work, including empirical validation through prospective studies, broader application in different organizational settings, and refinement of evaluation criteria to support more rigorous measurement. As a result, the generalizability of the framework and the level of confidence it provides for guiding decision-making in other startup contexts should be interpreted with caution.

6.5 Recommendations

For practitioners, particularly those in startup environments, the daBML framework aims to offer a lightweight structure to support the adoption of generative AI. Practitioners in this context include startup founders, product managers, innovation leads, and operations or engineering team members who are directly involved in evaluating and implementing new technologies. We do not present the framework as a complete solution but rather as a tool to guide early framing, encourage risk awareness, and promote iterative learning. One key implication is to begin with strategic clarity instead of jumping directly into technical experimentation. Teams may benefit from asking what value they seek, what internal capabilities are available, and which processes could realistically benefit from AI. The early stages of the framework—*Define* and *Analyze*—are designed to support this reflection. They offer a way to surface risks and constraints before resources are committed. This may help avoid premature or misaligned deployments. In applying the framework, teams are encouraged to define KPIs early and use them to shape small-scale pilots. Importantly, daBML is not meant to be prescriptive. It should be adapted to the context, resources, and maturity level of the organization using it.

Although the use cases focus on a later-stage startup, the daBML framework may also be relevant for earlier-stage teams. Its lightweight structure and emphasis on scoping and early risk reflection could support intentional experimentation when resources are limited. However, very early-stage startups may require further adaptation, and future work could explore how the framework performs in less mature organizational settings.

For researchers, this work highlights the need for adoption models that reflect the speed, uncertainty, and constraints typical of startup settings. While daBML builds on the well-known Build-Measure-Learn loop, it introduces upstream elements that are often overlooked. These include early-stage framing, typology classification, and lightweight risk analysis. Future research could explore whether these additions improve adoption outcomes. Future work could include validation through empirical studies. This might involve testing the framework across different domains, startup sizes, or AI maturity levels. Action research or field studies could help refine its components and assess its practical value. There is also room to examine how startups define success in AI adoption—particularly beyond technical implementation. This includes questions around strategic alignment, organizational learning, and ethical use. The daBML framework may provide a starting point for that discussion.

6.6 Conclusion

This chapter introduces daBML, a process-oriented toolset to support the adoption of generative AI in startup environments. The framework builds on the Build-Measure-Learn (BML) cycle and adds two upstream stages—*Define* and *Analyze*. These additions aim to bring more structure to early framing and risk consideration, especially in contexts where generative AI adoption carries organizational and ethical complexity.

The framework draws from existing literature and is illustrated through practical use cases. However, it remains conceptual. Its scope is limited to a specific organizational setting, and it has not yet been validated through broader empirical research. Practitioners are encouraged to view it as a starting point—something to adapt and test in their own context, rather than as a fixed recipe.

Future work could examine how the framework performs in different startup types or industries. Studies may also focus on how teams apply the framework in real time: how they define impact, how risk assessments shape implementation, and how KPIs evolve throughout the process. These insights could help improve the framework's structure and usability.

More broadly, this work speaks to a wider need for lightweight, startup-sensitive approaches to AI adoption. daBML does not aim to solve this challenge entirely but offers one contribution toward a more intentional and reflective adoption process—one that balances speed with strategic alignment and long-term value.

References

1. Antony, J.: Some pros and cons of six sigma: an academic perspective. TQM Mag. **16**(4), 303–306 (2004)
2. Baek, C.H., Kim, S.Y., Lim, S.U., Xiong, J.: Quality evaluation model of artificial intelligence service for startups. Int. J. Entrep. Behav. Res. **29**(4), 913–940 (2023). https://doi.org/10.1108/IJEBR-03-2021-0223
3. Baker, J.: The technology–organization–environment framework. In: Information Systems Theory, pp. 231–245. Springer, Berlin (2012)
4. Bettoni, A., Matteri, D., Montini, E., Gładysz, B., Carpanzano, E.: An AI adoption model for smes: a conceptual framework. IFAC-PapersOnLine **54**(1), 702–708 (2021). https://doi.org/https://doi.org/10.1016/j.ifacol.2021.08.082, 17th IFAC Symposium on Information Control Problems in Manufacturing INCOM 2021
5. Blank, S.: Why the lean start-up changes everything. Harv. Bus. Rev. **91**(5), 63–72 (2013)
6. Browder, R.E., Koch, H., Long, A., Hernandez, J.M.: Learning to innovate with big data analytics in interorganizational relationships. Acad. Manage. Discov. **8**(1), 139–166 (2022). https://doi.org/10.5465/amd.2019.0048
7. Butler, T., Espinoza-Limón, A., Seppälä, S.: Towards a capability assessment model for the comprehension and adoption of ai in organisations. J. AI Robot. Workplace Autom. **1**(1), 18–33 (2021). https://doi.org/10.69554/KLJJ4414
8. Chui, M., Roberts, R., Yee, L.: Generative ai is here: how tools like chatgpt could change your business (2022), https://www.mckinsey.com/capabilities/quantumblack/our-insights/generative-ai-is-here-how-tools-like-chatgpt-could-change-your-business. Accessed 04 Jan 2025
9. Company, M..: The state of AI in 2023: generative AI's breakout year (2023), https://www.mckinsey.com/capabilities/quantumblack/our-insights/the-state-of-ai-in-2023-generative-ais-breakout-year, Accessed 04 Jan 2025
10. Cook, D.A.: Evaluating education innovations rapidly with build-measure-learn: applying lean startup to health professions education. Med. Teach. **44**(12), 1338–1339 (2022). https://doi.org/10.1080/0142159X.2022.2118038
11. Cronin, I.: Understanding Generative AI Business Applications: A Guide to Technical Principles and Real-World Applications, 1 edn. Apress L. P, Berkeley, CA (2024)
12. Davis, F.D.: Perceived usefulness, perceived ease of use, and user acceptance of information technology. MIS Q. **13**(3), 319–340 (1989)
13. Deloitte Insights: How to quantify the value of generative ai investments (2023), https://deloitte.wsj.com/cio/how-to-quantify-the-value-of-generative-ai-investments-f79c2f79, Accessed 04 Jan 2025
14. Dumas, M., La Rosa, M., Mendling, J., Reijers, H.A.: Fundamentals of Business Process Management, 2nd edn. Springer, Berlin (2018)
15. Dwivedi, Y., Kshetri, N., Hughes, L., et al.: Opinion paper: "so what if chatgpt wrote it?" multidisciplinary perspectives on opportunities, challenges and implications of generative conversational ai for research, practice and policy. Int. J. Inf. Manage. **71**, 102642 (2023). https://doi.org/10.1016/j.ijinfomgt.2023.102642

16. Enholm, I.M., Papagiannidis, E., Mikalef, P., et al.: Artificial intelligence and business value: a literature review. Inf. Syst. Front. **24**(6), 1709–1734 (2022). https://doi.org/10.1007/s10796-021-10186-w, https://doi.org/10.1007/s10796-021-10186-w, published: 25 August 2021, Issue Date: October 2022
17. Gupta, V.: An empirical evaluation of a generative artificial intelligence technology adoption model from entrepreneurs' perspectives. Systems **12**(3) (2024). https://doi.org/10.3390/systems12030103
18. Gupta, V., Bjarnason, E., Gupta, C.: Strategic prototyping technology adoption in startups: framework, challenges, and opportunities. IT Prof. **24**(3), 88–95 (2022). https://doi.org/10.1109/MITP.2022.3172876
19. Hiatt, J.: ADKAR: a model for change in business, government, and our community. Prosci Res. **1**, 43–61 (2006)
20. Holmström, J., Carroll, N.: How organizations can innovate with generative AI. Bus. Horiz. **68**(5), 559-573 (2024). https://doi.org/https://doi.org/10.1016/j.bushor.2024.02.010
21. Hussain, A., Rizwan, R.: Strategic AI adoption in smes: a prescriptive framework. Preprint. arXiv:2408.11825 (2024). https://doi.org/10.48550/arXiv.2408.11825
22. IBM Institute for Business Value: The ingenuity of generative ai at scale (2023), https://www.ibm.com/thought-leadership/institute-business-value/en-us/report/scale-generative-ai?, Accessed 04 Jan 2025
23. Kanbach, D.K., Heiduk, L., Blueher, G., et al.: The genai is out of the bottle: generative artificial intelligence from a business model innovation perspective. Rev. Manager. Sci. **18**, 1189–1220 (2024). https://doi.org/10.1007/s11846-023-00696-z, published online: 13 September 2023
24. Kang, C., McLain, S., Adelberg, M.: How to quantify the value of generative AI investments. https://deloitte.wsj.com/cio/how-to-quantify-the-value-of-generative-ai-investments-f79c2f79 (2024)
25. Kitsios, F., Kamariotou, M.: Artificial intelligence and business strategy towards digital transformation: a research agenda. Sustainability **13**(4) (2021). https://doi.org/10.3390/su13042025
26. Kučević, E., Grünewald, F., Schanz, N.: Towards a simplified AI adoption framework: Success factors for the implementation of artificial intelligence information systems. In: HCI International 2024 – Late Breaking Papers: 26th International Conference on Human-Computer Interaction, HCII 2024, Washington, DC, June 29 – July 4, 2024, Proceedings, Part IX, pp. 88–106. Springer-Verlag, Berlin (2025). https://doi.org/10.1007/978-3-031-76827-9_6
27. Kumar, H.: Strategic adoption of artificial intelligence in modern enterprises: frameworks, applications, and future implications. Artif. Intell. Appl. **1**, 53 (2024)
28. Mahdjoubi, N., Owen, J.R.: Limitations of the lean startup methodology in technology-based ventures. J. Innov. Entrepreneurship **8**(1), 1–15 (2019)
29. Marshall, A., Bieck, C., Dencik, J., Goehring, B.C., Warrick, R.: How generative ai will drive enterprise innovation. Strateg. Leadersh. **52**(1), 23–28 (2024). https://doi.org/10.1108/SL-12-2023-0126
30. Master, S., Chirputkar, A., Ashok, P.: Unleashing creativity: the business potential of generative AI. In: 2024 2nd World Conference on Communication & Computing (WCONF), pp. 1–6 (2024). https://doi.org/10.1109/WCONF61366.2024.10692266
31. Microsoft Corporation: Adoption considerations for innovation (2024), https://learn.microsoft.com/en-us/azure/cloud-adoption-framework/innovate/considerations/adoption. Accessed 15 Apr 2025
32. Mohapatra, S., Kumar, A.: Developing a framework for adopting artificial intelligence. Int. J. Comput. Theory Eng. **11**, 19–22 (2019). https://doi.org/10.7763/IJCTE.2019.V11.1234
33. Moro-Visconti, R.: The Valuation of Artificial Intelligence-Driven Startups, pp. 293–344. Springer Nature Switzerland, Cham (2024). https://doi.org/10.1007/978-3-031-53622-9_5

34. Nguyen-Duc, A., Wang, X., Abrahamsson, P.: What influences the speed of prototyping? An empirical investigation of twenty software startups. In: Baumeister, H., Lichter, H., Riebisch, M. (eds.) Agile Processes in Software Engineering and Extreme Programming, pp. 20–36. Springer International Publishing, Cham (2017)
35. Perifanis, N.A., Kitsios, F.: Investigating the influence of artificial intelligence on business value in the digital era of strategy: a literature review. Information **14**(2), 85 (2023). https://doi.org/10.3390/info14020085
36. Ramaul, L., Ritala, P., Ruokonen, M.: Creational and conversational AI affordances: how the new breed of chatbots is revolutionizing knowledge industries. Bus. Horiz. **67**(5), 615–627 (2024). https://doi.org/https://doi.org/10.1016/j.bushor.2024.05.006
37. Reim, W., Åström, J., Eriksson, O.: Implementation of artificial intelligence (AI): a roadmap for business model innovation. AI **1**(2), 180–191 (2020). https://doi.org/10.3390/ai1020011
38. Ries, E.: The Lean Startup: How Today's Entrepreneurs Use Continuous Innovation to Create Radically Successful Businesses. Crown Business (2011)
39. Singh, A.: A study of role of mckinsey's 7s framework in achieving organizational excellence. Organ. Dev. J. **31**(3), 39–50 (2013)
40. Stanford: Artificial intelligence index report 2024 (2024), https://aiindex.stanford.edu/report/. Accessed 04 Jan 2025
41. Strobel, G., Banh, L., Möller, F., Schoormann, T.: Exploring generative artificial intelligence: a taxonomy and types. In: Proceedings of the Annual Hawaii International Conference on System Sciences, pp. 4546–4555 (2024). https://doi.org/10.24251/HICSS.2024.546
42. Sun, Y., Jang, E., Ma, F., Wang, T.: Generative AI in the wild: prospects, challenges, and strategies. In: Proceedings of the 2024 CHI Conference on Human Factors in Computing Systems. CHI '24. Association for Computing Machinery, New York (2024). https://doi.org/10.1145/3613904.3642160
43. Talebi, K., Ghasemi, Z., Nobari, N., Seraj, M.: Artificial intelligence adoption by digital startups in decision-making within uncertain business environments. In: Drăgan, F., Ivascu, L. (eds.) Entrepreneurship, chap. 1. IntechOpen, Rijeka (2025). https://doi.org/10.5772/intechopen.1007080
44. Tang, X., Du, S., Deng, W.: Business innovation in digital startups: a case study of an ai startup. Int. Rev. Econ. Finance **98**, 103898 (2025). https://doi.org/https://doi.org/10.1016/j.iref.2025.103898
45. Tornatzky, L.G., Fleischer, M.: The Processes of Technological Innovation. Lexington Books (1990)
46. Tursunbayeva, A., Chalutz-Ben Gal, H.: Adoption of artificial intelligence: a top framework-based checklist for digital leaders. Bus. Horiz. **67**(4), 357–368 (2024). https://doi.org/https://doi.org/10.1016/j.bushor.2024.04.006
47. Venkatesh, V., Morris, M.G., Davis, G.B., Davis, F.D.: User acceptance of information technology: toward a unified view. MIS Q. **27**(3), 425–478 (2003)
48. Waterman, R.H., Peters, T.J., Phillips, J.R.: Structure is not organization. Bus. Horiz. **23**(3), 14–26 (1980)
49. Zavrazhnyi, K., Kulyk, A., de Abreu, O.A.: The innovative impact of generative artificial intelligence on digital business transformation. Econ. Syst. Develop. **6**(2), 63–70 (2024). https://doi.org/10.32782/2707-8019/2024-2-9
50. Zhu, K., Kraemer, K.L.: Post-adoption variations in usage and value of e-business by organizations: cross-country evidence from the retail industry. Inf. Syst. Res. **16**(1), 61–84 (2005)

Theme II: Product Engineering

Chapter 7
Hypotheses Engineering in Software Startups: From Business to Architecture

Eduardo Guerra, Jorge Melegati, and Davide Montesin

Abstract Software startups operate in environments marked by high uncertainty and rapid innovation, yet many still prioritize technical excellence over validated customer needs. This chapter advocates for a shift toward hypotheses engineering: a systematic approach to uncover, test, and manage assumptions in startup development. We present an integrated application of two complementary techniques: HyMap, which supports early-stage identification and mapping of business hypotheses, and ArchHypo, which manages architectural uncertainties by treating them as hypotheses. Through a case study of a real-world startup integrating Generative AI into their product, we demonstrate how connecting business and architectural hypotheses enable traceable, strategic decision-making. The results show that combining HyMap and ArchHypo provides a more holistic, hypotheses-driven development process, improving a startup's ability to adapt, experiment, and align technical efforts with business goals.

Keywords Hypotheses engineering · Software architecture · Business assumptions · Software startups

7.1 Introduction

Software-enabled innovations that changed human life are ubiquitous in contemporary society. Web search engines, e-commerce Web sites, and social networks are just some examples. Many of these solutions were developed by emerging companies, the so-called startups. When the product or service is software intensive, these companies are called software startups [36]. Even though there are household

E. Guerra · J. Melegati (✉)
Faculty of Engineering, Free University of Bozen-Bolzano, Bolzano, Italy
e-mail: eduardo.guerra@unibz.it; jorge.melegati@unibz.it

D. Montesin
Catch Solve, Bolzano, Italy
e-mail: d@vide.bz

N. Tripathi et al. (eds.), *Advances in Software Startups*,
https://doi.org/10.1007/978-3-032-04294-1_7

names, e.g., Slack, Airbnb, and Instagram, representing successful software startups, more than 90% of startups fail [18]. There are various reasons for failure [36], but the lack of a structured business development process is a key determinant [6]. A key practice that could support these companies, by reducing the uncertainty involved in the process, is experimentation [1, 11]. This approach is characterized by continuously identifying critical product assumptions, transforming them into hypotheses, prioritizing, and testing them with experiments following the scientific method in order to support or refute them [20]. However, research has shown that the adoption of experimentation by software startups is still limited [17] because of an overfocus on technical aspects without considering the real needs of customers [23]. To tackle this issue, in previous work [22], we proposed the term "Hypotheses Engineering" to describe techniques to handle hypotheses in experiment-driven contexts, moving the focus from requirements.

Since then, several techniques have been proposed in the context of hypotheses engineering, not only for startups but also for consolidated companies. However, these techniques have been proposed for specific scenarios and steps of the development, still lacking a more comprehensive approach. Besides that, it has been observed that experimentation in software development has focused on what to develop, being closely linked to business development and customer development [20]. In this chapter, we focus particularly on HyMap, a hypotheses elicitation targeted to startups, and ArchHypo, a technique to handle uncertainties in software architecture by converting them into hypotheses and managing them throughout the development process. By combining these techniques, we aim to propose a full-fledged technique to support software startups with both business and architectural aspects. To evaluate our approach, we present the application of the techniques in a real software startup scenario.

The contribution of this work is the connection between HyMap and ArchHypo, proposed in Sect. 7.6, by extracting technical hypotheses related to the software architecture from the business hypotheses of the startup. Additionally, the proposed approach also suggests how to keep the related hypotheses connected, keeping the traceability among them and enabling the collaboration between the business and technical teams to handle the uncertainties. Another contribution is a case study, presented in Sect. 7.7, demonstrating the combined use of both techniques in a real scenario. It focuses on a startup that envisions the integration of Generative AI in its product, which is a scenario that captures what is happening in several other companies. In this sense, the way that the uncertainties were identified and handled can also be used as a reference in other cases. The originality of the work presented in this chapter lies in the consolidation of an approach that connects the uncertainty management, from the business to the technical hypotheses, which is not present in any technique proposed in the existing literature.

7.2 Experimentation in Software Startups

Despite being often used in research and practice, the term *software startup* does not have a clear definition [4, 29]. Based on a systematic mapping study (SMS) on the topic, Berg et al. [4] concluded that the most used terms in research to describe these organizations are innovation and uncertainty. Therefore, we will use the following definition throughout this chapter: software startups are companies that develop innovative, software-intensive products or services searching for a sustainable and scalable business model [36].

A natural objective for a startup endeavor is to be successful. In this context, a logical approach would be to distinguish the "technical" success of the software project, as a necessary condition, from the business success [21]. However, even the success or failure of a software project is a complex argument, as the literature shows. Ralph and Kelly [30] investigated the success concept in the software engineering context. First, they observed how the understanding of this concept evolved in project management literature. For a long time, a model used to describe such a phenomenon was the Iron, or Project, Triangle [30]. This metaphor postulates that the quality of a product (inner of the triangle) is constrained by three vertices: scope, budget, and schedule [2]. Then, the authors described a more comprehensive taxonomy proposed by Shenhar et al. [32], which describes success through four dimensions: project efficiency, impact on the customer, business success, and preparing for the future. Finally, the authors performed an empirical study with 191 design professionals, of whom 68 were in the software industry. The results indicated that practitioners understand software engineering success "as a multidimensional variable comprising project efficiency, artifact quality, market performance, and stakeholder impacts over time." This result is in line with findings in the information systems literature (e.g., [10]).

Therefore, software project success should not only concern the quality, scope, and schedule of the software system delivered. Following Shenhar et al.'s taxonomy, other measures that seem especially important for software startups are, for instance, fulfilling customer needs, commercial success, and creating a large market share. As Ralph and Kelly [30] observed in the discussions on software project development success, practitioners perceive the existence of a client who has problems to solve or needs to be fulfilled. Differently, software startups have to find these problems and even customers. Some types of pivots observed in software startups support such an argument. For instance, a customer segment pivot is a shift from one customer segment to another [3]. Zoom-ins are pivots where a single feature becomes the whole product, and as the opposite, zoom-out is when a product becomes only a feature of a bigger product. Consequently, software engineering in software startups, especially in the early stage, should focus on the overall goal of understanding how to apply its proposed innovation into a sustainable business model. Given the importance of software to the business model of a software startup, it is hard to separate software development from business in this context. Software development will inform how the company can create an innovative business model for a chosen customer or market segment. Meanwhile, the business model is constrained to what a software system can perform. In summary, especially in the context of software startups, business and technical successes are mingled together. The success of the project does not only regard technical aspects but also business development, which is associated with several uncertainties, such as whether they are able to fulfill real needs from customers. Therefore, to increase their chance of success, software startups need to handle and minimize uncertainties.

A common way to deal with these uncertainties has been experimentation, which is, for example, a key aspect of the Lean Startup, the most well-known startup development methodology [5, 14]. In the context of software engineering, experimentation is defined as a process of continuously validating product assumptions, transforming them as hypotheses, prioritizing, and testing them following the scientific method in order to support or refute them [20]. This notion comprises several techniques like iterations with prototypes, gradual rollouts, and controlled experiments [12] or even problem and solution interviews [20]. Therefore, in this context, the word "experiment" is not bound to the scientific meaning but points to a broader concept of data-driven rather than opinion-based decision-making [20].

Despite the scientific results pointing to the advantages of using experimentation and industry practices, such as the Lean Startup, research has shown that its adoption in these companies is limited [17, 23]. Instead, founders and other team members consider their ideas validated and focus on implementing them [17, 23]. It has also been observed that technical aspects were mostly overcome, and the major inhibitors for the adoption experimentation are at the individual level [20, 23]. To tackle this issue, Melegati et al. [22] proposed the term "hypotheses engineering," which will be described in detail in the next section.

7.3 Hypotheses Engineering

In the literature, there are models to describe how teams execute experimentation (e.g., HYPEX [27] and RIGHT [13]). Both models emerged from multiple case studies in software development companies applying experimentation. The models present a similar sequence of steps summarized as [22]:

1. Based on the current understanding of the customer, user, and market, identify, specify, and prioritize hypotheses.
2. Design an experiment to evaluate the hypothesis.
3. Execute the experiment and collect data.
4. Analyze the results and, based on the acquired learning, update the hypotheses and return to the first step.

Based on a parallel to requirements engineering (RE) in conventional software development, Melegati et al. [22] called this set of activities hypotheses engineering (HE), to stress the importance of properly handling hypotheses in experiment-driven software development.

Experimentation is strongly related to software development, and many experiments are pieces of software themselves. In other words, experimentation is a type of software development where the software produced is intended to evaluate previously defined hypotheses. Therefore, similar activities to those in conventional RE could be useful to handle hypotheses. In our view though, HE is not a substitute for RE but, instead, one activity, part of the experimentation process, to reach the final goal of defining software requirements. A hypothesis can be considered a type of higher-level requirement to guide experiments to understand the customer and market and, finally, reach requirements for the final software system. In other words, hypotheses are requirements for experiments, and since many of these are pieces of software themselves, using similar activities for hypotheses is reasonable. Nevertheless, since there is a shift from eliciting the customer needs in conventional RE to finding which product assumptions should be evaluated, RE's current practices and techniques may not be useful.

7.4 HyMap

In the context of RE, elicitation's primary goal is to define the requirements to reach the purposes for which a software system is intended [7]. For HE, a similar activity would identify on which assumptions a product is being built and transform them into hypotheses. These hypotheses can then be evaluated, being supported or refuted by an experiment, increasing the knowledge to support the decision-making process regarding the product and its features. HyMap [24] is a hypotheses elicitation technique developed for early-stage software startups. It is based on the Personal Constructs Theory by Kelly [19], which states that a person makes sense of the world through patterns or templates, the so-called constructs, created by the person. These constructs are also used to predict and control the course of events. HyMap's goal is to make these constructs evident and use them to identify the hypotheses to be tested. To this aim, HyMap defines a visual language to depict a map representing the constructs and their relationships and a process, based on an interview with founders or other decision-makers in a software startup, to build this map and derive hypotheses based on it. Figure 7.1 describes HyMap's visual language. The advantage of HyMap to alternatives, such as Assumption Mapping, is its scientific basis, i.e., Kelly's Personal Constructs Theory, and systematic development and evolution [24].

The creation of a HyMap starts by adding elements representing the product (on the bottom of the map in Fig. 7.1) and the foreseen customers (on the top of the map in Fig. 7.1). Right below the customers, boxes representing the customers' problems to be solved or mitigated by the proposed solution are added and linked with arrows to the respective customers. Similarly, above the representation of the product, boxes are added, representing the features that are expected to contribute to the solution of the customers' problems. These features are linked not only to the product but also to the respective problems. Then, in an iterative process, the interviewee, with the

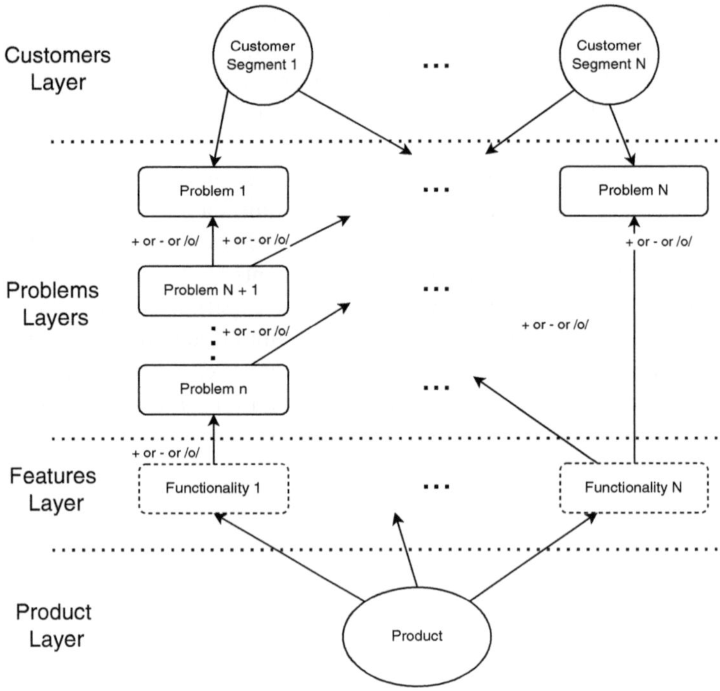

Fig. 7.1 HyMap's visual language

support of the facilitator, should evaluate each arrow to analyze if implicit concepts are used to explain that relationship. In this case, a new box should be included, which should be connected with arrows to the original boxes. The process should also be conducted on the arrows included in this step. The process ends when no new arrows are needed.

Once the map is complete, it is possible to create a hypothesis for each arrow. The elements being connected by the arrow will then define the type of the hypotheses. Arrows connecting the product to its features lead to "product hypotheses," which regard the team's capability of implementing that feature from a technical perspective. These hypotheses can be formulated using the following template: "the team developing <the product> is capable of implementing <the functionality>." Arrows connecting the features to problems or problems among themselves lead to "value hypotheses," which regard the relationship among different problems and problems with the features. These hypotheses can be formulated using the template: "<the functionality or the problem> <increases/decreases/ or has no effect> on <the problem>." Finally, arrows connecting problems to the customers lead to "problem hypotheses," which regard whether those are relevant problems for the customers. These hypotheses can be formulated using the template: "<The customers or a segment of them> <has/would like to solve> <the problem>."

7.5 ArchHypo

ArchHypo [34, 35] is a technique based on hypotheses engineering for managing uncertainties in the software architecture. It is based on a set of patterns for agile architecture [15, 37], in which the hypotheses are used as an implementation strategy for the pattern FIND WHERE IT HURTS,[1] based on the premise that architecture design should focus on points with higher uncertainty. The hypotheses can be stated as clear, straightforward assertions that reflect the development team's current assumptions.

After identifying the architectural hypotheses, each one should be assessed by the development team in terms of its level of uncertainty and its impact [33]. The level of uncertainty indicates how close the team is to either validating or disproving the hypothesis, while the impact reflects the potential consequences and costs of switching to an alternative solution. These two assessments are independent and are intended to encourage reflection on the hypothesis. They support a qualitative comparison with other hypotheses and assist in selecting appropriate techniques for addressing it. Since the goal is not to measure these characteristics with precision, a simple rating scale, such as five levels (Very Low to Very High), can be used. After this initial classification, the hypotheses are reviewed in each iteration, evaluating if they were accepted or rejected and, in case not, readjusting the uncertainty and impact assessment.

To handle the hypotheses, the team should elaborate a technical plan with actions to reduce uncertainty or impact. On the one hand, using techniques to obtain more knowledge about the hypothesis would reduce the uncertainty; on the other hand, introducing flexibility or modularization can reduce the impact. The technical plan is an implementation strategy for the pattern PLAN FOR RESPONSIBLE MOMENTS [15], and its action should be added to the project backlog to be prioritized and executed. The connection with the hypothesis should be considered when its prioritization is being discussed. The plan may consist of one or more actions intended to (a) conclusively confirm or reject the hypothesis; (b) decrease the level of uncertainty; (c) lessen the potential impact; or (d) establish criteria for deferring its resolution.

As an example, patterns related to software analytics [9] can be used to reduce uncertainty, and a PROTECTIVE GUIDELINE [28] can introduce coding practices and constraints to reduce the impact. It is important to highlight that the goal is not to solve all the hypotheses as soon as possible, since uncertainty is inherent to software projects, but to manage them to evaluate the right moment to make architectural decisions. In this sense, the technique provides a more systematic way to evaluate decisions that can be postponed, which is an important practice associated with continuous architecture [38].

---

[1] Pattern names are highlighted in small caps font, with capital letters.

ArchHypo is aligned with the idea that good solutions come with combining technical expertise with creativity [16, 25]. So, while these patterns present a set of practices for handling architectural hypotheses, the teams should not be limited to them and should also search for creative alternatives.

7.6 Building a Bridge Between the Techniques

On the one hand, HyMap produces a set of hypotheses related to the targeted customers, their problems, and if the product solves or mitigates the problems. On the other hand, ArchHypo's starting point is a set of hypotheses related to the software architecture. While the connection between the techniques might seem that it is just using the hypothesis identified by one technique and managing in the other, not all hypotheses found in HyMap might affect the architecture and be suitable to be handled in ArchHypo. In some cases, the connection or implications of the hypothesis might not be explicit. This connection must be considered in two different moments: (1) when the hypotheses are identified and (2) when creating a strategy for handling and managing the hypotheses. The next subsections go deep into each of these aspects.

7.6.1 Hypotheses Elicitation

When using HyMap, different types of hypotheses are generated after creating the map, considering the arrows from different layers in the model. Different implications for the software architecture might arise for each kind of hypothesis. Figure 7.2 presents the type of architectural hypotheses that would be generated, and the following explains the rationale of each one:

- **Product hypotheses** (*based on arrows from the product to the features layer*): This type of hypothesis can generate architectural hypotheses related to feasibility and team knowledge. In the first case, it should represent the uncertainty regarding the technical viability of implementing that functionality. In the second case, the hypotheses would be related to the team's lack of knowledge of the technology that would enable that functionality. In other words, by other means, it is possible to know the feasibility, but with some unknown consequences in other quality attributes. *Example: Consider the hypothesis "the team developing <product> is capable of implementing a 3D preview based on customer description." A feasibility hypothesis would represent the uncertainty related to the viability of implementing the feature. If the team does not have experience with the related technologies, other hypotheses can represent the uncertainties related to that, such as the impact on performance and the integration in a Web environment.*

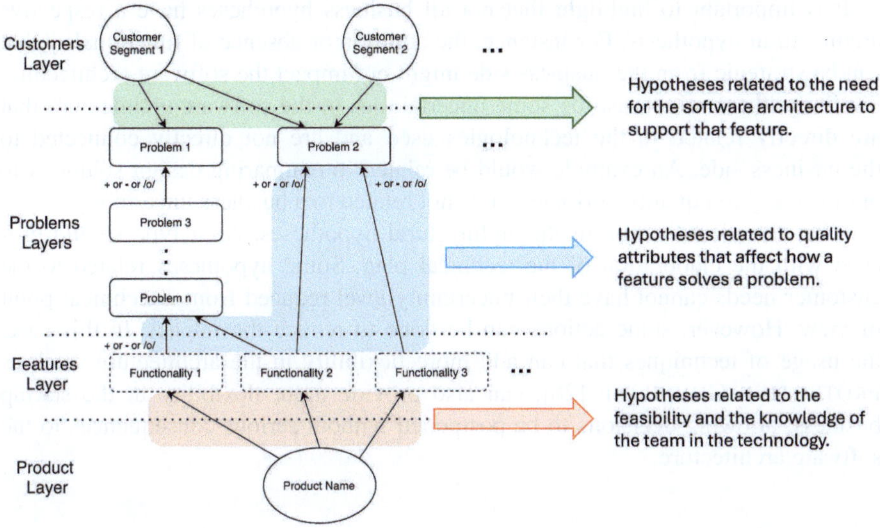

Fig. 7.2 Extracting the hypothesis related to the software architecture from the HyMap conceptual map

- **Value hypotheses** (*based on arrows from the features layer to the problem layers*): These hypotheses are related to the influence that the proposed features have on the problems. In this case, the hypotheses related to the software architecture are not direct but related to important quality attributes that might influence this causal relationship. In this case, the architectural hypothesis will be related to the influence of this requirement. *Example: Consider the hypothesis "importing the user's medical profile decreases the problem of the lack of information to make decisions." Given existing privacy regulations, security is an important quality attribute that would enable this causal relationship to be possible. Since the team has no knowledge about the security protocols that need to be implemented, an architectural hypothesis would represent this uncertainty.*
- **Problem hypotheses** (*based on arrows from the customers' layer to the problem layers*): These hypotheses are related to the necessity and importance of a given problem for the customers. The impact on the architecture happens if this feature has some influence on an important quality attribute, since the decision to implement it would depend on the hypothesis evaluation. *Example: Consider the hypothesis "<customer> has to follow the current state of the sensors managed by the system." This hypothesis is important to determine quality attribute requirements. Since accessing the current state of the system sensors would require receiving real-time information, performance, and availability requirements would be influenced by this hypothesis. In this case, the architectural solutions would be very different based on the hypothesis acceptance or rejection.*

It is important to highlight that not all business hypotheses have a respective architectural hypothesis. For instance, the addition or absence of functionality that can be strategic from the business side might not impact the software architecture. Similarly, there might also be some uncertainties in the software architecture that are directly related to the technologies used and are not directly connected to the business side. An example would be related to comparing design solutions to optimize a given quality attribute that is not related to a business uncertainty.

After the identification of the architectural hypotheses, ArchHypo should proceed with the elaboration of the technical plan. Some hypotheses related to the customer needs cannot have their uncertainty level reduced from a technical point of view. However, some actions can be done to reduce the impact. In this case, the usage of techniques that can add more flexibility in the architecture, such as PROTECTIVE GUIDELINE [28], can also provide more flexibility in the startup business, allowing decisions to be postponed without serious consequences to the software architecture.

7.6.2 Hypotheses Management

Even if the architectural hypotheses are more specific and related to technical aspects, keeping traceability between them and the business hypothesis is important. In this case, they can be different, but the source of uncertainty is the same. The strategy built to handle the uncertainty on the business and architectural sides should consider each other since one can highly influence the state of the other.

For instance, when the uncertainty on the business side is reduced, this fact should trigger a reduction in the uncertainty level of the respective hypothesis. On the other side, if an action reduces the impact related to a hypothesis in the software, it also reduces it on the respective business hypothesis. This connection can be used strategically by the startup to use actions on one side to support the other, as presented in Fig. 7.3.

As one example, when an important business hypothesis is difficult to evaluate in the short term, the technical plan to handle the respective architectural hypothesis might seek to reduce its impact. That will provide more flexibility on the business side, giving more time to explore the possibilities and make the decision. Accordingly, with a reduced impact, the risk of experimenting with one approach is reduced since it would be easier to change to the other. In this sense, an architectural solution can support the business by giving it more freedom to explore.

For an architectural hypothesis with a high impact, experimentation aiming at the reduction of the uncertainty from its business part can help to support technical decisions. By understanding where it is easier to have flexibility in the software architecture, the startup can prioritize actions to reduce the business uncertainties where it would have a larger impact.

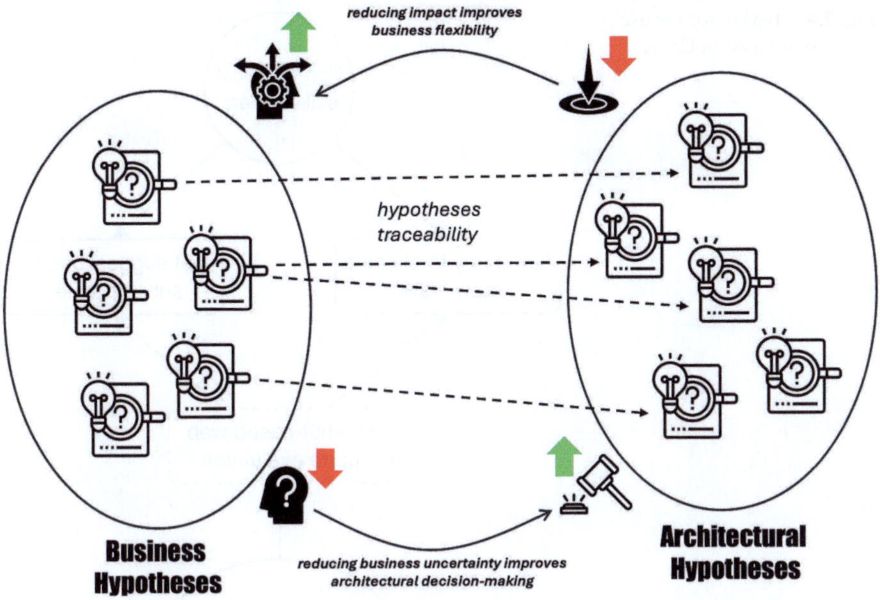

Fig. 7.3 Strategic actions in business and architectural hypothesis management

7.7 Case Study

To demonstrate the proposed technique, we verified how the combination of HyMap and ArchHypo would perform in the real context of a software startup called Catch Solve. This case was chosen because the startup owner is one of the authors of this chapter. Their product focuses on monitoring and testing Web applications, providing features to periodically run automated tests simulating real users to verify the functionality and availability of a Web application. One of the highlights of their platform is the functionality of providing reports with a screen recording of any error found. This startup already has previous experience in using hypotheses for architectural uncertainties [35].

7.7.1 Context and HyMap Application

The context considered is the possibility of incorporating artificial intelligence into the startup product. Given the rise of Generative AI [8, 31] and its potential in applications for software engineering [26], the startup owner considered that it would be strategic to integrate it into their platform. The integration would also open possibilities for participation in calls for funding related to the application of artificial intelligence. His idea was to have a conversational interface in which the

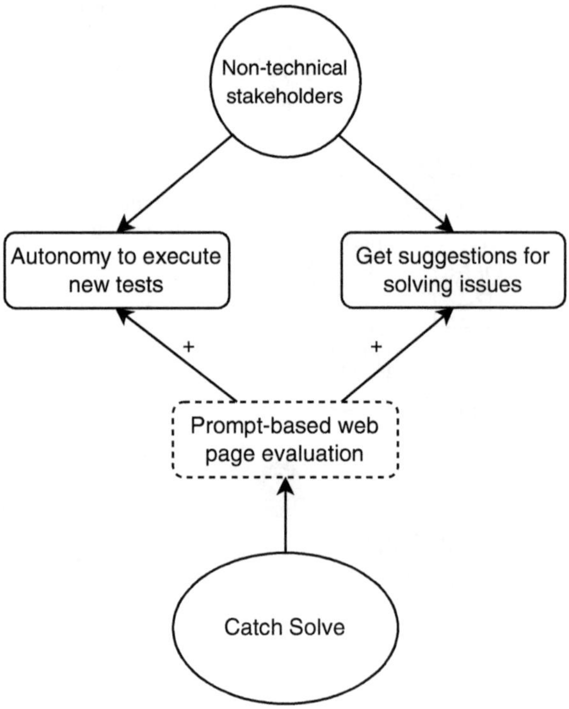

Fig. 7.4 HyMap for the use of Generative AI in Catch Solve

users could interact with a model in a way that it could invoke Catch Solve when appropriate. However, there was a lot of uncertainty related to the feasibility of that idea, how it could be implemented, and the consequences to the current software architecture.

To identify the hypotheses related to this change in the product, we developed a HyMap focused on this aspect, i.e., not representing the whole product but specifically the addition of AI to the product. The result of this exercise is presented in Fig. 7.4. The customer's need of *"autonomy to execute new tests"* comes from the fact that, in the current version of the product, all the tests need to be added by the startup, and allowing clients to create new tests would give more freedom to them and contribute to the business scalability. The other need represented in the figure, i.e., *get suggestions to solve issues*, depicts a functionality envisioned from the beginning of the product that had not been implemented yet.

Based on the generated HyMap (Fig. 7.4), we developed the following business hypotheses:

- BH1. Non-technical stakeholders want autonomy to execute new tests.
- BH2. Non-technical stakeholders want to get suggestions for solving issues.
- BH3. A prompt-based Web page evaluation would increase the autonomy to execute new tests.

- BH4. A prompt-based Web page evaluation would facilitate getting suggestions for solving issues.
- BH5. The Catch Solve development team is capable of implementing prompt-based Web page evaluation.

Since the product has been developed for some period of time, the team considered that it had enough data collected through interactions with customers to support the two problem hypotheses, namely, BH1 and BH2. Since the tests that monitor the Web application need to be developed by the startup team, BH1 would be important for product scalability. As stated in the startup name, Catch Solve, one of the initial goals was to already provide solutions to the problems detected. In this direction, even if currently the product only has the functionality of finding errors, BH2 is aligned with the initial startup vision. So, no architectural hypotheses related to these two hypotheses were added.

7.7.2 Translation into Architectural Hypotheses

Considering the value hypotheses, BH3 and BH4, it was evaluated if there is a quality attribute that could influence this causal relationship. In this case, reliability was pointed out as an important attribute since the product's APIs should be invoked appropriately, and the suggestions should make sense. The product hypothesis, BH5, was also considered in terms of the feature feasibility. Considering the intent to evaluate the usage of Generative AI in this context, the architectural hypotheses were also elaborated to express the assumption of the suitability of this technology. Based on this rational, the following architectural hypotheses were elaborated:

- AH1. Using Generative AI, the product APIs can be reliably invoked based on user prompts. (*mapped to BH3*)
- AH2. Using Generative AI, reliable suggestions can be given based on the problems found. (*mapped to BH4*)
- AH3. A prompt-based Web page evaluation can be implemented using Generative AI. (*mapped to BH5*)

Following ArchHypo, the next step was elaborating a technical plan to deal with the hypotheses. Since the startup did not have previous experience with Generative AI, they decided to start with an ARCHITECTURAL SPIKE [37] to handle AH3. The goal of it was to evaluate the ways in which the application could interact with the model and identify which was the most appropriate one. As a result of this step, the startup owner identified the *function calling* from the OpenAI API as the feature that would better fit into the Catch Solve platform.

The second step of the technical plan was to elaborate on a TRACER BULLET [15] that explores this integration in an end-to-end example. The startup owner chose two services from the platform: (a) one that evaluated the page regarding its accessibility, (b) another that verified specific regulations from the food industry (like the fact that allergens should always start with a capital letter). Based on that need, the TRACER BULLET implemented an agent that was connected to a Web page where a user can send prompts to interact with it. This agent used *function calling* to connect with the services. This implementation was also used to assess AH1 and AH2.

As a result of the TRACER BULLET, it was possible to confirm the feasibility of the integration of the Catch Solve platform with the Generative AI model through the *function calling*. In addition, a presentation about the implemented feature was done in a local event[2] for the software development community. During this event, not only the technical aspects but also other potential applications were discussed.

7.7.3 Hypotheses Handling

During this experience, AH1 was not accepted since, in some cases, the APIs were invoked using the wrong parameters. To overcome this, the user had to confirm the invocation of the APIs when necessary in this prototype. As a result, some additional mechanisms would need to be implemented to overcome this issue so that the feature can be incorporated into the product. For AH2, since the issues related to food industry regulations were straightforward to address, only the suggestions about the accessibility issues were evaluated. For this kind of problem, the suggestions were suitable and could be further explored with additional prompts. This hypothesis was kept open since an evaluation with other types of problems would be needed. However, this initial assessment was enough to reduce the associated uncertainty level.

Based on the implementation, the startup owner accepted hypothesis AH3, assessing that this feature is feasible by using Generative AI. However, one problem was found in this implementation: passing contextual information regarding the Web page, including its source code, in the prompts frequently surpassed the maximum number of characters. For the TRACER BULLET, a more "hard-coded" solution that could not be generalized for all cases was used to select relevant pieces of the page. Accordingly, a new hypothesis related to that was added: *AH4. It is possible to have a general solution to select relevant parts of a Web page source code to be added to the prompt.* This new hypothesis was also mapped to the business hypothesis BH5, since it would be important for the feasibility of that feature.

These initial steps reduced the general uncertainty regarding integrating Generative AI APIs with the startup software, but some hypotheses were still left open. One hypothesis was considered accepted, giving rise to a new one that captured a more specific problem. The startup owner considered it enough for its current needs since it gave him sufficient information to reason and better plan this future feature. Based on the type of API required for *function calling*, it was also possible to understand

[2] AI for Testing and Compliance, Software Developer's Thursday, https://noi.bz.it/en/events/software-developer-s-thursday/557a2b22-7b16-4d75-8270-ffcdfbf245b4.

better how to structure the software so that the impact of that future integration is reduced. Based on that, a PROTECTIVE GUIDELINE [28] was introduced to drive the system design in that direction.

7.7.4 Discussion

Based on the case study, it was possible to observe that the connection between HyMap and ArchHypo could guide the startup in identifying and handling hypotheses. In the first place, the set of hypotheses identified by HyMap captured the uncertainty that Catch Solve was experiencing from the business point of view. Further, the hypotheses that impacted the software architecture were extracted from them and managed with ArchHypo by elaborating and conducting a technical plan based on patterns suggested by the technique. The traceability among business and architectural hypotheses kept them connected, even when a new architectural hypothesis arose. Considering this evidence, combined with the previous results in adopting the techniques in isolation [24, 34, 35], it is possible to state that the proposed approach is a promising technique for software startups to manage their uncertainties.

For startups with fewer resources, it might be difficult to prioritize more technical tasks that are not converted to a new feature or to a more immediate product enhancement. The hypotheses assessment proposed by ArchHypo can support the development of a more strategic vision and the prioritization of actions. This assessment might also be useful for more mature startups with a further developed product, in which a higher number of uncertainties might arise. In this case, understanding the potential impact is important to understand where the available resources might be applied. In the end, a local adaptation of the techniques would be needed according to the startup's priorities and resources. For instance, to define the pace at which the techniques' steps should be applied would depend on the availability of resources that can be dedicated to them.

A professional with software architecture expertise is necessary for the application of the technique, since ArchHypo has a long learning curve [34] and it requires experience to choose and implement the techniques to handle the uncertainties. As future work, tool support can provide guidance and reduce the expertise needed for the use of the technique.

The presented case study had the scope of demonstrating the use of the proposed technique. However, it has some limitations. First, it inherently has a limited generalization: even though we might expect that the results would be similar in comparable contexts, we cannot guarantee that they would be valid for all startups. Second, there is a risk of confirmation bias given the involvement of the authors of this study with the techniques and the startup. To mitigate this issue, we followed the techniques as they have been previously published in peer-reviewed venues. We also described in detail, considering the limitation of space, the steps conducted in the research.

7.8 Conclusions

This chapter focused on techniques to manage uncertainty in software startups using hypotheses engineering. Uncertainty is an inherent aspect of businesses that seek innovative and disruptive solutions. Because of that, identifying and managing uncertainties is important to explore the alternatives in a more systematic way. In this direction, hypotheses engineering is a discipline that proposes the usage of hypotheses to represent this uncertainty in an explicit way. HyMap is a technique based on hypotheses engineering that uses a conceptual map to identify potential customer needs and map them to candidates of the startup software features. This map is used to elicit potential business hypotheses. ArchHypo is a technique, not exclusively focused on software startups, that uses the concepts from hypotheses engineering to manage software architecture uncertainties.

In this chapter, we proposed the combination of both techniques to provide a more complete toolset for software startups to manage their uncertainties. Based on the type of hypotheses generated by the HyMap, we proposed an approach for identifying possible impacts in the software architecture to create a bridge between them. In the case where these impacts were found, these hypotheses are assessed and managed using ArchHypo. By keeping traceability between hypotheses, it is possible for the technical side to support the business side and vice versa, building a more strategic approach to uncertainty management. The Catch Solve case study presented how this combination of both techniques would be applied in a real case. As future work, more case studies could be conducted in software startups regarding the application of both techniques combined. Based on the results, the technique can be refined and adapted to more specific contexts. Additionally, considering the strong foundation of ArchHypo in patterns, new patterns regarding the conversion of business hypotheses into architectural hypotheses can be identified and documented.

References

1. Andries, P., Debackere, K., van Looy, B.: Simultaneous experimentation as a learning strategy: business model development under uncertainty. Strateg. Entrep. J. **7**(4), 288–310 (2013). https://doi.org/10.1002/sej.1170
2. Atkinson, R.: Project management: cost, time and quality, two best guesses and a phenomenon, its time to accept other success criteria. Int. J. Project Manage. **17**(6), 337–342 (1999). https://doi.org/10.1016/S0263-7863(98)00069-6
3. Bajwa, S.S., Wang, X., Nguyen Duc, A., Abrahamsson, P.: "Failures" to be celebrated: an analysis of major pivots of software startups. Empir. Softw. Eng. **22**(5), 2373–2408 (2017). https://doi.org/10.1007/s10664-016-9458-0
4. Berg, V., Birkeland, J., Nguyen-Duc, A., Pappas, I.O., Jaccheri, L.: Software startup engineering: a systematic mapping study. J. Syst. Softw. **144**(February), 255–274 (2018). https://doi.org/10.1016/j.jss.2018.06.043
5. Bortolini, R.F., Nogueira Cortimiglia, M., Danilevicz, A.d.M.F., Ghezzi, A.: Lean Startup: a comprehensive historical review. Manage. Decis. **59**(8), 1765–1783 (2021). https://doi.org/10.1108/MD-07-2017-0663

6. Cantamessa, M., Gatteschi, V., Perboli, G., Rosano, M.: Startups' roads to failure. Sustainability **10**(7), 2346 (2018). https://doi.org/10.3390/su10072346
7. Cheng, B.H.C., Atlee, J.M., Joanne, M.: Research directions in requirements engineering. In: Proceeding FOSE '07 2007 Future of Software Engineering, pp. 285–303 (2007). https://doi.org/10.1109/FOSE.2007.17
8. Chiu, T.K.: The impact of generative AI (GenAI) on practices, policies and research direction in education: A case of chatGPT and midjourney. Interact. Learn. Environ. **32**(10), 6187–6203 (2024)
9. Choma, J., da Silva, T.S., Guerra, E.M.: Pattern Language for Lightweight and Interactive Software Analytics Process, pp. 162–189. Springer, Berlin/Heidelberg (2025). https://doi.org/10.1007/978-3-662-70810-1_4
10. Dwivedi, Y.K., Wastell, D., Laumer, S., Henriksen, H.Z., Myers, M.D., Bunker, D., Elbanna, A., Ravishankar, M.N., Srivastava, S.C.: Research on information systems failures and successes: status update and future directions. Inf. Syst. Front. **17**(1), 143–157 (2015). https://doi.org/10.1007/s10796-014-9500-y
11. Eisenhardt, K.M., Tabrizi, B.N.: Accelerating adaptive processes: product innovation in the global computer industry. Adm. Sci. Q. **40**(1), 84 (1995). https://doi.org/10.2307/2393701
12. Fabijan, A., Dmitriev, P., McFarland, C., Vermeer, L., Holmström Olsson, H., Bosch, J.: Experimentation growth: evolving trustworthy A/B testing capabilities in online software companies. J. Software: Evol. Process **30**(12), e2113 (2018). https://doi.org/10.1002/smr.2113
13. Fagerholm, F., Sanchez Guinea, A., Mäenpää, H., Münch, J.: The RIGHT model for continuous experimentation. J. Syst. Softw. **123**, 292–305 (2017). https://doi.org/10.1016/j.jss.2016.03.034
14. Frederiksen, D.L., Brem, A.: How do entrepreneurs think they create value? A scientific reflection of Eric Ries' Lean Startup approach. Int. Entrep. Manag. J. **13**(1), 169–189 (2017). https://doi.org/10.1007/s11365-016-0411-x
15. Guerra, E., Wirfs-Brock, R., Yoder, J.: Patterns for initial architectural design on agile projects. In: 4th Asian Conference on Pattern Languages of Programs (AsianPLoP) (2015)
16. Gutbrod, R., Wiele, C.: The Software Dilemma: Balancing Creativity and Control on the Path to Sustainable Software. Springer Science & Business Media, Berlin (2012)
17. Gutbrod, M., Münch, J., Tichy, M.: How do software startups approach experimentation? Empirical results from a qualitative interview study. In: Felderer, M., Méndez Fernández, D., Turhan, B., Kalinowski, M., Sarro, F., Winkler, D. (eds.) Product-Focused Software Process Improvement, pp. 297–304. Springer International Publishing, Cham (2017). https://doi.org/10.1007/978-3-319-69926-4_21
18. Herrmann, B.L., Marmer, M., Dogrultan, E., Holtschke, D.: Startup ecosystem report 2012. Telefonica Digital and Startup Genome (2012)
19. Kelly, G.: The Psychology of Personal Constructs: Volume One: Theory and Personality. Taylor & Francis, Oxfordshire (2002)
20. Lindgren, E., Münch, J.: Raising the odds of success: the current state of experimentation in product development. Inf. Softw. Technol. **77**, 80–91 (2016). https://doi.org/10.1016/j.infsof.2016.04.008
21. Melegati, J.: Towards a framework to guide the creation of development practices for software startups. In: Gregory, P., Kruchten, P. (eds.) Agile Processes in Software Engineering and Extreme Programming – Workshops, pp. 155–164. Springer International Publishing, Cham (2021)
22. Melegati, J., Wang, X., Abrahamsson, P.: Hypotheses engineering: first essential steps of experiment-driven software development. In: IEEE/ACM Joint 4th International Workshop on Rapid Continuous Software Engineering and 1st International Workshop on Data-Driven Decisions, Experimentation and Evolution (RCoSE/DDrEE), pp. 16–19 (2019). https://doi.org/10.1109/RCoSE/DDrEE.2019.00011
23. Melegati, J., Edison, H., Wang, X.: XPro: A model to explain the limited adoption and implementation of experimentation in software startups. IEEE Trans. Softw. Eng. **48**(6), 1929–1946 (2022). https://doi.org/10.1109/TSE.2020.3042610

24. Melegati, J., Guerra, E., Wang, X.: Hymap: eliciting hypotheses in early-stage software startups using cognitive mapping. Inf. Softw. Technol. **144**, 106807 (2022)
25. Mohanani, R., Ram, P., Lasisi, A., Ralph, P., Turhan, B.: Perceptions of creativity in software engineering research and practice. In: 2017 43rd Euromicro Conference on Software Engineering and Advanced Applications (SEAA), pp. 210–217 (2017). https://doi.org/10.1109/SEAA.2017.21
26. Nguyen-Duc, A., Cabrero-Daniel, B., Przybylek, A., Arora, C., Khanna, D., Herda, T., Rafiq, U., Melegati, J., Guerra, E., Kemell, K.K., et al.: Generative artificial intelligence for software engineering–a research agenda. Preprint. arXiv:2310.18648 (2023)
27. Olsson, H.H., Bosch, J.: From opinions to data-driven software R&D: a multi-case study on how to close the 'open loop' problem. In: 2014 40th EUROMICRO Conference on Software Engineering and Advanced Applications, pp. 9–16. IEEE, Piscataway (2014)
28. Paris, A., Guerra, E., Silveira, F., Silva, K.: Patterns for small adjustments in the development process to deal with architectural uncertainties. In: Proceedings of the 29th European Conference on Pattern Languages of Programs, People, and Practices, pp. 1–8 (2024)
29. Paternoster, N., Giardino, C., Unterkalmsteiner, M., Gorschek, T., Abrahamsson, P.: Software development in startup companies: a systematic mapping study. Inf. Softw. Technol. **56**(10), 1200–1218 (2014). https://doi.org/10.1016/j.infsof.2014.04.014
30. Ralph, P., Kelly, P.: The dimensions of software engineering success. In: Proceedings of the 36th International Conference on Software Engineering, pp. 24–35. ACM, New York (2014). https://doi.org/10.1145/2568225.2568261
31. Semujanga, B., Mikalef, P.: Exploring the productivity impacts of generative AI in organizations. In: Conference on e-Business, e-Services and e-Society, pp. 103–111. Springer, Berlin (2024)
32. Shenhar, A.J., Dvir, D., Levy, O., Maltz, A.C.: Project success: a multidimensional strategic concept. Long Range Plan. **34**(6), 699–725 (2001). https://doi.org/10.1016/S0024-6301(01)00097-8
33. Silva, K., Adolfo, L.B., Coppe, A., Silveira, F.F., Ferreira, M., Guerra, E.: Patterns for using hypothesis engineering to manage architectural uncertainties. In: Proceedings of the 29th European Conference on Pattern Languages of Programs, People, and Practices, pp. 1–8 (2024)
34. Silva, K., Melegati, J., Silveira, F., Wang, X., Ferreira, M., Guerra, E.: Archhypo: managing software architecture uncertainty using hypotheses engineering. IEEE Trans. Softw. Eng. **51**(2), 430–448 (2024)
35. Silva, K., Melegati, J., Wang, X., Ferreira, M., Guerra, E.: Using hypotheses to manage technical uncertainty and architecture evolution in a software start-up. IEEE Softw. **41**(4), 7–13 (2024)
36. Unterkalmsteiner, M., Abrahamsson, P., Nguyen-duc, A., Baltes, G.H., Conboy, K., Dennehy, D., Sweetman, R., Edison, H., Shahid, S., Wang, X., Garbajosa, J., Gorschek, T., Hokkanen, L., Lunesu, I., Marchesi, M., Morgan, L., Selig, C., Oivo, M., Shah, S., Kon, F.: Software startups - a research agenda. e-Informatica Softw. Eng. J. **10**(1), 1–28 (2016). https://doi.org/10.5277/e-Inf160105
37. Wirfs-Brock, R., Yoder, J., Guerra, E.: Patterns to develop and evolve architecture during an agile software project. In: Proceedings of the 22nd Conference on Pattern Languages of Programs, pp. 1–18 (2015)
38. Woods, E., Erder, M., Pureur, P.: Continuous Architecture in Practice: Software Architecture in the Age of Agility and DevOps. Addison-Wesley Professional, Boston (2021)

Chapter 8
Experimentation Practices in Indie Game Startups

Elizabeth Bjarnason, Johan Linåker, and Fabian Fagerholm

Abstract Small independent (indie) game startups face fierce competition when developing games with limited time, budget, and resources. Continuously testing and experimenting with new ideas, features, and content is essential to validate and guide development toward a viable and successful game. Such continuous experimentation (CE) requires access to users and user data, which is often very limited in the early stages of development, both in general and in particular for indie game companies. We provide insights and recommendations on how to perform experimentation and game testing in pre-release stages of indie game development based on an exploratory interview survey with 10 independent game developers from different companies. We provide a framework for CE that highlights key parts to consider when planning and implementing an experiment. Current practices for experimentation within indie game development are also described for the early development stages of ideation, preproduction, feature production, and content production.

Our empirical findings offer insights and recommendations into how to conduct experiments during pre-release stages of game development, specifically for indie game companies. Other software startups, particularly those with a value proposition centered around interactive and satisfying user experiences, can also benefit from our research.

Keywords Game development · Continuous experimentation · User research · User data · Indie game company

E. Bjarnason (✉) · J. Linåker
Lund University, Department of Computer Science, Lund, Sweden
e-mail: elizabeth.bjarnason@cs.lth.se; johan.linaker@cs.lth.se

F. Fagerholm
Aalto University, Helsinki, Finland
e-mail: fabian.fagerholm@aalto.fi

N. Tripathi et al. (eds.), *Advances in Software Startups*,
https://doi.org/10.1007/978-3-032-04294-1_8

8.1 Introduction

The game industry is thriving with increasing yearly turnarounds and number of employees. For example, in Sweden, the game industry represents 4% of the national gross service export with a yearly turnaround of 86 billion SEK (including international subsidiaries) and a workforce of around 25,000 people globally, including 8,500 employees in 939 companies located in Sweden, of which a significant portion are small indie companies [10]. The industry is fiercely competitive, and game development companies are pressured by short deadlines and need to stay cost-efficient [17]. Therefore, betting on a wrong idea or a feature that is not technically or commercially viable poses a significant business risk.

In the broader industry, software-intensive organizations have increasingly adopted Continuous Experimentation (CE) practices [15] to mitigate the risk of releasing products with weak market viability. With this experiment-driven development approach, features and qualities are continuously evaluated based on user feedback [7] with hypotheses defined upfront based on expected technical and/or commercial viability [3]. Ideally, experimentation should be performed throughout the entire game development process, from ideation and pre-release to post-launch. This approach guides development and product planning to create an engaging game experience that maximizes the value creation [20]. The pre-release stages are extra critical, as they include the majority of development activities. As development progresses, the cost and impact of pivoting increases.

CE requires access to user data to test hypotheses [7], which is especially challenging prior to release. At this stage, the number of users, and thus user data and feedback, is naturally limited [20]. This challenge is especially taxing for gaming startups with limited resources and without the backing of larger game publishers. These companies, known as independent (*indie*) game companies, are typically small and new, with limited resources, experience, and practice comparable to established game companies and studios [8].

In this chapter, we provide a framework of CE that highlights five key parts to consider when planning and implementing experimentation in game development based on our previous work [13]. We also outline how experimentation practices can vary over development stages from ideation to beta release. Our results are based on an exploratory semi-structured interview survey with 10 game developers from different indie game companies. We have synthesized our findings into a revised version of our framework of continuous experimentation and provide recommendations for experimentation practices within game development based on current practices as described by our interviewees. In the future, we aim to further explore experimentation practices through case studies of a wider range of companies including larger game companies and companies in other business domains and to investigate how our recommendation can support companies in improving their development practices.

8.2 State of the Art

While many CE-like activities can be observed in game development, there is limited research of experimentation in the game industry and for indie game studies [6] with some notable exceptions [5, 20]. Game analytics is a widely adopted practice within game development used for purposes such as in-game balancing, identifying bottlenecks in game levels, detecting bugs, reducing costs and risks, and negotiating with investors and publishers [19]. Leveraging field data to inform decision-making is a fundamental aspect of CE. Some specific aspects of CE have received direct attention in game development [6], e.g., the exploratory use of prototyping in the requirements engineering process [5], and monetary feature-optimization in post-deployment. The area of user research also provides some input into how user feedback can guide game development [14]. User research shares with CE the overall idea of basing development on an empirical approach.

Research describes a need to match experimentation practices to the different stages of game development [1]. Qualitative methods are primarily used in early development stages when the amount of quantitative user data is limited [20]. Play-testing is highlighted as the main overarching method, while A/B testing is common in the later post-production stages [9]. Identifying and isolating features for evaluation is a challenge [12], especially in the early development stages [11]. The evaluated feature set needs to be comprehensive enough to retain all essential aspects required for game-play while still allowing the experiment to assess the defined Key Performance Indicators (KPIs) [9].

A distinction can also be noted in relation to the game genre and context. For example, in the mobile game context and freemium-type games [12], there is a strong belief in quantitative methods. Andersen et al. demonstrate the potential of quantitative experimentation in guiding feature development in gaming [2]. However, while this approach is applied within game development, in particular for mobile games, our research indicates that there are game companies where feature development tends to be opinion based instead of based on the outcome of game testing.

Depending on the purpose and aspects being experimented on, different metrics are required, such as game mechanics (the rules of the game), game dynamics (what happens when the game is played), and aesthetics (the feeling of fun experienced by the player) [11]. When designing an experiment, each aspect requires specific consideration regarding the technical implementation and commercial viability [16]. Validation of aesthetics, or fun factor (regardless of technical or commercial viability), is specifically highlighted as a key challenge, due to the need to connect with a relevant target audience [17] while limiting the risk of leaking differentiating ideas and details to the public and potential competitors [1]. Therefore, play-testing is usually performed with internal developers or trusted associates, despite the risk of cognitive and confirmation biases [20]. Chueca et al. point to the need for new methods, tools, and processes to identify and validate requirements relating to the user experience of games [4].

8.3 Research Method

Our findings are based on an interview survey of how CE is applied within indie game development prior to releasing a game. We interviewed representatives from ten indie companies to gain a broad understanding of practices across different game startups. Seven of the startups have fewer than 5 employees, two have 8–9 employees, and one has over 50 employees. Our interviewees' experience of game development ranges from four to fourteen years and covers roles such as founder, co-founder, game producer, game director, lead game developer, and lead game designer. Six of the interviewees were currently based in Sweden, two in Netherlands, one in Switzerland, and one in Ukraine. The interviews were performed online for about 30 minutes each and consisted of open questions regarding the use and experience of CE and related practices such as game user research, testing, and requirements engineering. Further details of our research method can be found in [13].

8.4 Continuous Experimentation Framework

Our framework for CE consists of five key components that outline the rationale and methodology behind experimentation. These components are *goal definition*, *experiment object*, *sampling strategy*, *design strategy*, and *execution strategy* (see Fig. 8.1). The current version of the framework includes some dimensions specific to game development, such as game experience. However, most of the dimensions are general, such as understandability, sketches, and executables, and may apply to software development in any business domain.

Goal definition	**Experiment object**	**Design strategy**	**Sampling strategy**	**Execution strategy**
Purpose - Scoping, Validation - Idea, Feature Game experience - Playability - Fun factor - Understandability	Medium - Sketches - Videos - Executables Maturity - Area (*Aesthetics, Mechanics, Content*) - Level (*Conceptual, Playable, Polished*)	Method - Split testing - Sequential testing - Exploratory testing Cadence - Systematic - Ad-hoc Length	Participants - Internal team - Friends and family - Publishers - External unknowns - Dedicated community - Streamers Number of participants	Data collection technique - Observation - Survey - Interview - Analytics - Telemetry

Fig. 8.1 Overview of our framework for CE in game development including key parts of experimentation in the early stages of game development

8.4.1 Goal Definition

The goal of experimentation consists of a combination of the **purpose** of an experiment and the aspect of the **game experience** that is being evaluated. The purpose concerns *scoping* and *validating* of *game ideas* and *features*. The *game experience* [18], or user experience, that is evaluated concerns the *playability*, *fun factor*, and *understandability* experienced by the user while playing. Evaluation of these aspects is closely coupled to the design and development of the mechanics, aesthetics, and content of a game. For example, experimenting with *mechanics like weapons and items... [enables exploring] what kinds of choices players are making and if they feel that those are satisfying*. The importance of understandability varies depending on the type of game. For example, for a strategy game, the player needs to *learn... and understand the basic game mechanisms* to play and enjoy the game and thus has a steeper learning curve compared to a first-shooter game.

8.4.2 Experiment Object

The experiment object refers to the artefact that is used to evaluate the game experience. The **medium** that is used (sketches, videos, or executable prototypes) and the aspect and level of **maturity** of the experiment object need to be aligned to the goals of the experiment. *Sketches* of the art and imagined game play can be used to evaluate the overall game idea. *Videos* demonstrating game play are often used to communicate new game ideas and concepts. *Executable prototypes* are used to evaluate the actual game experience by observing participants playing the game. For this reason, experimenting with an executable prototype is often preferred even if this requires more time and effort than, e.g., sketching or prototyping a new idea in isolation. One interviewee motivated this preference with a desire to *get it [the change] into the game as quickly as possible ... to see if it works with the rest*. The maturity of the experiment object can vary regarding its *level* of detail for different *aspects* of the game, such as *aesthetics*, *mechanics*, and *content*. The aesthetics relate to the graphical style and artwork of the game, while game mechanics concern the dynamics, features, and physical mechanics as experienced when playing a game. The content relates to game level design and extending the game play with more levels and variation in using the mechanics. The maturity *level* of the experiment object varies from *conceptual* to *playable* to a *polished* representation of one or more of the aspects. Sketches that illustrate the aesthetics and mechanics of an envisioned game at a *conceptual level* can be used to evaluate high-level game ideas and visions. In contrast, a rough executable prototypes with *playable mechanics* and *aesthetics* can be used to demonstrate and evaluate the core mechanics and loop of a game. Similarly, as level design progresses, the *content* is refined and expanded, and the overall game experience is evaluated through experimentation.

8.4.3 Design Strategy

When designing and setting up experiments, three main types of **methods** are used, namely, *split*, *sequential*, and *exploratory testing*, with variations in **cadence** and **length** of experiments. The choice of strategy depends on the experimentation goal, type of game, current development stage, and available resources. *Split testing* involves comparing multiple versions and is often limited to two versions (i.e., A/B testing). This limitation for indie game development is due to the high cost of developing multiple variants of the game. *Sequential testing* is the most common experimentation method used when developing features and content. In this method, the option considered to have the best potential is evaluated first, and if the feedback is negative, the alternative solution is implemented and evaluated. For example, when improving on functionality that is not working, developers *just test the new version and see if the reactions have improved. Exploratory testing* is a less formal experimentation method where there is no predefined hypothesis that is used either for a general and open evaluation or to focus on a specific aspect such as game mechanics or fun factor. One game developer describes this as *"If we have something that we know we want to know more about, then it is really focused... if it is more ... how does the game play experience feel ... then it is more open."* The *cadence* with which experiments are performed varies through *structured systematic experimentation* to *ad hoc experimentation* with a *length* commonly ranging between a weekend to a week. Sometimes, longer experiments, spanning up to several weeks, are performed, though updates during this period make it hard to draw clear conclusions from the experiment since the feedback *at the beginning of the playtest and ... at the end of the playtest is actually feedback on two different builds*.

8.4.4 Sampling Strategy

Participants of an experiment are selected, or sampled, to represent a certain population, which involves selecting the **demographics** and **number of participants**. Indie game companies engage various types of participants, including their *internal team* and *publishers*, *friends and family*, *external unknowns*, and *dedicated communities*. *Streamers*, i.e., individuals who play and comment on games while simultaneously recording and sending live, are also included. Other game developers can provide *feedback [that is] even more useful ... [since] they have some development knowledge* and tend to *see things that regular gamers do not think about*. The type and number of participants used typically depend on the current stage of game development and the availability of participants. The sampling also needs to align with the type of experiment (goals, design strategy, and experiment object). For physical playtests, indie game developers generally are satisfied with 8–10 individuals. For online and external playtests with players from the community or unknown externals, a larger number of participants are often used. For example, A/B test can be performed within a dedicated community of around 60–70 participants. Valuable insights can be gained from as little as *10 players [which can] often get you... [a] visible micro trend*. In other cases, 100 testers or more testers may be required for the input to be significant and trustworthy. However, indie game companies face major challenges in recruiting larger numbers of participants and in attaining un-biased participants with a good representativeness of the target audience. For example, friends and family often have a positive bias and are predisposed to approve of the company's work. So, the representativeness of those selected for the experiment needs to be considered to mitigate the risk of biases, inconclusive, and misleading results.

8.4.5 Execution Strategy

Feedback is gathered from experiments through *data collection techniques* such as *observations*, *surveys*, *interviews*, and *telemetry data*. Indie game companies commonly use **observations** of participants performing game play to gain insights into how the game is played and if participants get stuck or do not understand certain aspects of the game. Often the screen is recorded to allow for later analysis and also enables recruiting participants irrespective of physical location. Watching people play can also be useful in mitigating biases, for example, in friends and family, or when game players know that they are talking to the developer and are less likely to criticize. When observing participants during live game play testing, it is important not to interfere by asking leading questions or helping them, since this may influence their behavior and responses. Follow-up *surveys* and *interviews* are commonly used to complement observations. Surveys can consist of a mix of open and closed questions about the user experience but also specific questions on game aspects in focus for the experiment, such as *"Did you do this? Dig there? Press that button?"* Such specific questions can reveal how well the gamer has understood the game logic and mechanics. Similar types of questions are used in interviews that allow for follow-up questions, which can provide richer answers and deeper insights into game play behavior and experience. However, interviews are time-consuming and can *take up too much time for ... sole developers*. Balancing cost and benefit of experimentation poses a constant challenge. While experimenting with external participants takes time from development, it also reduces the risk of *running into problems that are very hard or costly to correct*.

8.5 Pre-release Development Stages

Game development is an iterative and gradual process through which new ideas, features, and content of the game are explored, validated, refined, and expanded into a final public release. We have identified four main pre-release stages, namely, *Ideation*, *Pre-production*, *Feature production*, and *Content production*. The experimentation practices for indie game development vary throughout these stages, and experiments are carried out with a broadening set of participants and with a gradually extended and refined representation of the game from early sketches and designs to vertical slices through to alpha, beta, and final release. Figure 8.2 provides an overview of experimentation practices for all stages categorized using our CE framework (described in Sect. 8.4.)

8.5.1 Ideation Stage

In this initial stage, the **goal** of experimentation is primarily to identify and *scope the idea* of the game by validating its *fun factor* and potential for market success. This stage is especially critical for indie game companies since this affects the use of very limited development team resources. The game idea that is selected at this stage can determine the success or failure of the whole company. For example, showing a very early sketch to a publisher can lead to adjusting the scope and resulting in a game that *sells better in the end.*

Simpler non-executable **experiment objects** are used to visualize a *conceptual* representation of the envisioned *aesthetics* and *mechanics* of the game. This typically involves using *sketches* and conceptual designs of the art and imagined game play to evaluate the game ideas and design options. *Videos* can also be used in this stage to demonstrate game play and to communicate an envisioned idea or game concept, e.g., to publishers and investors.

The **design strategy** in this stage often consists of *ad hoc* experimentation using *explorative testing* in short experiments that run for one or more days. *Split testing* is also commonly used in this stage to explore multiple ideas in parallel, due to the relatively low cost of producing sketches and conceptual artwork. For example, several alternative versions of a game are often experimented with by showing conceptual art and designs to potential publishers to present their game ideas and art designs. The feedback is used to guide the indie game companies in selecting which idea to pursue and invest further development effort in. However, if several publishers are involved, this can lead to challenges with inconclusive feedback, which forces the indie game company to make decisions based on other criteria, e.g., lowest development cost.

Sampling of participants in this stage is limited to *publishers* and the *internal team*, and the **execution strategy** for experiments primarily relies on *observations* and informal *interviews*. At this stage, before the game idea and concept is set, it is very important for indie game companies to include *publishers* in the testing to ensure their support. For example, an experiment consisting of presenting conceptual sketches of different game ideas to a potential publisher can provide feedback that guides the decision on which idea to pursue and to develop further. This can prevent wasting scarce development resources on unviable game ideas.

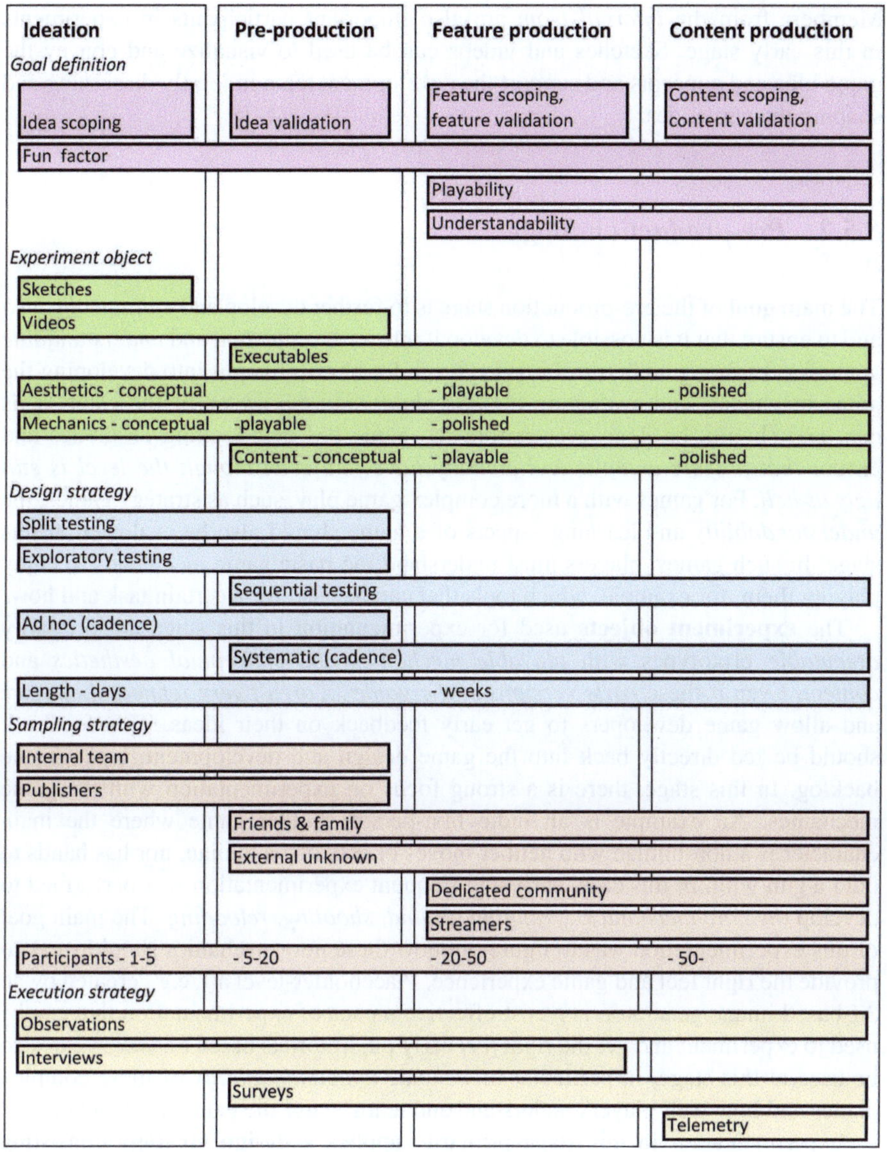

Fig. 8.2 Overview of experimentation practices in pre-release development stages

Members from the *internal team* are also important participants in experiments in this early stage. Sketches and videos can be used to visualize and convey the game idea and concepts and support the development team in jointly discussing and shaping the game idea.

8.5.2 Pre-production Stage

The main **goal** of the pre-production stage is to further develop and *validate the idea* and to ensure that it is possible to develop it into a *playable*, *fun*, and *understandable* game for the target audience. In this stage, a lot of effort is put into developing the game mechanics and evaluating the *playability* and *fun factor* of the game. This can, and should, be done even before the game has nice-looking aesthetics and ensure *that players enjoy it and actually have fun, even though the level is still ugly as hell.* For games with a more complex game play, such as strategy games, the *understandability* and learning aspects of a game should also be evaluated at this stage. In such games, players must understand the basic game mechanics to enjoy playing them, for example, which tools that can be used for a certain task and how.

The **experiment objects** used for experimentation in this stage are primarily *executable* prototypes with *playable mechanics* and *conceptual aesthetics* and *content*. Even if these *early versions of the game ... aren't very refined, they work* and allow game developers to get early feedback on their ideas. This feedback should be fed directly back into the game design and development, e.g., via the backlog. In this stage, there is a strong focus on experimentation with the game mechanics. An example is an indie first-person-shooter game where the main character is a non-human who neither moves or acts like a human, nor has hands to hold a gun with. In this case, early and frequent experimentation was performed to develop *the core mechanics... running around, shooting, reloading*. The main goal of this experimentation was to figure out how these new mechanics should work to provide the right feel and game experience. Placeholder-level art, e.g., created by an AI-based image generator, is a cost-effective means of experimentation that can be used to experiment and get the right *feel* early on. Tutorials based on *videos* can also be used at this stage, in particular to evaluate *understandability* of more complex games and how well players understand and learn to use the game mechanisms.

Experimentation in this stage primarily applies a **design strategy** consisting of *systematic experimentation* through a combination of methods over small and quick iterations, typically 1–2 weeks. *Split* and *exploratory* testing are used as the game mechanics are evolved, though for different purposes. *Split testing* is useful for experimenting with new features. As one indie game developer described their use of A/B testing in this stage, *"we build a quick and dirty version of the one and the other and let them test."* One indie company experimented with advanced AI functionality by developing two versions of their game, one with the AI functionality. In the experiment, the participants selected which version they preferred to play. Based on the feedback, the company decided to adopt the new AI functionality. Testing multiple versions at the same time also comes with challenges, especially for indie companies who have access to a limited number of players. Questions arise, such as *"should they all play both versions? And if so, in what order? And does it influence them?"* The sampling of participants and planning of the experiment then needs to be considered to mitigate biases and reduce the risk of incorrect or inconclusive feedback.

A **sampling strategy** based on convenience and availability tends to be used in the pre-production stage, and experimentation is primarily carried out with participants from the *internal team* and the *publishers*. A small set of easily available participants from within the teams co-working space can also be used as play testers. Internal experimentation is often performed on a weekly basis, e.g., through *show-and-tell sessions* that then continue also throughout later development stages. At the end of this stage, as the prototype becomes more mature, early versions of the game can be shown to *friends and family*, and *external participants* can be recruited through publishing small demos as previews on gaming platforms such as Itch.io and Steam. These kinds of experiments can be used to poll interest and can provide valuable *feedback from people who explore the game*. However, experimenting with such early versions of the game with external gamers can also yield *very divided feedback from enthusiastic to very disappointed.* Drawing conclusions from such diverse feedback can be very challenging and should not be used as the sole source of feedback for major decisions about the game.

8.5.3 Feature Production Stage

The main **goal** of experimentation turns to *feature scoping* and *feature validation* as development shifts into developing a complete set of features and working toward an alpha release. In this stage, *the decision on what to include in the game* is based on experimentation results, both regarding which features to include and the detailed scoping of these. As the game matures, all aspects of the game are important to consider and validate including *fun factor*, *playability*, and *understandability*.

The **object** that is experimented with is primarily a version of the game under development. Experimentation is then performed with an *executable* that has *playable aesthetics* and *content* and gradually *maturing mechanics*.

The predominant **design strategy** in this stage is *sequential* testing using play testing in a *systematic* manner over a period of 1–2 *weeks* with predefined hypothesis or questions for the playtest. Lessons and takeaways from experimentation are used to inform the backlog and prioritize feature development and bug fixing. An example is experimentation with replacing a gun with an alternative mechanism. In this case, the goal of the experiment was to evaluate a hypothesis that the gun was used too repetitively and impacted negatively on the user experience. In this case, the experiment revealed that the users enjoyed, and preferred, the gun, which led to re-implementing it in the game. *Split testing* is also used in this stage when experimenting with specific new features, but to a limited degree due to the cost of implementing multiple options. An example of a split test is an experiment where alternative *playable game mechanics* and *playable aesthetics* in the form of alternative artwork were added to a limited prototype based on the main game. In this case, the alternative variant was compared to the main game, and the ideas that were successful according to the participants' feedback were re-implemented in the main game. The *length* of experiments typically shifts to longer iterations in this stage, as more development is conducted between tests, and the maturity level increases for the mechanics and aesthetics of the game. This is sometimes mixed with shorter and more intense periods of experimentation. Shifting the *cadence* allows for both experimenting with more strategic features that require *more long-term decisions and introduction of larger feature implementations, followed by more intense testing* of smaller changes to optimize the game mechanics or details in a feature.

In this stage, the **sampling** of participants shifts to involve a larger number of *external unknowns*, while the **execution strategy** remains similar to pre-production with an increase in *surveys* and recorded *observations* of game play. Indie game companies often recruit external participants by publishing early game versions, or demos, on platforms such as Itch.io and Steam to attract attention and to invite players into their Discord channels (a chat platform). The Discord channels serve as an infrastructure for growing and facilitating *dedicated communities* of fans and potential play testers that can be used in experiments on a reoccurring basis. If indie companies have the funds, they can also acquire external play testers from third-party platforms. These platforms provide recruitment of game players with specific characteristics. While experimenting with "the correct" audience reduces the risk of biases in the outcome, it also comes with a monetary cost. Another cheaper source of valuable insights into game play can be obtained by observing *streamers* and their audience or by letting *friends and family* evaluate early demos of the game.

8.5.4 Content Production Stage

As development shifts to working toward a beta release, the main **goal** of experimentation turns to *content scoping* and *content validation* in the content production stage. Developing content can be seen as *stretching out that fun and putting these features in varied situations* and *making actual story levels that use all of these features and tools that we've built, but... [with] variations .. so that the game stays interesting*. This requires a lot of experimentation to find out *which combinations of mechanics that work and are interesting*.

Similarly to the feature production stage, the main **experiment object** in this stage is the game under development, which at this point is an *executable* with a full set of features with *polished mechanics*. The *aesthetics* of the game are primarily conceived and evaluated in this stage through producing the final artwork and developing this game aspect from a *conceptual* to a *polished* level of maturity.

A *sequential* approach is the predominant **design strategy** currently used by indie companies in the content production stage. Level designers design and create game situations that are then experimented with, and *if people actually struggle there, we'll try the other [alternative] next*."

The **sampling** of participants shifts as the game matures, and play testing is performed with larger numbers of *external unknowns* and *dedicated community*. These are complemented by continuous game testing with the *internal team* since play testers with game development experience can smoke out issues that normal gamers may not observe. The opposite is also true: an external game tester may find issues and bugs that the internal team is blind to.

The number of participants allows shifting the **execution strategy** toward increased use of *telemetry*, meaning data generated by players' interactions with the game. Telemetry data, such as duration and progress of game play, can provide insights about game play including difficulties, engagement, bugs, etc. In the mobile context, game events are tightly connected to analytics, e.g., to record time from one game action to another to tell how quickly a player progresses compared to an average user. Frameworks such as Google Analytics can provide certain metrics such as the number of active users, new players, monthly active users, day-one retention, and day-seven retention. While these general KPIs are helpful, more detailed in-game metrics can provide more value. However, this requires indie companies to implement analytics tooling such as data pipelines and processing infrastructure of the back-end, in their development environment. However, the *telemetry data* needs to be complemented by *interviews* and *observations* in order to evaluate the fun factor since *fun is so subjective*. For example, observing how players move around and interact with the game environment provides insights into the game experience, how the game mechanics are working, and how much *fun* the participants are having. This qualitative feedback is especially time-consuming to gather and to analyze, and game developers should strive for a good cost-benefit balance, e.g., by limiting this data collection to a subset of the participants of an on-line experiment.

8.6 Recommendations and Advice for Practice

We provide the following recommendations and advice to practitioners on how to improve on their experimentation practices. These are based on our empirical insights and on previous research on continuous experimentation.

Adopt an experiment-driven mindset based on continuous experimentation with game ideas, features, and content. Be prepared to pivot and change direction and even kill favorite game ideas, if experimentation results indicate that they are unviable.

Systematically and consciously perform experimentation throughout the game development effort, from ideation, through pre-production, to production and beyond. Define hypothesis and clear goals for each experiment, and design the experiments and the evaluation factors to match this.

Mix and combine different types of experiments to maximize the value of the feedback and reduce the risk of inconclusive or incorrect conclusions. By varying and combining the strategy for sampling participants, and designing and executing experiments, multiple triangulating data points can be obtained, which increase the reliability and validity of the data.

Involve external participants as early as possible, ideally already in the ideation stage. Feedback from external unknowns and dedicated community participants often provides un-biased feedback on new game ideas and mechanics, in contrast to the feedback from internal testers and friends and family. Such feedback enables detecting problems early on and enables efficient development of features and content with a high game experience factor. This avoids spending development resources on major changes in later development stages.

Select the execution strategy to match available number of participants. Focus on observations and interviews when you have a limited number of participants. And use telemetry data when you have access to a larger number of participants. We also recommend complementing telemetry data with observations and interviews for a smaller number of participants to provide insights into how to interpret the quantitative data.

Adapt your design strategy to the current design stage of the item under development and the overall game development stage and the number of available participants. In early design stages, e.g., of a new feature, we recommend experimenting with multiple variants through split testing, if there are sufficient participants for this and prototypes can be produced cheaply. For example, experimenting with multiple variants of sketches (for content and aesthetics) and smaller executable demos can provide a cost-effective initial evaluation of multiple design options in a short period of time. As the design of a feature matures, or if the cost of producing multiple variants is very high, sequential testing is the most cost-effective choice. Explorative testing is recommended as a complement to the other testing strategies, in particular for later development stages and of later design stages, when the feature under development is mature.

Be aware of and mitigate biases by using mixed experimentation strategies, for example, by varying the data collection methods, the number and type of participants used, or the cadence and execution strategy of experiments. For example, combine telemetry with observations and interviews to gain explanations to the measured behavior. The risk of drawing incorrect conclusions can be reduced both by combining different types of data and data from multiple sources. Such triangulation can also mitigate the risk of biases and increase the value obtained from experiments.

Finally, we recommend **continuously improving experimentation practices** through regular retrospectives of performed experiments to capture insights gained from specific experiment designs and setups. Our framework can serve as a basis for team discussions on how to improve on experimentation practices. Questions to consider include the following: Could similar value have been obtained with a simpler and cheaper prototype (experiment object)? How did the number and type of participants (sampling strategy) affect the cost and outcomes? Was the data collection method appropriate (execution strategy)? Also, consider the current development stage and reflect on how experimentation can be tailored to provide the most valuable feedback and insights for that stage.

8.7 Conclusions

Indie companies face significant challenges due to limited time and resources compared to larger and more established game companies with well-known game titles. To succeed, these startups must adopt a cost-benefit mindset and effective experimentation practices. Our research highlights the importance of continuous experimentation in indie game development, and we identify key aspects such as goal definition, experiment object, design strategy, sampling strategy, and execution strategy. We also describe current experimentation practices for the pre-release development stages of ideation, pre-production, feature production, and content production. Experimentation is crucial in pre-release stages to scope and validate the business viability of game ideas, features, and content. By continuously evaluating the game experience through experiments with external gamers (users), problems with playability, fun factor, and understandability can be caught early on. The feedback can be used to guide design decisions and enable effective use of scarce development resources.

Future work will delve deeper into the key aspects of experimentation practices and factors influencing them in order to identify best practices in this area and means to further improve game development practices. Special attention will be given to the resource and efficiency needs of indie game companies and how to support game developers in optimizing their cost-benefit balance. This involves investigating tools and processes for experimentation and exploring and validating the usefulness of our recommendations. Additionally, the perspectives and practices of more established and larger game companies will be explored to contrast with the findings from indie game companies.

Finally, our findings and recommendations can provide insights and practical advice on how to apply experimentation practices. We encourage game developer both within indie companies and more established game companies to consider our findings and how to strengthen their experimentation practices in the pre-release stages of game development. Also other software-intensive industries, in particular those with a strong focus on user experience, may gain from considering our advice.

Acknowledgments This work was support by the Wallenberg AI, Autonomous Systems and Software Program (WASP) funded by the Knut and Alice Wallenberg Foundation and the Research Council of Finland (project no. 349574, Naturalistic decision-making in Continuous Experimentation).

References

1. Aleem, S., Capretz, L.F., Ahmed, F.: Game development software engineering process life cycle: a systematic review. J. Softw. Engin. Res. Dev. **4**, 1–30 (2016)
2. Andersen, E., Liu, Y.E., Snider, R., Szeto, R., Cooper, S., Popović, Z.: On the harmfulness of secondary game objectives. In: Proceedings of the FDG '11, pp. 30–37 (2011)
3. Auer, F., Ros, R., Kaltenbrunner, L., Runeson, P., Felderer, M.: Controlled experimentation in continuous experimentation: Knowledge and challenges. Inf. Softw. Technol. **134**(2021), 106551 (2021). ISSN 0950-5849. https://doi.org/10.1016/j.infsof.2021.106551
4. Chueca, J., Verón, J., Font, J., Pérez, F., Cetina, C.: The consolidation of game software engineering: a systematic literature review of software engineering for industry-scale computer games. Inf. Softw. Technol. 107330 (2023)
5. Edison, H., Melegati, J., Bjarnason, E.: Experimentation in early-stage video game startups: practices and challenges. In: Hyrynsalmi, S., Münch, J., Smolander, K., Melegati, J. (eds.) Software Business. ICSOB 2023. Lecture Notes in Business Information Processing, vol. 500. Springer, Cham (2024). https://doi.org/10.1007/978-3-031-53227-6_25
6. Engström, H.: Game development research (2020)
7. Fagerholm, F., Guinea, A.S., Mäenpää, H., Münch, J.: The right model for continuous experimentation. J. Syst. Softw. **123**, 292–305 (2017)
8. Grabarczyk, P.: Is every indie game independent? towards the concept of independent game. Game Stud. **16**(1) (2016). https://gamestudies.org/1601/articles/gardagrabarczyk
9. Hyrynsalmi, S., Klotins, E., Unterkalmsteiner, M., Gorschek, T., Tripathi, N., Pompermaier, L.B., Prikladnicki, R.: What is a minimum viable (video) game? Towards a research agenda. In: 17th IFIP WG 6.11, pp. 217–231 (2018)
10. Industry, S.G.: Swedish Games Industry 2023 Game Developer Index. Swedish Games Industry (2023)
11. Järvi, A., Taajamaa, V., Hyrynsalmi, S.: Lean software startup–an experience report from an entrepreneurial software business course. In: Software Business: 6th International Conference 2015, Proceedings 6, pp. 230–244. Springer, Berlin (2015)
12. Koskenvoima, A., Mäntymäki, M.: Why do small and medium-size freemium game developers use game analytics? In: 14th IFIP WG 6.11, pp. 326–337 (2015)
13. Linåker, J., Bjarnason, E., Fagerholm, F.: Pre-release experimentation in indie game development: an interview survey. In: Proceedings of ICSOB. Springer, Berlin (2024)
14. Pagulayan, R.J., Gunn, D.V., Hagen, J.R., Hendersen, D.J., Kelley, T.A., Phillips, B.C., Guajardo, J., Nichols, T.A.: Applied user research in games. Wiley Handbook Hum. Comput. Inter. **1**, 299–346 (2018)
15. Ros, R., Runeson, P.: Continuous experimentation and a/b testing: a mapping study. In: Proceedings of the 4th RCoSE, pp. 35–41 (2018)
16. Rosenfield Boeira, J.N., Rosenfield Boeira, J.N.: MVPS: do we really need them? Lean Game Dev: Apply Lean Framew to the Proc of Game Dev, pp. 33–48 (2017)
17. Schmalz, M., Finn, A., Taylor, H.: Risk management in video game development projects. In: 47th HICSS, pp. 4325–4334. IEEE, Piscataway (2014)
18. Stahlke, S.N., Mirza-Babaei, P.: Usertesting without the user: opportunities and challenges of an ai-driven approach in games user research. Comp. Ent. **16**(2), 1–18 (2018)
19. Su, Y., Backlund, P., Engström, H.: Comprehensive review and classification of game analytics. Service Oriented Comp. Appl. **15**(2), 141–156 (2021)
20. Yaman, S., Mikkonen, T., Suomela, R.: Continuous experimentation in mobile game development. In: Proceedings of 44th SEAA, pp. 345–352 (2018)

Chapter 9
Getting Started with Product Management in Software Startups

Gerardo Matturro and Josefina Fernández

Abstract Product management has become critical for modern organizations, from small startups to corporate enterprises. Due to the usual limitations of software startups in terms of the size and experience of the founding team, financial resources, and high technical and business risks, this organizational function does not exist in its early stages. Still, the need for a differentiated role in dealing with product management slowly arises. This chapter addresses the study of the emerging product manager role and the product management function in software startups. For this purpose, semi-structured interviews were conducted with a group of experienced founding partners and product managers of software startups to know (a) what circumstances led to the establishment of the product management function in software startups and (b) what the most relevant product management activities associated with the emerging role of product manager. Additionally, a series of focus group meetings were conducted to define the content of a set of role guides to assist the emerging product manager in performing the main early-stage product management activities. Circumstances like bad product-market fit and negative user feedback from the first launch led to establishing the emerging role, while communicating product learnings and participating in product prototyping belong to the usual early-stage activities. The role guides were evaluated as suitable and very useful for assisting emerging product managers.

Keywords Software startups · Product management · Product manager · Role guides

G. Matturro (✉) · J. Fernández
Universidad ORT Uruguay, Montevideo, Uruguay
e-mail: matturro@fi365.ort.edu.uy; jf231636@fi365.ort.edu.uy

N. Tripathi et al. (eds.), *Advances in Software Startups*,
https://doi.org/10.1007/978-3-032-04294-1_9

9.1 Introduction

A software startup is a newly created company with minimal or no operating history, focused on creating and developing an innovative, software-intensive product or service as a basis for creating business value [1].

Since this software-based product or service is essential for the survival and growth of the new venture, it is crucial to manage it effectively.

Product management is defined as the organizational function within a company dealing with the thoughtful and proactive management of a product or group of products throughout all stages of the product lifecycle (conception, planning, development, testing, launch, delivery, and withdrawal) [2].

This role is often well defined in established companies, but not so in new ventures, particularly during their early stages. In early-stage software startups, the role of product manager typically does not formally exist; rather, it gradually emerges as the company grows. Initially, founders make product decisions and collaborate closely to define the vision, prioritize features, and gather user feedback. However, due to specific events or circumstances, as the product evolves, the need for a dedicated product management function becomes more apparent—especially to coordinate cross-functional efforts, streamline development, and ensure alignment with market demands.

On the other hand, software startups often face several well-known challenges, such as a lack of resources, being made up of small teams with limited experience, and relying on a single product [3]. In this scenario, it is not a good strategy for an emerging product manager to try to meet LeMay's characterization that "as a product manager, you are responsible for doing whatever needs to get done to ensure the success of your team and your product" [4]. On the contrary, it is crucial for the emerging product manager to prioritize actions and focus on a few core activities rather than attempting to manage every possible task.

The objectives of this study are as follows:

O1—to understand how the organizational function of product management originates in software startups

O2—to identify the key activities performed by the individual in the role of Product Manager

O3—to develop a set of role guides tailored to the context of software startups to assist a novice product manager in executing essential product management activities

O4—to validate the previously developed guides

The results of the study are of interest to (a) software entrepreneurs, who will be able to identify their particular circumstances for creating the software product management function and the activities on which to focus first, (b) researchers who want to delve deeper into the study of this function and its associated role, and (c) business incubators aiming to better support and train software entrepreneurs in the creation and evolution of the product management function.

The remainder of this chapter is organized as follows: Sect. 9.2 introduces the concept of product management, outlines the role of the product manager, and reviews the literature on product management in the software industry in general and in software startups in particular. Section 9.3 details the study's methodological design, while Sect. 9.4 presents and discusses the main findings. Section 9.5 offers a series of recommendations for practitioners, and Sect. 9.6 concludes with suggested future research actions.

9.2 State of the Art

This section focuses on presenting relevant concepts regarding the origin and characteristics of the product management function, along with a concise narrative review of the responsibilities and primary activities related to the product manager's role in software organizations and startups.

9.2.1 Product Management and the Role of a Product Manager

The concept of product management originated in the 1930s at Procter & Gamble (P&G) when Neil H. McElroy, a marketing manager, wrote a memo advocating for "brand men" who would take full responsibility for a product's success. This idea laid the foundation for modern product management by emphasizing a dedicated role focused on understanding customer needs, coordinating cross-functional teams, and driving product success.

As with many concepts across disciplines, there is no single definition of product management or the role of a product manager. For product management, definitions vary from very "diffuse" ones, such as "if it needs to be done, and it isn't anyone else's job, then it's your job" [4], to the more extensive and detailed "...a management concept that focuses on the need for cross-functional and cross-divisional control and coordination of products or product groups. ... In addition to the functional alignment of the functional areas, product management must ensure product-related alignment. ... is thus a kind of information, coordination, and control platform for all product-relevant topics within and outside the company" [5].

Beyond a concrete definition, what is relevant is to know the primary responsibilities associated with product management and the most common activities a product manager usually performs.

The concept of "activity" refers to any deliberate action or series of actions performed to achieve a specific goal, while "responsibility" denotes the duty to manage and be accountable for the outcomes of those actions. While the general idea of responsibility might be easier to grasp, the exact steps or activities needed to achieve it can sometimes be more complex and less immediately apparent.

Mainstream product management literature often fails to distinguish between the two concepts and tends to characterize the product manager specifically according to their responsibilities.

Thus, according to Anderson and colleagues, a product manager's key responsibilities are understanding the customer experience, developing vision, building and following the product roadmap, driving the product launch, participating in the promotion plan development, and contributing to product pricing and positioning strategies [6].

Cagan mentions that a good product manager is responsible for having a deep knowledge of the actual users and customers, a deep understanding of the business and how it works, the role the product plays in the business, and the market and industry in which the company is competing [7].

9.2.2 Product Management in New Ventures

Product management in startups has its particularities due to the specific characteristics of this type of new company.

In the opinion of Banfield and colleagues, if successful product leaders are a rare breed in the product universe, then successful startup product managers are even more [8]. To these authors, startup product leaders face intense challenges, needing both market expertise and the ability to build and lead teams from scratch. The chaotic early stages often prioritize tactical wins over strategic plans, with small, ambiguity-tolerant teams focused on rapid experimentation and customer feedback. As startups mature, processes become more structured, metrics are tracked, and inter-team alignment improves. The product team then shifts its focus to detail-oriented optimizations, aiming for precise improvements in key areas like customer acquisition and lifetime value.

As Ahuja advises, implementing proper product management practices early in a startup can broaden perspectives beyond merely having an excellent UX; it enables an understanding of user needs, focuses on product-market fit, and helps reach more customers [9].

9.2.3 Software Product Management

When reviewing the more specialized literature on software product management, one notices a shift in emphasizing activities over responsibilities when describing the product manager's role. As mentioned earlier, a responsibility indicates what needs to be achieved, while activities describe how to achieve it.

Managing software products involves overseeing software product development, launch, and continuous improvement. This role includes, among others, defining product vision, gathering and prioritizing customer requirements, and working closely with engineering, marketing, and sales teams to ensure the product meets market needs and business goals.

In a study by Maglyas and colleagues, they identified vision creation, product lifecycle management, release planning, and product requirements engineering as core activities associated with a product manager, while strategic planning, portfolio management, product analysis, product launches, product support, and product development were identified as supporting ones [10].

Pattyn conducted a Systematic Literature Review to identify the specific tasks commonly associated with the responsibilities of a product manager [11]. Results show that 662 unique tasks have been identified across 122 activities related to the product manager's role.

A well-known framework for software product management is the one proposed by the International Software Product Management Association (ISPMA). Its reference architecture outlines the essential components and best practices for effective software product management [12]. According to this framework, software product managers have direct responsibility for the activities under the areas of "Product strategy" and "Product planning." In contrast, activities under "Development," "Marketing," "Sales and Fulfillment," and "Delivery Services and Support" have more of an orchestrating role as the direct responsibility typically lies with other units in the company.

9.2.4 *Product Management in Software Startups*

Based on its general framework presented above, the ISPMA has also proposed an adaptation called "SPM for startups" tailored to address the unique needs of software product managers and founders in startup environments. This adaptation covers essential practices and processes that assist startups in navigating the early and growth stages of their development [13].

Under each of the seven areas that structure this framework, some activities are more relevant for the early stages of startups, while others are better suited for implementation during their growth phase. For instance, in the Product Strategy area, activities like product definition and delivery model are pertinent at an early stage, whereas ecosystem management and financial management become increasingly critical during the growth phase.

In a recent study, Melegati and colleagues found that the product manager role in software startups is an ill-defined, multidisciplinary one focused on technical duties and communication, strategy, and leadership [14]. To the best of these authors' knowledge, there is no work in literature specifically focused on product management within the context of software startups. A research gap exists in identifying the tasks a product manager should perform and whether there is a minimum set of practices related to software development that are typically, if not always, executed by the product manager.

9.3 Research Method

For this study, key informants [15] were founding partners or representatives of software startups with experience in product management.

To address the objectives outlined at the beginning of this chapter, the study was organized into three phases, as illustrated in Fig. 9.1.

In Phase 1, which aimed to address objectives O1 and O2, semi-structured interviews were conducted with key informants.

During Phase 2, which aimed to address objective O3, the focus group technique was used to define the overall structure of the role guides and specify their content. The authors and four interviewees from Phase 1 participated in this focus group, along with two business mentors who joined in a supporting and advisory role.

Finally, in Phase 3, which aimed at addressing objective O4, the focus group technique was also applied, with the participation of the authors and the interviewees who had not participated in the Phase 2 focus group.

All interviews and focus group sessions were recorded to capture participants' discussions and perspectives, as well as to document the rationale behind the decisions made. Excerpts from the interviews and discussions held in the various focus group sessions will be included in the following section to illustrate how the results were obtained.

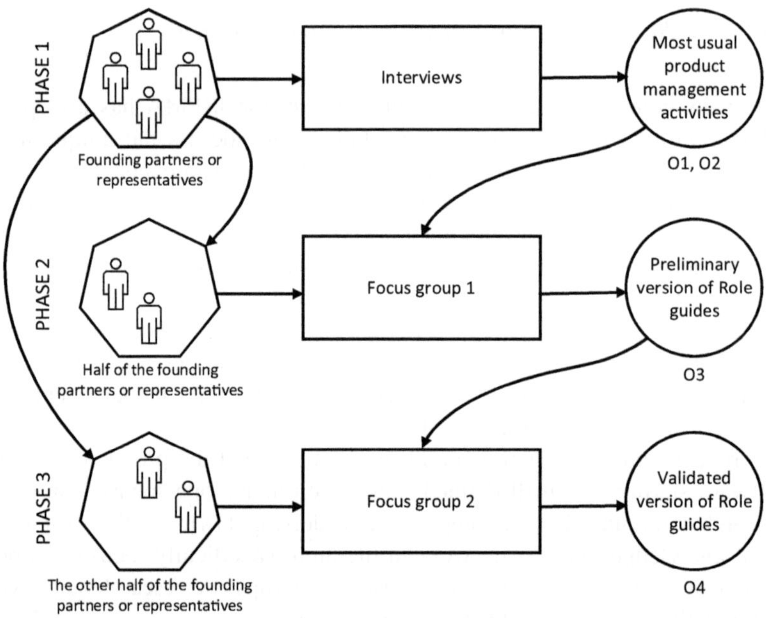

Fig. 9.1 Stages of data collection and creation of role guides

9.4 Key Findings

This section presents the study's primary results, derived from the interviews in Phase 1 and the focus groups in Phases 2 and 3.

9.4.1 Participating Software Startups

During the data collection stage for Phase 1, semi-structured interviews were conducted with founding partners or representatives of eight software startups at different stages of development, as shown in Table 9.1. The participating startups have been or are being incubated at the Center for Innovation and Entrepreneurship (CIE), the university business incubator of Universidad ORT Uruguay (https://cie.ort.edu.uy).

Table 9.1 shows, for each participating startup, the number of founding partners as well as their knowledge and experience backgrounds prior to establishing the respective venture. "Graduated" means that the venture completed the incubation process and now operates normally in the market, "In incubation" indicates that the venture is still undergoing the incubation process in the business incubator, and "Terminated" signifies that the startup has ceased its operations.

9.4.2 Reason for Establishing Product Management Function

Regarding objective O1, to find out the events or reasons that led to establishing a differentiated role for product management, the interviewees were asked to describe the particular situation or circumstances that led them to recognize the need for this role. Based on the content analysis of the responses obtained, Table 9.2 shows the main events or reasons mentioned by the interviewee.

Table 9.1 Software startups participating in the study

Name	Stage	Number of founders	Study background
CIE1	Graduated	3	Systems engineer (2), economist (1)
CIE2	Graduated	4	Systems engineers (2 graduates, 2 students)
CIE3	Graduated	2	Clinical psychologists
CIE4	Terminated	1	Industrial engineer
CIE5	Graduated	2	Systems engineers (1 graduate, 1 student)
CIE6	In incubation	2	Systems engineer (1), programmer (1)
CIE7	Graduated	1	Systems engineer
CIE8	In incubation	3	Systems engineer

Table 9.2 Reason or circumstance for creating the product management function

Reason or circumstance	Definition (based on interviewees' descriptions)
Bad product-market fit	It occurs when a product fails to effectively meet the needs or solve the problems of its target market, resulting in low customer engagement, poor adoption, and, ultimately, insufficient revenue to sustain the business
During product creation	This is the phase in a startup's lifecycle where a product transitions from an initial concept to a tangible, functional solution. It includes activities such as ideation, design, development, and iterative refinement based on testing and feedback
For economic survival	It refers to the company's ability to generate sufficient revenue to cover its operational costs, sustain its activities, and remain solvent during its early stages
Foreseeable depletion of money	It refers to the anticipated scenario where a startup's available financial resources are expected to run out based on current spending trends and revenue generation patterns
Increase in the number of users	It refers to a significant and measurable growth in the startup's user base, indicating that more individuals or organizations are adopting the software-based product or service
Negative feedback from the first production launch	It refers to the adverse responses from early users after the initial release of a software product. This feedback highlights issues such as functionality problems, usability challenges, or misalignment with market needs, indicating that the product may require adjustments or improvements

From Table 9.2, it emerges that the reasons can be business related (e.g., For economic survival), product related (e.g., During product creation), or a combination of both (e.g., Bad product-market fit).

To arrive at those reasons or circumstances, the open coding and axial coding techniques were applied to the interview transcripts. With open coding, interview transcripts are broken down into discrete segments and examined closely to identify meaningful concepts. Then, labels, or "codes," were assigned to sections of text to capture those important concepts. Once the codes to be used have been defined, the axial coding technique was applied in the second stage of the interview analysis. In this phase, the codes are reassembled to grouping them into broader categories that reveal underlying patterns or themes in the data.

To illustrate the process followed, consider the category of "Bad product-market fit" as an example, along with the following excerpts from the interview transcripts and their corresponding assigned open codes:

- **Interview 2**: "We spent six months developing features we thought were essential, but when we demoed it to potential customers, they said they didn't need half of what we'd built." **Open code**: Features and customer needs mismatch.
- **Interview 3**: "Our platform was designed for freelancers, but the more we talked to them, the more we found out they already had their own ways of handling

those tasks and weren't actively looking for alternatives." **Open code**: Wrong target market.

- **Interview 5**: "After our launch, the user acquisition was way lower than expected. The feedback we got was basically: 'cool idea, but not something I'd pay for.'" **Open code**: Low perceived value.

The assigned codes "Features and customer needs mismatch," "Wrong target market," and "Low perceived value" are conceptually linked through their shared implication: the product did not align well with market needs, behaviors, or expectations. Thus, they were grouped into the axial category "Bad product-market fit."

To establish the other categories in Table 9.2, the same type of analysis and coding process was applied using additional segments of the interview transcripts.

9.4.3 Activities Associated with a Product Manager Role

To address objective O2, respondents were presented during the interviews with a list of 24 activities typically associated with product management, drawn from the general literature on software product management. The interview questions in this case aim to determine which activities are most necessary during the emergence of the product management role. Each item on the list was rated on a Likert scale with the options "Not required," "Rarely required," "Occasionally required," "Frequently required," and "Always required".

Table 9.3 illustrates the ten most essential product management activities along with their corresponding definitions obtained from the interviews. The Score column indicates the number of "Frequently required" and "Always required" responses from all respondents.

As seen in Table 9.3, these required activities are related to the product (e.g., Participate in software testing) to the business (e.g., Identify opportunities and threats) or to both (e.g. Define product and marketing strategy).

The identified activities contribute to varying degrees to the overall responsibilities of a product manager described in Sect. 9.2. In particular, many early-stage startup activities align with both Anderson's and Cagan's views of product management. There is a strong emphasis on understanding the customer, defining product strategy, and grasping the business and market.

Anderson emphasizes that a product manager should have a profound understanding of the customer experience. This understanding is obtained through activities such as conducting customer interviews to collect direct feedback and sharing product learnings with the team to keep everyone updated on customer interactions with the product. To this author, it's also essential to create a clear product vision, which includes defining the product and marketing strategy and recognizing potential opportunities and challenges market. Additionally, the product

Table 9.3 Most required product management activities

Activity	Score	Definition (based on interviewees' descriptions)
Customer interviews	8	Engage with users to understand their experiences, challenges, and expectations
Define improved versions of the product	8	Define updates and enhancements to address user needs, fix issues, or stay competitive
Monitor, assess, and refine release activities	8	Oversee product launches, gather feedback, and make adjustments for smooth deployment and adoption
Participate in software testing	8	Actively evaluate the product to ensure it meets quality, functionality, and user expectations
Communicate product learnings	7	Share insights, lessons, and data to inform stakeholders and improve future decisions
Cost optimization and control	7	Manage resources efficiently to balance product quality and profitability
Define product and marketing strategy	7	Develop a plan to position the product effectively in the market and reach target customers
Define product requirements	7	Specify features, functionalities, and technical needs to guide product development
Identify opportunities and threats	7	Analyze market trends and competition to uncover growth prospects and mitigate risks
Participate in product prototyping	7	Collaborate on creating and refining early versions of the product to validate concepts

manager is tasked with creating and adhering to the product roadmap. This involves specifying enhancements for the product and detailing its requirements.

Another crucial responsibility highlighted by Anderson is steering the product launch, which includes actions like monitoring, evaluating, and fine-tuning release activities to guarantee a successful launch. Additionally, the product manager participates in the development of promotion plans by contributing to the product and marketing strategy and plays a role in shaping product positioning strategies. Finally, activities such as participating in product prototyping and testing help ensure that the product reflects user expectations and meets the standards required for a successful launch.

Cagan, on the other hand, emphasizes that a product manager must possess a deep knowledge of the actual users and customers. This is directly supported by activities such as customer interviews, communicating product learnings to the team, and participating in product testing, all of which provide valuable insights into user behavior and feedback. To this author, a good understanding of the business and how it works, along with the product's role within the business, is also essential. This is reflected in activities such as cost optimization and control and defining improved versions of the product. Lastly, Cagan highlights the importance of having deep knowledge of the market and industry, which is demonstrated through activities such as defining the product and marketing strategy, as well as identifying opportunities and threats in the competitive landscape.

9.4.4 Role Guides Structure and Contents

Regarding objective O3, the general structure of the role guides and the specific content for each of the ten activities presented in Table 9.3 were developed from the focus group meetings of Phase 2. To accomplish this task, five focus group meetings took place between April and May of 2024.

Defining the Structure of the Guides

The initial session occurred in person with all participants, mainly focusing on the overall structure (template) of the guides, as outlined in Table 9.4.

The template's structure arose from a desire to develop a practical and comprehensive tool for product managers at early-stage software startups. The goal was to go beyond abstract definitions and provide actionable guidance.

The definition of the template structure emerged from an iterative and collaborative process during the focus group session. Participants began with an open discussion about the core challenges and responsibilities faced by early-stage product managers in software startups. They then shifted their focus to identifying the information that would be most valuable to someone new to product management or working in a rapidly evolving startup environment. The participants stressed the need for clarity on what each activity entails, why it is important, and how it fits into a broader framework. The discussion also underscored the importance of understanding the necessary skills and having resources for further learning. Regarding the reference to the ISPMA framework, the group agreed that linking activities to it would provide a valuable connection to established best practices.

Participants discussed various ways to present the information and agreed on the current structure to ensure clarity, conciseness, and practicality. For instance, they debated whether to include examples within the "Description" section but decided against it to keep the template concise, opting instead for bibliographic references to provide a more in-depth understanding. The "Skills required" section involved a detailed discussion about the specific skills and knowledge needed for each type

Table 9.4 Template for the role guides

Section	Purpose
Activity	Name of the activity
Description	Defines what the proposed activity consists of (What is it?) and its benefits (What is it for?)
ISPMA framework	The process of the ISPMA framework that this activity is associated with
Skills required	A list of necessary skills to carry out the proposed activity and a brief explanation of their importance are included
To learn more	A set of bibliographical references to the literature used to build the card, which the reader can use for support if necessary

of activity. The participants drew upon their own successes and failures to identify the crucial competencies. The inclusion of bibliographic references in the “To learn more” section stemmed from a desire to provide a solid theoretical foundation and encourage further learning.

Defining the Contents of the Guides

To develop the content of the guides, the work was divided into two subgroups consisting of two entrepreneurs, one business mentor, and one of the authors. Each group created preliminary versions of the guides for five of the activities.

To illustrate how the content of the guides was defined, Fig. 9.2 presents excerpts from the discussion and brainstorming session about the Communicate product learnings guide.

The mandate for each session was: “We (the researchers) seek a brief, concise, and easy-to-read document, perhaps in outline format with short sentences, covering the essentials that a novice product manager should know about the activity.”

The resulting preliminary versions were then presented and discussed in the general sessions of the focus group with all its members. In each session, two or

Brainstorming session during subgroup 1 meeting

Josefina (Facilitator): Guiding the discussion and capturing key points.
Carlos (Participant 1): Founder/Product Manager of an early-stage e-commerce platform.
Susana (Participant 2): Product-focused, concerned with implementation.
Juan: (Participant 3): Business mentor.

Josefina: “*Good morning. Let's begin today's meeting by defining the content of the Communicate product learnings activity guide. ... Our first task is to define the DESCRIPTION section. Let's start with 'What it involves.*'”.
Carlos: "*From my perspective, it's about understanding what our users are actually doing and saying. So, gathering user feedback is crucial. Also, looking at the numbers – analytics – to see how features are used.*"
....
Susana: "*I agree with the data part. We also need to consider things like A/B testing results. Are our changes actually making a difference? And don't forget team discussions; .... Market research also plays a role in understanding the broader landscape...*"
Josefina: "*Good points. So, we have user feedback, analytics, market research, A/B testing, and internal team discussions as sources of information. Now, once we have all this information, what do we do with it? How do we make it understandable and usable for others?*"
....
Juan: "*From a business standpoint, simply having raw data isn't enough. It needs to be presented in a way that allows for informed decision-making. So, creating clear and concise reports is key.*"
....

Fig. 9.2 Excerpts from discussion session for Communicate product learnings guide content

three of the guides are analyzed, and adjustments and improvements to their content are discussed and defined to achieve a final agreed-upon version. Thus, after four sessions, the guides corresponding to the ten activities were completed and ready for evaluation in the next phase of the study.

9.4.5 Role Guides Evaluation

To evaluate the quality and usefulness of the role guides in assisting novice product managers, as posed in objective O4, a new round of focus group meetings was conducted as part of Phase 3 of the study.

The authors served as moderators for this focus group, which included the four interviewees from Phase 1 who did not take part in the Phase 2 focus group. At the first meeting, the purpose of the focus group was communicated, and its evaluative function was explained, as described in [16]. The exchange of opinions and experiences in product management among the participants led to new improvements to the guidelines, resulting in a final version agreed upon by all.

The final versions of all role guides are available online for download from https://github.com/germat/PMinSS.

At the end of the last meeting, participants were asked to complete a short survey regarding the overall evaluation process. Among the various questions and statements included in this survey, the following two are particularly relevant to each role card:

(S1) "The guide's content for the <ACTIVITY> activity closely relates to what it means to carry out the activity and the responsibilities associated with its execution in our startup."

(S2) "It would have been beneficial to have the <ACTIVITY> role guide when I started with product management in my startup."

Each statement was rated on a Likert scale with the options "Strongly disagree," "Disagree," "Neutral," "Agree," and "Strongly agree."

A summary of the survey results is presented in Table 9.5. For statements S1 and S2, the total number of responses (40) matches the number of role guides (10) evaluated by the representatives (4) of the startups in the focus group.

Table 9.5 indicates that participants hold a very positive attitude toward the content of the role guides and find them useful as support for novice product managers.

Table 9.5 Distribution of responses to survey statements

Statement	Strongly disagree Disagree	Neutral	Agree Strongly agree
S1	1	5	34
S2	0	0	40

For instance, one participant who rated the S1 statement for the "Communicate product learnings" activity guide as "Strongly Agree" explained his rating in the following terms:

> I find this activity guide to be well-aligned with my experience, and I consider its content to be useful and effective. The ability to synthesize information from various sources, like user feedback and market research, and then communicate those learnings clearly is critical. ... The guide correctly emphasizes the importance of not just gathering data, but also creating reports and presentations to share insights across the team. This has been essential for us in ensuring that everyone ... is on the same page. ... The emphasis on skills such as data visualization, storytelling, and active listening reflects the reality of the job. Although there are some "details" that can be improved, I think the guide captures the essence of this activity, and I see it as a useful starting point for anyone who has to do this at their startup.

9.5 Recommendations

Of the eight software startups participating in the study, only one had a founding partner with experience in product management, having worked in the software industry before starting the new venture (CIE2). Consequently, the typical situation appears to be that there is often no member on the founding team with product management experience.

Since the need to establish product management as a distinct role develops gradually during the initial stages of software ventures, the reasons or circumstances outlined in Table 9.2 may provide insight into the appropriateness of its implementation. Considering these reasons or circumstances, Table 9.6 recommends the most suitable product management activities to address them.

For example, consider again the reason or circumstance "Bad product-market fit." The rationale supporting the suggestion to implement the three corresponding activities listed in Table 9.6 emerged from discussions among participants in the Phase 3 focus group.

The summary of those discussions, generated from the session's recordings and field notes, is as follows:

> Poor product-market fit signals a mismatch between what we are building and what the market actually needs or wants. Customer interviews directly confront this by providing first-hand insights into user pain points, unmet needs, and desires. By actively listening to potential customers, product management can uncover the discrepancies between the current product and market expectations. Communicating product learnings, especially from these interviews and early product usage, ensures the entire team understands the issues and the "why" behind necessary changes. Finally, defining improved versions of the product, informed by customer feedback and market analysis, allows the startup to iterate and pivot towards a stronger alignment with market demands, ultimately striving for that elusive product-market fit.

Similar discussions took place to connect the identified activities to the other reasons or circumstances.

Table 9.6 Suggested activities to deal with reasons or circumstances

Reason or circumstance	Related activities
Bad product-market fit	Customer interviews Communicate product learnings Define improved versions of the product
During product creation	Define product and marketing strategy Define product requirements Participate in product prototyping
For economic survival	Identify opportunities and threats Define improved versions of the product Cost optimization and control
Foreseeable depletion of money	Identify opportunities and threats Cost optimization and control
Increase in the number of users	Monitor, assess, and refine release activities Define improved versions of the product
Negative feedback from the first production launch	Customer interviews Participate in product testing Introduction of improved versions of the product Communicate product learnings

Table 9.7 Alignment of activities with the ISPMS framework

	Core	Orchestration
Early stage	Communicate product learnings (Product requirements engineering) Customer interviews (Customer Insight) Define product and marketing strategy (Positioning and Product Definition)	Define product requirements (Detailed Requirements Engineering) Participate in product prototyping (User Experience Design) Participate in product testing (Quality Management)
Growth stage	Cost optimization and control (Financial Management) Define improved versions of the product (Release Planning) Identify opportunities and threats (Market Analysis)	Monitor, assess, and refine release activities (Product launches)

The activities identified in this study can be put in correspondence with the classification proposed by the ISPMA general framework (introduced in Sect. 9.2) regarding whether the product manager's involvement is direct (core) or more of orchestration. On the other hand, the adaptation of this framework to the startups' environment (also introduced in Sect. 9.2) suggests that some of its processes are more relevant in the early stage, while others are more pertinent during the growth stage, even though it is challenging to establish a clear boundary between one stage and the other.

Nevertheless, the classification of the identified activities, based on the definitions presented in Table 9.3 and the descriptions of the components of both frameworks, is shown in Table 9.7 for both dimensions.

Since the aforementioned models are not prescriptive, software startups should assess their specific circumstances and begin implementing the product management activities they find most appropriate. To support these implementations, the role guides presented in Sect. 9.4.4 serve as a valuable resource for initiating product management, even before the initial "symptoms" of the role's necessity emerge.

To interpret and act on the role guides, a novice product manager should consider each element from the "Description" section one at a time and reflect on how to implement it in practice, considering the potential benefits and the suggested skills needed to achieve them.

For instance, let us examine the Communicate Product Learnings guide. The first item in its "Description" section emphasizes the importance of consistently gathering and synthesizing information from various sources, including user feedback, analytics, and internal team discussions. In this case, if you feel overwhelmed by the breadth of sources, it is better to prioritize the most accessible ones first, such as direct user conversations or readily available Web site analytics. Once you have initial findings, create clear and concise reports or presentations to share key insights with your development team and other relevant stakeholders. Even a simple, well-structured document can be highly effective. A key benefit of this approach is ensuring that decisions are data driven rather than based on assumptions, which helps the startup build a product that truly meets user needs. Focus on clear communication and developing fundamental data visualization skills, as presenting information visually can significantly enhance understanding for the audience. The goal is to establish a habit of sharing insights, fostering a shared understanding of the product and its goals within the team.

> To interpret and act on an activity guide, consider each element in its "Description" section one by one, and think about how to implement it, considering the potential benefits and the skills needed to achieve them.

Going beyond a single activity, let's now explore how to use the role guides to implement a series of activities that address one of the reasons for establishing the product management function; for example, "Bad product-market fit." To tackle this critical and frequent problem, a structured approach involving "Customer interviews," "Communicate product learnings," and "Define improved versions of the product" is essential for resolution, as suggested in Table 9.6. These activities are interdependent and create a continuous feedback loop crucial for evolving the product to truly meet market demands.

The initial step in addressing poor product-market fit is to conduct "Customer interviews." This activity aims to gain a firsthand understanding of customer needs, pain points, and motivations. It includes identifying and recruiting target customers from the desired user segments, defining clear objectives for the interviews, and developing a structured interview script with relevant questions. During these one-on-one or small group conversations, it is crucial to engage with customers and actively listen to their experiences. Detailed notes, audio recordings, and other relevant data should be collected, with a focus on understanding customer motivations and needs. Conducting interviews throughout the product development lifecycle enables the refinement of questions and approaches based on previous findings, which helps in continually grasping the market. This direct engagement with customers is essential for testing product assumptions and hypotheses with real users, uncovering hidden needs, and ultimately tailoring the user experience to customer preferences.

Once raw customer insights are gathered, the next critical step is to "Communicate product learnings." This involves collecting and synthesizing information from various sources, including invaluable user feedback obtained from customer interviews, as well as analytics, market research, and internal team discussions. The essence of this activity for addressing product-market fit lies in creating clear and concise reports, presentations, and documentation that effectively convey key findings and insights to the development team, designers, and other relevant stakeholders. Establishing a central repository ensures that knowledge is captured and accessible for future reference, fostering a shared understanding of the product and its goals, which enhances team collaboration. Regularly sharing these insights and implementing mechanisms for gathering feedback on product learnings ensure that decisions are based on data rather than assumptions. Rapid dissemination of learning facilitates quicker product iteration and adaptation to market needs, directly accelerating the journey to product-market fit.

Finally, equipped with clearly communicated product insights, the focus shifts to "Define improved versions of the product." This directly addresses the poor product-market fit by synthesizing customer feedback, usage data, and market analysis to pinpoint specific areas for enhancement. The emphasis is on identifying which improvements will have the most significant impact on user satisfaction and business goals, ensuring that enhancements promote the product's long-term success. For each identified improvement, it is essential to define the functional requirements, user stories, and acceptance criteria. Collaborating closely with engineers and designers ensures that these improved versions are technically feasible and user-friendly. Importantly, after implementation, feedback and data must be collected to confirm that the improvements meet the intended goals. This ongoing refinement based on user feedback and market trends is what ensures the product satisfies the needs of the target audience, addresses user pain points, and ultimately results in higher customer satisfaction and a stronger product-market fit.

This iterative process of listening, learning, and improving is, then, fundamental to overcoming the challenge of "Bad product-market fit," as suggested in Table 9.6.

Regarding business incubators and accelerators, they play a significant role in creating and promoting new ventures by offering a range of support services. These services include business training, guidance on developing business and marketing plans, building management teams, and providing general business services such as accounting and advertising, among others [17].

The reasons and circumstances identified in this study serve as a starting point for business incubator support programs to focus on training activities related to software product management in general, if they do not already have them, and on methods to plan and implement the activities suggested in Table 9.6 to address these issues. Business mentors can provide personalized guidance, share their expertise, and assist startups in applying these research findings to their specific software products.

For researchers on entrepreneurship and software startups, the findings of this study offer a foundation for future research.

First, there may be additional reasons or circumstances beyond those identified in this study that contribute to the need to establish the product management function. These other factors will lead to various activities relevant to the initial stages. Therefore, exploring other circumstances surrounding role creation will help expand the list of activities and their corresponding role guides.

Second, the proposed role guides have been validated retrospectively, drawing on the knowledge and experience of the participants in this study. Retrospective validation refers to evaluating a resource or intervention after it has been applied in practice, focusing on its content and effectiveness. This kind of validation calls for further research to validate their current implementation. Prospective validation would allow for real-time observation of the guides' impact on new ventures, identifying current gaps, measuring tangible outcomes, and understanding the practicalities of user adoption and usability.

Finally, considering the external validity of this study, although the participants are experienced entrepreneurs in product management within software startups, the role guides may not be suited to the needs and specifics of other software startups. By using them as starting points, examining their practical implementation should help improve and expand the role guides with "alternative courses" for specific situations.

9.6 Conclusions

In software startups, the need to establish the organizational function of product management arises in its initial stages due to certain events or circumstances related to the product, the business, or both.

Through interviews and focus groups with founding partners and product managers of software startups, we identified a set of factors that drive the need to create this organizational function and the most common product management activities during the early stages of these ventures. The identified activities represent a step toward addressing the research gap highlighted by Melegati and colleagues (mentioned in Sect. 9.2.4), regarding the need to know the tasks to be performed by a product manager in the context of software startups.

To support the implementation of these activities, we developed a set of role guides to assist emerging product managers in executing these initial activities, as also suggested in the study by Melegati and colleagues. The evaluation of these role guides by experienced product managers was very positive, highlighting their relevance and usefulness.

The findings are of interest to entrepreneurs, researchers, and business incubators, offering a basis for supporting and improving the product management function in software startups.

References

1. Unterkalmsteiner, M., Abrahamsson, P., Wang, X., Nguyen-Duc, A., Shah, S.: Software startups: a research agenda. e-Inform. Softw. Eng. J. **10**(1), 89–123 (2016). https://doi.org/10.5277/e-Inf160105
2. Association of International Product Marketing and Management: The Guide to the Product Management and Marketing Body of Knowledge. Product Management Educational Institute (2013)
3. Giardino, C., Unterkalmsteiner, M., Paternoster, N., Gorschek, T., Abrahamsson, P.: What do we know about software development in startups? IEEE Softw. **31**(5), 28–32 (2014). https://doi.org/10.1109/MS.2014.129
4. LeMay, M.: Product Management in Practice. O'Reilly, Sebastopol (2018)
5. Aumayr, K.: Successful Product Management. Springer, Berlin (2023)
6. Anderson, A., McAllister, C., Harris, E.: Product Development and Management Body of Knowledge, 3rd edn. Wiley, Hoboken, NJ (2024)
7. Cagan, M.: Inspired. How to Create Tech Products Customers Love, 2nd edn. Wiley, Hoboken, NJ (2018)
8. Banfield, R., Eriksson, M., Walkingshaw, N.: Product Leadership. O'Reilly, Sebastopol (2017)
9. Ahuja, B.: Product management for early-stage startups. Forbes Bus. Council. (2022)
10. Maglyas, A., Nikula, U., Smolander, K., Fricker, S.: Core software product management activities. J. Adv. Manag. Res. **14**(1), 23–45 (2017). https://doi.org/10.1108/JAMR-03-2016-0022
11. Pattyn, F.: The critical role of product managers and their responsibilities in software startups: a systematic literature review. Am. J. Eng. Technol. Manag. **9**(4), 66–91 (2024). https://doi.org/10.11648/j.ajetm.20240904.11
12. Kittlaus, H.-B.: Software Product Management, 2nd edn. Springer, Berlin (2022)
13. International Software Product Management and Association: Software Product Management for Startups. International Software Product Management and Association (2023)
14. Melegati, J., et al.: Product managers in software startups: a grounded theory. Inf. Softw. Technol. **174** (2024). https://doi.org/10.1016/j.infsof.2024.107516
15. Marshall, M.: The key informant technique. Fam. Pract. **13**(1), 92–97 (1996)
16. Acocella, I., Cataldi, S.: Using Focus Groups. Theory, Methodology, Practice. Sage Publications, London (2021)
17. Albort-Morant, G., Oghazi, P.: How useful are incubators for new entrepreneurs? J. Bus. Res. **69**, 2125–2129 (2016). https://doi.org/10.1016/j.jbusres.2015.12.019

Chapter 10
Product Feature Prioritization Practices in Software Startups: A Survey Study

Frédéric Pattyn, Usman Rafiq, and Peter Goetz

Abstract Software startups operate in resource-constrained environments and under extreme uncertainty. Such challenges highlight the need for effective product feature prioritization, which is critical to the success of startups. This book chapter examines how software startups prioritize product features and explores whether this differs from the feature prioritization practices of established companies. We identify key factors that influence startup prioritization decisions by analyzing 171 survey responses from experienced product managers. Our findings reveal that startups prioritize cost-related factors and time to market (TtM) significantly higher than established companies. Furthermore, the results show that financially informed prioritization can serve as a critical runway management tool for startups. Therefore, startups that fail to integrate these considerations might face premature scaling, cash flow crises, and shortened runways. This book chapter contributes to developing an initial understanding of feature prioritization for startups, providing actionable insights to practitioners aiming to make sustainable product feature prioritization decisions.

Keywords Requirements engineering · Requirements prioritization · Requirements prioritization Criteria · Runway · Startup

F. Pattyn
Department of Business Informatics and Operations Management, Ghent University, Ghent, Belgium
e-mail: Frederic.Pattyn@ugent.be

U. Rafiq (✉)
Faculty of Engineering, Free University of Bozen-Bolzano, Bolzano, Italy
e-mail: Usman.Rafiq@unibz.it

P. Goetz
New Data Vision Ltd, London, UK
e-mail: management@newdatavision.com

N. Tripathi et al. (eds.), *Advances in Software Startups*,
https://doi.org/10.1007/978-3-032-04294-1_10

10.1 Introduction

Software startups operate in a fast-paced, uncertain, and resource-constrained environment [6], where survival depends on managing runway—the time before cash reserves are depleted. Despite their innovative potential, these ventures face numerous challenges, including premature scaling, cash flow mismanagement, difficulty in securing investments, and funding shortages [12, 13]. These challenges, particularly financial ones, contribute to a high failure rate, with 63% of startups ultimately shutting down [13] and 25% failing within the first year alone [12]. Given these constraints, prioritizing product features can become a critical aspect, alongside other success determinants, in the management of these innovative ventures.

While extensive research has been conducted so far to improve the odds of success for software startups [33], less attention has been given to how startups manage and prioritize their product features. Existing research centers around proposing the engineering practices tailored for startups, yet it lacks specific guidance on how requirements prioritization criteria (RPC) are selected and applied in such a context. Moreover, it becomes particularly relevant to explore when we consider a plethora of research proposing feature prioritization practices for established companies [21]. Requirements prioritization (RP) is considered a critical decision-making activity in requirements engineering (RE) [30]. Thus, it determines which software features should be developed first, directly influencing product development and strategic decisions of startups. Therefore, despite the importance of selecting context-appropriate RP methods and criteria, there is little empirical evidence on how startups practice this prioritization.

To address this research gap, our study aims to understand and contrast the perceived relevance of different RPCs in the context of startups and established companies. Accordingly, the primary research question (RQ) that we explored in this chapter is:

RQ: How do product management practitioners perceive the relevance of different requirements prioritization criteria in startups and established companies?

We employed a mixed-methods survey [14] to answer our RQ. This means that we incorporated both closed-ended questions to collect quantitative data and open-ended questions to collect qualitative data. Overall, we collected responses from 171 experienced product management practitioners. To ensure a structured comparison, the survey respondents were tested A/B, with some answering questions from a startup perspective and others from an established company perspective. This classification enabled the study to systematically analyze which RPCs are perceived as more relevant in different contexts, particularly within startups. By analyzing these insights, our study seeks to contribute in building an initial understanding of how startups should possibly approach feature prioritization differently and whether their choices align with broader perceptions of significance. These findings offer a foundation for developing more context-appropriate RP methods for startups and set the stage for future research. Additionally, this chapter contributes to ongoing discussions among startup practitioners regarding how prioritization approaches evolve in dynamic, resource-constrained environments.

10.2 Background and Related Work

10.2.1 Requirements Engineering

Requirements engineering (RE) is a foundational software development process, guiding project feasibility assessment, risk evaluation, and strategic planning [19]. It consists of various activities such as product planning (including vision, business case analysis, requirements classification, prioritization [18], road mapping, and release planning), stakeholder negotiation (including communication and stakeholder agreement [18, 19]), requirements elicitation, analysis, and management [18, 19, 28]. While all RE activities are important for development, this chapter focuses particularly on requirements prioritization (RP). This activity determines which product features to develop first based on various constraints [10]. It discusses two main topics: (1) the requirements prioritization methods (RPM) and (2) the requirements prioritization criteria (RPC). Despite extensive research on RPM in general, limited attention has been given to RPC selection, particularly in startup contexts. Therefore, in the following sections of this chapter, we explore both RPM and the most relevant RPC for software startups.

10.2.2 Requirements Prioritization Methods

Requirements Prioritization for Established Companies

Over the years, several studies [11, 26, 29, 31] have proposed multiple RP methods. These methods range from structured decision-making models to more heuristic or collaborative approaches. Traditional decision-support techniques include multi-criteria decision-making methods, multi-attribute utility theory, and analytic hierarchy process, all of which rely on quantitative weighting mechanisms to rank requirements [3]. Other mathematical and computational approaches, such as data envelopment analysis, SMART, ELECTRE, PROMETHEE, SAW, and TOPSIS, provide optimization-based solutions for prioritization, often leveraging historical data and predefined evaluation metrics [34].

In contrast, agile and lightweight frameworks have gained traction in modern software development, emphasizing iterative prioritization and stakeholder collaboration. Approaches such as MoSCoW, dot voting, buy-a-feature, impact/effort matrix, Kano model, and story mapping aim to streamline prioritization through stakeholder input and business-driven decision-making [3]. Additional heuristics, such as ICE, RICE [25], round the group prioritization [2], top ten requirements [1], and weighted scoring offer structured but adaptable scoring models to balance value. Meanwhile, game-theoretic models like planning game, value-oriented prioritization, and $100 allocation (often referred to as cumulative voting) [4], hypothesis prioritization canvas [32], dot voting [3], eclipse framework [3], and integrated prioritization approach [10] introduce participatory decision-making elements [9, 24, 27]. More sophisticated prioritization approaches, including fuzzy logic-based techniques [16], case-based reasoning, e^3-value [7], interactive genetic algorithms [31], Lanchester theory [3], ranking based on product definition [26], quality functional development [27], quantitative win-win [29], RePizer [11], Wieger's matrix approach [26], aggregated DM methods [17] or aggregated indices randomization method [5], and aggregated decision-making methods, have also been proposed to address uncertainties and dependencies in software development [23]. These techniques utilize advanced computational models to enhance prioritization accuracy, particularly in complex and large-scale projects.

Prioritization in a Startup Context: Gaps and Challenges

While various RP methodologies exist, most have been designed with established enterprises and established software projects in mind, as one might have noticed. Their applicability in a startup context remains underexplored. Startups work with speed, adaptability, and observe rapid iterations; thus, these elements take precedence over formalized, data-heavy prioritization models discussed in the section, as mentioned earlier. Traditional RP techniques, particularly those requiring extensive stakeholder alignment or historical data, may not align with the fast decision cycles and market-driven pivots common in startups.

Existing literature has largely focused on the theoretical effectiveness of RP models, but empirical research on how startups implement prioritization strategies in practice is scarce. For instance, studies by Ma [15] and Hujainah et al. [10] provide insights into general prioritization techniques, yet they do not account for the specific pressures and constraints faced by startups. On the other hand, a recent study by Gupta et al. [8] emphasizes startup-specific prioritization challenges but offers only descriptive insights, without linking the findings to practitioner-driven prioritization criteria or decision frameworks. This gap highlights the need for a focused analysis of how prioritization methods and criteria can be adapted to support startup survival and growth.

10.2.3 Requirements Prioritization Criteria

The diversity of possible requirements prioritization criteria (RPC) is vast, while the focus is limited. Overall, all these RPCs can be classified into ten categories [22]. These categories are listed in Table 10.1:

Table 10.1 Requirements prioritization criteria (RPC) categories and factors

RPC category	Factors
Cost-related factors	Expected cost (development), budget constraints, cost-benefit ratio, maintenance, budget process, cost-importance ratio
Revenue and financial impact	Estimated expected revenue, profitability, return on investment (ROI), payback period, net present value (NPV), breakeven point, cash flow analysis, internal rate of return (IRR)
Business and strategic impact	Estimated market share, competitive intensity, strategy alignment, strategic fit, signed contracts, market maturity (growth rate), proprietary position, cultural alignment, brand value, company synergies, need to demonstrate product, existence of market need, feature promised
Stakeholder and customer considerations	Stakeholder preferences, customer value, importance, user-friendly, user engagement, contribution to user task, user loyalty, frequency of use
Technical factors and constraints	Complexity, technical constraints, code change, re-usability, modifiability, technology, compatibility (incl. technical), scalability, standards
Resource constraints and availability	Resource constraints (incl. HR)
Quality and performance metrics	Documentation quality, level of ambiguity, reduce errors, consistency, durability, traceability, testability, non-functional characteristics
Risk assessment	Risks (incl. dev, business, failure), penalties, prioritization (incl. features, bugs), predictability (incl. commercial, info), volatility, security, feasibility, regulations, legal mandate, harm avoidance
Time constraints and scheduling	Time constraints, time to market (TtM), MVP feature set coverage
Dependency and Interdependency Factors	Dependencies, similarity

10.3 Research Method

We employed a survey research design [14] to address the RQ of this book chapter. This research method is commonly used in the field of software engineering when a large sample of data needs to be collected. In our case, we needed data from product management practitioners across both types of organizations, i.e., startups and established companies. Therefore, the survey enabled us to collect empirical data from a wide range of product management practitioners engaged in requirements prioritization (RP) within both types of organizations. The data and insights discussed in this chapter are part of a large survey aimed at proposing product management practices for software startups. Moreover, data analysis methods in survey research allowed us to find patterns and differences between startups and established companies regarding RP criteria. The overall research design is shown in Fig. 10.1. It outlines how we created the survey instrument, evaluated it, revised it, collected and analyzed data, and ultimately interpreted the results.

10.3.1 Survey Design

The survey instrument consisted of three key components: (1) a preface communicating objectives of the research, a brief profile of researchers, and informed consent; (2) demographic questions; and (3) core questions defined to address the RQ.

At the beginning of the survey, we introduced participants to the purpose of the research and the introduction of the researchers. In the same section, we informed all participants about the voluntary participation and asked them to give informed consent. This step was taken following GDPR and data privacy guidelines. Upon giving consent, participants were briefed about the segments, that is, either a startup or an established company. Therefore, survey participants selected one of these categories when responding to the survey.

To ensure transparency and develop context, we collected demographic data. This data is considered essential for interpreting the results within the startup and product management landscape. A balanced approach was taken in designing this section, capturing relevant background information while minimizing survey fatigue to optimize completion rates. Therefore, the demographic section consisted of generic attributes, such as gender, age, highest educational qualification, country of residence, and primary language. In addition, role-specific questions were included to establish professional experience and relevance to the study's scope. In summary, the demographic questions collect data regarding:

- Years of experience in product management
- Years specifically serving as a product manager
- Current role as a product manager for a software or SaaS product

To further contextualize respondents' familiarity with startup environments, additional questions gathered direct exposure to startups, including:

- Experience working in a startup
- Number of startups worked at
- Duration of involvement in startup settings
- Experience as part of a founding team

By collecting these demographic insights, we ensured that findings are based on the segment analysis and truly reflect the opinions of relevant product management professionals. Therefore, this background data helped make our findings more accurate and useful for startups.

Finally, the key section of the survey was presented. This section was focused on targeted questions according to our RQ. There were two primary questions in this component. The first key question prompted respondents to identify the

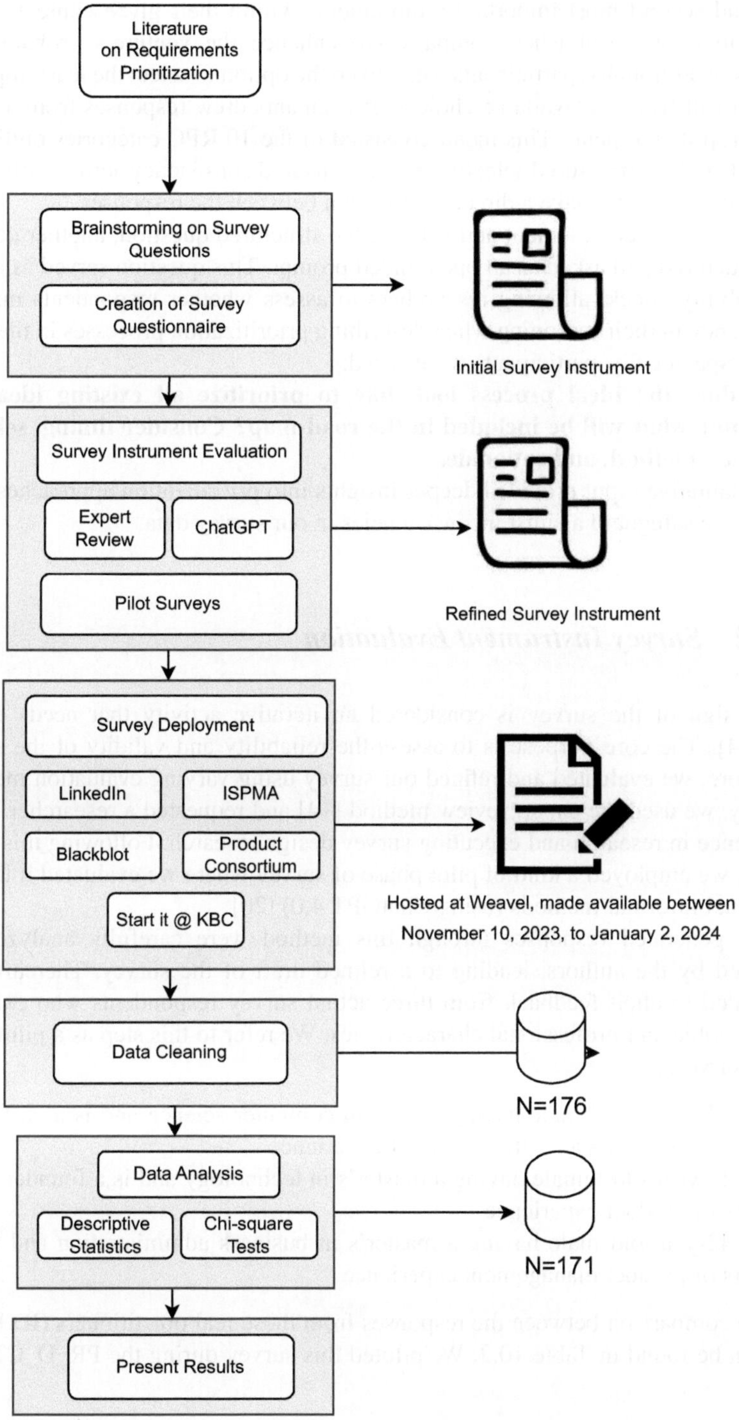

Fig. 10.1 Survey design

most and second most important requirements within their given context—either a startup or an established company—to enhance the venture's probability of success. Additionally, participants were given the option to select the least important requirement from the available choices. Participants drew responses from a predefined drop-down menu. This menu consisted of the 10 RPC categories outlined in Table 10.1. This structured selection process ensured consistency across participants and facilitated us to make a direct comparison between the responses.

Moreover, to complement and validate the structured question, another question was structured and asked as an open-ended prompt. This question served as a built-in reliability check, allowing researchers to assess whether respondents maintain consistency in their reasoning when describing prioritization processes in their own words. Specifically, participants were asked:

What does the ideal process look like to prioritize all existing ideas and determine what will be included in the road-map? Consider timing, selection variables, method, and rationale.

This qualitative input provided deeper insights into prioritization approaches while acting as a safeguard against inconsistencies in our survey data.

10.3.2 Survey Instrument Evaluation

The design of the survey is considered an iterative activity that needs evaluation [14]. The core purpose is to assess the reliability and validity of the survey. Therefore, we evaluated and refined our survey using varying evaluation methods. Initially, we used the expert review method [14] and requested a researcher having experience in research and executing survey design research. Following this expert review, we employed a kind of pilot phase of survey where we evaluated it through additional informal methods (using ChatGPT 4.0) [20].

The generated responses through this method were carefully analyzed and validated by the authors, leading to a refined draft of the survey. Thereafter, we proceeded to elicit feedback from three actual survey respondents who exhibited demographic and professional characteristics. We refer to this step as a pilot phase of the survey.

- P1: 37-year-old female having a PhD in computer science and is a co-founder and product manager with 9 years of experience
- P2: 27-year-old female having a master's in technology and is a founder with 4 years of product experience
- P3: 42-year-old male having a master's in business administration and has 10 years of product management experience

The comparison between the responses from these real practitioners (ID P1, P2, P3) can be found in Table 10.2. We piloted this survey during the PR_D_CT DAY

Table 10.2 Pre-survey responses from participants

ID	Q1	Q2
P1	Technical factors and constraints	I would look at the data we have regarding our business and customers first. We will have this maybe from quant/qual research, maybe from trackers, sales records, and so on. Judging by this, we'd be able to see what the valuable items are. And then you consider the complexity. You talk with your developers/engineers to get their opinion on the matter. And then consider the urgency as well, for example, if there is a new regulation that forces the company to make some changes to the software, then that should be implemented ASAP. This is, in my opinion, a good way to prioritize because it's data-driven, considers complexity/feasibility, as well as urgency/timing
P2	Stakeholder and customer considerations	Determine which initiatives cover multiple product areas: business, vision, customer, strategy. Then prioritize based on RICE
P3	Revenue and financial impact	In all cases, it depends on the severity of the problem that the idea is solving and the potential for ROI. Going deeper into the different ideas depends on whether it's a new idea (v1) or an improvement on the existing product (v2+). For new ideas, it is essential to build something small, ship it, and evaluate it. Why? Because empirical evidence is the only thing that counts. The skill is to learn to make something small enough. Prioritization of new ideas should not be overcomplicated. Timebox it and go to work
P4	Business and strategic impact	What is our vision ⇒ what is the strategy to achieve that vision ⇒ what are the objectives to achieve that strategy? ⇒ analyze data, talk to users and stakeholders
P5	Cost-related factors	Empty
P6	Business and strategic impact	Allocating a percentage of resources to 2–5 pre-selected areas of the business (about once per year, based on the overall strategy) and then optimizing within each area. The latter can be done by the PM and the development team in order to reach an objective

conference hosted by Sirris in Ghent (Belgium) on September 11, 2023.[1] During this event, one of the authors had the opportunity to invite 120 product managers to complete the survey, seek their feedback, and verify the results. On the conference day, however, there were only three respondents (refer to Table 10.2, ID, P4, P5, P6):

- P4: 28-year-old male having a master's degree and is currently a product manager with 1 year of experience
- P5: 26-year-old, undisclosed gender, with a master's degree and 5 years of experience in product management

[1] https://www.sirris.be/en/agenda/prdct-day-2023-unconference-and-digital-product-managers

– P6: 50-year-old male with a master's degree, who has been a founder three times, and has 1 year of experience in product management

All responses collected on that particular conference day were excluded from the final data analysis. In general, the instrument evaluation results, by various means, showed considerable similarity between informal methods using ChatGPT and those of the test participants. Table 10.2 shows responses from the participants in the pilot phase. At this point, we decided to formally conclude the survey design and considered it ready for actual data collection.

10.3.3 Survey Deployment for Formal Data Collection

Following the survey instrument evaluation and refinement, we deployed the survey to begin the data collection phase. We hosted the survey on an advanced Web-based and AI-supported tool called Weavely.[2] We then distributed the survey to the target population and employed a convenience sampling method [14] to achieve this step. Therefore, we used our professional networks and associated organizations to distribute the survey. In particular, we used LinkedIn to approach product management professionals as well as requested the International Software Product Management Association (ISPMA), Blackblot, the Product Consortium, and Start it @KBC to float our survey. The majority of responses (62%, or 107 in total) were garnered via LinkedIn, utilizing both existing and newly formed connections with pertinent backgrounds to optimize response rates. Out of 664 individuals contacted, 412 (62%) viewed the message, and 182 provided feedback, whether positive or negative. The overall feedback rate for the LinkedIn channel was 27.4%, while the success rate stood at 16.11%, translating to 107 successful responses out of 664 contacted connections. Figure 10.2 presents the sources of the survey data collected between November 10, 2023, and January 2, 2024.

10.3.4 Data Analysis

We collected 176 survey responses in total at the end of the data collection phase. After data cleaning and applying our inclusion criteria, we included 171 responses for further data analysis. During data cleaning, we removed responses that were invalid or where participants were ineligible to answer the survey questions.

To analyze the data, we applied descriptive statistics and p-value analysis. We used descriptive statistics to summarize the demographic statistics of the survey participants and to provide an overview of the distribution of responses regarding

[2] https://app.weavely.ai/

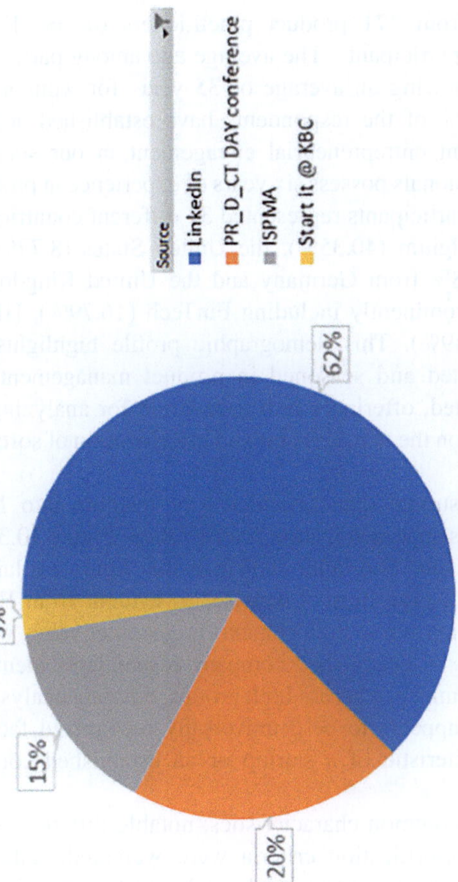

Fig. 10.2 Sources of survey responses ($N = 171$)

RPC applied by product management practitioners. Moreover, we used p-value analysis to understand the association of RPC in the contexts of startups and established companies. We followed the guidelines proposed by Linåker et al. [14] to analyze the survey data.

10.4 Results and Discussion

We collected data from 171 product practitioners ($n = 171$), with 29.76% identified as women participants. The average age among participants is 38 years, with a breakdown showing an average of 35 years for women and 40 years for men. Notably, 36.84% of the respondents have established at least one startup, reflecting a significant entrepreneurial engagement in our survey. Similarly, on average, these professionals possess six years of experience in product management. Geographically, the participants represented 37 different countries, with the largest contingents from Belgium (40.35%), the United States (8.77%), India (6.43%), and a combined 4.68% from Germany and the United Kingdom. They span 51 distinct industries, prominently including FinTech (16.79%), HR Tech (10.95%), and IT services (9.49%). This demographic profile highlights a group that is not only well educated and seasoned in product management but also diverse and globally distributed, offering a rich foundation for analyzing the influence of various backgrounds on the management and prioritization of software development requirements.

The analysis of survey data provided key insights into how startups and established companies approach feature prioritization. Figure 10.3 presents an aerial view of this comparison. The delta shown in this figure explains how priorities of these companies diverge most. Likewise, as evident from Fig. 10.3, the most frequently cited criterion across both contexts is customer value, with 36% of startup respondents and 33% of established company respondents identifying it as a top priority. Given its prominence across both groups, our data analysis further revealed that customer value appears to be a universally recognized factor, rather than a distinguishing characteristic of a startup or an established company's decision-making process.

Aside from these common characteristics, notable differences emerged in how other requirements prioritization criteria were weighted, reflecting the distinct strategic considerations of startups and established companies. A comparative analysis of data highlighted that startups prioritize cost efficiency, rapid market entry, and lean product development, whereas established companies focus more on financial performance, strategic alignment, and long-term stability.

To further investigate these distinctions, we performed a p-value analysis to assess the statistical significance of the differences in prioritization tendencies between startups and established companies. The results highlight several critical divergences:

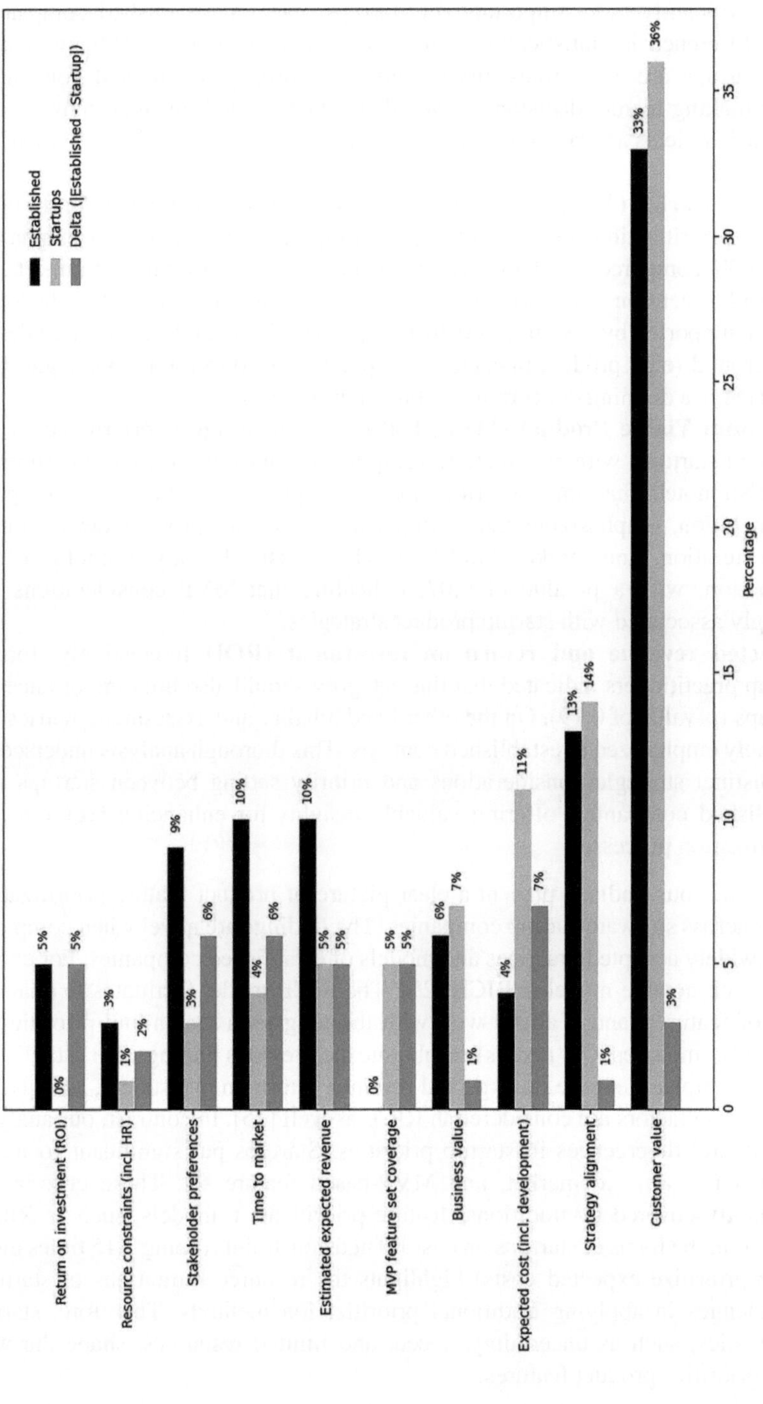

Fig. 10.3 Requirements prioritization criteria: established companies vs startups

- **Cost-related factors**, particularly expected costs (including development costs), are significantly more important for startups than for established companies. This difference is statistically significant, with a p-value of 0.05, indicating that startups are 2.15 times more likely to prioritize cost-related constraints when making feature decisions. Given their often-limited financial runway, this emphasis reflects an urgent need to optimize expenditures and allocate resources efficiently.
- **Time-to-Market (TtM)** is another criterion that holds greater weight in startups' feature prioritization decision-making. Startups are more likely to emphasize TtM (6%) compared to established companies (4%), reinforcing the importance of rapid execution and early market entry. The significance of this factor is further supported by p-values of 0.36, 0.25, and 0.12, depending on respondents' background (e.g., product managers and previous startup founders), suggesting that TtM is a defining concern in startup environments.
- **Minimum Viable Product (MVP) feature set coverage** is prioritized exclusively in startups, with 5% of startup respondents selecting it as a top criterion. We also noted that this criterion does not appear in established company prioritization, emphasizing the startup's need for lean product development, rapid iteration, and market validation. The statistical analysis confirms this distinction, with a p-value of 0.07, indicating that MVP considerations are strongly associated with startup product strategies.
- **Expected revenue and return on investment (ROI)** Interestingly, formal startup practitioners indicated that this category should also hold importance for startups (*p*-value of 0.19). On the other hand, quality and assessment metrics are uniquely emphasized in established contexts. This thorough analysis underscores the distinct strategic considerations and priority setting between startups and established companies, offering valuable insights for enhancing requirements prioritization processes.

In general, our findings present a clear picture of product feature prioritization practices across software startup companies. The findings are novel when compared with the widely accepted practices and models of established companies. For example, one such notable model is RICE [25]. The RICE model facilitates to quantify scoring of features, and it aligns well with the long-term vision and priorities of established companies. Our results corroborate the previous findings that established companies emphasize more on expected revenue, return on investment, and quality metrics. These factors are considered in RICE as well [25]. In contrast, our analysis reveals several divergences in startup priorities. Startups put significant focus on cost efficiency, time to market, and MVP-based feature set. These criteria are not explicitly covered by traditional feature prioritization models, such as RICE. Furthermore, the focus of startups on cost-related constraints (being 2.15 times more likely to prioritize expected costs) highlights the resource limitations of startups and challenges in applying traditional prioritization methods. Therefore, startup characteristics, such as uncertainty, speed, and limited resources, shape the way startups prioritize product features.

Lastly, it is important to acknowledge a few limitations of our chapter. We collected survey data through convenience sampling via LinkedIn and other professional networks. While this data collection methodology was effective in reaching a broad audience, it also introduces the potential for self-bias. It means that survey participants who chose to participate may differ from those who did not. Although our sample is diverse based on the demographics of the participants, the non-randomness approach limits the generalizability of our findings. We plan to address this limitation in our future work through qualitative interviews with a more diverse and purposeful sampling.

10.5 Practical Recommendations

Based on the findings of this chapter, we provide a number of practical recommendations to startup practitioners. In particular, the recommendations are intended for product managers, startup founders, product owners, and development teams at startup companies.

- **Use time to market as a filter:** If a feature cannot be developed and validated quickly, it could be too risky for early-stage development. Therefore, practitioners shall prioritize features that can be delivered in a short time frame unless they see a critical advantage in developing them.
- **Avoid vision-only decisions:** While vision is essential in guiding startups, relying solely on vision could be disastrous. This kind of visionary prioritization can lead to runaway costs and product misfit. Our findings show that prioritization must be influenced by customer value, cost, efficiency, and speed. However, startups might adopt and implement a vision-based prioritization only after a feature passes cost and time feasibility filters.
- **Quantify the startup runway impact:** Each prioritization decision should be evaluated in terms of how it extends (or shortens) the financial runway of the startup. Therefore, startups should encourage and prioritize runway-based quantification of features. A helpful tactic might be to ask questions, for instance, "Will this feature generate revenue or validation before we need our next raise?" This approach can help quantify the runway impact and support efforts to directly attract investments.
- **Validate with customers, yet filter with costs:** While customer needs are crucial, features must also pass a feasibility and affordability test. Therefore, to achieve this, startups should assess a must-have value and then prioritize high-value features with the lowest cost and shortest build time first.
- **Use feature prioritization to delay scaling risks:** Prioritizing features can help validate hypotheses before investing in expensive scaling. Therefore, startups should defer scalability until core hypotheses are validated through the absolute MVP tests.

- **Track real vs. expected impact post-launch:** Another recommendation that we think significant to consider is the learning from the post-mortem of feature prioritization. As a startup, one must compare prelaunch estimates with actual results. This reflection will help bring accuracy to future prioritization.
- **Educate investors on lean prioritization strategy:** Lastly, startups must proactively share how they prioritize features, i.e., focus on customer value, MVP, cost, and time to market, to investors. This will result in building investor confidence and promoting fundraising activities.

10.6 Conclusions

This book chapter aimed to understand how startup companies prioritize product features and how it is different from established companies. The analysis revealed few approaches to startup product management where these innovative companies are seen shifting the focus of feature prioritization from traditional product-driven decision-making to a financially aware, runway-conscious methodology. Along the same lines, while existing literature has explored feature prioritization extensively, much of it has been developed without considering the unique constraints of early-stage ventures. Startups operate in an environment where resource scarcity, time pressure, and uncertainty dictate survival. This book chapter underscores the critical role of financially informed requirements prioritization criteria in optimizing decision-making, mitigating risk, and extending a startup's financial runway.

The findings challenged conventional wisdom that prioritization should solely be customer driven or based on visionary intuition. Instead, startups that incorporate cost, time to market, return on investment, and expected revenue into their feature prioritization decision-making processes tend to outperform their peers in terms of funding secured, runway longevity, and overall business sustainability. The study highlighted how gut-feeling-based prioritization, an overemphasis on product vision, and a failure to consider the cost of development could contribute to premature scaling, cash flow crises, and eventual failure in multiple startups. In contrast, those that integrate a structured, financially aware approach to feature selection demonstrate stronger market validation and better financial health.

This book chapter laid the foundation for a paradigm shift in how startup founders and product teams shall approach prioritization. By introducing a runway-conscious, opportunity-cost-driven perspective, this research advocates for a new framework where startups treat feature prioritization as a financial strategy not just a product development decision. For startups, adopting this approach means:

- Maximizing survival odds by extending the runway through financially aware decision-making
- Minimizing costly missteps by ensuring features align not only with customer demand but also with financial sustainability

- Making data-driven trade-offs between short-term gains and long-term growth, balancing customer needs with financial impact

For researchers, this book chapter opens up new avenues in requirements engineering for startups, particularly in exploring financially predictive prioritization frameworks that could help early-stage companies navigate uncertainty more effectively. On the contrary, regarding implications for startup management, our results demonstrated that financially driven feature prioritization plays a decisive role in startup longevity. However, further research is needed to refine this decision-making model into a repeatable, scalable framework. Future avenues could investigate:

- How different stages of startup growth influence the evolution of prioritization criteria
- The role of investor expectations and external financing in shaping prioritization decisions
- The scalability of financially aware prioritization frameworks beyond early-stage ventures

References

1. Aasem, M., Ramzan, M., Jaffar, A.: Analysis and optimization of software requirements prioritization techniques. In: 2010 International Conference on Information and Emerging Technologies, pp. 1–6. IEEE, Piscataway (2010)
2. Achimugu, P., Selamat, A., Ibrahim, R.: A clustering based technique for large scale prioritization during requirements elicitation. In: Recent Advances on Soft Computing and Data Mining: Proceedings of The First International Conference on Soft Computing and Data Mining (SCDM-2014), Universiti Tun Hussein Onn Malaysia, Johor, June 16th–18th, 2014, pp. 623–632. Springer, Berlin (2014)
3. Achimugu, P., Selamat, A., Ibrahim, R., Mahrin, M.N.: A systematic literature review of software requirements prioritization research. Inf. Softw. Technol. **56**(6), 568–585 (2014)
4. Alhenawi, E., Awawdeh, S., Khurma, R.A., García-Arenas, M., Castillo, P.A., Hudaib, A.: Choosing a suitable requirement prioritization method: a survey. Preprint. arXiv:2402.13149 (2024)
5. Aruldoss, M., Lakshmi, T.M., Venkatesan, V.P.: A survey on multi criteria decision making methods and its applications. Am. J. Inf. Syst. **1**(1), 31–43 (2013)
6. Giardino, C., Bajwa, S., Wang, X., Abrahamsson, P.: Key challenges in early-stage software startups. In: Agile Processes in Software Engineering and Extreme Programming, pp. 52–63. Springer, Berlin (2015). https://doi.org/10.1007/978-3-319-18612-2_5
7. Gordijn, J., Akkermans, J.: Value-based requirements engineering: exploring innovative e-commerce ideas. Requir. Eng. **8**, 114–134 (2003)
8. Gupta, V., Fernandez-Crehuet, J.M., Hanne, T., Telesko, R.: Requirements engineering in software startups: A systematic mapping study. Appl. Sci. **10**(17), 6125 (2020)
9. Herrmann, A., Daneva, M.: Requirements prioritization based on benefit and cost prediction: an agenda for future research. In: 2008 16th IEEE International Requirements Engineering Conference, pp. 125–134. IEEE, Piscataway (2008)
10. Hujainah, F., Bakar, R.B.A., Abdulgabber, M.A., Zamli, K.Z.: Software requirements prioritisation: a systematic literature review on significance, stakeholders, techniques and challenges. IEEE Access **6**,71497–71523 (2018)

11. Khan, S.U.R., Lee, S.P., Dabbagh, M., Tahir, M., Khan, M., Arif, M.: Repizer: a framework for prioritization of software requirements. Front. Inf. Technol. Electron. Eng. **17**(8), 750–765 (2016)
12. Kolmar, C.: 20+ must-know startup statistics [2023]: average time to reach profitability at a startup (2023), https://www.zippia.com/advice/start-up-profitability-statistics. Accessed 04 Apr 2025
13. Kotashev, K.: Startup failure rate: how many startups fail and why (2022), https://www.failory.com/startup-failure-rate. Accessed 04 Apr 2025
14. Linåker, J., Sulaman, S.M., Maiani de Mello, R., Höst, M.: Guidelines for conducting surveys in software engineering v. 1.1, vol. 50, pp. 1–64. Lund University (2015)
15. Ma, Q.: The effectiveness of requirements prioritization techniques for a medium to large number of requirements: a systematic literature review. Auckland University of Technology (2009)
16. Ma, Y., Dou, Y., Xu, X., Tan, Y., Yang, K.: Requirements prioritization for complex products based on fuzzy associative predicate representation learning. Adv. Eng. Inf. **62**, 102621 (2024)
17. Mardani, A., Jusoh, A., Nor, K., Khalifah, Z., Zakwan, N., Valipour, A.: Multiple criteria decision-making techniques and their applications–a review of the literature from 2000 to 2014. Econ. Res.-Ekonomska istraživanja **28**(1), 516–571 (2015)
18. Melegati, J., Goldman, A., Kon, F., Wang, X.: A model of requirements engineering in software startups. Inf. Softw. Technol. **109**, 92–107 (2019)
19. Nuseibeh, B., Easterbrook, S.: Requirements engineering: a roadmap. In: Proceedings of the Conference on the Future of Software Engineering, pp. 35–46 (2000)
20. Pattyn, F.: Improving software startup viability: addressing requirements prioritization challenges amid increasing interest rates. In: Conference: 14th International Conference on Software Business (ICSOB) (2023)
21. Pattyn, F.: Overcoming the limitations: a research agenda towards a pragmatic framework for product managers at software startups. Ghent University (2023)
22. Pattyn, F.: Critical requirements prioritization criteria for survival at software startups. Preprint for Journal of Information and Software Technology (2024)
23. Pattyn, F., Rafiq, U.: Smart scaling for software startups through financial requirements prioritization criteria. In: International Conference on Software Business, pp. 454–460. Springer, Berlin (2024)
24. Perini, A., Susi, A., Ricca, F., Bazzanella, C.: An empirical study to compare the accuracy of ahp and cbranking techniques for requirements prioritization. In: 2007 Fifth International Workshop on Comparative Evaluation in Requirements Engineering, pp. 23–35. IEEE, Piscataway (2007)
25. ProductPlan: Rice scoring model. https://www.productplan.com/glossary/rice-scoring-model/ (nd). Last Accessed 20 May 2025
26. Racheva, Z., Daneva, M., Buglione, L.: Supporting the dynamic reprioritization of requirements in agile development of software products. In: 2008 Second International Workshop on Software Product Management, pp. 49–58. IEEE, Piscataway (2008)
27. Racheva, Z., Daneva, M., Herrmann, A., Wieringa, R.J.: A conceptual model and process for client-driven agile requirements prioritization. In: 2010 Fourth International Conference on Research Challenges in Information Science (RCIS), pp. 287–298. IEEE, Piscataway (2010)
28. Rafiq, U., Bajwa, S.S., Wang, X., Lunesu, I.: Requirements elicitation techniques applied in software startups. In: 2017 43rd Euromicro Conference on Software Engineering and Advanced Applications (SEAA), pp. 141–144 (2017). https://doi.org/10.1109/SEAA.2017.73
29. Ruhe, G., Eberlein, A., Pfahl, D.: Trade-off analysis for requirements selection. Int. J. Softw. Eng. Knowl. Eng. **13**(04), 345–366 (2003)
30. Svensson, R.B., Torkar, R.: Not all requirements prioritization criteria are equal at all times: a quantitative analysis. J. Syst. Softw. **209**, 111909 (2024)
31. Tonella, P., Susi, A., Palma, F.: Interactive requirements prioritization using a genetic algorithm. Inf. Softw. Technol. **55**(1), 173–187 (2013)

32. Trieflinger, S., et al.: How to prioritize your product roadmap when everything feels important: a grey literature review. In: 2021 IEEE International Conference on Engineering, Technology and Innovation (ICE/ITMC). IEEE, Piscataway (2021)
33. Unterkalmsteiner, M., Abrahamsson, P., Wang, X., Nguyen-Duc, A., Shah, S., Bajwa, S., Baltes, G., Conboy, K., Cullina, E., Dennehy, D., Edison, H., Fernandez-Sanchez, C., Garbajosa, J., Gorschek, T., Klotins, E., Hokkanen, L., Kon, F., Lunesu, I., Marchesi, M., Morgan, L., Oivo, M., Selig, C., Seppänen, P., Sweetman, R., Tyrväinen, P., Ungerer, C., Yagüe, A.: Software startups - a research agenda. e-Informatica Softw. Eng. J. **10**(1), 89–123 (2016). https://doi.org/10.5277/e-Inf160105
34. Velasquez, M., Hester, P.T.: An analysis of multi-criteria decision making methods (2013), https://api.semanticscholar.org/CorpusID:6891121

Chapter 11
AI-Powered Toolchain Framework for Agile Software Development in Startups

Obaid Khan, Nirnaya Tripathi, Yueqiang Xu, and Anh Nguyen Duc

Abstract The integration of AI-powered tools into Agile methodologies within startups is explored in this chapter, emphasizing how AI-driven tools enhance efficiency, innovation, and team collaboration. Drawing from interviews with professionals from six software startups, it highlights the transformative impact of tools like GitHub Copilot, ChatGPT, and Fireflies.ai in streamlining Agile practices, such as task automation, code quality assurance, sprint planning, and backlog management. The study examines AI-powered tool's role in boosting productivity, reducing workloads, and accelerating delivery through automated documentation, predictive insights, and real-time analytics. An AI-enhanced Agile toolchain framework is introduced, showcasing strategies for backlog prioritization, continuous integration and delivery (CI/CD), and workflow optimization. It also addresses challenges like balancing automation with Agile's human-centric values, ethical concerns, and resource constraints.

Keywords Generative AI · AI-powered tool · Agile methods · Startup · Software development

11.1 Introduction

Startups play a crucial role in driving technological innovation. Operating in competitive markets, these companies rely on their ability to adapt quickly and deliver solutions that meet changing demands. Digital technologies, particularly

O. Khan · N. Tripathi (✉) · Y. Xu
M3S Research Unit, University of Oulu, Oulu, Finland
e-mail: Obaid.Khan@student.oulu.fi; Nirnaya.Tripathi@oulu.fi; yueqiang.xu@oulu.fi

A. N. Duc
University of South-Eastern, Bø, Telemark, Norway

Norwegian University of Science and Technology, Trondheim, Norway
e-mail: anh.nguyen.duc@usn.no

N. Tripathi et al. (eds.), *Advances in Software Startups*,
https://doi.org/10.1007/978-3-032-04294-1_11

software, have become essential for startups, helping them streamline processes and scale their operations [30]. This dependency highlights the shift of software from a technical tool to a core driver of business growth [12].

Over the years, software development has moved away from rigid methods like the Waterfall model, which struggled to adapt to changing needs, to flexible approaches like Agile. Introduced in 2001, Agile focuses on collaboration, adaptability, and iterative development, making it especially suitable for startups [13, 17]. These principles allow startups to respond quickly to feedback, deliver incremental improvements, and manage their limited resources effectively [32]. At the same time, artificial intelligence (AI) is transforming how startups work. AI-powered tools automate repetitive tasks, analyze data, and support decision-making to enable teams to focus on creativity and strategy [29]. A toolchain, defined as a set of interconnected tools, can assist not only technical activities, i.e., design, coding, testing, and deploying, but also managerial tasks, i.e., sprint planning, and backlog management, allowing startups to work more efficiently and scale faster [7, 21]. However, integrating AI-powered tools into Agile methodologies presents unique challenges. While AI-powered tools can enhance efficiency, their reliance on automation may conflict with Agile's emphasis on human collaboration and adaptability [28]. Moreover, startups face barriers like resource constraints and the complexities of adopting AI-powered tools, which require careful planning to address [16]. Understanding how to balance AI's benefits with Agile's values is crucial for startups aiming to stay competitive and innovative.

11.2 Background

This section presents background on software development, Agile methodologies, software startups, AI in startups, integration of AI tools with Agile approaches, and AI tools and relevant work on AI-driven toolchain.

11.2.1 Evolution of Software Development and Methodologies

Early software development relied on rigid models like the Waterfall model, introduced by Royce in the 1970s. While structured, it was inflexible, with each phase of requirements, design, implementation, and testing, occurring sequentially, making it difficult to accommodate changing needs [15]. Royce himself suggested iterative approaches like the Sashimi model to address some limitations [18]. As software became central to industries, especially in fast-paced sectors like startups, the need for more flexible, iterative methodologies led to the rise of Agile. Agile development, emphasizing adaptability, continuous feedback, and close collaboration, contrasts with Waterfall's rigidity. Frameworks like Scrum and XP allow for quick iterations and continuous improvement. The Agile Manifesto [17] formalized these principles, emphasizing flexibility and responsiveness over rigid planning.

Agile's early focus on small teams soon expanded to address challenges in larger organizations. Frameworks like SAFe and LeSS emerged to scale Agile for larger teams, focusing on alignment and collaboration across multiple teams [14]. The shift toward Agile and hybrid methodologies reflects the industry's response to increasing complexity, unpredictability, and the demand for faster, more flexible development cycles [10, 19].

11.2.2 Agile Methodologies: Core Principles and Practices

The formalization of Agile methodologies in the early 2000s marked a turning point for software development. The Agile Manifesto, created in 2001, emphasized values like collaboration, adaptability, and continuous delivery. The core principles of prioritizing individuals and interactions, delivering working software, collaborating with customers, and responding to change reflect a commitment to customer-centric development [17]. These principles are supported by twelve specific guidelines that encourage sustainable development, customer collaboration, and technical excellence. Within Agile, frameworks like Scrum, Kanban, and Extreme Programming (XP) provide different approaches for managing workflows. Scrum organizes work into time-boxed sprints for regular reassessment, while Kanban focuses on visualizing tasks and limiting work in progress to maximize efficiency [1].

11.2.3 Software Startups

Startups are distinct for their focus on innovation, risk tolerance, and rapid growth. These companies, often characterized by new, technology-driven business models, are constantly challenged to develop unique solutions quickly to gain market traction [7]. With limited resources, startups require methodologies that enable fast iteration and adaptability to both market demands and customer feedback. The early phases of startups, especially the "startup stage," are crucial in determining their survival and growth [26]. Due to this uncertainty and the evolving nature of their business and engineering, many startups struggle in the "valley of death," where financial and operational challenges are critical [11, 31]. Agile methodologies, with their iterative cycles and flexibility, are particularly suited to this environment, enabling startups to pivot and adjust quickly in response to new information and changing market conditions [32].

11.2.4 Artificial Intelligence in Startups: Enhancing Efficiency and Innovation

Artificial intelligence (AI), particularly technologies like machine learning (ML) and neural networks (ANNs), is revolutionizing the software development landscape. AI's ability to analyze vast amounts of data and identify patterns makes it indispensable in data-driven decision-making and automating complex tasks [2, 29]. For startups, AI provides a powerful tool for automating routine processes, gaining insights into customer behavior, personalizing products, and predicting market trends. These capabilities not only increase efficiency but also enhance innovation, enabling startups to remain competitive and agile [32]. AI can also alleviate operational bottlenecks, allowing teams to focus on high-value tasks that contribute to overall innovation [7].

11.2.5 Integrating AI-Powered Tool with Agile Methodologies

The integration of AI-powered tool with Agile presents both opportunities and challenges. AI-powered tool can optimize several aspects of Agile practices, such as automating routine tasks, improving decision-making with data insights, and improving predictive accuracy. For instance, Generative AI (GenAI) can help streamline backlog management by identifying critical tasks based on feedback and historical patterns [28]. AI-powered tools can automate testing, reducing the manual effort required for quality assurance, and enabling teams to focus on more strategic, creative aspects of development [8]. However, integrating AI-powered tool into Agile is not without its complications. Agile methodologies emphasize human-centric values, such as collaboration and adaptability, which can sometimes conflict with AI's automation-driven approach. As AI-based systems take over tasks like sprint planning or backlog management, there is the risk of reducing the human touch that Agile values so highly, particularly the creativity and collaboration that drive successful development teams [9]. Moreover, ethical considerations, such as data privacy and transparency in AI-driven decision-making, complicate this integration [16].

GenAI for Software Development in Startups
The advent of Generative AI (GenAI) requires a paradigm shift for software engineering as it has been reshaping how software is designed, developed, and maintained, especially with startups operating in agile and resource-constrained environments. This review below demonstrates GenAI's role in relation to software development toolchains, exploring productivity, automa-

(continued)

tion, code quality, collaboration, governance, and future adoption trajectories while highlighting the practical gaps.

Recent literature highlights GenAI tools, notably AI pair programmers like GitHub Copilot or Cursor AI, on their potential for tremendous productivity enhancements in software development. Studies report significant gains, with some evidence suggesting up to a 55.8% increase in developer productivity for specific coding tasks [23, 34]. This productivity gain is significant with analysis projecting that such AI-powered developer life cycles can contribute to boosting economic growth, especially by accelerating the output of developers, including those less experienced [5]. The potential to boost software engineering productivity is a recurring theme, with tools like ChatGPT and Copilot frequently cited [6]. As such, the general discussion is that GenAI tools can enhance individual software development productivity across various activities [20] and improve overall developer output [33].

However, this narrative of high productivity faces counterarguments. Existing research addresses that these productivity effects can be difficult to ascertain due to issues like imperfect compliance with tool usage in experimental settings or uncertainties about whether certain improvements in studies truly capture the full scope of developer productivity [4]. Furthermore, while individual task completion might accelerate, concerns over potential increased dependence on these AI tools arise [25]. Thus, the current literature often skims past the long-term implications of this cognitive offloading and the balance between productivity boost and GenAI dependency.

11.2.6 From Integrating AI/GenAI Tools to Toolchain-Based Framework

As aforementioned [23, 34], the single tool use of AI can indeed generate syntactically correct code; however, these models' grasp of broader project architecture, complex business logic, or evolving requirements remains underdeveloped and requires ongoing human oversight and intervention. This challenges the idea of end-to-end automation, and individual GenAI tools still require further advancement [20].

From an empirical viewpoint, we argue that the AI toolchain-based approach can help mitigate the existing weakness in the siloed AI tool use approach, such as focusing on individual AI tools. Our literature review of current discussions and conceptual frameworks identified several key streams, just to name a few:

(1) AI augmentation stream: Pangavhane et al. [22] explore AI-augmented software development, detailing how AI tools can support various development phases like DevOps optimization, testing automation, and code generation. They

also present an evaluation of AI performance across different SDLC stages; (2) AI automation stream: Raghi et al. [24] focus on SDLC automation using GenAI and Large Language Models (LLMs). They propose an approach to streamline the entire software development process, from planning to deployment, by minimizing human intervention; (3) Practitioner's AI tool use: Ebert and Louridas [6] discuss GenAI technologies and usage within the empirical context of software industry. Their work covers specific tools such as ChatGPT and Copilot, their impact on software productivity, and the associated risks and benefits for software practitioners.

However, while these studies provide findings on AI-augmented SDLC, GenAI automation in SDLC, and practical GenAI tool use, they often tackle these aspects separately. We identified a significant gap: existing approaches provide little systematic assistance, and there is little understanding of a holistic, empirically based AI toolchain framework. Such a framework is needed to coherently integrate diverse AI-based tools across the agile SDLC. As such, current research has not fully explored the empirical viewpoint of agile startup practices, how individual AI tools can be combined into a coherent toolchain to support and optimize key operations within agile development. Such framework is developed and presented in this study by synthesizing and building on the empirical results.

Overall, successfully integrating AI/GenAI into an organization's (such as software startup) operations and norms is a tremendous challenge [6]. This suggests that beyond the technical capabilities of the tools themselves, significant challenges exist in terms of organizational readiness as well as the development of new roles to orchestrate AI-enhanced development processes [27]. Therefore, the current GenAI research streams often highlight the "what if" scenarios without sufficiently detailing the "how to" of addressing the adoption practicalities for diverse organizational contexts like startups. Overall, in this study, we present the AI-driven toolchain concept and an empirical approach for practitioners, especially in software startups.

11.3 Method

This study used empirical interviews to investigate how Agile methodologies integrate with AI-powered tools and sought to provide a deeper insight into the experiences of the participants. To address the study objective, a purposive sample of participants was selected using convenience sampling from startups specializing in software development. This included software developers, product owners, product managers, and Agile coaches, all of whom have experience with both Agile methodologies and AI-based tools.

Startup Cases and Study Details
The study involved six startup cases (C1–C6), each represented by software engineers (I1–I6) with varying technical backgrounds and Agile experience. Participants included full-stack and mobile app developers with expertise ranging from MERN, Python, Ruby on Rails, and cloud technologies to Flutter and Java, spanning industries such as healthcare, finance, and e-commerce. Agile methodologies were consistently applied across the startups, predominantly Scrum and Kanban, with customizations based on specific project needs. Agile experience among interviewees ranged from 2.5 to 3 years, often combining frameworks to manage product delivery, bug fixes, and deployment pipelines. The business domains reflected a strong focus on AI-driven, user-centric, and secure software solutions, developed within diverse environments from US-based startups to Finnish ventures. Data was collected through semi-structured interviews via videoconferencing. Throughout the study, ethical standards were upheld. Informed consent was obtained from all participants, and confidentiality was maintained through data anonymization. The study used the thematic analysis mapping [3] to interpret qualitative data.

11.4 Result

We organize the insights of our interviews into a thematic map, as shown in Fig. 11.1, and discuss in the following sections.

11.4.1 AI-Powered Tools Adopted in Software Startups

AI-powered tools mentioned across the interviews and how they were applied to different Agile practices:

GitHub Copilot

GitHub Copilot[1] assisted in Agile practices, including refactoring, unit tests, code reviews, and task automation, and was widely employed, as evidenced by interviews 1, 2, 3, 4, 5, and 6. These practices enhanced the development process using GitHub Copilot by enabling developers to generate code, automate unit tests, and

[1] GitHub Copilot: https://github.com/features/copilot.

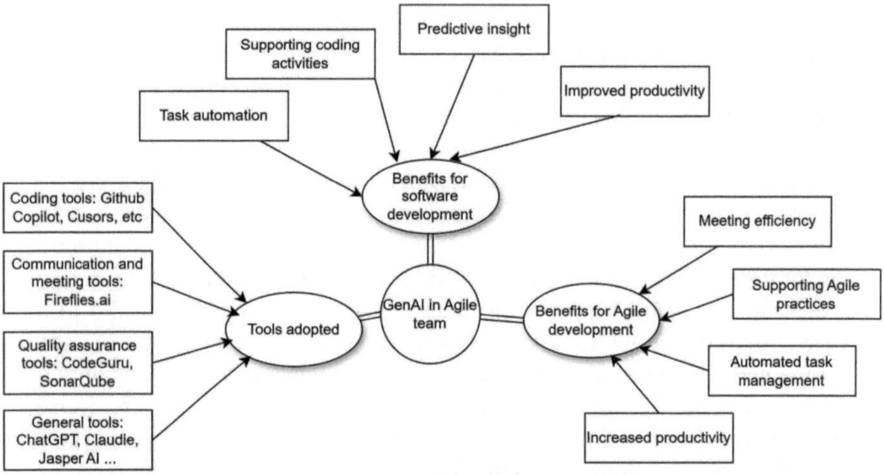

Fig. 11.1 Thematic map obtained from data analysis

suggest improvements efficiently. GitHub Copilot played a crucial role in assisting developers by learning the codebase early, which boosted productivity during code reviews and accelerated onboarding processes for new team members. One interviewee (I6) emphasized the importance of integrating tools like GitHub Copilot at the project's outset, stating, "Before kicking off the development of a project, I would definitely integrate GitHub Copilot so that it learns what's happening in the codebase."

ChatGPT/GPT-Based Tools

ChatGPT and GPT-based tools[2] have significantly contributed to agile practices, including task automation, documentation, story mapping, backlog grooming, and usability testing, as noted in interviews 1, 2, 4, and 5. These tools streamlined routine tasks by automating the drafting of documentation, summarizing meeting minutes, and grooming backlogs, allowing teams to focus on high-value activities. Additionally, they provided AI-driven insights that enhanced usability testing. One interviewee (I5) highlighted their effectiveness, stating, "I just copy all the text, put it in ChatGPT, and tell it to give me all the important points from our meeting."

[2] ChatGPT: https://chatgpt.com/.

Fireflies.ai

Fireflies.ai[3] has proven to be a valuable tool in supporting agile practices such as daily standups, meeting summaries, and documentation, as highlighted in interview 6. Its ability to automate note-taking and generate concise meeting summaries has significantly reduced manual effort. Furthermore, Fireflies.ai streamlines the creation of action items and facilitates task management by directly generating tickets for tools like JIRA. One interviewee emphasized its impact, stating, "Fireflies takes meeting notes and even creates tickets, reducing manual tasks for QA teams and project managers."

Amazon CodeGuru

Amazon CodeGuru[4] has been instrumental in supporting agile practices such as code reviews, continuous integration, and testing, as noted in interview 6. It provides automated code reviews that effectively detect bugs, inefficiencies, and security vulnerabilities, ensuring high-quality code. By integrating seamlessly into CI pipelines, CodeGuru enhances development efficiency and supports iterative workflows. Interviewee (I6) highlighted its value, stating, "It goes through your code base and learns what's happening, then gives you prompts for improvements."

SonarQube

SonarQube,[5] particularly its AI-enhanced features, plays a critical role in agile practices such as automated code reviews and continuous integration, as emphasized in interview 4. By detecting bugs, security vulnerabilities, and code smells early in the development pipeline, it significantly improves code quality and reduces technical debt. Interviewee I4 highlighted its effectiveness, stating, " AI-driven tools like SonarQube help us catch bugs and code smells early."

Jasper AI

Jasper AI[6] has proven valuable in agile practices such as documentation, user stories, and task assignment, as noted in interview 4. By streamlining the drafting of user stories and technical documentation, Jasper AI enhances the clarity and efficiency of project planning. Additionally, it supports task assignment and fosters

[3] Fireflies: https://fireflies.ai/.

[4] CodeGuru: https://aws.amazon.com/codeguru/.

[5] SonarQube: https://www.sonarsource.com/products/sonarqube/.

[6] Jasper AI: https://www.jasper.ai/.

improved team communication. Interviewee I4 highlighted its utility, stating, "Jasper AI helps us draft concise explanations and generate user stories efficiently."

11.4.2 Benefits of AI-Powered Tool Adoption in Software Development

AI-driven tools are transforming agile practices by enhancing productivity and streamlining workflows across various aspects of software development.

Task Automation emerged as a major benefit, with interviewees highlighting how AI-powered tool automates repetitive tasks such as writing unit tests, code refactoring, and generating user stories. This allows developers to focus on more complex and strategic work, significantly improving efficiency. **Meeting Efficiency** has also seen improvement with tools like Fireflies.ai and Firefly, which automate note-taking and action item assignments during daily standups, sprint planning, and retrospectives. P6 remarked, "AI-powered tools like Firefly automate meeting notes and task assignments," showcasing how these tools ensure transparency and foster collaboration.

In the area of **Testing and Code Quality**, AI-assisted tools such as SonarQube, Amazon CodeGuru, and automated testing frameworks ensure robust code quality while streamlining CI/CD pipelines. These tools enhance efficiency by detecting issues early and automating routine testing and deployment tasks. As P6 explained, "The continuous integration and continuous deployment processes... automatically take all the code and deploy it," highlighting how these tools reduce manual effort and accelerate releases. **Predictive Insights** provided by AI-driven dashboards also improve sprint planning and execution. These dashboards offer valuable data on team velocity, task prioritization, and sprint performance, enabling better decision-making. Generative AI assistants further support **Sprint Planning** by helping Scrum Masters and Product Owners prioritize tasks more effectively.

AI-powered tools play a pivotal role in **Documentation**, with LLMs and cognitive document tools streamlining the drafting of requirements, descriptions, and technical specifications. P5 shared, *"C5 use LLMs for writing descriptions, titles, and technical specifications,"* which speeds up the process while ensuring clarity and precision. In **Code Reviews**, AI-driven tools identify issues and provide improvement suggestions, maintaining high code quality and supporting continuous improvement. P2 noted, *"C2 use AI-driven tools for code reviews and automatic testing, which helps us maintain high quality,"* underlining the reliability these tools bring to development workflows.

11.4.3 Advantages of Integrating AI-Powered Tool in Agile Methodologies and Approaches

Supporting Agile Practices

AI-driven tool significantly enhances the efficiency of Agile processes, spanning tasks from documentation to deployment. By incorporating cognitive document search applications and AI-driven CI/CD tools, teams experience improved workflows and reduced manual effort. For instance, P1 noted, "C1 use LLMS for writing descriptions, titles, and technical specifications," demonstrating how an AI-powered tool shortens meetings and automates repetitive tasks. P3 highlighted the strategic benefits, stating, "I get more time to think of new ideas instead of creating summaries or meeting notes," underscoring how AI enables time savings for higher-value work. Additionally, P2 remarked, "Processes have led to faster delivery times and improved code quality," reflecting the transformative impact of an AI-powered tool in accelerating delivery and enhancing routine tasks in Agile environments.

Automated Task Management

AI-powered tools automate repetitive tasks, enabling teams to concentrate on innovation and tackling complex problems. P3 highlighted this benefit, stating, "Before using AI, I was manually creating documentation and user stories; now AI generates them for me," illustrating how automation improves accuracy and minimizes errors. Similarly, P6 shared, "Firefly takes meeting notes, creates tickets, and streamlines task management," showcasing how AI enhances productivity by optimizing routine workflows and freeing up time for more strategic activities.

Increased Productivity

AI-driven tool significantly boosts productivity by enabling teams to accomplish more in less time. P1 emphasized this, stating, "AI positively affects my work by allowing me to accomplish more in less time," highlighting its role in task acceleration. P2 noted the collaborative benefits, sharing, "We now have extra time for feedback and brainstorming, integrating new ideas," demonstrating how AI saves time for creative and strategic discussions. Additionally, P4 remarked, "With AI handling routine tasks, I can focus on complex problem-solving," illustrating how AI frees up mental bandwidth for critical, high-value tasks.

11.5 Discussion and Recommendation

Basing on the empirical insight, we propose a framework of AI-powered toolchain for Agile software project (Sect. 11.5.1) and discuss future directions for startups to adopt the toolchain in their Agile projects (Sect. 11.5.2).

11.5.1 Proposing an AI-Powered Toolchain Framework

Driven from our interview insight, to achieve enhanced productivity and optimized workflows, AI-driven toolchains can provide competitive advantages to startups operating under resource constraints and demanding development schedules. Through the use of AI-powered tools, the startups are able to reduce repetitive tasks and gain real-time insight for better decision-making while achieving greater efficiency in their agile development work.

Table 11.1 presents our proposed empirical AI-powered toolchain framework for Agile startup context, which consists of five main categories:

C1—Core Components of the AI-Powered Toolchain Framework

This includes Backlog and task management tools and code assistance tool. Agile workflows require efficient backlog management, and AI-enhanced solutions like Asana and Amazon Queue can increase productivity by automating task, prioritizing feedback integration, and minimizing manual intervention. Practitioners gain from AI's algorithmically driven generation and modification of requirements, addressing typical human error as well as enhancing task management. AI solutions like Cursor AI, Amazon CodeGuru, and GitHub Copilot provide AI-based interventions for maintaining code effectiveness and quality. By producing code snippets and making recommendations based on best practices, GitHub Copilot facilitates pair programming, speeding up development cycles and reducing potential implementation errors. To further improve code quality and lower vulnerabilities, Amazon CodeGuru and Cursor AI provide automatic code reviews and intelligent bug repair.

AI-augmented CI/CD systems like CodeMagic show a paradigm shift in software deployment strategies. These automated CI/CD systems manage automated testing, expedite build procedures, and enable smooth deployments. On the other hand, AI-enabled tools like SonarQube ensure continuous code quality monitoring during each sprint development cycle. On top of this, regular releases and strict test-driven development can be maintained with the use of AI-driven CI/CD solutions.

Table 11.1 Empirical AI-powered toolchain framework used by Agile startup and startup scalability aspect

Major category	AI-powered tool category	AI-powered tools from the interview	AI-powered tools role
Core parts of the AI-enhanced Agile toolchain	Backlog and Task Management Tools	Asana, Amazon Queue, Linear	Task Prioritization, Feedback Integration
	Code Assistance and Quality Assurance Tools	GitHub Copilot, SonarQube, Amazon CodeGuru, Cursor	Code Generation, Quality Checks
	Continuous Integration and Delivery (CI/CD)	CodeMagic	Build Processes, Automated Testing
Task automation and workflow optimization	Automated Task Management	Firefly.ai.ai, Jasper AI	Task Automation, Workflow Streamlining
	AI-Driven Documentation	Jasper AI, Different LLMs	Document Creation, Real-Time Updates
	Reduced Meeting Time and Improved Collaboration	Firefly.ai.ai, Different LLMs	Meeting Notes, Actionable Insights
Development and quality assurance	Automated Testing and Code Review	GitHub Copilot, SonarQube, Amazon CodeGuru	Test Writing, Code Review
	Intelligent Bug Detection and Resolution	Amazon CodeGuru, Cursor	Bug Detection, Code Vulnerabilities
Knowledge sharing	Collaborative Planning Tools	Firefly.ai, Jasper AI	Story Mapping, Workflow Planning
Real-time performance monitoring	Productivity and Performance Analytics	Different LLMs	Team Productivity, Resource Allocation
	Workflow Bottleneck Detection	Wood	Bottleneck Identification, Real-Time Fixes

C2—Task Automation and Workflow Optimization

Recent AI-powered task management solutions demonstrate significant potential in reducing administrative overhead. Firefly.ai, as an example, automates processes like creating tickets and collecting notes. Interview participants of our study echoed this notion, pointing out that AI-driven solutions have reduced manual work, channeling the development team's focus toward high-value development work. The use of advanced large language models (LLMs) like Claude to automate the creation of technical material to ensure (close to) real-time updates on the development documentation contributes to improved documentation process efficiency. To put it another way, these advanced LLMs replace some of the traditional manual documentation processes, potentially improving overall documentation quality. Our interview data highlights that AI-driven documentation has led to increased overall productivity.

AI-driven collaboration tools also demonstrate promising capabilities in optimizing the communication and coordination aspects of startup development processes. Our empirical evidence shows that these LLMs are capable of summarizing meeting discussions, generating actionable insights, and intelligently assigning collaborative responsibilities. This new AI-supported coordination practice reduces the need for lengthy meetings and enhances collaboration, especially for geographically dispersed, remote, or hybrid teams.

C3—Development and Quality Assurance

Emerging AI-enabled tools such as GitHub Copilot, SonarQube, and Amazon CodeGuru are starting to play important roles in quality assurance. These tools are focusing on areas like automated testing, code review, and problem identification processes, allowing developers to create test cases and reorganize code, providing continuous and algorithm-based feedback to enhance efficiency within the development workflows.

Predictive analytics powered by AI embodies a more proactive software quality management approach than traditional reactive quality assurance practices. These AI-driven tools find code flaws and vulnerabilities before they become serious, improving product stability. Smart bug identification (e.g., by Amazon CodeGuru) gives developers useful information to stop problems from getting worse, ultimately improving overall software system stability and reliability.

C4—Knowledge Sharing and Retrospective

AI-based collaborative planning and retrospective tools demonstrate capabilities in cross-functional teams. Platforms like Asana enable sophisticated visual workflow planning, enhancing cross-functional collaboration. These tools ensure that all members have a clear and holistic understanding of project goals and dependencies.

C5—Real-Time Performance Monitoring

Different LLMs (e.g., Claude) contribute to the generative capabilities of building sophisticated, data-driven insights into team performance metrics, enabling agile teams to implement dynamic resource allocation. Our interviews informed that AI-driven analytics have helped teams identify workload imbalances and prevent burnout of individual developers.

11.5.2 *Future Direction: Trustworthy, Compliance-Enhanced, and Ethic AI in Startup Software Development*

Data security and compliance have been top priorities of the regulators and AI policies. Especially with the use of sensitive data in mission-critical industries and application areas, data security is a major concern for startup companies utilizing AI-driven tools. As such, selecting the adequate AI-powered tools with robust data protection guidelines reduces the chance of data exposure.

In order to comply with regulations such as the AI Act (EU),[7] GDPR (EU),[8] and HIPAA (USA),[9] startups active in regulated industries have increasing pressure to use secure and trustworthy AI-powered tools that support encryption and traceable control among others. Our research shows that software startups should emphasize the need for strong protocols to protect sensitive data and raise issues with data security and dependability in connection with the use of AI tools or adopting an AI-driven toolchain approach.

In addition to security and compliance, ethical use and development of AI require further attention from industry, academia, and policymakers. The ethical deployment of AI involves managing biases, ensuring transparency, fairness, and explainability of the AI models.

11.6 Conclusion

Referring to the discussion above, the state-of-the-art development clearly shows AI's impact on automation, workflow optimization, knowledge sharing, and analytics aspects for agile software startups.

AI Native Augmentation Across the SDLC Building on this research, we propose that the trend of AI-driven augmentation in task management, documentation, testing, and code review is likely to further expand: AI tools will manage more complex, end-to-end SDLC processes with increasing autonomy. Cursor AI and several alternatives are clear examples. As we move toward more advanced AI or GenAI tools, it is expected to shift from mere coding assistance to active augmentation; in this vein, AI not only performs tasks but also anticipates needs, suggests solutions, and collaborates with developers as a proactive partner instead of a passive tool. For example, Cursor AI and some existing multi-agent solutions could autonomously generate and adapt application modules based on high-level requirements. Although

[7] AI Act (EU): https://www.europarl.europa.eu/topics/en/article/20230601STO93804/eu-ai-act-first-regulation-on-artificial-intelligence.

[8] GDPR (EU): https://gdpr.eu/.

[9] HIPAA (USA): https://www.hhs.gov/hipaa/for-professionals/privacy/laws-regulations/index.html.

considered part of a toolchain, these GenAI tools are expected to evolve and become key in automating more code generation, refactoring, and enhancement processes, eventually freeing up developers to focus more on highly strategic and complex problem-solving.

Proactive Software Development Lifecycle (or Proactive SDLC) While current AI tools provide real-time analytics for performance monitoring and bottleneck detection, the future points to scenarios where AI can be increasingly used to forecast potential project risks and predict defects with greater accuracy, for example, identifying potential security vulnerabilities before they are introduced into the codebase. This proactive approach will allow software startups to mitigate issues early on, leading to more stable products and efficient resource utilization.

Continuous Security, Compliance, and Ethical Alignment and Explainable AI (XAI) The security, compliance, and ethical implications of GenAI in software development include, and are not limited to, algorithmic bias and lack of transparency. They present an important issue: the future requires AI models to continuously align with ethical standards and legal regulations as they evolve. In this stream of development, GenAI systems will need to be designed for ongoing monitoring and automatic adjustment to prevent unethical or noncompliant behavior. This is key in agile practices with rapid iteration, critical for both software startups and industry incumbents.

Concluding Remark

We envision that the AI toolchain for software engineering is expected to undergo substantial changes, transforming from a collection of discrete assistance tools into an integrated, intelligent, and autonomous ecosystem. For AI/software startups and entrepreneurs, embracing this transformation is not just an opportunity but a necessity to maintain agility and promote innovation. If we take a collaborative, forward-looking perspective into the future, a symbiotic relationship can be between human developers and AI/GenAI, where these AI agents handle repetitive and computationally intensive tasks while enabling engineers and entrepreneurs to focus on creativity, strategy, and ensuring software development remains human centric, ethical, and compliant. Therefore, by proactively tackling the current AI-related challenges, capturing GenAI opportunities, and creating new value, software startups can unlock new levels of productivity and build a more solid foundation for success in the age of AI and GenAI.

References

1. Agile Alliance: Manifesto for agile software development (nd), retrieved from https://agilemanifesto.org
2. Belharet, A., Bharathan, U., Dzingina, B., Madhavan, N., Mathur, C., Toti, Y.D.B., Babbar, D., Markowski, K.: A study on the impact of artificial intelligence on project management (2020)
3. Braun, V., Clarke, V.: Using thematic analysis in psychology. Qual. Res. Psychol. **3**(2), 77–101 (2006)
4. Cui, K.Z.: The productivity effects of generative ai: Evidence from a field experiment with github copilot. An MIT Exploration of Generative AI (likely a working paper series or report series) (2024)
5. Dohmke, T.: Sea change in software development: economic and productivity analysis of the ai-powered developer lifecycle. GitHub Blog (interpretation based on typical dissemination for such reports by CEOs) (2023)
6. Ebert, C., Louridas, P.: Generative AI for software practitioners. IEEE Softw. **40**(4), 30–38 (2023)
7. Ehsan, Z.A.: Defining a startup-a critical analysis. Available at SSRN 3823361 (2021)
8. Fitzgerald, B., Stol, K.J.: Continuous software engineering: a roadmap and agenda. J. Syst. Softw. **123**, 176–189 (2017)
9. Highsmith, J.: Agile Project Management: Creating Innovative Products. Pearson Education, London (2009)
10. Hoda, R., Noble, J.: Becoming agile: a grounded theory of agile transitions in practice. In: 2017 IEEE/ACM 39th International Conference on Software Engineering (ICSE), pp. 141–151. IEEE, Piscataway (2017)
11. Hudson, J., Khazragui, H.F.: Into the valley of death: research to innovation. Drug Discov. Today **18**(13–14), 610–613 (2013)
12. Klotins, E., Unterkalmsteiner, M., Chatzipetrou, P., Gorschek, T., Prikladnicki, R., Tripathi, N., Pompermaier, L.B.: A progression model of software engineering goals, challenges, and practices in start-ups. IEEE Trans. Softw. Eng. **47**(3), 498–521 (2019)
13. Klotins, E., Unterkalmsteiner, M., Chatzipetrou, P., Gorschek, T., Prikladnicki, R., Tripathi, N., Pompermaier, L.B.: Use of agile practices in start-up companies. e-Informatica Softw. Eng. J. 15(1), 47–64 (2021). https://doi.org/10.37190/e-Inf210103
14. Leffingwell, D.: Agile Software Requirements: Lean Requirements Practices for Teams, Programs, and the Enterprise. Addison-Wesley Professional, Boston (2010)
15. Lehman, M.M., Ramil, J.F.: Software evolution and software evolution processes. Ann. Softw. Eng. **14**, 275–309 (2002)
16. Leijnen, S., Aldewereld, H., van Belkom, R., Bijvank, R., Ossewaarde, R.: An agile framework for trustworthy AI. In: NeHuAI@ ECAI, pp. 75–78 (2020)
17. Manifesto, A.: Manifesto for agile software development (2001). https://agilemanifesto.org/
18. Matković, P., Tumbas, P.: A comparative overview of the evolution of software development models. Int. J. Ind. Eng. Manage. **1**(4), 163 (2010)
19. Misra, S.C., Kumar, V., Kumar, U.: Identifying some important success factors in adopting agile software development practices. J. Syst. Softw. **82**(11), 1869–1890 (2009)
20. Modi, M. D. B.: Transforming software development through generative AI: a systematic analysis of automated development practices. Int. J. Sci. Res. Comput. Sci. Eng. Inf. Technol, **10**(6), 536–547 (2024). https://doi.org/10.32628/CSEIT24106197
21. Nguyen-Duc, A., Khanna, D.: Value-based adoption of ChatGPT in Agile software development: a survey study of Nordic software experts. In: Nguyen-Duc, A., Abrahamsson, P., Khomh, F. (eds.) Generative AI for Effective Software Development, pp. 257–273. Springer Nature Switzerland, Cham (2024)

22. Pangavhane, S., Raktate, G., Pariane, P., Shelar, K., Wakchaure, R., Kale, J.: AI-augmented software development: Boosting efficiency and quality. In: 2024 International Conference on Decision Aid Sciences and Applications (DASA), pp. 1–5 (2024). https://doi.org/10.1109/DASA63652.2024.10836523
23. Peng, S., Kalliamvakou, E., Cihon, P., Demirer, M.: The impact of AI on developer productivity: evidence from GitHub copilot. ArXiv (2023). https://arxiv.org/abs/2302.06590
24. Raghi, K.R., Sudha, K., Sreeram, A.M., Joshua S, S.: Software development automation using generative AI. In: 2024 International Conference on Emerging Research in Computational Science (ICERCS), pp. 398–403 (2024). https://doi.org/10.1109/ICERCS63125.2024.10894980
25. Sajja, A., Thakur, D., Mehra, A., Sajja, A., Thakur, D., Mehra, A.: Integrating generative ai into the software development lifecycle: Impacts on code quality and maintenance. Int. J. Sci. Res. Arch. **13**(1), 1952–1960 (2024)
26. Salamzadeh, A.: Innovation accelerators: emergence of startup companies in Iran. In: 60th Annual ICSB World Conference June, pp. 6–9 (2015)
27. Sauvola, J.: Future of software development with generative AI. In: International Conference on Automated Software Engineering (2024)
28. Schwaber, K.: Scrum 2017. Steinhardt, Gabriel. "Agile Software Development." The Product Manager's Toolkit®, pp. 131–147. Springer International Publishing, New York City (2017)
29. Shaikh, M., Vayani, A.H., Akram, S., Qamar, N.: Open-source electronic health record systems: a systematic review of most recent advances. Health Inf. J. **28**(2), 14604582221099828 (2022)
30. Tarr, P.L., Wolf, A.L.: Engineering of Software: The Continuing Contributions of Leon J. Osterweil. Springer Science & Business Media, Berlin (2011)
31. Tripathi, N., Klotins, E., Prikladnicki, R., Oivo, M., Pompermaier, L.B., Kudakacheril, A.S., Unterkalmsteiner, M., Liukkunen, K., Gorschek, T.: An anatomy of requirements engineering in software startups using multi-vocal literature and case survey. J. Syst. Softw. **146**, 130–151 (2018)
32. Tripathi, N., Oivo, M., Liukkunen, K., Markkula, J.: Startup ecosystem effect on minimum viable product development in software startups. Inf. Softw. Technol. **114**, 77–91 (2019)
33. Ulfsnes, R., Moe, N.B., Stray, V., Skarpen, M.: Transforming software development with generative AI: Empirical insights on collaboration and workflow. In: Generative AI for effective software development, pp. 219–234. Springer Nature Switzerland, Cham (2024)
34. Whitaker, A.: Who Owns AI?. Artivate **13**, 1–21 (2024)

Chapter 12
Do Agile Practices Inhibit Innovation?

Mario Simaremare, Henry Edison, and Nirnaya Tripathi

Abstract Innovation is an essential ingredient of successful software startups. Startup teams often adopt Agile practices in their startup journey, finding innovative solutions to address specific market-driven challenges. The goal of this chapter is to establish the state of the practice of how Agile methods (including practices, ceremonies, and rituals) leverage innovation in the context of software startups. Ten software startup practitioners working with Agile practices were interviewed. Based on the results, we conclude that the core Agile practices, such as iterative feedback loops, daily standups, periodic retrospectives, and reasonable sprint assignments, encourage Agile teams to innovate continuously. However, overfocusing on sprint completion and switching between sprints hinder Agile teams from pursuing innovative solutions. The adoption of Agile methods or practices depends on various influencing factors, such as team leadership, team conduciveness, task distribution strategy, and knowledge. We also found that Agile teams use various metrics to measure the output and the impact of their innovation, such as the number of introduced features and product quality to measure the output of innovation, while customer satisfaction and subscription are used to measure the impact of innovation. We use the innovation measurement model to better understand the relationship between the influencing factors and the measurement metrics. We also provide six recommendations on how to adopt Agile methods and practices into Agile teams.

Keywords Agile · Agile practices · Innovation · Software startups

M. Simaremare (✉) · H. Edison
Blekinge Institute of Technology, Karlskrona, Sweden
e-mail: mario.simaremare@bth.se; henry.edison@bth.se

N. Tripathi
M3S Research Unit, University of Oulu, Oulu, Finland
e-mail: nirnaya.tripathi@oulu.fi

N. Tripathi et al. (eds.), *Advances in Software Startups*,
https://doi.org/10.1007/978-3-032-04294-1_12

12.1 Introduction

Innovation is one of the strategic options companies need to decide what unique value they want to bring to the market [30]. Through innovation, companies can open new markets, disrupt industry leaders and gain a competitive edge. However, in a fast-changing world, only a few companies have shown the ability to innovate continuously. Deregulation, empowered customers, emerging technology and digitization, globalization, uncertain economic situations, and rapid product development have further challenged companies' innovation capabilities. In the past, companies focused on establishing a systematic process for managing innovation (i.e., using the stage-gate innovation model) or long-term strategic planning. However, these approaches offer insufficient capabilities and flexibility under such highly dynamic and uncertain situations.

The concept of agility is considered a relevant approach for managing innovation [9, 27]. The principles of Agile emphasize the role of iteration and learning mechanisms in coping with complexity and uncertainty that cannot be predicted. Companies such as General Electric, Amazon, and Spotify have adopted agility as the fuel of innovation and part of their culture [3, 15, 23]. Since its introduction to software development, Agile methods have proven effective in improving how we develop high-quality software with regard to changes and uncertainties [10], thus contributing to a company's growth [5].

Agility has also been considered the most suitable process model in the context of software startups [20]. Software startups are newly created companies that aspire to grow fast in extreme uncertainty. In software startups, software plays an important role as an outcome of entrepreneurial operations and as a ubiquity, becoming the business model itself [29]. Fast release with an iterative and incremental approach, which shortens the lead time from idea conception to market, enables startups to respond to the challenges they are confronted with.

Even though Agile seems to be able to prescribe how to develop a product faster, it cannot answer what product should be developed [4]. The iterative and incremental way of building software only works when the problem is well understood, but the solution is not [4]. In an innovation context, however, neither the problem nor the solution is well understood. Thus, Lean Startup emphasizes the importance of understanding the problem before developing the solution [24]. Software startups should "get out of the building" from day one to understand what customers perceive as value. Then, a minimum viable product is built iteratively and tested frequently by the customers to validate assumptions about values. In this way, the focus is always on delivering customer value, and the risk of being too solution-oriented is minimized.

Existing literature has accumulated a growing body of knowledge of the application of Agile methods in emerging companies such as startups (e.g., [18, 20, 28]). However, how Agile methods inspire and hinder innovation still lacks empirical evidence [7, 12]. In this sense, this chapter aims to establish the state of the practice of how Agile methods (including practices, ceremonies, and rituals) leverage innovation in the context of software startups. Therefore, in this chapter, we aim to discuss (i) how Agile practices inspire and hinder innovation, (ii) the factors that influence innovation in an Agile environment, and (iii) the metrics used to measure innovation in an Agile context.

The remainder of the chapter is organized as follows. Section 12.2 discusses the background concepts and related work. Sections 12.3–12.5 present the findings of the study. Discussion and recommendations for Agile teams can be found in Sect. 12.6. Lastly, we conclude this chapter in Sect. 12.7.

12.2 Agile and Innovation in Software Startups

As the most adopted development methods in software startups [21], Agile methods[1] emphasize delivering valuable software solutions through iterative development and close collaboration [20]. Agile methods prioritize close interactions, customer collaboration, working software solutions, and rapid responses to customers' evolving needs. In the startup context, the adoption of Agile practices usually happens gradually from ad hoc to structured [14] and is not strictly bound to a particular method (e.g., Kanban, Scrum, and XP). This means that in the early days of a startup team, it is common to adopt practices that work with the team culture and address the team's needs. In practice, software startups often combine Agile practices with the Lean principle to conserve resources through continuous experimentation to find a valid problem, a viable solution, and a market [10, 24].

There are positive correlations between the adoption of Agile practices and software startups' ability to perform, innovate [18, 22], and achieve project success [25]. Agile practices, such as continuous integration and quick iterative cycles, can significantly improve product quality [18]. Startup teams can also make use of various technologies, such as artificial intelligence (AI) [32], to further enhance their ability to perform and innovate.

Team leadership holds a central role in maintaining team cohesiveness while adopting Agile practices. High team cohesiveness can uncover resource and budgeting issues that can hinder Agile teams from innovation [18, 31] and keep team members' excitement and motivation [31]. To maintain team cohesiveness, the leadership needs to actively promote open communication, define team vision, establish a clear planning strategy, and maintain regular iterative delivery [22, 31]. On the other hand, team leadership is also expected to give team members enough freedom to learn and explore alternative solutions [16].

Adopting Agile practices that foster innovation can be challenging [1, 2]. Hindrances such as insufficient resources, technological limitations, and low team maturity can prevent Agile teams from effectively implementing these practices [1]. Overemphasizing short-term releases, conflicting internal visions, overly cross-

[1] Agile Manifesto: https://agilemanifesto.org/.

functional roles, lack of process-product documentation, and low team efficacy often cripple Agile teams' ability to deliver innovative solutions and reach the market in timely manner [2]. Additionally, inadequate sprint planning, excessive meeting overhead, insufficient customer involvement, and frequent rework pose further challenges [19].

Innovation is vital for software startups but is challenging to achieve [13], and so is measuring it. Measuring innovation means finding out if the innovative solutions produced by startup teams are actually creating value, making a significant difference, and disrupting the markets [26]. Innovation is often measured through a combination of "fixed" and "relative" metrics [26]. While the former focuses on measuring how much revenue the innovation generates, the latter emphasizes how much improvement in terms of quality the innovation brings, such as greater efficiency and better user experience [26].

From a broader context, an innovation can be modeled into three interrelated and measurable aspects, namely, team capability, innovation output, and innovation performance [11] as depicted in Fig. 12.1. Team capability measures the available resources, knowledge, technology, research and development activities, and various determinant factors, such as team vision, culture, trust, and managerial approach [11]. Having a certain set of team capabilities will enable a team to innovate and produce outputs in the form of software that can be measured through, for example, the number of new features and improvements, which are also reflected by the product quality [11]. Innovation output will further induce impact in the form of, for example, improved customer satisfaction and product sales [11]. Consequently, both innovation output and performance inform decisions on the input. We use the measurement model to frame our findings in this chapter.

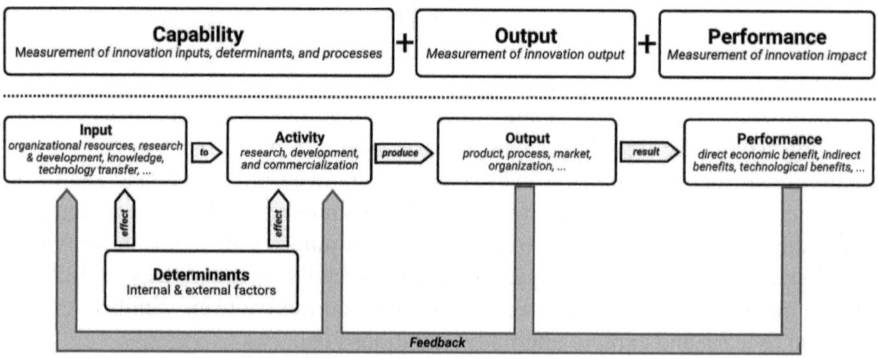

Fig. 12.1 Innovation measurement model [11]

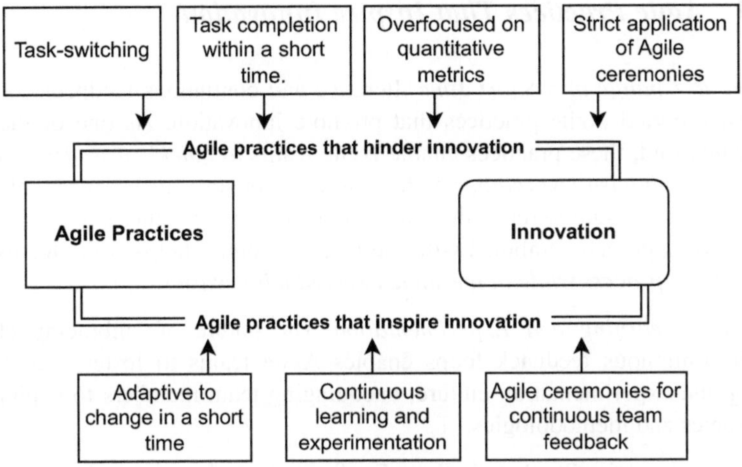

Fig. 12.2 Thematic analysis

Research Method

This chapter is based on ten semi-structured interviews with software startup practitioners from various industries, such as health, finance, AI, and embedding systems in Europe and Asia. The interview participants have three to seven years of experience in various roles, such as founders, developers, and researchers. Each interview lasted between 30 and 50 minutes through the Zoom platform. Sessions were recorded with interviewees' consent and transcribed using OpenAI's Whisper. We contacted candidates through LinkedIn messages, startup events, and our professional network.

We employed thematic analysis [6, 8] to capture patterns and more profound insights from interview qualitative data. We initially defined four preliminary themes based on the research aims, namely, *Agile practices that inspire innovation*, *Agile practices that hinder innovation*, *influencing factors of innovation*, and *metrics used to measure innovation*. Codes emerged organically throughout the analysis and were mapped to the themes (see Fig. 12.2).

12.3 How Agile Practices Inspire and Hinder Innovation

This section contains our findings on how Agile practices can both inspire and hinder software startup teams from innovating.

12.3.1 Agile Practices That Inspire Innovation

Adaptive to Change in a Short Time Iterative and continuous feedback loops are the most reported Agile practices that promote innovation. As one of the study participants said, these practices enable Agile teams *to quickly test new ideas and pivot if something isn't working*, which is essential for software startups with scarce resources and pressure to reach the market immediately. Another participant stated the iterative approach combined with the Lean principles helps Agile teams focus *on optimizing process while at the same time reducing wastes.*

Continuous Learning and Experimentation The nature of embracing changes through continuous feedback loops enables Agile teams to foster a continuous learning and experimentation culture, encouraging team members to explore new technologies and methodologies.

Agile Ceremonies for Continuous Team Feedback Participants mentioned the benefit of Agile ceremonies, such as daily standups and retrospectives, which encourage continuous team feedback and idea sharing, leading to more collaborative and innovative solutions. These ceremonies also motivate open communication across all team members, whether juniors or seniors, where everyone can say their opinion, ensuring everyone feels heard and valued.

12.3.2 Agile Practices That Hinder Innovation

Task Switching Oftentimes, a team member needs to work on multiple tasks or sprints and switch between them in response to, for example, requirement changes and sprint priority. The participants felt this practice significantly lowered their productivity and, to some extent, hindered them from exploring alternative solutions. A participant shared his experience: "Let's say I'm working on a sign-up flow, and suddenly my clients informed me to do another high-priority task. I will leave the sign-up flow and continue working on that again later. When I return to the first feature (sign-up), my productivity will decrease. It (i.e., the task switching) hinders me from innovating."

Task Completion Within a Short Time The study participants mentioned their difficulties in crafting creative solutions when their teams hurried them to complete tasks at hand as soon as possible, *because creative exploration needs time.*

Overfocused on Quantitative Metrics The study participants felt more pressure when their productivity was measured by the number of completed sprints, for example, in ticket-based systems where the number of completed tickets indicates how many tasks are completed. Overfocusing on quantitative metrics discourages the participants from producing quality results since they want to be seen as productive people with high outputs.

Strict Application of Agile Ceremonies Another reported hindrance is when the team leadership uses Agile ceremonies. such as daily stand-ups and retrospectives, as *a way to check team members' work.* Moreover, from the study participants' perspectives, a strict execution of these ceremonies brings discomfort and anxiety to the team. A participant expressed his experience with "a lot of back and forth meetings ... I don't like these daily standups because it mostly becomes a boring kind of meeting. It's mandatory, and you have to be there, but you have nothing to present because you were in another meeting yesterday." The study participants felt that oversupervising is correlated with trust issues between the team leadership and team members. The participants emphasized the importance of developing a team with a strong *sense of responsibility and capability to work independently and collaboratively.*

12.4 Influencing Factors of Innovation

This section lists various factors that the study participants believed to be important in adopting Agile methods and practices.

Justification Behind the Adoption The decision to implement a particular Agile method or practice should be sufficiently justified to indicate that an Agile team is well aware of their decision. For example, according to his experience, a study participant argued that Agile methods would *work better in small teams. When the project is small, with clear goals and has no time constraints, a traditional waterfall is preferable.*

Team Cohesiveness Most of the study participants highlighted the importance of having a cohesive team to foster innovation. The participants felt that having good relations with other colleagues would improve the internal team communication and induce idea exchanges. Moreover, being cohesive enables team members to share opinions, knowledge, and perspectives openly. These positive vibes make team members feel accepted and have a sense of belonging, fostering an organic willingness to support each other and collaborate.

Knowledge Acquisition Having adequate knowledge is a crucial innovation catalyst because *a person can never be more innovative if he lacks knowledge.* Most of the study participants believed that every team member must be encouraged to seek knowledge from various sources and platforms, such as Udemy[2] and Coursera.[3] Being knowledgeable opens team members to new alternative solutions.

Technology Utilization The study participants pointed out the importance of utilizing existing technology to support Agile practices. For example, when a team

[2] Udemy: https://www.udemy.com/.

[3] Coursera: https://www.coursera.org/.

member cannot attend in-person meetings, they can post an update on group chat and Jira.[4] Agile teams can also adopt AI into their unique workflow, for example, to provide immediate feedback to the stakeholders and team members.

12.5 Metrics to Measure Innovation

This section lists various reported metrics used by the study participants in their respective teams to measure their innovation output and impact.

The participants used different metrics to measure the innovation output. These metrics include (1) the number of new processes or techniques introduced, (2) ideas converted into products, and (3) new features or improvements delivered. Innovation can also be measured by the product's quality, including (4) how well the solution scales in response to changing requirements, (5) the reduction of technical debts, and (6) the overall product performance.

Positive outputs of innovation eventually bring positive impacts that are commonly measured through (1) positive user feedback, (2) improved user experiences, (3) improved user engagement, and (4) customer satisfaction, which ultimately (5) improve customer retention and generate (6) more customers. A study participant summed, "We measure how much user retention we are getting, how much positive feedback from the user we are getting, and obviously how good the responses we're getting from the investors are." The improved impacts of innovation are also appreciated in various forms within Agile teams or companies in a broader context, for instance, as one of the practitioners pointed out, "public announcements, (an opportunity to give) talks, and some kind of cheering up celebration." The list of the reported metrics in this book chapter is shown in Table 12.1.

Table 12.1 A mapping between reported metrics and elements of innovation [11]

Reported metrics	Type of measurement
Focus on new customers	Internal determinant
Number of introduced processes or techniques, converted ideas into products, produced artifacts (e.g., codes), and new or improved features; overall solution quality: scalability and performance, technical debts	Innovation output
User engagement, user feedback, user experience, user satisfaction, customer retention, and new customer subscriptions	Innovation impact

[4] Jira: https://www.atlassian.com/software/jira.

12.6 Discussion

This section discusses our findings in relation to the aims of this chapter. Following that, this section also provides a list of recommendations for practitioners and Agile teams on adopting Agile practices into their workflows.

12.6.1 Agile Practices and Innovation

Our findings indicate that the core Agile practices can inspire and hinder Agile teams from innovation. The nature of quick iterative feedback loops in Agile practices allows teams to experiment with new ideas, learn new approaches, and quickly pivot when something does not go as expected [18]. Agile ceremonies, such as daily standups and retrospectives, enable Agile teams to gather feedback from the internal team and positively improve team performance while at the same time maintaining team conduciveness [16, 22, 31]. During these ceremonies, a team member can discuss, for example, difficult problems and receive suggestions for viable solutions from more experienced colleagues. However, a strict implementation of these ceremonies potentially blocks Agile teams from self-efficacy [16] and innovation. For example, repetitive meetings cause unnecessary time overhead and work interruption, deterring team members from working on their sprints and potentially lowering their productivity [16]. The iterative loops also indicate that an Agile team is attempting to quickly adapt with the changing customer and market needs.

The study participants reported to usually work with multiple sprints simultaneously with a tight time budget. This practice is common in the startup context, where resources are scarce and requirements are evolving. This situation often forces team members to constantly juggle between sprints, switching from one sprint to another. Sprint juggling potentially disrupts team members from focusing on a problem at a time, exploring various options, and producing an innovative solution [19]. These findings align with an earlier work that suggests every Agile team should have a proper sprint planning [22] to control the project progress while at the same time inspiring team members to innovate by minimizing sprint juggling. Proper sprint planning also helps Agile teams manage the delivery pressure [19] and improve self-efficacy [16].

Measuring team performance with quantitative metrics encourages team members to complete their sprints on time [31]. These measurements help team leadership track the project progress [31]. However, our findings suggest a negative perception of this practice where team members felt disincentivized for spending more time and effort to explore better solutions since their performance is not measured qualitatively. For example, a team member can produce a working solution in a short time, but to ensure its quality, additional costly reviews and refactoring are required [19]. For the sake of completing his or her sprints, the team member would prefer to move on and come back later only if time allows.

12.6.2 Influencing Factors of Innovation

Adopting Agile practices requires strong team-wide commitment. Our findings indicate that startup teams should have clear justifications before selecting any specific Agile practice. For instance, factors such as project complexity, team size, and team maturity should guide this decision [2]. When full adherence to a single Agile method is impractical, teams can experiment with practices drawn from multiple Agile approaches and tailor them to fit their unique culture and workflow [14]. Having a sufficient rationale behind a decision indicates that the team leadership knows what they are doing, which improves team's confidence, efficacy, and commitment [31].

Our findings underline the important role of team leadership in maintaining team cohesiveness, aligning with earlier work [31]. High team cohesiveness correlates with team members' excitement and motivation, innovation's essential ingredients [31]. The leadership is responsible for guiding the team and encouraging team members to acquire and use contemporary knowledge and technology, such as AI, to support Agile practices. For instance, a developer specializing in mobile platforms might receive targeted training on emerging technologies to deepen their expertise.

Table 12.2 maps the identified influencing factors and internal determinant taxonomy [11].

12.6.3 Metrics to Measure Innovation

The study participants mentioned various metrics used in their specific contexts for specific purposes. These findings confirm what has been reported in the prior work. For example, the number of new features [11] to measure innovation output and sales to measure innovation impact [26]. Most of the metrics identified in this study are related to one another. For example, the number of converted ideas into a product may correlate with the number of produced artifacts (i.e., codes), and the number of new or improved features are used to measure the implementation progress of a product. Table 12.1 lists all of the identified metrics and maps them to the goal of the metrics according to the innovation measurement model [11].

Table 12.2 Reported factors and internal determinant taxonomy of innovation [11]

Reported factor[a]	Determinant taxonomy
Customer orientation; customer acceptance; responsive to the customer and the market	Customer orientation
Training, flexible working hours; skill and experience	Human resources
Visionary and team-oriented leadership	Leadership
Cohesive and supportive team; team feedback; opportunity to give opinions	Team collaboration, communication, and culture
Transparent and trustworthy team; oversupervision through meetings (−)	Trust
Knowledge acquisition and sharing within team members	Knowledge management
Expertise-based task distribution; strict Agile practices (−)	Empowerment
Willingness to take ownership and responsibility	Commitment
Opportunity to research and experiment with creative solutions	Research and development
Seek and utilize technologies to support team workflow, e.g., AI and seamless collaboration tools	Tool support
Embracing customer feedback	Marketing
Collaboration with customer	External collaboration
Communication	Communication

[a] Factors marked with (−) indicate negative influence to innovation

Recommendation for Practitioners and Agile Teams

Based on our findings, we propose the following six recommendations as additions to earlier studies [1, 2, 16, 17]. These recommendations should be useful for software startups and Agile practitioners to mitigate Agile practices from blocking innovation. Even though the recommendations were extracted from interviews with software startup practitioners, they are applicable to other domains and company maturity (i.e., medium enterprise).

1. Construct a cohesive team through open, transparent, and democratic leadership. Agile teams should be open to opinions and make decisions transparently to make team members feel included and challenged.
2. Equip team members with knowledge relevant to their expertise and encourage knowledge sharing within the team.
3. Distribute tasks or sprints wisely, and more importantly, task assignments should be made based on agreements with team members to foster ownership and excitement.
4. Finding suitable method fragments or Agile practices is a journey. An Agile team should actively seek method fragments or practices that align with the team's values. The team could adapt the method's fragments or practices to the team's specific needs and culture.

(continued)

5. Seek and utilize available technology to enhance and streamline the team's workflows. For example, AI can be used as an automatic notetaking tool and feedback generation.
6. Imposing metrics to measure team performance is beneficial for tracking the project progression. However, emphasizing too much on achieving these metrics distracts team members from developing innovative solutions. We recommend Agile teams to find the balance between metric achievements and flexibility in how to achieve them. The list of commonly used metrics is shown in Table 12.1.

12.7 Conclusion

Software startups operate in an evolving market with high uncertainty and limited resources. Yet they also possess a unique ability to create innovative solutions that address market needs. To navigate this challenging environment, startup teams often adopt Agile methods and practices, which provide them with flexibility in responding to market changes.

This chapter aims to explore how Agile practices support and hinder innovation, the factors that impact innovation in an Agile environment, and the metrics used to measure innovation in an Agile context. We conducted semi-structured interviews with ten software startup practitioners practicing Agile methods.

Our findings show that the core Agile practices, such as iterative feedback loops, daily standups, periodic retrospectives, and reasonable sprint assignments, encourage Agile teams to innovate continuously. However, overfocusing on tasks or sprint completion distracts Agile teams from exploring innovative solutions. Switching between sprints too often to satisfy customers' ever-changing requirements also hinders Agile teams from producing quality solutions.

Moreover, the experience in adopting Agile methods or practices may vary from team to team with various influencing factors, including team leadership, team conduciveness and transparency, task distribution strategy, acquired and circulated knowledge, the opportunity to learn and experiment with new solutions, ability to seek and use technology to support team workflow, team members' commitment, willingness to take ownership, and team orientation toward customers' satisfaction.

Agile teams use various metrics to measure the output and impact of their innovation. For example, the number of introduced processes, features, codes, and overall product quality are used to measure the output of innovation. On the other hand, customer satisfaction and subscriptions are used to measure the impact of innovation.

To better understand the relationship between the influencing factors of innovation and the reported measurement metrics, a map is formed based on the innovation measurement model. Last but not least, we also provide a list of recommendations on how to adopt Agile methods and practices into Agile teams.

Acknowledgments This work has been endorsed by ELLIIT, the Swedish Strategic Research Area in IT and Mobile Communications.

References

1. Abrantes, P.C., Furtado, A.P.: Agile development practices applied to software startups: a systematic mapping review. In: 16th Iberian Conference on Information Systems and Technologies (CISTI), pp. 1–6 (2021)
2. Annosi, M.C., Foss, N., Martini, A.: When agile harms learning and innovation: (and what can be done about it). Calif. Manag. Rev. **63**(1), 61–80 (2020)
3. Bäcklander, G.: Doing complexity leadership theory: how agile coaches at Spotify practise enabling leadership. Creat. Innov. Manag. **28**(1), 42–60 (2019). https://doi.org/10.1111/caim.12303
4. Bosch, J., Olsson, H.H., Björk, J., Ljungblad, J.: The early stage software startup development model: a framework for operationalizing lean principles in software startups. In: Proceedings of 4th International Conference on Lean Enterprise Software and Systems (2013)
5. Bouncken, R.B., Kraus, S., Roig-Tierno, N.: Knowledge- and innovation-based business models for future growth: digitalized business models and portfolio considerations. Rev. Manag. Sci. **15**, 1–14 (2021)
6. Braun, V., Clarke, V.: Using thematic analysis in psychology. Qual. Res. Psychol. **3**(2), 77–101 (2006)
7. Conboy, K., Wang, X., Fitzgerald, B.: Creativity in agile systems development: a literature review. In: International Federation for Information Processing Working Group 8.2 Information and Organizations, pp. 122–134 (2009)
8. Cruzes, D.S., Dyba, T.: Recommended steps for thematic synthesis in software engineering. In: 2011 International Symposium on Empirical Software Engineering and Measurement, pp. 275–284 (2011)
9. Denning, S.: The next frontier for agile: strategic management. Strateg. Leadersh. **45**(2), 12–18 (2017)
10. Dybå, T., Dingsøyr, T.: Empirical studies of agile software development: a systematic review. Inform. Softw. Technol. **50**(9–10), 833–859 (2008)
11. Edison, H., bin Ali, N., Torkar, R.: Towards innovation measurement in the software industry. J. Syst. Softw. **86**(5), 1390–1407 (2013). Issn: 0164–1212. https://doi.org/10.1016/j.jss.2013.01.013. https://www.sciencedirect.com/science/article/pii/S0164121213000058
12. Edison, H., Jabangwe, R., Duc, A.N., Wang, X., Abrahamsson, P.: An investigation into software product innovation: a systematic literature review. In: Proceedings of 2016 International Conference on Engineering, Technology and Innovation/IEEE International Technology Management Conference (ICE/ITMC) (2016)
13. Fiorentino, R., Longobardi, S., Scaletti, A.: The early growth of start-ups: innovation matters. Evidence from Italy. Eur. J. Innov. Manag. **24**(5), 1525–1546 (2021)
14. Giardino, C., Paternoster, N., Unterkalmsteiner, M., Gorschek, T., Abrahamsson, P.: Software development in startup companies: the greenfield startup model. IEEE Trans. Softw. Eng. **42**(6), 585–604 (2016)
15. Goldstein, V., Euchner, J.: Transformation for growth at GE: An interview with Viv Goldstein. Res. Technol. Manag. **60**(6), 14–19 (2017). ISSN: 08956308, 19300166. Taylor & Francis, Ltd. 2025-10-19

16. Huck-Fries, V., Spitzer, R., Thatcher, J., Krcmar, H.: (no) need to apply agile? Bus. Inf. Syst. Eng. **67**(1), 55–81 (2025)
17. Javdani Gandomani, T., Zulzalil, H., Bahsoon, R.: Empowering software startups with agile methods and practices: a design science research. Softw.: Pract. Exper. **55**(2), 220–242 (2025)
18. Klotins, E., Unterkalmsteiner, M., Chatzipetrou, P., Gorschek, T., Prikladnicki, R., Tripathi, N., Pompermaier, L.B.: Use of agile practices in start-up companies. e-Informatica Softw. Eng. J. **15**(1), 47–64 (2021)
19. Meckenstock, J.N., Wallmichrath, V.: Adapt and overcome - how agile practitioners adapt to issues that impede the delivery of value: an interview study. In: Peter, S., Kropp, M., Aguiar, A., Anslow, C., Lunesu, M.I., Pinna, A. (eds.) Agile Processes in Software Engineering and Extreme Programming, pp. 245–264. Springer Nature Switzerland, Cham (2025)
20. Pantiuchina, J., Mondini, M., Khanna, D., Wang, X., Abrahamsson, P.: Are software startups applying agile practices? The state of the practice from a large survey. In: Proceedings of International Conference on Agile Software Development (2017)
21. Paternoster, N., Giardino, C., Unterkalmsteiner, M., Gorschek, T., Abrahamsson, P.: Software development in startup companies: a systematic mapping study. Inf. Softw. Technol. **56**(10), 1200–1218 (2014)
22. Peeters, T., Van De Voorde, K., Paauwe, J.: The effects of working agile on team performance and engagement. Team Performance Manage.: An Int. J. **28**(1/2), 61–78 (2022). https://doi.org/10.1108/TPM-07-2021-0049
23. Pisano, G.P.: You need an innovation strategy. Harv. Bus. Rev. **93**(6), 44–54 (2015). https://www.hbs.edu/faculty/Pages/item.aspx?num=49244
24. Ries, E.: Lean Startup: How Today's Entrepreneurs Use Continuous Innovation to Create Radically Successful Businesses. Crown Business, New York City (2011)
25. Serrador, P., Pinto, J.K.: Does agile work? — a quantitative analysis of agile project success. Int. J. Project Manage. **33**(5), 1040–1051 (2015). https://doi.org/10.1016/j.ijproman.2015.01.006
26. Shapiro, A.R.: Measuring innovation: beyond revenue from new products. Res.-Technol. Manage. **49**(6), 42–51 (2006)
27. Sharma, S., Singh, G., Jones, P., Kraus, S., Dwivedi, Y.K.: Understanding agile innovation management adoption for smes. IEEE Trans. Eng. Manage. **69**, 3546–3557 (2022)
28. Souza, R., Rocha, L., Silva, F., Machado, I.: Investigating agile practices in software startups. In: Proceedings of the 32rd Brazilian Symposium on Software Engineering, pp. 317–321. ACM, New York (2019)
29. Steininger, D.M.: Linking information systems and entrepreneurship: a review and agenda for it-associated and digital entrepreneurship research. Inform. Syst. J. **29**(2), 363–407 (2019)
30. Treacy, M., Wiersema, F.: The Discipline of Market Leaders: Choose Your Customer, Narrow Your Focus, Dominate Your Market. Addison-Wesley, Reading (1995)
31. Whitworth, E., Biddle, R.: Motivation and cohesion in agile teams. In: Agile Processes in Software Engineering and Extreme Programming, pp. 62–69. Springer, Berlin/Heidelberg (2007)
32. Zhang, C., Zhang, C., Zheng, S., Qiao, Y., Li, C., Zhang, M., Dam, S.K., Thwal, C.M., Tun, Y.L., Huy, L.L., kim, D., Bae, S.H., Lee, L.H., Yang, Y., Shen, H.T., Kweon, I.S., Hong, C.S.: A complete survey on generative AI (AIGC): is chatgpt from gpt-4 to gpt-5 all you need? CoRR abs/2303.11717 (2023). https://doi.org/10.48550/ARXIV.2303.11717

Theme III: Business Development and Growth

Chapter 13
Designing a SaaS Pricing Strategy Canvas: Guiding Startups Towards Structured Decision-Making

Yannick van Oord, Slinger Jansen, Andrey Saltan, and Gerard Wagenaar

Abstract This chapter introduces the Pricing Strategy Canvas, designed to help startups develop a structured pricing approach for their software-as-a-service (SaaS) product. Current literature indicates that SaaS pricing often lacks structure and relies heavily on ad hoc methods, highlighting the need for a specialized tool. The proposed canvas integrates essential elements from the Business Model Canvas, Lean Canvas, and other **SaaS pricing** literature. Expert interviews and insights from SaaS practitioners further shaped the tool, ensuring it effectively bridges theory with practical application. Validated through workshops, the Pricing Strategy Canvas fosters meaningful discussions among founders, encourages critical thinking, and supports the iterative and experimental nature of startups, ultimately guiding more informed, data-driven pricing decisions.

Keywords SaaS pricing · Canvas · Pricing strategies

13.1 Introduction

SaaS startups are new companies that focus on developing and offering SaaS products. They are characterized by their high uncertainty and risk-tolerant behavior, limited resources, and rapid decision-making processes [2]. Typically, they offer software products through diverse pricing models. Common approaches include the **freemium model**, where basic features are offered for free alongside premium paid versions; **dynamic pricing**, which adjusts according to customer demand; and **pay-per-use**, which charges customers based on their actual consumption [21].

Y. van Oord (✉) · S. Jansen · G. Wagenaar
Utrecht University, Utrecht, Netherlands
e-mail: yannickvanoord3@gmail.com; slinger.jansen@uu.nl; g.wagenaar@uu.nl

A. Saltan
LUT University, Lappeenranta, Finland
e-mail: Andrey.Saltan@lut.fi

N. Tripathi et al. (eds.), *Advances in Software Startups*,
https://doi.org/10.1007/978-3-032-04294-1_13

To shape the pricing model and make other pricing-related decisions, startups often rely on an underlying pricing strategy. A pricing strategy is the foundation upon which all pricing decisions are made, for example, the pricing model as described above [18]. However, determining the price and pricing strategy remains particularly challenging for startups due to conflicting guidance and the complexity involved in pricing SaaS products [19]. For instance, startups often face a dilemma between adopting value-based pricing or market-based pricing approaches. Furthermore, SaaS startups are often heterogeneous in the way they approach their product pricing and are very limited in what they share [19].

Several existing tools, known as canvases, have become widely used for structuring and visualizing startup business models, notably the Business Model Canvas and the Lean Canvas. Among other things, these canvases include information on costs, target customer, the value of the product, and distribution and marketing channels [15]. While the Business Model Canvas (BMC) is very popular for a lot of businesses, the Lean Canvas has a better focus on startups [9]. Nevertheless, these canvases are limited in the amount of information regarding the pricing strategy of a software product. Currently, only cost and revenue are taken into account, and a specific, scientifically grounded pricing canvas does not exist. With many factors at play when determining the price of an SaaS product [11], it would be beneficial to have a canvas as a tool to approach the pricing strategy. One of the reasons being that pricing has a major impact on the success of an SaaS startup [18].

The research presented in this chapter thus explores how a pricing strategy canvas might effectively assist SaaS startups. Despite the popularity of canvases, there remains ambiguity about their conceptual foundations, practical efficacy, and rationale behind their existence [8]. By investigating existing pricing practices and identifying challenges specific to SaaS startups, this study addresses the research question: *How can a comprehensive canvas be designed to guide SaaS startups in determining optimal pricing for their software products?*

Research Methodology

To address the research question and develop the Pricing Strategy Canvas, a practical, three-step approach inspired by Osterwalder's Business Model Canvas development [6, 14] was employed (Fig. 13.1):

1. **Multivocal Literature Review:** Multivocal review of academic and industry literature on SaaS pricing to establish a theoretical foundation
2. **Expert Interviews:** Semi-structured interviews with startup founders and SaaS pricing experts, refining the canvas iteratively
3. **Validation Workshops:** Practical testing through workshops with startups, assessing usability and effectiveness in real-world scenarios

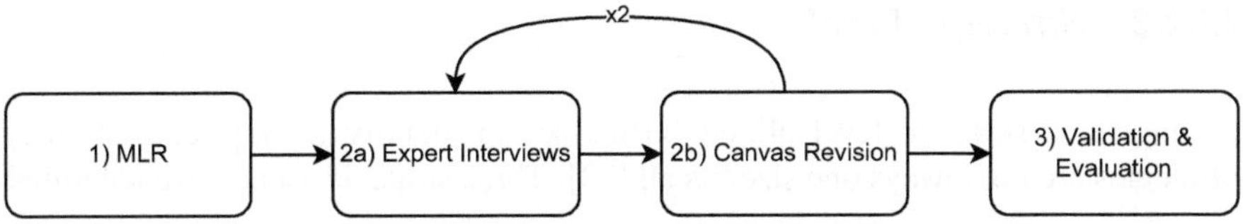

Fig. 13.1 Pricing canvas development process

13.2 Multivocal Literature Review

This multivocal literature review serves as the initial phase of a research process, synthesizing both academic and industry literature on SaaS pricing to establish a robust theoretical foundation. Saltan and Smolander [18] define SaaS pricing as the scope of the decisions, practices, underlying conditions, and processes in determining the monetary value of the offered SaaS service, with a pricing strategy being the foundation upon which all pricing decisions are made. However, terminology across various studies is inconsistent, with terms like pricing model, pricing structure, pricing policy, and pricing approach often used interchangeably [16]. Below, we present the results from the multivocal literature review, discussing pricing activities, specific pricing strategies, and a change of scope for the pricing canvas based on theoretical data.

13.2.1 SaaS Pricing Activities

Two previous multivocal literature reviews have been performed in order to grasp the complexity of SaaS pricing [16, 17]. These studies emphasize that gray SaaS literature is often more valuable to the industry than well-formed academic literature [16], and in this case, there are significantly more gray than academic sources. In addition, research states there is an obvious separation between academia and industry [16], causing SaaS literature to be scattered across multiple dimensions, which could cause different implementations of pricing strategies [17], highlighting the need for a tool, like a pricing canvas to bring theoretical and practical side of SaaS pricing closer together.

Saltan and Smolander [19] have summarized the findings from their literature reviews resulting in three levels in which SaaS pricing activities are performed [16]. The three identified levels are *strategic*, *tactical*, and *operational*. Each level has their own activities that contribute to the goal of said level. It is said if there is a lack of focus in the strategic, tactical, or operational levels, the product and the company are likely to fail [18]. Therefore, it is important that the SaaS pricing process is carefully considered to ensure the success of the startup.

13.2.2 Strategic Level

Pricing on a strategic level allows businesses to identify their pricing strategy. Strategies are not always one size fits all [23]. Three strategic aspects are identified:

Competitive Research and Market Positioning:
Leveraging pricing to shape consumer perception and differentiate itself from competitors [19], similar to the *unique value proposition* from Lean Canvas, where businesses propose where their unique values lie and how they can differentiate themselves from the rest of the market [9].

Market Segmentation and Value Proposition:
Identifying and segmenting potential customers to align the value offered to specific segments [19], similar to the BMC and Lean Canvas, where filling in the *customer segments*, *value proposition*, and *unfair advantage* lead to their uniqueness from other parties, hence identifying their market strategy [9, 14].

Pricing Structure, Strategies, and Models:[1]
Defining objectives, pricing logic, and business models, including commonly recognized structures such as flat-rate, pay-as-you-go, tiered, user-based, feature-based, variable, and hybrid pricing models [19].

The strategic level is not limited to the mentioned strategies; additional approaches, such as those described by Mohout in his pricing strategy book [11], may also be applied. It can further incorporate the business model, for example, freemium, subscription based, pay-per-use, or dynamic pricing from Saputra [21], along with the corresponding monetization strategies outlined by Mohout.

13.2.3 Tactical Level

The tactical level of SaaS pricing involves translating strategic pricing decisions into specific offerings and actions [19]. It includes the design and implementation of the pricing strategy in a way which directly affects how the product is presented and sold to the customers. There are three activities that the tactical level of SaaS pricing considers:

[1] Here, the term *pricing strategy* does not refer to the overall pricing strategy of the product but to a specific tactic or method to come to a price or a sales strategy. This will be discussed later in this chapter.

Offering Design, Versioning, and Bundling:
Translating strategic decisions into specific offers, including the number and functions of offered versions and their pricing [19]. This aspect concerns how the product will be designed; what versions of it exist, such as a free and a paid version; and if bundles can be sold. Pricing strategies here often rely on pricing metrics such as user numbers, features, usage intensity, consumer characteristics, and outcome achievements [19].

Transparency, Promotion, and Communication:
How SaaS companies inform customers about their offerings and promote their services to increase customer interest [19]. This aspect considers the marketing part for the sales and promotion of the product, similar to the *channels* and *customer relationships* in the Business Model Canvas and Lean Canvas respectfully [9, 14].

Customer Acquisition, Retention, and Usage Analytics:
How pricing is used to manage customer acquisition, retention, and analyze usage. One theory that can be applied here is the Pirate Funnel by McClure [10], which describes and captures activities and campaigns to allow for excellent customer acquisition and retention.

13.2.4 Operational Level

At the operational level, day-to-day activities to maintain and monitor the pricing strategy are performed. Factors such as ownership and control highlight how pricing decisions are organized within a company and how responsibility is distributed among the responsible team [19]. Monitoring the performance of the pricing strategy, as well as the influence of external forces on the pricing strategy, is a common activity on this level [19]. For example, inflation is an external factor influencing the performance of a current pricing strategy. Finally, resources and cost planning ensure pricing is aligned with the overall management of resources and expenses [14], which can include looping back to the strategic level, and checking if everything is aligned there, or going further to, for example, the filled-in BMC or Lean Canvas and seeing if everything conforms to the strategies identified.

13.2.5 SaaS Pricing Strategies

Interestingly, Osterwalder describes several pricing strategies that he refers to as *mechanisms* [14]. A pricing mechanism is a specific tactic a business applies within their overall SaaS pricing process, following the definition by Saltan and Smolander [18]. Unfortunately, these mechanisms never received a spot in the Business Model Canvas, causing pricing to be excluded massively from the canvas. In addition,

Mohout [11] describes another 11 different pricing mechanisms (called *methods* in his book) that SaaS startups can use to determine a specific software price.

There are many specific pricing strategies businesses can use. In total, we have found 23 different pricing strategies in two papers, but there exist many more. Two examples of specific strategies are:

- **Silicon Valley Rule-of-Thumb (fixed pricing)** This strategy is essentially value-based pricing, focusing on financial and customer value. It applies a multiplier, often set at 10x, to the cost of delivering the product or service. For example, if an SaaS product costs $100 to develop and deliver, it would be priced at $1,000, as the perceived customer value justifies the markup. The entrepreneur has the flexibility to determine this value based on market perception [7, 11, 12].
- **Anchor Pricing (value-based pricing)** This strategy involves setting a price based on a comparison with another product or reference point. By providing a frame of reference, customers perceive the anchored price as reasonable. Referencing is particularly useful in new markets where no existing price benchmarks exist [11, 13]. For instance, an SaaS product might be priced alongside a competitor's offering to establish a psychological reference for value.

13.2.6 Scoping Towards the Strategic Layer

Startups frequently struggle with formulating and implementing effective pricing strategies, often due to strategic undermanagement [3]. Addressing the strategic layer enables startups to make informed decisions about their pricing, which is the focus of this research. It also helps startups position themselves effectively by aligning their pricing with their value proposition, differentiating them from competitors. Saltan and Smolander [18] claim that pricing is integral to software business strategy and should not fail. By emphasizing the strategic layer, startups can develop pricing models that respond to market conditions while ensuring that new employees understand the overarching strategy. Therefore, we name the proposed canvas the Pricing Strategy Canvas. For additional input for the Pricing Strategy Canvas, Saltan and Smolander [20] have identified four factors that affect the pricing strategy of the SaaS product:

- **Willingness to pay**: Customer's price tolerance and elasticity [1]
- **Customer segments**: Distinction between B2B, B2C, and B2G markets, influencing the choice of pricing approaches
- **Complexity of product**: Pricing adjustments depending on the extent of required customer support and product service levels
- **Nicheness of product**: Impact of targeting specific industries, regions, or regulatory environments on product pricing

Table 13.1 Unique factors influencing SaaS pricing

Category	Factors
Market	Market size and demand (or maturity)
	Market structure and competition
	Types of customers
	Barriers and constraints
	Delivery and sales channels
	Dynamics of technological progress
Company	Business goals and opportunities
	Company size and maturity
	Resources availability
	Costs and cost structure
	Ownership and financing
Consumers	Perceived value and willingness-to-pay
	Information asymmetry and customer uncertainty
	Customer satisfaction and loyalty
	Customer acquisition costs
	Adoption readiness
	Customer usage patterns
	Switching and migration costs
	Network effect
Product	Life cycle stage
	Competitive advantage
	Functions and features
	Quality attributes
	Software architecture
	Lease and usage period
	Product category
	Experience required
	Scalability potential

In addition to internal (company) factors, external (non-company or market) factors also influence the effectiveness and success of the pricing process and strategy [17]. Saltan and Smolander [18] and Saltan [16] provide a combined total of 28 factors that influence SaaS pricing, divided into four categories: market, company, consumers, and product. The list of all factors is provided in Table 13.1. These factors will further inform the subsequent expert interviews in this study.

13.3 Pricing Strategy Canvas Development

This section details the empirical findings derived from semi-structured interviews with SaaS startup founders and pricing experts, the development of the Pricing Strategy Canvas based on these findings, and subsequent validation workshops.

13.3.1 Expert Interviews

Table 13.2 summarizes the backgrounds of the interviewed experts, providing context for the detailed discussion of the interview findings below.

Know Your Product

The first interviews revealed that *pricing SaaS is challenging due to its intangibility*, as discussed with experts E1 and E2. This theme persisted in later interviews, with E3 and E4 echoing similar concerns.

The perceived value of SaaS is difficult to define, especially for the creators. Experts E1 and E2 explained that "co-founders often view their product through a biased lens". Consequently, the element of *value proposition*, adopted from BMC, was considered overly broad. A perceived value should focus more on customer benefits such as time and cost savings, rather than the cost to the business. Experts E3 and E4 stressed further that "startups often focus too much on cost-based pricing", which they view as incompatible with SaaS. Thus, the value proposition is refined to highlight the customer's advantages more clearly.

Understanding your customer is also crucial. Expert E3 highlighted a common mistake among startups: replicating competitor pricing models without sufficient customer insight. Additionally, E5 emphasized the significance of demonstrating customer Return on Investment (ROI), notably in industries such as cybersecurity, where the measurable value includes cost reductions or effort savings. In their example, a competitor added an ROI calculator to show the returns for the customer, which were a blind guess.

Table 13.2 List of interviewee demographics

Expert	Role/function	Sector	Product type
E1[a]	Startup co-founder	Consultancy	Process management tool
E2[a]	Startup co-founder	Consultancy	Process management tool
E3	Small-size company CEO and co-founder	Fintech	Payment and billing platform
E4	Independent SaaS advisor	Consultancy	Several SaaS product types
E5	Scale-up co-founder and CEO	Cybersecurity	Cybersecurity awareness tool
E6	Scale-up co-founder and director	Cybersecurity	Cybersecurity platform
E7	Startup founder	Metal industry	CRM tool
E8	Startup co-founder and CEO	Healthcare	Transcription tool
E9	Medium-sized company co-founder and CEO	Online retail	E-commerce platform

[a] Experts 1 and 2 work for the same startup

The Devil Is in the Details

While the literature review identified 28 relevant SaaS pricing factors, expert interviews revealed the inherent complexity of SaaS pricing. Expert E3 noted, "These factors cover most things, but miss many more." Experts E1 and E2 emphasized factors like product scalability and migration costs, which were particularly relevant to their startup. E3 described the challenge as *the devil is in the details*, pointing to the need for a more detailed Pricing Strategy Canvas.

SaaS pricing is complex and situational, and pricing consultants often exist to help startups navigate these intricacies. Experts E3, E4, and E5 criticized the first concept draft of the Pricing Strategy Canvas to be too abstract and called for more details on how factors interrelate, especially how elements like customer segments influence pricing models.

Four Dimensions of SaaS Pricing

Expert E4 introduced four key dimensions for a successful pricing strategy. The first is *product value*, which requires a deep understanding of customer needs and how the product addresses them. The second dimension is *market and competition*, emphasizing the need to assess competitors and market conditions. E4 specifically cautioned: "Many startups overlook competition, assuming they will become the next unicorn."

The third dimension is *iterative pricing*, with expert E1 suggesting that the canvas should be an evolving document, revisited as market conditions change. The fourth dimension is *future-proof pricing*, with E4 noting that pricing strategies should allow growth but remain flexible to adapt as the business matures.

SaaS Pricing as an Experiment

For SaaS startups, pricing is often approached as an experiment. E5 explained that their startup frequently relied on "ballparking" followed by A/B testing, due to limited resources for thorough market research. An iterative approach enables startups to refine pricing strategies based on customer feedback.

While A/B testing can be costly in terms of time and money, it allows startups to experiment with different pricing models. For example, E3's startup tested upfront costs versus a pay-per-use model and found that upfront payments encouraged faster adoption, aligning better with growth objectives.

Customer Retention

Customer retention is crucial in SaaS pricing, particularly with respect to switching costs. Experts E1 and E2 were curious about future migration costs as they hadn't yet encountered them, while Expert E3 proposed the *angler fish method* to identify features that could lock customers in. The ability to increase switching costs can enhance product stickiness and customer loyalty, which is vital for long-term growth.

Understanding customer retention factors is essential for developing a sustainable pricing strategy, especially in competitive markets. By increasing switching costs, startups can strengthen customer loyalty and foster growth.

Company Strategy

The initial interview results revealed that the 28 SaaS pricing factors from the academic literature are not enough to capture the complexities of SaaS pricing strategies. While they remain relevant, practical applications often go beyond these factors. However, the factors provide a useful framework for discussing key elements in SaaS pricing.

A recurring theme was the importance of company strategy. Expert E6 highlighted, "What I am missing is the overall company strategy, that is what will lead to my pricing strategy," underlining the role of a business's strategy in shaping its pricing decisions. E7 agreed, stating, "With this, you can dive deeper into each part and give more value to each aspect (of SaaS pricing)," emphasizing how strategy influences pricing, whether for startups or large enterprises. Similarly, E9 stressed, "My vision and mission determine my pricing strategy."

Startups often adopt an iterative approach to pricing, testing different models aligned with their mission. Experts E1 and E8 noted that open negotiations with customers help startups refine their pricing and understand what drives conversions, illustrating the impact of a startup's strategy on pricing decisions.

Price Timing

Payment timing plays a crucial role in startup success and customer relationships. Experts E3 and E6 highlighted that payment timing affects cash flow and customer commitment. Specifically, E3 mentioned using an upfront fee as an incentive to ensure customer commitment, especially with pay-per-use models. Considering price timing reduces the risk of non-payment when usage is inconsistent. As Expert E6 explained, "Starting the business is very thirsty when it comes to cash. Therefore, capital is needed," and upfront payments help secure necessary resources for growth.

Know Your Customer

The importance of understanding your product and customers was confirmed in the second round of interviews. Expert E8 explained, "As it makes the job of our customers less stressful," highlighting the challenge of pricing such a product.

Moreover, knowing your target customer is vital. E6 noted the absence of a customer column in the Pricing Strategy Canvas, suggesting its inclusion to better understand customer problems and market structure. Expert E9 similarly emphasized that "your product has a price in a specific market," with market factors influencing pricing decisions. They proposed changing the canvas order, addressing market factors before pricing to ensure a clearer focus on the customer segment and market specifics, which are crucial for pricing decisions.

13.3.2 The Final Pricing Strategy Canvas

In total, interviews with nine experts from eight Dutch SaaS startups and SMEs informed the development of the final Pricing Strategy Canvas (Fig. 13.2). This final canvas integrates theoretical insights from MLR and empirical expert feedback. A clear alignment between the theoretical factors in Table 13.1 and practical canvas columns demonstrates effective integration of theory and practice.

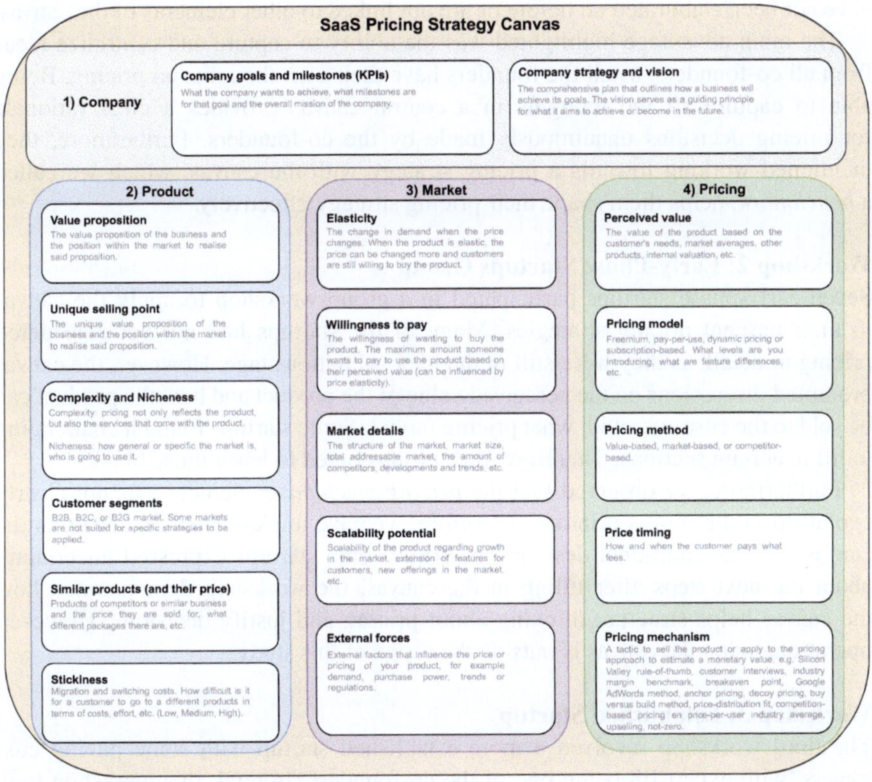

Fig. 13.2 The SaaS Pricing Strategy Canvas

13.3.3 Workshops

To apply and test the Pricing Strategy Canvas in practice, we conducted workshops with a total of nine startups. We have applied the canvas in different startup phases to test the canvas in different startup scenarios. We evaluated the canvas based on its usability and effectiveness in the current landscape of the startups. Below, we summarize the findings from these workshops:

Workshop 1: Pilot-Phase Startup
The co-founders of this startup, having already seen the first draft of the canvas, were able to use the Pricing Strategy Canvas naturally, due to their familiarity with similar tools like the Business Model Canvas. With their product being in the pilot phase, the Pricing Strategy Canvas gave insight into the pricing strategy the co-founders want to implement to convert their pilot customers to paying customers. The canvas facilitated discussions about pricing elements such as elasticity and price timing, which had not previously been considered due to the product being in the pilot phase. This led to the idea of them setting the boundaries for the Service-Level Agreement contract. We observe the canvas sparking discussions on elements that have not been elaborated on before or are not linked to other elements of the canvas.

The main advantage highlighted was the ability to capture and centralize ideas from all co-founders, as all the founders have their own thoughts on pricing. Being able to capture all the thoughts in a central canvas provides a clear rationale for pricing decisions unanimously made by the co-founders. Furthermore, they mentioned working towards a pricing strategy with the canvas, which we called a *benchmark*, helps them shape their pricing strategy effectively.

Workshop 2: Early-Phase Startups Group
Seven early-phase startups participated in a group workshop to apply the canvas to their nascent pricing strategies. Many of the startups had not yet considered pricing in detail, as they were still in the idea validation stage. However, the canvas prompted discussions on the perceived value of the product and how the product can be sold to the customer with what pricing model. Some startups found it challenging to fill in certain sections. Therefore, the startups opted to leave those blank.

Furthermore, we observed that the *pricing mechanism* element was not clearly explained in the canvas printout. Therefore, we have implemented an update in the canvas with an additional description. While some startups expressed uncertainty about the next steps after filling in the canvas, the workshop demonstrated how the canvas helps structure thinking about pricing and justify decisions. However, operationalizing the canvas is outside the scope of this study.

Workshop 3: Established Startup
The third workshop involved a more established startup with some paying customers, with expert E8 being one of the co-founders. In total, this workshop took two and a half hours. The canvas prompted detailed discussions between the CEO

and the researcher about their current pricing strategy and future goals. The startup find that the canvas helped them reflect on their value proposition, perceived value, and competitive positioning as a rationale to their choices of their current pricing. We refer to this as a *snapshot* of their current pricing strategy.

The canvas also revealed that their product provided substantial value but is harder to sell due to unclear benefits to the customers, leading to further reflection on how to communicate value effectively while justifying higher prices compared to competitors, which is one of their current pain points. With the competition laid out in the canvas, they know how to price their product based on their own, and the customer's, perceived value.

Ultimately, E8 finds that the canvas adds value to their current business. Now, it has showed them why their pricing is currently the way it is. However, they also mentioned that the canvas has potential in the future to guide them towards different pricing strategies, for example, when some competitors do not exist anymore.

13.4 Discussion

13.4.1 Canvas Use-Case Scenarios

During the interviews, we have found several scenarios in which the Pricing Strategy Canvas can be effectively used. One such scenario is A/B testing, as mentioned by expert E5, where the canvas serves as a structured way to compare two versions of a pricing strategy (A and B), testing them against prospects. A/B testing with the Pricing Strategy Canvas allows startups to visualize and analyze their pricing options and refine it if needed.

However, there are more scenarios in which the Pricing Strategy Canvas can be used by startups. Many startups struggle to determine an optimal pricing strategy. Without a structured approach, pricing decisions often become guesswork, which we have seen during the interviews. Guesswork leads to missed revenue opportunities or pricing models that fail to attract customers. By applying the Pricing Strategy Canvas, the SaaS startup may realize the factors that are needed to develop a sound pricing strategy. By mapping out these factors, the canvas helps startups make informed pricing decisions instead of relying on intuition alone. Another scenario is that startups need to adjust their pricing strategies as they grow and scale. As they transition from early-stage validation to expansion, their customer base, market positioning, and revenue goals evolve. The Pricing Strategy Canvas helps startups systematically assess and refine their pricing approach to ensure alignment with their growth stage, for example, a startup moving from an initial product-market fit phase to a broader market expansion. Another critical use-case scenario is investor and stakeholder communication. The Pricing Strategy Canvas provides a clear framework for presenting pricing rationale, making it easier to justify pricing decisions in pitch meetings or board discussions. It can also serve

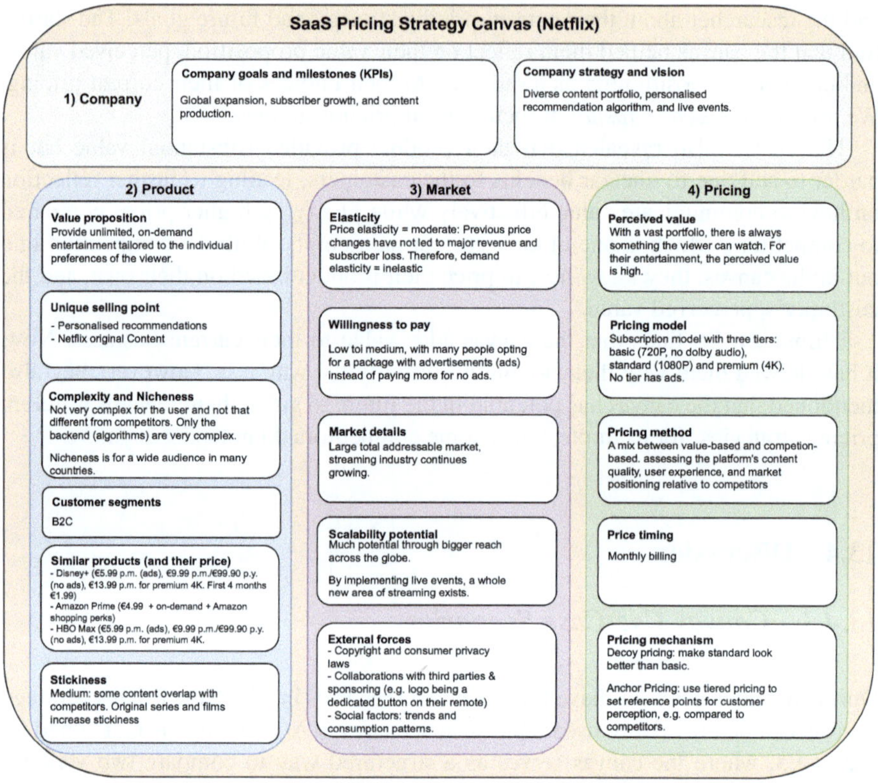

Fig. 13.3 The Pricing Strategy Canvas filled in for Netflix

as a reference point for ongoing pricing reviews, allowing startups to iteratively refine their strategies based on market evolution and internal growth.

13.4.2 Application of the SaaS Pricing Strategy Canvas

With the Pricing Strategy Canvas completed, we want to show how the canvas performs. For this, we have filled in the canvas for the popular SaaS organization *Netflix*. Figure 13.3 shows the test case for Netflix of the canvas. We use the canvas to describe the current pricing strategy of Netflix, that is, to make a snapshot. For startups, a snapshot can be used to look back at the captured pricing strategy and see what has changed or needs to change in the new pricing strategy. Additionally, the canvas can be used to determine a new pricing structure based on the input in the first three columns, which we call a benchmark.

13.4.3 Canvas Guidance

To effectively fill in the Pricing Strategy Canvas, its users can resort to different tools to identify each of the elements. In the best case, the Pricing Strategy Canvas should be filled in after filling in the Business Model Canvas (BMC) because we argue that the Pricing Strategy Canvas is an extension of the BMC.

It needs to be said that compared to other canvases, for example, the BMC, the Pricing Strategy Canvas is considerably larger. With the complexity of SaaS pricing, as seen in the literature, this expanded format allows for a more comprehensive and nuanced exploration of strategic pricing considerations. Unlike the BMC, which fits onto a single page with high-level blocks, the Pricing Strategy Canvas dives deeper into pricing-specific elements, which requires more space. To maintain clarity and usability, certain sections of the canvas are laid vertically rather than horizontally, not because vertical or horizontal positioning implies different categories but to ensure the layout remains readable and does not become overly wide or visually overwhelming. The choice of orientation simply supports better structure and visual balance, such as the company block representing the overarching strategy over the other three columns. Furthermore, each expert agreed on the structure of the canvas, which they all contributed to. This consensus not only validates the relevance of the identified categories and factors but also highlights their importance to increase the practical ability of the Pricing Strategy Canvas.

If the BMC has been filled in before working on the Pricing Strategy Canvas, several elements are already known, such as the company strategy, company goals, value proposition, unique selling point, and customer segments. Therefore, it is also the easiest to start filling in the canvas starting with the company column: the overarching company strategy influences product development, which, in turn, influences its market and, therefore, its pricing.

Below, we suggest some existing tools that startups can use to effectively fill in several Pricing Strategy Canvas elements:

- By performing a *competitor analysis*, the **similar products** can be identified, and the **switching and migration costs** can be determined if a customer wants to migrate to a competitor.
- **Elasticity** can be estimated with the *Van Westendorp Price Sensitivity Meter* [22], which helps determine the optimal price point and acceptable price range by surveying customers on their perception of value at different price levels.
- Together with a *conjoint analysis* [5] or *customer interviews*, the **willingness to pay** can be identified by considering customer trade-offs between product features and price.
- To describe the **market**, a *TAM-SAM-SOM-analysis* ([4] gives some methods and examples of how the analysis is performed) helps understand the total, serviceable, and obtainable market, ensuring that the pricing will align with market demand and growth potential. Such an analysis also helps identify where the product is scalable.

- Identifying the **perceived value of the product** is easy for its creators, but it is harder to identify for the customer. By, for example, holding *customer interviews*, their perceived value can be identified or can be calculated through *mathematical reasoning*, for example, the product saves two hours per day, multiplied by the salary of the employee.
- The canvas already gives some options on specific **pricing models and methods** that startups can choose. However, they would need to see, for example, through a *competitor analysis* and *customer interviews* what model is best to sell the product. Then, they can determine how they want to monetize their product, either through the customer value identified earlier or a competitive approach. Startups can determine the **timing of their price** *based on the pricing model they have chosen*. The startup can opt for an upfront fee (starting capital), usage based, monthly, or yearly billing. The timing depends on the preferences of the startup. In a competitive market, the pricing approach of a bigger competitor can be used as guidance.
- The canvas is completed by stating if and what **pricing mechanisms** are used to determine or use the price. The canvas provides many options and is not limited to these. These can be simple mechanisms, for example, anchoring a specific product tier. For guidance, startups can have a look at the work of Mohout (2015) [11], which provides many mechanisms startups can use.

For startups and businesses, we have deployed the Pricing Strategy Canvas online for them to download and use it themselves. The canvas template can be found on https://doi.org/10.5281/zenodo.17643140. Additional information on the canvas can be found on https://pricingstrategycanvas.wordpress.com.

13.4.4 The Gap Between Theory and Practice

The interviews revealed a significant gap between theoretical knowledge and practice in the SaaS domain. While SaaS is crucial in today's digital landscape, its rapid evolution has outpaced the development of corresponding theoretical frameworks. Input from the interviews showed that while simplifying SaaS into 28 factors is helpful, it does not capture its full complexity. These factors offer guidance for a systematic approach to SaaS pricing, and the Pricing Strategy Canvas similarly provides a structured way to consider elements that might otherwise be overlooked.

This research aimed to bridge the gap between theory and practice, showing how practical concepts can inform theory (gain an understanding of SaaS pricing) and vice versa (developing a canvas for SaaS pricing). The Pricing Strategy Canvas demonstrates how a theoretical framework can offer actionable insights, similar to the Business Model Canvas and Lean canvas.

Our findings confirm that SaaS pricing is largely practice oriented, often based on experience or logic rather than theory. Many entrepreneurs simply base prices on competitors' rates or experiment with it, raising the question whether SaaS pricing should remain a practice-driven domain. This research offers a practical tool for businesses and insight into current SaaS pricing processes for academia to satisfy both areas.

Given that SaaS and its pricing strategies are continuously evolving, particularly with the integration of AI, the future of SaaS pricing remains uncertain. As AI becomes increasingly integral to SaaS platforms, pricing strategies, but also canvases, may reach new complexities with, for example, an AI-based canvas.

13.5 Recommendations and Implications

The SaaS Pricing Strategy Canvas offers substantial benefits for both startups and established businesses by providing a structured framework for pricing decisions. Many startups currently rely on intuition, often guessing prices without solid foundations, as software pricing lacks the tangible cost metrics seen in physical products. The Canvas breaks pricing down into key components, helping teams develop thoughtful, collaborative strategies and avoid common pitfalls.

A Structured Pricing Decision Framework
As discussed throughout this chapter, the Pricing Strategy Canvas brings structure to the SaaS pricing process, especially with the pricing strategy. The interviews revealed that many startups set prices arbitrarily, often guessing what might work. Unlike physical products with tangible costs, software products are harder to put a price on and are therefore priced on intuition.

By breaking pricing into key components, the canvas helps businesses develop sound pricing strategies while avoiding common pitfalls. With this input, the pricing strategy becomes more solid and thought-out. Additionally, the structured approach facilitates internal discussions and cross-team collaboration.

Enabling Experimentation
Startups operate in an uncertain environment, which would require flexible and responsive pricing strategies. The Pricing Strategy Canvas supports adaptability by allowing SaaS startups to experiment with different pricing models before committing to a final approach.

A key method for such experimentation is A/B testing, where different pricing strategies are tested on distinct customers to evaluate their impact on conversion rates and retention. The canvas helps visualize the pricing versions, enabling startups to document, compare, and refine pricing variations systematically.

An Iterative Approach to Pricing
The interviews revealed that many SaaS startups treat pricing as a one-time decision, rarely revisiting or adjusting it unless major issues arise. Pricing should be an ongoing process that evolves alongside the product, for example, with the introduction of new features. Participants in this study likened the canvas to metaphorically be

a "gold plaque on the wall," meant to be taken down and reassessed at set intervals to determine whether the pricing strategy remains effective or requires adjustments. Putting the pricing strategy under the spotlight in a set interval allows the startup to reassess the pricing where necessary, reducing the risk of the product failing because of its price.

Enhanced Investor and Stakeholder Communication
To secure funding, startups often seek investment from venture capitalists or other stakeholders. A well-structured pricing strategy can be crucial for gaining investor confidence, as pricing impacts revenue generation, market positioning, and long-term scalability. Investors seek assurance that a startup's pricing model supports sustainable growth leading to profitability, ultimately ensuring a return on their investment. Some investors, however, may prioritize growth over short-term profitability. The Pricing Strategy Canvas strengthens credibility by demonstrating a structured, data-driven approach to pricing, improving investor confidence and alignment with business objectives.

13.5.1 Conclusion

This chapter and underlying research aimed to design and validate a comprehensive Pricing Strategy Canvas through iterative co-creation with industry experts and SaaS startup founders. The expert interviews and practical validation workshops confirmed that the canvas is valuable, effective, and practical for guiding strategic pricing decisions. Drawing inspiration from the widely successful BMC, this Pricing Strategy Canvas bridges theoretical foundations and practical usability, equipping SaaS startups with a clear, adaptable, and strategic pricing framework.

Looking ahead, the integration of artificial intelligence (AI) presents exciting possibilities for enhancing the canvas. Machine learning capabilities could analyze canvas elements dynamically, offering data-driven pricing recommendations that improve accuracy, responsiveness, and efficiency in decision-making. The current canvas provides a robust foundation upon which future AI-enhanced tools can be developed, potentially transforming SaaS pricing strategies and further empowering startup success.

References

1. Anderson, P.L., McLellan, R.D., Overton, J.P., Wolfram, G.L.: Price elasticity of demand. MacKinac Center for Public Policy (1997). Accessed April, 2025. Available at: https://www.mackinac.org/1247
2. Azeem, M., Khanna, A.: A systematic literature review of startup survival and future research agenda. J. Res. Mark. Entrep. **26**(1), 111–139 (2024)

3. Bontis, N., Chung, H.: The evolution of software pricing: from box licenses to application service provider models. Int. Res. **10**(3), 246–255 (2000)
4. Davalas, A.: The importance of the tam-sam-som model and how big data and ai help. Int. J. Soc. Sci. Econ. Res. **8**(12), 3936–3944 (2023)
5. Green, P.E., Rao, V.R.: Conjoint measurement-for quantifying judgmental data. J. Mark. Res. **8**(3), 355–363 (1971)
6. Hevner, A.R., March, S.T., Park, J., Ram, S.: Design science in information systems research. MIS Quart. **28**, 75–105 (2004)
7. Hinterhuber, A.: Towards value-based pricing—an integrative framework for decision making. Ind. Mark. Manag. **33**(8), 765–778 (2004)
8. Jansen, S.: What is a canvas anyway? The canvas as a mechanism for research communication and impact in information systems (2025, March 28). Available at SSRN: https://ssrn.com/abstract=5196852 or http://dx.doi.org/10.2139/ssrn.5196852
9. Maurya, A.: Running Lean. O'Reilly Media, Santa Rosa (2022)
10. McClure, D.: Startup metrics for pirates (2007). https://growthlabs.com.br/wp-content/uploads/2024/06/startup-metrics-for-pirates-long-version463.pdf. This source is a slidedeck
11. Mohout, O.: Lean Pricing: Pricing Strategies for Startups. Die Keure Publishing, Bruges (2015)
12. Nagle, T.T., Holden, R.K.: The Strategy and Tactics of Pricing: A Guide to Profitable Decision Making. Prentice Hall Upper Saddle River, NJ (2002)
13. Northcraft, G.B., Neale, M.A.: Experts, amateurs, and real estate: an anchoring-and-adjustment perspective on property pricing decisions. Organiz. Behav. Human Decis. Process. **39**(1), 84–97 (1987)
14. Osterwalder, A.: The business model ontology a proposition in a design science approach. Ph.D. thesis, Université de Lausanne, Faculté des hautes études commerciales (2004)
15. Osterwalder, A., Pigneur, Y.: Business Model Generation: A Handbook for Visionaries, Game Changers, and Challengers, vol. 1. Wiley, Hoboken (2010)
16. Saltan, A.: Do we know how to price saas: a multi-vocal literature review. In: Proceedings of the 2nd ACM SIGSOFT International Workshop on Software-Intensive Business: Start-Ups, Platforms, and Ecosystems, pp. 7–12 (2019)
17. Saltan, A., Smolander, K.: Towards a saas pricing cookbook: a multi-vocal literature review. In: Software Business: 10th International Conference, ICSOB 2019, Jyväskylä, Finland, November 18–20, 2019, Proceedings 10, pp. 114–129. Springer (2019)
18. Saltan, A., Smolander, K.: Bridging the state-of-the-art and the state-of-the-practice of saas pricing: a multivocal literature review. Inf. Softw. Technol. **133**, 106510 (2021)
19. Saltan, A., Smolander, K.: How saas companies price their products: insights from an industry study. In: Software Business: 11th International Conference, ICSOB 2020, Karlskrona, November 16–18, 2020, Proceedings 11, pp. 1–13. Springer (2021)
20. Saltan, A., Smolander, K.: Saas pricing practices typology: A case study. In: Agile Processes in Software Engineering and Extreme Programming–Workshops: XP 2021 Workshops, Virtual Event, June 14–18, 2021, Revised Selected Papers 22. pp. 87–95. Springer International Publishing (2021)
21. Saputra, D.I.S., Indartono, K., Handani, S.W.: Business models based on technology for startup. J. Innov. Bus. Econ. **3**(02), 91–98 (2019)
22. van Westendorp, P.: NSS Price Sensitivity Meter (PSM) – A new approach to study consumer-perception of prices. In: Proceedings of the 29th ESOMAR Congress, pp. 139–167. ESOMAR Publications, Amsterdam (1976)
23. Zhang, Z.: Competitive pricing strategies for software and saas products. Inf. Manag. **57**(8), 103367 (2020)

Chapter 14
From Classrooms to Social Commerce: How 5G Is Turning Educators into Software Entrepreneurs

Nan Yang, Yu Cui, and Sami Hyrynsalmi

Abstract The commercialization of 5G and related technologies not only enhances speed and connectivity but also accelerates business model transformation, such as the emergence of social commerce platforms and influencer economics. With years of experience in the accounting professional training and substantial industry influence, five educators developed an influencer-educator model, providing educational services as commodities on social commerce platforms. This report explores the first five years (2019–2024) of this model as implemented by SierEDU, a software startup founded by educators without a software background. Rather than creating entirely new software business models, they strategically adapted existing social commerce models to reshape the traditional education industry. They sell modularized and standardized educational services by leveraging both their private influence and public traffic on social commerce platforms. To gain full control over traffic and customer relationships, they developed their own SierEDU App and several backend systems for service delivery and customer retention, serving as a private traffic pool. Building on their influencer-educator model and the private traffic pool they established, they successfully launched three AI-powered features through effective innovation attempts, reaching a cumulative total of 4 million paid customers by May 2024. The founders, who used to be traditional educators, became software entrepreneurs while continuously shifting between the roles of exploitative influencers and explorative software product owners. This case contributes to our understanding of ambidextrous startups and leadership, navigating the tension between seeking new business opportunities brought by advanced technologies and exploiting existing strengths for early-stage survival.

N. Yang (✉) · S. Hyrynsalmi
LUT University, Lahti, Finland
e-mail: nan.yang@lut.fi; sami.hyrynsalmi@lut.fi

Y. Cui
SierEDU, Beijing, China
e-mail: hans.cui@sieredu.com

N. Tripathi et al. (eds.), *Advances in Software Startups*,
https://doi.org/10.1007/978-3-032-04294-1_14

Keywords Software startup · Ambidextrous organization · Entrepreneur · Social commerce · 5G · Online education

14.1 Introduction

When people think about software startup founders, technical skills and engineering backgrounds are often considered essential attributes—or at least, it is expected that someone from the founding team has such expertise. Although this understanding holds true for some contexts, particularly for deep tech startups, it constrains our understanding of how software entrepreneurs start and succeed.

In this report, we present the five-year journey of SierEDU,[1] a software startup providing online educational products and services for finance and accounting professional customers, approximately 80% of whom are working professionals, with the remainder being university students. Founded in 2019, SierEDU broke away from the traditional pre-recorded model of finance and accounting professional education in China, which had dominated for over two decades. They adopted a fully live-stream model led by influencer-educators under 5G-powered social commerce. In 2021, the CEO of SierEDU was named to the Forbes 30 Under 30 Asia list, an annual recognition by Forbes magazine that honors young leaders and innovators [4].

We share how a non-technical founding team successfully transitioned into software entrepreneurs in the 5G era; all the founders come from professional education or investment backgrounds and without software field experience. This report reflects the insights from three authors: one strategic advisor of SierEDU, one co-founder of SierEDU, and one academic expert in software business; this co-founder is the business lead of SierEDU for sales, operations, and marketing execution. Our reflection is from a management and leadership perspective, toward exploring and exploiting 5G and AI for business innovation.

5G, the fifth generation of cellular network technology, was commercially launched in 2019, with China among the first countries to deploy it. 5G enabled a wider range of scenarios for mobile and real-time services, including live-stream commerce and education. Building on this technical backdrop, SierEDU was founded and released its first product in the same year. Starting with a founding team of five in 2019, SierEDU has grown into a medium-sized software company by 2024. In the process of being mature [11], SierEDU is also impacted by AI, like nearly all other software companies. But in contrast to most of their peers who began exploring AI only after the public release of ChatGPT in late 2022, SierEDU was an early adopter [10] of large language models. They launched their first AI-powered feature, an automated grading system for accounting mock examinations, in the second half of 2022.

[1] http://sieredu.com/

While 5G technology played an important role in the founding of SierEDU and AI for accelerating its maturity, this report does not aim to evaluate their business model or the commercial success of 5G and AI. Instead, we hope to encourage more practitioners from diverse backgrounds to think of and engage in today's software business, rather than feeling constrained by technical barriers. SierEDU's founders abstract social commerce patterns, with influencer-driven economics as the core business logic, from underlying technical advances. By leveraging their identity as long-standing educators in finance and accounting professional training with strong personal branding, they successfully entered the social commerce business. Shifting from the slow and deliberate mindset of traditional educators to the agile and iterative logic of software development, they become software entrepreneurs. The necessity of technical expertise in software entrepreneurship has become increasingly polarized. In the past, a certain level of technical skills was essential for building software startups. However, under current technological abundance, technical capabilities serve as a core competitive advantage in some new software businesses but are no longer essential for others.

14.2 New Patterns of Consumer Behavior and Growth of Social Commerce Under 5G

From a technical perspective, 5G is designed to deliver ultrafast data transmission speeds—about 100 times faster than 4G—along with significantly reduced latency and support massive device connections [9]. Beyond these technical indicators, for SierEDU, 5G has had a profound impact on user behavior when interacting with digital services. As non-technical entrepreneurs, founders of SierEDU know that, while remaining attentive to these technical advancements, it is more crucial to envision the deeper shifts triggered in user behaviors and market dynamics. It is within these user behavior changes that new business opportunities emerge.

In both the US and Chinese e-commerce markets, the impact of 5G-enabled transformation is significant. Although SierEDU is mainly concentrated in the Chinese market, we also include the US market here to help a broader audience better understand the context as well as the global trends. According to KPMG's report, "Towards Seamless Commerce" [6], e-commerce is driving the future of US retail and powered largely by younger generations, particularly millennials and Gen Z. Meanwhile, China is one of the world's most advanced e-commerce market, worth more than 1.4 trillion USD, accounting a 40% share in the global market. The widespread adoption of 5G and AI has fostered a more liquid, immersive, mobile-first, and live-stream shopping experience. These consumer behavioral shifts paved the way for social commerce (s-commerce) [1] based on influencer-driven marketing.

14.2.1 From Fragmented Customer Journeys to Integrated Social Commerce Experience

The strategic advisor of SierEDU, also the first author of this report, founded and led the international business division of Raycloud Technology (stock code: 688365), China's first listed SaaS company serving global e-commerce sellers. According to her experience, we describe the traditional e-commerce customer journey as follows, before social commerce emerged. It is fragmented across multiple platforms, requiring customers to jump between off-platform advertising, search engines, brand Web sites, social media, instant messaging apps, phone calls, emails, e-commerce platforms, and more. Each transition introduces friction and increases the risk of customer dropoff.

Taking purchasing an accounting book online as an example, the typical e-commerce journey might involve:

- Discovery and awareness, through social media or search engine advertisements
  Emma, a recent university graduate preparing for her CPA exam (a professional accounting certification exam), browses LinkedIn for career advice. She noticed that one of her connections has shared a recommendation for a CPA preparation book. Although the post is relevant to her, she does not immediately click it because there are tons of recommendations there every day. The next day, while looking for study materials on Google, she sees the advertisement for the same book. Influenced by repeated exposure, this time she clicks the ad and is forwarded to the publisher's Web site.
- Engagement and consideration, on brand Web sites
  Arriving at the publisher's Web site, she finds detailed descriptions, reviews, and free sample chapters. With the interest in purchasing, she proceeds to checkout, only to realize that she needs to register a new account first before checking out. Feeling the extra step too cumbersome, she abandons the purchasing process and decides to check Amazon, where she already holds an Amazon Prime membership.
- Decision-making, on e-commerce platforms and through phone calls
  Landing on Amazon and entering the book name, she finds many sellers. Some offer discounts but have long delivery times, while others have faster shipping but higher prices. She takes some time on comparison and balance, considering as well sellers' ratings and reviews. She also has an additional question: whether this book includes any online lectures. She contacted the seller through Amazon messaging assistant, and it is said the response with be in 48 hours. She does not want to wait anymore and directly calls Amazon customer service to ask. After receiving a positive answer, she places the order.
- Service, on e-commerce platforms and through emails
  After receiving the book, she noticed that the access code for the online lectures is missing from the package. She attempts to resolve the issue by contacting Amazon customer service but is informed that the book was sold by a third-party

seller. She gets the suggestion to research the seller via email. Following this instruction, she sent an email with her Amazon order information and photos of the received package. Then, she received the missing code after 2 working days.

– Retention, on off-platform advertising or e-commerce platforms or emails
After purchasing, she continues to receive promotional ads for the same book everywhere, as those external advertising systems cannot know her purchase history. It makes her annoyed. Additionally, the seller provides her with a discount coupon for their Amazon store, but she has little incentive to return soon.

In the purchasing journey above, Emma interacts with at least *six* different platforms or channels: LinkedIn, Google, the publisher's Web site, Amazon, phone calls, and emails. Notably, we use the book—a standardized product—to illustrate the customer journey in a relatively simple way. If considering non-standardized products, such as education services, the whole journey will be even more complex, with additional steps for evaluation, comparison, decision-making, and long-term continuous service. Based on this traditional model, before 5G was launched, it was impractical for SierEDU to offer education services for professional customers through e-commerce channels. Such a fragmented and multi-touchpoint journey makes it difficult to establish trust, provide personalized pre-sales consultation, and long-term after-sales service.

This is where social commerce emerged with a solution. Social commerce brings such a fragmented e-commerce experience into an integrated one, with a full affiliate marketing feature set, transactions, payment, and order tracking. On social commerce platforms, for example, TikTok in the USA and Douyin in China, the entire customer journey is completed within a single platform. Also, with live-stream selling on mobile devices, it enables the customers to make purchasing decisions more quickly with trust and enjoy the embedded after-sales service whenever they need. Furthermore, personalized recommendations, based on historical data and social relations, ensure a smoother customer experience and enhance customer loyalty.

14.2.2 Influencer-Led Consumer Decision-Making in Social Commerce

Social commerce integrates elements of social media and e-commerce, but it also creates something fundamentally new. The abovementioned affiliate marketing is driven by influencers, who form the core of the social commerce ecosystem. Rather than customers actively searching for products or clicking on-site/off-site advertisements, today, influencers guide purchasing decisions through trust-based recommendations aimed at their followers [7]. One key transaction format led by influencers is live-stream selling, which is the most direct and with the highest conversion rate.

Live-stream selling emphasizes scenario-based demand activation, where influencers vividly present real-life contexts and directly address customer pain points. It enhances emotional resonance, shortens decision-making time, and creates more instant purchasing behaviors, primarily through mobile devices. Starting from 5G launched and accelerated significantly by COVID-19, live-stream e-commerce experienced explosive growth in the first half of 2020, from fast-moving consumer goods (FMCG) categories such as cosmetics to travel, financial services, and education. According to AliResearch (Alibaba's research institute) and KPMG's joint report [5], in those six months in 2020, over 10 million live-streaming sessions were conducted across China, with more than 400,000 active influencers, over 50 billion cumulative views, and more than 20 million products listed for sale.

14.3 How Influencers Lead the Closed Loop of Social Commerce

Social commerce operates as a B2C (business-to-consumer) model. In the context of education, the "B" represents educators, while the "C" refers to students. After examining the behavioral shifts on the consumer side and understanding how social commerce emerges, we now turn our attention to the seller's, specifically SierEDU's, perspective.

14.3.1 Closing the Data Loop and Enabling Traceable Marketing Investments

In the e-commerce journey, the fragmented experience perceived by customers is not merely a matter of inconvenience; for business sellers, it poses an even tougher and more critical challenge—the inability to monitor, control, and close the data loop.

Figure 14.1 shows that customers transit between platforms within one purchase process: discovery and awareness on Google, engagement and consideration on the seller's independent Web site built upon Shopify, decision-making on Amazon, after-sales service through phone calls, and retention via emails. The data is lost between each transition in this open loop. Sellers are unable to track the full purchasing process, nor establish a clear attribution between marketing efforts and final transactions of each customer. Although sellers can see the overall marketing Return on Investment (ROI) metrics, they lack customer-level or channel-level ROI measurement. In addition, recent changes in privacy regulations have further reduced the effectiveness of off-site ad tracking. Without such precise data, sellers encounter difficulties in optimizing marketing strategies or allocating budgets efficiently.

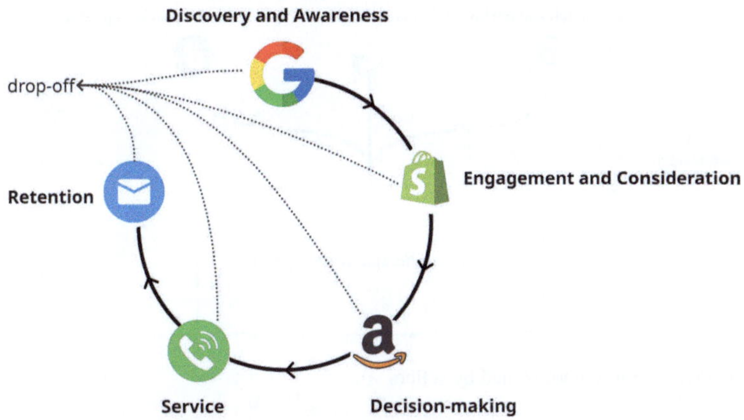

Fig. 14.1 Open-Loop in E-Commerce Journeys

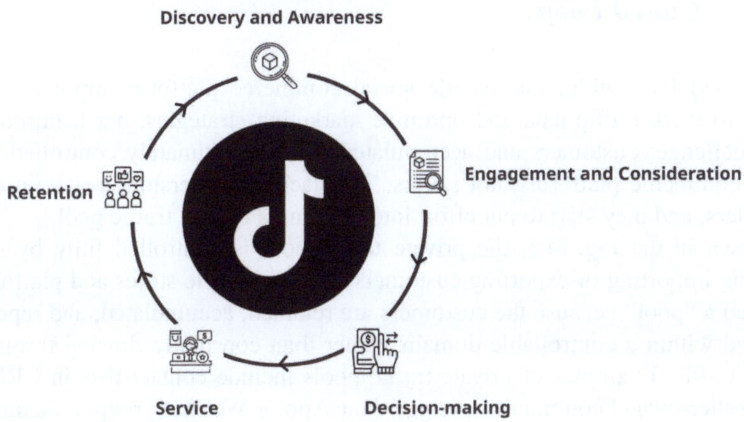

Fig. 14.2 Closed loop in social commerce platforms

Social commerce is closing the loop in Fig. 14.1. As illustrated in Fig. 14.2, social commerce platforms, such as the current TikTok, integrate the whole journey into a unified closed loop in their platform, with continuous data flow. TikTok, practically through its counterpart DouYin for China, has successfully implemented the closed loop, while still a large number of social commerce platforms remain only partially closed—better than e-commerce's open loop, but still some parts are missing. For example, Meta has been accelerating its transition toward a closed loop across Facebook and Instagram since 2023. Beginning on April 24, 2024, Meta will make the in-site checkout feature with Facebook and Instagram mandatory for all US sellers; the payment must be completed there rather than anywhere outside their platforms [2].

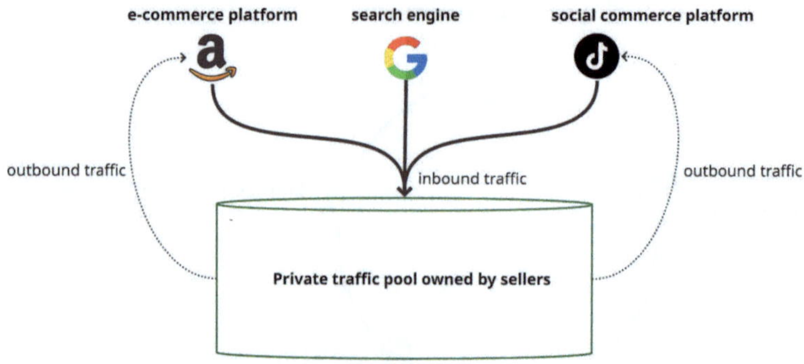

Fig. 14.3 Private traffic pool owned by sellers

14.3.2 Building Private Traffic Pools and Breaking Free from Closed Loops

The closed loop within one single social commerce platform improves sellers' ability to track traffic data and optimize marketing strategies, but it introduces a new challenge: customers and accumulated data are ultimately controlled by the social commerce platforms, not sellers. This lack of ownership creates insecurity for sellers, and they start to put effort into building a private traffic pool.

Shown in the Fig. 14.3, the private traffic pool is controlled fully by sellers, allowing importing or exporting customers across multiple stores and platforms. It is called a "pool" because the customers are retained, accumulated, and repeatedly engaged within a controllable domain, rather than constantly flowing through the public traffic. Examples of private traffic pools include contact lists in CRM systems, seller-owned communities (e.g., WhatsApp or WeChat groups), membership programs, seller-owned apps or Web sites, etc. In contrast, public ones refer to algorithm-driven exposure like Amazon search results, Instagram's Explore feed, or TikTok's For You page. The core difference between private and public traffic lies in whether sellers can reach the same group of people repeatedly without costs.

14.3.3 Influencers as the Trust Engine of Private Traffic Pools

Influencers help sellers build private traffic pools, and sellers pay them based on marketing results. They act as bridges between public and private traffic, as well as anchors within private traffic pools to retain customers over the long term.

As bridges, influencers guide followers or customers to join their private communities, such as groups of instant messaging apps. In doing so, the one-way broadcast of public traffic is transformed into bidirectional interaction. Customers may enter the private communities either before purchase to seek advice or assess credibility or after purchase to access repeat-purchase incentives or share user experiences. Despite the enclosed nature of private traffic pools, a degree of member flow ability still exists.

Influencers not only attract new people joining their pools but also need to pay attention to the outflow management. They need to ensure that inflow exceeds outflow, sustaining overall private traffic growth. While initial entry is typically driven by the trust in influencers, it is a long-term social trust among the whole community of members. In addition to the trust built by influencers, experience sharing, peer recommendation, and emotional resonance also reinforce people's willingness to stay in the private traffic pools.

14.4 Educators Were Influencers Before It Was Cool

Influencer-led social commerce offers a potential entry point for SierEDU. Through years of experience in professional education before establishing SierEDU, the founders have unintentionally become influential figures, building social media accounts followed and trusted by thousands of professionals and students.

14.4.1 Internal Proof of the Influencer-Educator Model

Weibo, referred to as "China's X (formerly Twitter)," is one of the most influential social media platforms in China. As of May 19, 2025, SierEDU's official Weibo account had 287,700 followers, listed first in Fig. 14.4; the rest of the accounts are all top educators from SierEDU. In addition to its official account, SierEDU's network of influencer-educators also maintains their individual Weibo accounts, collectively amassing over 7.582 million followers.

When SierEDU was founded with five co-founders in 2019, three of them had already accumulated a follower base through years of teaching experience, while the other two had no such background. Both the current CEO of SierEDU, Jinnan Guo, and the second author of this report, Yu Cui, were part of the founding team, with Jinnan having teaching experience and Yu starting with none. From the very beginning, SierEDU developed and validated a model within its founding team, where experienced influencer-educators mentored and cultivated new ones. This approach was first proven effective among the five co-founders and later extended to the newly recruited teachers. As illustrated in Fig. 14.4, Yu began building his follower base from scratch in 2019 and has become a recognized influencer with 480,900 followers on Weibo as of May 2025.

The founding members of SierEDU have balanced their multiple roles as entrepreneurs, educators, and influencers. On January 3, 2025, during SierEDU's annual public event, CEO Jinnan Guo announced that he would step back from the role of educator and focus fully on company management. By that time, SierEDU

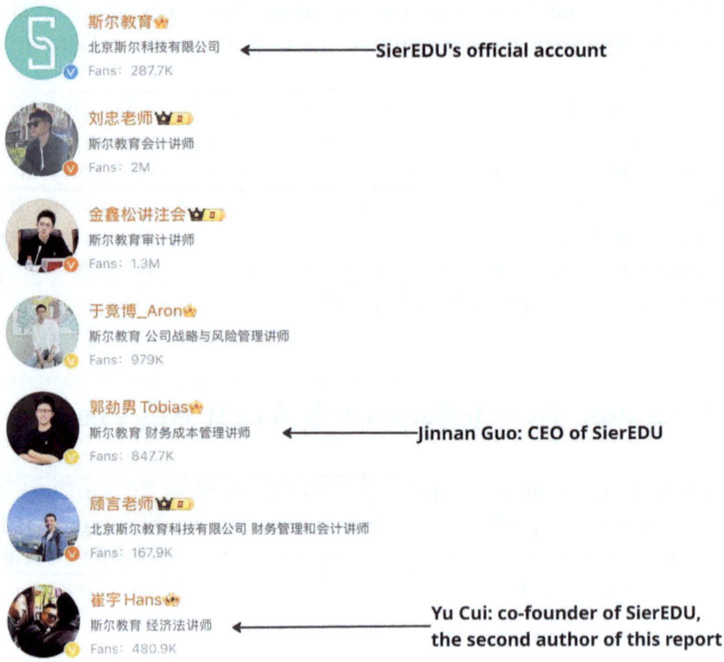

Fig. 14.4 Number of followers for selected Weibo accounts affiliated with SierEDU, as of May 2025

had already grown significantly—from the original five co-founders to hundreds of employees. This decision was driven by two main considerations. First, more and more new influencer-educators in SierEDU had emerged, some of them receiving even higher customer satisfaction ratings than Jinnan himself. Second, he worried that his continued presence in teaching might hold back younger teachers' career development and limit their growth.

Despite stepping away from educational activities, Jinnan's public influence in the field of finance and accounting professional education remains strong. As shown in Fig. 14.4, his Weibo account continues to attract followers, reaching 847,700 followers by May of 2025.

14.4.2 Scaling the Social Commerce Loop of Influencer-Educators

Within the influencer-educator model, teachers at SierEDU are involved in the entire social commerce loop—from attracting through live-stream sessions to teaching material development, live-stream course delivery, community engagement, and after-class Q&A. In SierEDU's early stage, the founding members participated in each step of the process in such a loop.

With a fast-growing customer base, nearly tens of thousands of cumulative paid customers by 2021, as well as SierEDU's continued commitment to live-stream teaching rather than pre-recorded courses, it becomes tough for SierEDU's founders to manage the full social commerce loop on their own. To maintain the service quality while customer number growing, they hire more full-time and contract-bound teachers for training under the influencer-educator model. Rather than recruiting educators with existing influence from the market, SierEDU focuses on cultivating its own influencer-educators. One reason is that high-profile educators who are easily poached may also leave just as easily. More importantly, SierEDU considers the cultivating process and capability as a core of its long-term competitive advantages.

Besides, the founders decided to have a more structured internal division of labor. The same as other social commerce businesses, SierEDU employs customer service representatives. Moreover, they also introduced new roles such as course consultants, study planners, and class mentors. These roles replicate the offline sales and service functions in the traditional education field within a social commerce environment.

14.5 Private Traffic Ecosystem Is Where the Real Game Happens

As the role of influence-educators became increasingly central to SierEDU's identity and operations, its founders are also clear that personal influence alone is not enough to support long-term business growth. In Sect. 14.2.1, we have discussed how social commerce platforms are increasingly evolving toward full closed-loop ecosystems. As a seller on those platforms, SierEDU has access to a vast amount of platform-generated data, but it doesn't own or control such data. Besides the ownership, changes in platform algorithms and politics could also impact SierEDU's accessibility of data stored in those social commerce platforms. As a result, in early 2021, SierEDU's founders decided to build their own app (both mobile and laptop versions) for their textbook products and educational service delivery, also serving as a centralized private traffic pool. For a founding team without software technical backgrounds, building a software application and corresponding backend systems posed significant challenges. To lead this effort, they brought in a CTO with deep experience in large-scale platform development and AI. Under this new technical leadership, an in-house software development team was formed and built one customer-end app (SierEDU App) and around ten backend systems for internal operation. The three most important backend ones are listed below:

- Teaching and Research System, supporting the standardized development and delivery of both course and book content

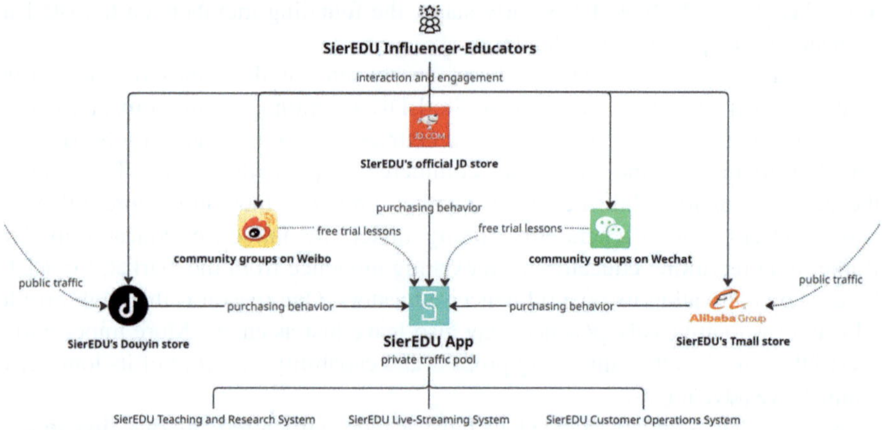

Fig. 14.5 SierEDU's app-centered private traffic ecosystem

- Live-streaming System, enabling a seamless switch from generic third-party live-streaming tools to a self-developed scenario-based system
- Customer Operations System, tracking each customer's learning progress and providing data-driven personalized support

Figure 14.5 presents SierEDU's private traffic ecosystem, with its customer-end SierEDU App at the center. Influencer-educators serve as the initial point of contact; meanwhile, social commerce platforms such as Douyin and Tmall also bring public traffic. Through trusted interactions with influencer-educators, potential customers are directed either to community groups or toward social commerce storefronts. Within these community groups, leads continue communicating with influencers, being encouraged to download the SierEDU App and attend free live trial lessons. On those social commerce platforms, once a purchase is made, customers transition from the closed-loop social commerce into the SierEDU App, where they receive ongoing services, such as planning their study and participating in live-stream lectures. Customers at all stages of their learning journey, from trial to repeat purchase, are aggregated within one app, the SierEDU App. Here, they can access free trial sessions, enroll in a course or purchase textbooks, attend live-stream lectures, engage in Q&A, complete mock exams, etc. Several internal backend systems support such an integrated user experience, among which the Teaching and Research System, the Customer Operations System, and the Live-Streaming System are the most representative.

While Fig. 14.5 outlines the main components and relationships of SierEDU's private traffic ecosystem, the actual operational environment is far more dynamic and complex, continuously evolving in response to user behaviors, platform changes, and strategic decisions.

14.6 Private Traffic as the Foundation for AI Exploration

When SierEDU established its in-house software development team in 2021, its founders had already sensed that a wave of AI-driven transformation was approaching. Their awareness was largely shaped by observing leading players in the whole online education industry, such as one of the biggest unicorns, VIPKID [3] in the K12 (from kindergarten to 12th grade) market. VIPKID began incubating AI-powered teaching tools as early as 2018 and launched an AI teaching assistant in 2019. Therefore, after the SierEDU App was launched and stable for a few months, the SierEDU founding team began to explore AI-powered features in 2022. By the end of that year, they introduced the first AI grading feature in the finance and accounting education sector. Over the next two years, SierEDU continued to develop more AI features, such as AI subtitles and AI Q&A. All these AI-powered features are integrated into SierEDU's private traffic pool, SierEDU App.

In the following, we illustrate three representative scenarios of SierEDU's AI features, showing how AI exploration happens in SierEDU.

14.6.1 AI Grading in 2022: A Lesson in High-Concurrency Scenario

For many SierEDU's customers preparing for finance and accounting professional exams, attending mock tests is a key approach for assessing their learning progress and exam readiness. There are lots of subjective questions in these exams. *As examinees, they want to know whether their written answers in mock exams would actually earn marks under official grading standards and why so that they can identify weaknesses and improve before the real exam comes.*

Before the AI grading feature, the SierEDU App provided customers with standard answers and scoring rubrics, allowing them to self-grade. However, the participation interest is really low, and many customers lack the motivation to do self-grading. Moreover, compared with experts' grading results, those who score themselves have only around a 50% accuracy rate. They always tend to overestimate their scores, leading to overly optimistic judgments about their learning progress and more failures in the real exams.

In late 2022, SierEDU introduced the AI grading feature, embedded within the SierEDU App. Based on domain-specific scoring rubrics and historical experts' grading data, it delivers more reliable and accurate results than self-grading, within 5-minute responding time and over 90% accuracy rate. While the AI grading significantly improved user experience and the accuracy of mock test results, it brought infrastructure and cost challenges for SierEDU.

Unlike general-purpose AI tools with relatively stable traffic, this AI grading feature is tightly coupled with exam seasons. When the exam data is approaching, tens of thousands of customers submit answers simultaneously, causing a sudden data peak, and the response time is far more than the promised 5 minutes. It creates a dilemma: allocating enough servers to meet the concurrency requirements in the peak time but at a higher cost and with idle capacity during off-peak non-exam seasons or optimizing the resources based on average usages and risking customers' dissatisfaction.

The deployment of the first AI feature led SierEDU's founders to start thinking about how to make AI at the platform level and general-purpose scenarios, rather than a vertical scenario breakthrough. Such horizontal general scenarios need to be highly reusable, contributing to the foundational capability of the SierEDU app.

14.6.2 AI Subtitles in 2023: Improving Usability, But Not Monetization

Back in 2019, when SierEDU first launched, it offered subtitles across all courses. The goal was straightforward: to help learners better comprehend new finance or accounting terminology and make course content easier to review. Although this feature was welcomed by customers, it was soon taken offline. The reason was not a lack of demand but a lack of scalability. The subtitles correction required heavy manual review and correction. As a startup, the operational cost of making accurate subtitles became unaffordable for SierEDU, yet the need never disappeared. *As working people who attend the live-stream lecture during daily commuting, they want accurate subtitles for their courses, so that they can follow the content and understand new terms better despite the background noise on the bus.* Studying in noisy public environments on mobile devices is a common scenario for SierEDU, as over 80% of its customers are working people.

In 2023, aiming for a more general AI feature, SierEDU reintroduced subtitles. This time, it is powered by AI and trained on SierEDU's own materials with minimal human labor. The AI subtitle feature improves user experience with a small cost and achieves a platform-level AI feature. But it did not directly attract new customers or generate revenue. It makes the SierEDU App more user-friendly, but not more competitive and marketable.

14.6.3 AI Q&A in 2024: Second, Not Hours for Customers

Real-time interaction has always been one of SierEDU's core strengths. Insisting on live-stream lectures provides customers with opportunities to ask questions and get answers right away. However, not all customers can attend live sessions. Also, for those who watch the recording for review purposes, the Q&A process was complex for them. *As asynchronous learners relying on lecture replays, they want to ask questions in context, without explaining much where they get stuck, so that they can get fast and accurate help.*

Before AI was introduced in Q&A session, customers had to jump to a separate Q&A section in the SierEDU App and describe both context and question using texts and images. The average turnaround time for receiving answers was within 24 hours. For customers who asked questions, such a lad often reduced their motivation to ask questions again; for educators, answering questions was really time-consuming.

To address this for both customers' and educators' ends, SierEDU launched an AI Q&A feature directly integrated into both live-stream lectures and after-lecture exercise pages. Now, wherever the customer encounters confusion, they describe the questions and submit them on those pages, without explaining in which course or which part they have these questions. AI Q&A feature captures the relevant context info as well as customers' historical learning data to analyze the questions and generate answers in 30 seconds. If the proposed questions contain only text, without images, the response time is only 10 seconds on average.

Making a 24-hour response time to seconds, AI Q&A dramatically improves user experience and learning results for existing customers while attracting more trials. Importantly, speed did not come at the cost of accuracy. In the first month after launching this feature, only 10% of the questions were transferred back to educators, meaning 90% were resolved without human intervention. Moreover, user satisfaction scores for AI responses averaged 3.76 out of 4, close to the historical 3.8 score from educators' manual responses.

14.7 Strategic Reflection on the First Five Years of SierEDU

From its inception, SierEDU has been navigating the finance and accounting professional education field by layering one strategic insight atop another. Through the exploitation of accumulated influence through founders' prior educational experience, it began by capitalizing on the rise of 5G-enable social commerce and influencer-driven economics. While many sellers on social commerce platforms remained confined within closed loops, SierEDU broke through by investing in its own app, turning public traffic into private traffic pools. With these foundations in place, SierEDU moved quickly into AI exploration, launching an AI-powered feature at a very early stage.

None of this exploitation and exploration would have been possible without the founders' mindset, a software-native orientation emphasizing modularity, standardization, user-centricity, rapid iteration, and readiness to change.

14.7.1 Software Mindset as the Hidden Engine for the Founding Team

SierEDU's founders have been trying to make traditional non-standardized education services into standardized content from the establishment. Although for many people AI technology was just a recent breakthrough, the founders are quite clear that the groundwork for AI features had been laid since day one.

It may seem that SierEDU built AI features quickly and smoothly. But noted by its founders, the truth is that they have been working on standardizing all educational content from the very beginning. The general AI model on the market is difficult to deal with domain-specific financial exams. Take SierEDU's AI Q&A feature as an example; it was trained on millions of standardized user queries accumulated across multiple exam sessions. Each of these queries has been cleaned, rephrased, and tagged by educators according to SierEDU's internal taxonomy, well before AI emerged. By treating every interaction between teacher and student as data, SierEDU built a rich training corpus. Such a dataset is not only used for AI model training but also for the improvement of human-delivered content, such as textbooks and lectures.

Taking users as the center also indicated SierEDU's software mindset. Beyond the user-driven iterations within the SierEDU App, their commitment to user centricity has extended to both digital and physical product lines. For example, when releasing new AI features, they continue to monitor user satisfaction scores. Also, in their offline textbooks publishing business, SierEDU applied the same user-centered philosophy; the recent revisions of its flagship accounting textbook incorporated feedback from over 6,500 customers.

While operating in a fast-paced software market driven by rapid iteration, SierEDU's team remains both the "fast logic" of software and the "slow logic" of education, focusing on agile development as well as long-term accumulation of educational capability and customer trust.

14.7.2 Dynamic Balance Between Exploitation and Exploration

In today's fast-evolving technology and more complex business environment, the ability to balance exploitation and exploration, also called organizational ambidexterity, has become a strategic imperative for startups from their establishment. In the past, early-stage startups could rely on one single successful innovation to gain momentum. Such a breakthrough in exploration would be transformed into a stable exploitation model, supporting the startup through the survival phase till maturity.

However, the current pace of change demands more. For today's startups, continuous innovation and continuous exploitation are no longer optional; rather, the dynamic balance between them is crucial for survival. Recognizing this dynamic process, SierEDU's founding team, who remain the current core management, proposed the concept of effective innovation from a strategic perspective. It refers to the breakthrough that delivers business outcomes and lays the foundation for following exploitation, avoiding pursuing novelty for its own sake, wasting resources, or disconnecting from customers. Each effective innovation brings the foundation for the next business exploitation.

In 2024, an empirical article on Harvard Business Review analyzed 35 attempts at breakthrough innovation in large enterprises [8]. It suggests that the strategic intents behind exploitation should be cost and profit, while exploration should aim for innovation and growth. Yet in SierEDU's experience, this line is far less clear.

During exploitation, innovation continues. For example, SierEDU strategically leveraged the existing influence of its educators to attract customers and drive sales, establishing the new influencer-educator model. During exploration, cost optimization remains a strategic focus. For example, novel AI grading, subtitle, and Q&A features were designed to reduce internal operational costs and free up human resources. In this sense, the boundaries between exploitation and exploration blur.

Moreover, ambidexterity in startups tends to concentrate in the founding team itself, rather than separate departments. At SierEDU, every lead has consistently held multiple roles. Some of them are exploitative, such as an educator or influencer, while others are exploratory, such as a software product owner or community operation expert.

Especially, such ambidextrous roles are mostly embodied in one of SierEDU's leaders, Yu Cui, who is also the second author of this report. He has consistently operated at both exploitative and explorative businesses, helping refine internal capabilities while driving new opportunities. He brings the ambidextrous idea and topic to the management level, leading strategic decision-making.

14.7.3 Risks and Ongoing Challenges

While SierEdu's success in the first five years offers many positive insights, we have to admit that several underlying risks and unresolved challenges remain. The two prominent issues are platform dependency and regulation compliance. Although owning its private traffic pool, SierEDU's current business model still highly relies on social commerce platforms, from new customer acquisition to repeat purchasing. Providing AI-powered education services has not been regulated in China yet, as well as most other countries, but the discussion of regulations in AI-related software development has started. Especially for the sectors that needed to be regulated, such as medical care, education, banking, etc., regulation compliance will be mandatory in the following years and impact the current business model.

14.8 What's Next

From educators to entrepreneurs, the founders of SierEDU have undergone a complete transformation. Lacking software backgrounds was never a limitation for them, because software is more than a delivery format but always a way of thinking. Such an agile mindset becomes the core strategic value for SierEDU.

Now, SierEDU defies simple labels. It can be regarded as an online education company, a software company, an e-commerce company, or more. To its leadership, this ambiguity opens more future possibilities. In the future, SierEDU may expand into new verticals in professional education, such as law or healthcare; may build an SaaS platform and evolve into a B2B service, providing training to auditing companies; or may apply the influencer-led social commerce to new product categories, taking advantage of the existing supply chain. After 5G and AI, 6G and agentic AI are approaching. For SierEDU, this will not change their core strategic principle—under ambidextrous leadership, keeping effective innovation at a pace that matches or exceeds the rate of external change.

14.9 Recommendations for Entrepreneurs

Based on this five-year journey and our own reflection, we distill the following actionable insights for practitioners, especially entrepreneurs without a technical background, who are or consider presuming ambidexterity.

- **Software business can begin with a mindset, not just technical skills.** Success in software-intensive startups requires founders' agile thinking, user-centric design, and continuous innovation, more than technical expertise. Software business is a mindset more than a technical skill.
- **Entrepreneurs must stay curious and sensitive to emerging patterns.** Remain alert to technological enablers, behavioral shifts, and emerging business models. Innovation often comes not from full invention but from recognizing and adapting to changes.
- **Startups' internal knowledge accumulation, modulization, and standardization should start on day one.** Knowledge management is not only essential for mature companies but also a long-term foundation for startups' scalability and innovation. Even in the earliest phase of a startup when facing serious survival problems, internal knowledge development should not be ignored.
- **Pursue effective innovation instead of innovation for its own sake.** Prioritize innovations that deliver tangible business or customer value. Avoid chasing trends or hype without clear strategic alignment.
- **Startup ambidexterity is rooted in leadership, nowhere else.** The balance between exploration and exploitation lies within founders, who must simultaneously foresee the future and survive the present.

Acknowledgments This research was funded by the Business Finland project 6G Bridge—6G software for extremely distributed and heterogeneous massive networks of connected devices (8516/31/2022)—and supported by FAST, the Finnish Software Engineering Doctoral Research Network, funded by the Ministry of Education and Culture, Finland.

References

1. Baghdadi, Y.: A framework for social commerce design. Inf. Syst. **60**, 95–113 (2016)
2. Ecwid Support: Checkout methods for Facebook and Instagram shops (2024). https://support.ecwid.com/hc/en-us/articles/10123681731100-Checkout-methods-for-Facebook-and-Instagram-Shops. Meta changed checkout methods starting April 24, 2024
3. EdTech China: How vipkid became the biggest unicorn in China's fiercely competitive edtech market (2020). https://edtechchina.medium.com/how-vipkid-became-the-biggest-unicorn-in-chinas-fiercely-competitive-edtech-market-9969602705bd. Published on Medium
4. Forbes: Jinnan Guo - Forbes 30 under 30 Asia (2021). https://www.forbes.com/profile/guo-jinnan/?list=30under30-asia-consumer-technology
5. KPMG China: Live-streaming e-commerce: Towards a trillion market (2020). https://assets.kpmg.com/content/dam/kpmg/cn/pdf/zh/2020/10/live-streaming-e-commerce-towards-trillion-market.pdf
6. KPMG International: Towards seamless commerce (2022). https://assets.kpmg.com/content/dam/kpmgsites/xx/pdf/2022/02/towards-seamless-commerce.pdf
7. Lin, X., Wang, X.: Towards a model of social commerce: improving the effectiveness of e-commerce through leveraging social media tools based on consumers' dual roles. Eur. J. Inf. Syst. **32**(5), 782–799 (2023)
8. O Reilly, C.A., Tushman, M.L.: The ambidextrous organization. Harvard Bus. Rev. **82**(4), 74–83 (2004)
9. Oyeniran, C., Adewusi, A.O., Adeleke, A.G., Akwawa, L.A., Azubuko, C.F.: 5g technology and its impact on software engineering: new opportunities for mobile applications. Comput. Sci. IT Res. J. **4**(3), 562–576 (2023)
10. Prescott, M.B.: Diffusion of innovation theory: borrowings, extensions, and modifications from it researchers. ACM SIGMIS Database DATABASE Adv. Inf. Syst. **26**(2–3), 16–19 (1995)
11. Wang, X., Edison, H., Bajwa, S.S., Giardino, C., Abrahamsson, P.: Key challenges in software startups across life cycle stages. In: Agile Processes, in Software Engineering, and Extreme Programming: 17th International Conference, XP 2016, Edinburgh, May 24–27, 2016, Proceedings 17, pp. 169–182. Springer International Publishing (2016)

Chapter 15
Digital Health Entrepreneurship: A Founder's Perspective on Ecosystem-Supported Growth

Guido Giunti, Sharon Guardado, and Nirnaya Tripathi

Abstract Health-tech startups are a type of software startup that uses advanced technologies to develop personalized health solutions for digital health. However, they face challenges such as high failure rates, lack of investor trust, and insufficient market demand. This study aims to explore how the ecosystem influences the development of mHealth applications in health-tech startups and to understand the critical factors contributing to their success in bringing products to market. The research employs autoethnography and archival documentation as data collection techniques. These methods are used to examine the mHealth app development process within the context of a health-tech startup and its ecosystem. The study identifies key phases in the mHealth app development process and evaluates the roles of different startup ecosystem elements in each phase. The findings reveal that ecosystem support is crucial at every stage of development, impacting the startup's ability to launch and sustain its product successfully. This study offers practical recommendations for professionals in the field and proposes directions for future research to enhance the success and sustainability of health-tech startups.

Keywords Software startup · Health-tech startups · Startup ecosystem · mHealth apps · Digital health · Entrepreneurship

G. Giunti (✉)
Faculty of Medicine, University of Oulu, Oulu, Finland

School of Medicine, Trinity College Dublin, Dublin, Ireland
e-mail: guido.giunti@oulu.fi

S. Guardado · N. Tripathi
M3S Research Unit, University of Oulu, Oulu, Finland
e-mail: Sharon.GuardadoMedina@oulu.fi; Nirnaya.Tripathi@oulu.fi

N. Tripathi et al. (eds.), *Advances in Software Startups*,
https://doi.org/10.1007/978-3-032-04294-1_15

15.1 Introduction

Health-tech startups are a type of software startup that are transforming healthcare by utilizing advanced software technologies to create personalized health strategies [2, 4]. There is mounting evidence for the benefits that digital health solutions can bring compared with, and complementary to, traditional in-clinic approaches [38]. The most common example of health-tech companies is perhaps those that provide mobile applications to support healthcare delivery (mHealth). Health-tech startups are pivotal in transforming the healthcare landscape and are known for addressing areas in which traditional healthcare systems may be lacking to improve efficiency and cost-effectiveness in care delivery [6, 29]. However, the journey to generate solutions that empower patients and healthcare professionals (HCPs) is not without its challenges, such as fierce competition, the ever-expanding need for more resources, and support from ecosystem stakeholders [8].

Despite the initial promise of many health-tech startups, these often shut down within their first two years. While there are as many reasons behind each failure as there are companies, a bulk of the problems seem to stem from a combination of a lack of market-fit understanding, an unsuitable team, and the inability to secure trust and long-term support from funding agencies and investors [30]. For a mHealth product to successfully enter the market, startups require a supportive ecosystem right from the conceptualization stage to the product's launch (see Fig. 15.1) [36, 37]. Specialized incubators are crucial for helping startups avoid failure, and a shortage of health-tech incubators may be a contributing factor. There is a need to understand the role of various elements of a startup ecosystem in shaping a health-tech startup's journey and its product development process [36]. The current situation led us to consider the research question (RQ): "How do the different elements of a startup ecosystem influence the development of mHealth products in health-tech startups?"

15.2 State of the Art

Health-tech startups, a booming sector, are reshaping healthcare by employing breakthrough technologies to improve care and reduce costs [2, 4, 6]. These solutions allow the use of data analytics to provide tailored, data-driven health interventions [36]. In fact, Fortune Business Insights projects the Compound Annual Growth Rate (CAGR) of the digital health market to grow 23.3% from 2023 to 2030, with the market expected to grow from USD 452.79 billion in 2023 to USD 1,965.30 billion by 2030 [14].

The potential of digital health and mHealth solutions is enormous and yet the integration of these technologies into clinical pathways remains an ongoing challenge [26]. One of the challenges is failing to properly meet users' needs, as over 20% of all apps are abandoned after only a single use [31, 35], raising the

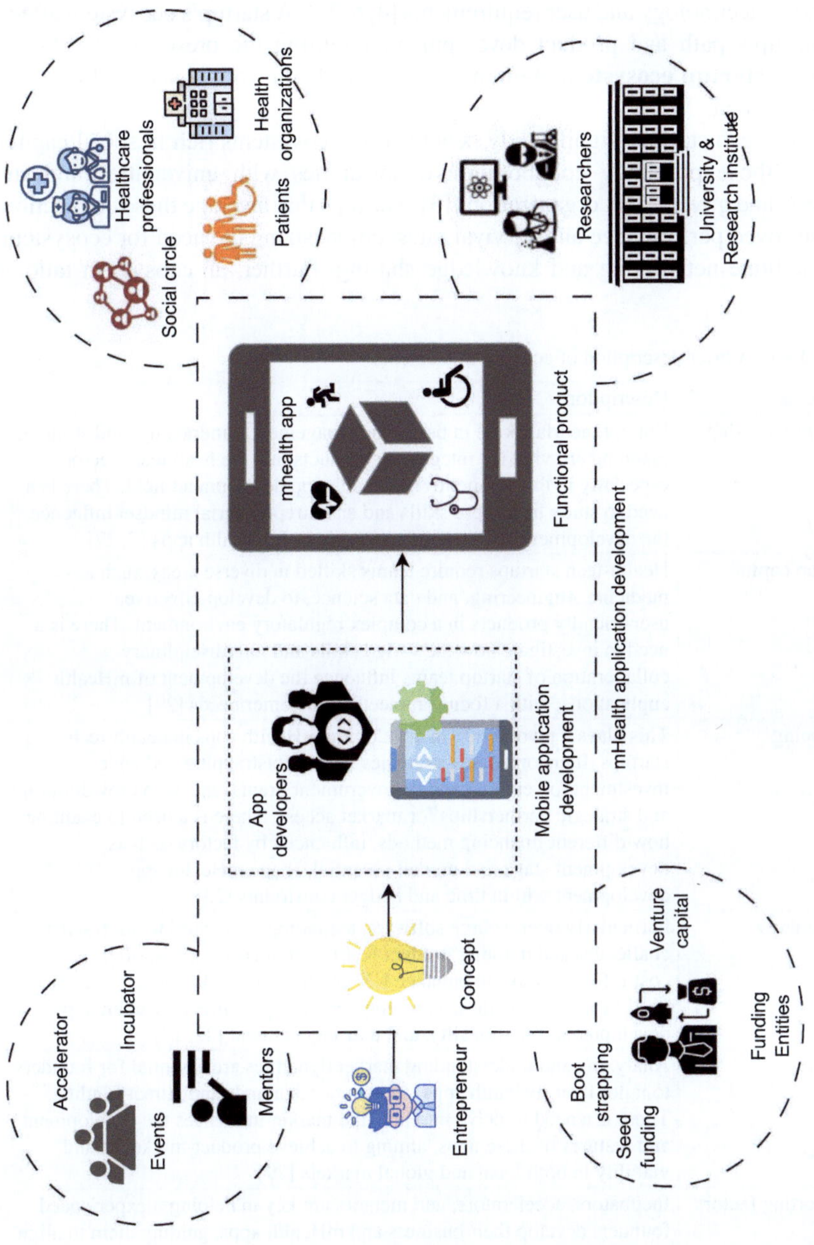

Fig. 15.1 mHealth app development in a health-tech startup and its ecosystem stakeholders

stakes for mHealth solutions. Further, these solutions must provide evidence-based benefits and be safe to use. Startups in this field are in constant pursuit of funding, attempting to form partnerships, and trying to adapt to the dynamic landscape of healthcare technology and user requirements [4, 6, 34]. A startup's ecosystem affects the startup's path and product development, requiring the presence of different nurturing **startup ecosystem elements** (see Table 15.1) from conceptualization to product launch.

Health-tech startups significantly benefit from ecosystems rich in social capital, such as those providing collaboration opportunities with universities, industry partners, and government organizations [3]. Startups that leverage these connections see improved performance and survival rates, emphasizing the need for ecosystems that facilitate networking and knowledge sharing. Further, an ecosystem tailored

Table 15.1 A brief description of ecosystem elements

Elements	Descriptions
Entrepreneurship	Entrepreneurial skills in business management, fundraising, and strategic planning are vital for integrating products into the healthcare sector, especially in the competitive mHealth app development field. There is a need to study how these skills and an entrepreneurial mindset influence the development and customer reception of mHealth apps [7, 27]
Human capital	Health-tech startups require teams skilled in diverse areas, such as medicine, engineering, and data science, to develop effective, user-friendly products in a complex regulatory environment. There is a need to investigate how the varied skills and interdisciplinary collaboration of startup teams influence the development of mHealth applications, with a focus on meeting customer needs [29]
Financing	This plays a pivotal role in developing mHealth apps in health-tech startups. It encompasses strategies from bootstrapping and angel investment to venture capital, government grants, and even crowdfunding and strategic partnerships for market access. There is a need to examine how different financing methods, influenced by factors such as development stage and market potential, shape mHealth app development within time and budget constraints [23]
Technology	Particularly open-source software, technology is central to addressing challenges and defining product features in mHealth apps, offering cost-effective ways to enhance UX and hasten development. There is a need to assess how these emerging technologies affect mHealth apps' development, functionality, and user engagement [22, 27]
Market	Analyzing and understanding market dynamics are essential for founders to tailor their mHealth apps to customer demands and attract funding. There is a need to delve into how the market influences the development and features of these apps, aiming to achieve product-market fit and viability in both local and global markets [29]
Supporting factors	Incubators, accelerators, and mentors are key in helping inexperienced founders develop their business and mHealth apps, guiding them to align products with market demands. Thus, there is a need to investigate the impact of these supporting entities on the development of mHealth apps, focusing on young and emerging founders

to address healthcare requirements can bridge gaps, such as connecting startups with healthcare providers and facilitating the technical validation of innovations, which is crucial for market penetration [5]. Access to robust digital infrastructure and a diversity of support agents, such as technology providers and R&D labs, are essential for health-tech innovation [32]. Ecosystems that offer these resources help health-tech startups stay competitive by enabling scalable solutions and promoting continuous technological advancement.

15.3 Research Method

The research employed a mixed-methods approach centered on DTx Co, a health-tech spin-off from Oulu, Finland, which specializes in developing digital health solutions for chronic disease management. The case focused particularly on More Stamina,[1] an mHealth application designed to aid people with multiple sclerosis (MS) in managing fatigue. Data collection was carried out through autoethnography—leveraging the personal experiences of the company's CEO—and an in-depth review of archival documentation from DTx Co's internal repositories. These materials included development logs, media reports, and outputs from tools such as Confluence and Jira. The archival evidence was supplemented by scientific publications that tracked the design and development journey of the More Stamina app [18, 19, 21].

Autoethnography

Autoethnography uses personal experience ("auto") to interpret and describe ("graphy") cultural beliefs, experiences, practices, and texts ("ethno") [11]. This approach has been used in software engineering studies in the past [9, 25]. In this instance, the autoethnographic method was used to understand the sociological and practical aspects underlying mHealth app development and the ecosystem roles in it, from the perspective of the CEO and leader of DTx Co.

For data analysis, thematic coding was applied to interpret the materials from both data sources, focusing on key ecosystem dimensions such as entrepreneurship, technology, market forces, support systems, finance, and human capital. The analysis followed the chronological phases of the product's evolution—conceptualization, development, and final implementation—to provide structured insights into the software development process. The study's validity was reinforced

[1] More Stamina app: https://www.morestaminaapp.com/.

by this triangulation of qualitative and documentary data, enabling both insider and evidence-based perspectives. However, the dual role of the researcher as both CEO and subject introduces potential bias despite mitigation efforts. Additionally, since the case pertains to a single Finnish startup, the broader applicability of the findings is limited, though the methodology offers a valuable lens for similar digital health innovation studies.

15.4 Findings

This section will first present an overview of DTx Co and More Stamina's development process in a chronological manner to provide context, followed by an exploration and analysis of the relevant startup ecosystem elements and how they influenced the process.

Startup Description
DTx Co's value proposition focuses on providing evidence-driven, patient-centered, effective solutions. For this purpose, it developed a design and development method that combines design thinking, agile methodologies, artificial intelligence, and behavioral change sciences. The method relies on active patient involvement early, often, and throughout the process, considering patients not as subjects but as partners, and on building a strong scientific publication base to support design and development decisions.

The organization is relatively small, with 12 team members, including a steering board group with a patient representative. DTx Co follows a lean startup approach with core activities focusing on research and software development. The development team works following the Scrum methodology, in two-week long sprints, while the research team follows a waterfall model, in which planning and execution are approached in a more sequential manner.

15.4.1 More Stamina Development

Conceptualization

The idea for the solution emerged as a combination of various factors, including need identification during DTx Co's founder's doctoral studies [16], limitations in current mHealth solutions, and market requirements. An analysis of the MS mHealth landscape revealed a significant gap in available solutions [17, 18], particularly in features related to energy and resource management and remote

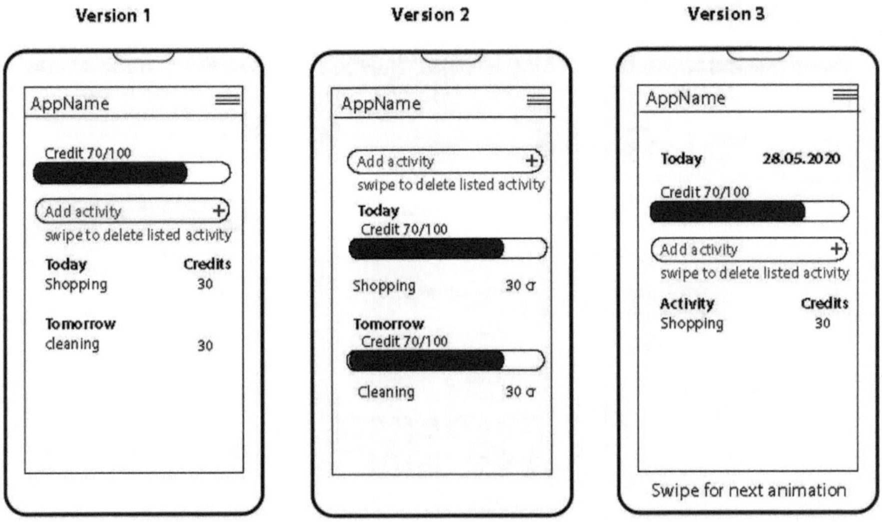

Fig. 15.2 Initial concepts of More Stamina during usability testing iteration

monitoring, underscoring the unmet needs in this area. Direct engagement with MS patients and HCPs helped understanding their specific needs to ensure solution fit [19], and co-creation sessions defined product requirements and features [15]. The conceptualization stage utilized low-fidelity mock-ups and paper prototypes to validate the hypotheses and problem-solution fit.

mHealth Design

Insights from interviews, focus groups, and co-design sessions were converted to user requirements for software development. Different iterations were tested and improved upon using Nielsen heuristics (see Fig. 15.2). Once a unique mHealth design concept that met the needs of people with MS was determined [20], steps were taken toward the creation of a working prototype. The University of Oulu Innovation Center (UIC) played a pivotal role at this stage in supporting researchers interested in commercializing their research. This support encompassed a range of activities, including courses, workshops, competitions, and events focused on entrepreneurship and idea commercialization. Additionally, mentors at UIC offered guidance on entrepreneurial aspects and provided assistance in securing funding. Eventually, a hybrid app was created through iterative collaboration between the founder and a senior full-stack software developer.

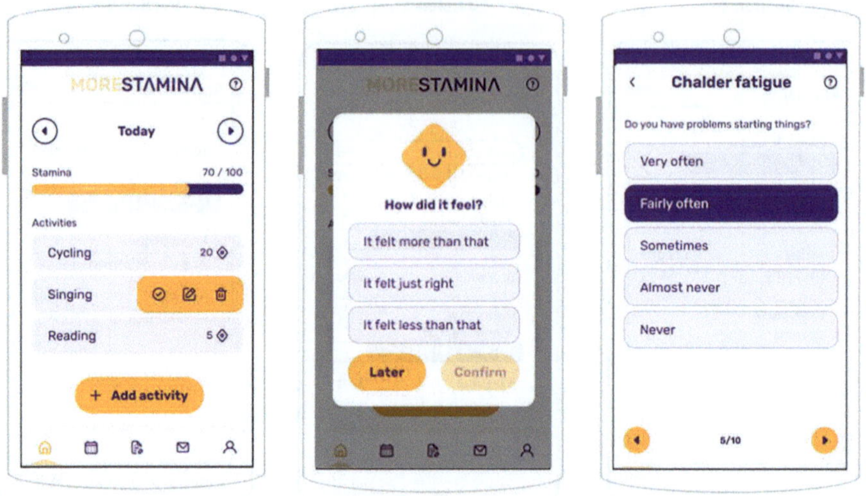

Fig. 15.3 Screenshots of the More Stamina mHealth app

Working Prototype

The team developed a functional product by prioritizing requirements based on cost, time and availability, expanding the product scope to target global MS solution needs (see Fig. 15.3). To accomplish this, the founder underwent specialized training in digital transformation, agile development, and team management to support complex product development. The organization used patient and public involvement (PPI) to ensure that the product matched expectations. PPI refers to the active engagement of patients, caregivers, and the general public in the planning, design, conduct, and dissemination of research or healthcare initiatives, ensuring that their perspectives and experiences are incorporated into decision-making processes to make outcomes more relevant and effective. More Stamina used PPI in a number of ways, from co-design partners to strategy board leadership [39]. Further, it followed strict usability standards before releasing the first product, and to take advantage of the target market. A working product was constructed using ad hoc and third-party components.

15.4.2 Ecosystem Elements Influence

Based on an analysis of the available data and the third author's experience, this section assesses the contributions of various elements, such as entrepreneurship, technology, market dynamics, support organizations, financing, and human capital, to the development of the More Stamina app.

Entrepreneurship

The development of the product concept was significantly influenced by the founder's skill set and entrepreneurial qualities. The founder is a trained HCP and accomplished researcher pursuing evidence-based solutions, with prior experience with startups in roles as employee and co-founder. This combination provided fertile ground for innovation, as an existing entrepreneurial mindset was supported with healthcare expertise. The founder's background is linked to the rigorousness of the process for validating the different stages with patients and HCPs. As the complexity of initiative and development grew, the founder participated in various entrepreneurial training and boot camps, to improve his understanding of value propositions, the business models, and other entrepreneurial frameworks to support the initiative.

Technology

The research team generated user requirements that were translated into the backlog by the product owner. The software development team used an agile development approach to incrementally add new features until a fully functional application was developed. The role of the product owner was crucial, bridging the gap between the research and development teams and translating research findings into development requirements. A cumulative flow diagram from More Stamina's Jira is shown in Fig. 15.4, representing the progress and flow of work during the period analyzed.

DTx Co developed a smartphone hybrid application that uses Node.js and React for the frontend. React is used to create a dynamic and responsive user interface, while Node.js handles the frontend's server-side logic. The backend is built with Express, a framework for building RESTful APIs, released as free and open-source

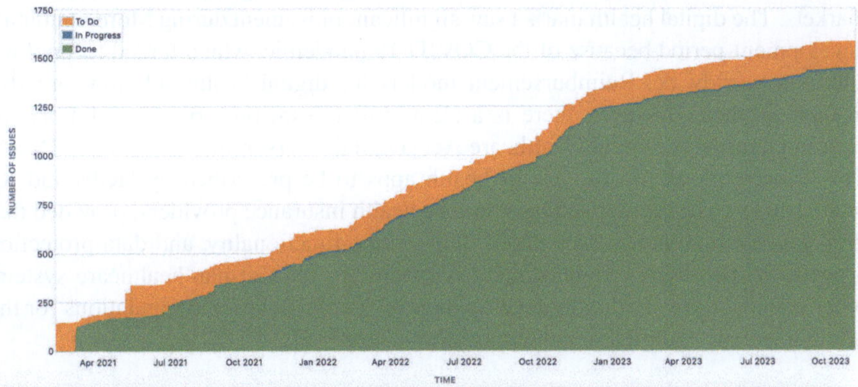

Fig. 15.4 More Stamina cumulative flow diagram, extracted from Jira reports covering the period of February 2021 to October 2023

software under the MIT License. The app integrates with OpenWeather APIs to provide up-to-date weather information and connects with Google Fit to track user activity data. This setup allows the app to function efficiently across various devices and platforms.

As mentioned earlier, development management utilizes the Atlasian suit with Jira platform for tracking issues and sprints, while software versioning used GitHub. The development strategy was determined by a combination of PPI participation and the use of early-stage health-technology assessment using the Digi-HTA framework [21]. Further, in order to provide secure data environments and high-performance computing, the More Stamina platform is hosted in Finland's CSC Center for Science,[2] a state-owned company that provides IT services, computing resources, and data management solutions to the Finnish research community.

Market

The development of More Stamina relies heavily on interactions with the market and customers, particularly HCPs and patients. Patients are crucial sources of feedback, and the healthcare sector expects standardized processes during the development phase. Therefore, the nature of the target market significantly affects the More Stamina development process. During the conceptualization stage, the founding team conducted an in-depth analysis of health apps available to consumers in app stores and found the MS mHealth landscape highly immature. They compared these apps to the needs reported by MS patients. Only 30 apps out of thousands of health-related apps were identified for MS, and the majority of these apps lacked features on energy and resource management strategies or remote monitoring options. Instead of conducting an extensive market analysis in advance to assess market fit, the founding team approached local patients and HCPs to test the concept.

Engaging in conversations with patients is crucial to refining ideas and identifying features that appeal to the widest range of target patients, HCPs, and markets. The digital health market saw significant movement during More Stamina's development period because of the COVID-19 pandemic, which forced technology adoption worldwide. Reimbursement models for digital health solutions are still in their infancy. However, there is a clear shift toward prescribable solutions, as seen in Germany's Digital Healthcare Act (Digitale-Versorgung-Gesetz) for DiGA. This framework allows the use of health apps to be prescribed by HCPs and for related costs to be reimbursed by statutory health insurance providers, provided that they pass evaluation assessments of their safety, functionality, and data protection aspects. While DiGA reimbursement is specific to the German healthcare system, other countries are starting to develop their own approaches and regulations for the reimbursement of digital health application usage [13].

[2] CSC https://csc.fi/en/.

Incubators, Mentors, and Events (Supporting Factors)

During the initial phases of development, the startup received support from various external organizations that significantly influenced the shaping of its product concepts and business strategies. Accelerators, such as UIC, played a crucial role in boosting the confidence of the team and providing essential business and prototype development knowledge through their more intensive, short-term programs that fast-tracked the startup's development. Mentors provided valuable support in areas such as business, technical, and customer discovery. This support was vital for More Stamina's development process. Furthermore, UIC provided a range of courses, workshops, competitions, and events related to entrepreneurship and idea commercialization, as well as entrepreneurial advice and support for developing and funding business ideas. They supported the funding application process and offered valuable networking opportunities by connecting founders with contacts that could aid in prototype development, a task that is often challenging to undertake independently. In collaboration with Business Finland, UIC promoted meetings with angel investors and venture capitalists, facilitating pitching and discussion. The startup team also participated in industry and entrepreneurship events, such as Slush,[3] in which they sought to validate the value proposition, obtain funding, and receive expert feedback. Mentors within these programs were invaluable in guiding prototype development and identifying potential customers for further validation.

Finances

Developing More Stamina required different types of funding at different stages of product development. Pre-seed funding played a crucial role in shaping the development of the app, especially in the early stages of the startup journey. The need discovery and requirement gathering was part of doctoral studies funded by the Horizon 2020 Connected Health Early Stage Researcher Support System Initial Training Network. The work was partly supported by FinCEAL Plus BRIDGES and the European Network for the Joint Evaluation of Connected Health Technology COST action.

The initial prototyping and usability testing were covered by two rounds of funding from a UIC accelerator through its proof-of-concept scheme. Further development and commercialization studies were funded through Business Finland's research-to-business funding scheme. This allowed the startup to offer basic salaries, enabling founders to commit full time to rapidly developing a prototype and the initial version of their product. This was later compounded with additional funding from the Finnish Innovation Fund. Venture capital firms, providing more substantial capital, can further support the transition of product development (Fig. 15.5).

[3] Slush https://slush.org/.

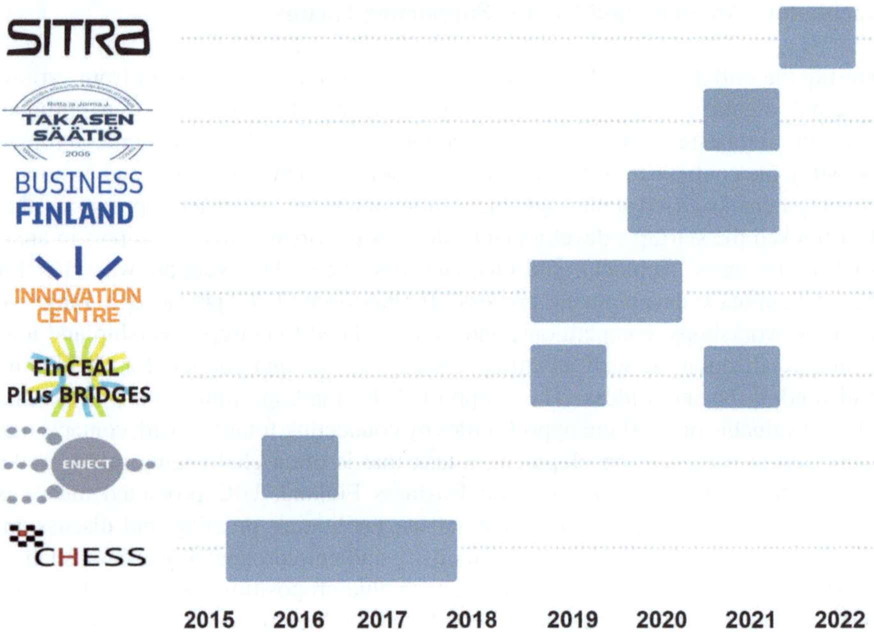

Fig. 15.5 Funding timeline

Human Capital and the Team

The founder and the team possess the required healthcare, technical, and entrepreneurship skills to craft concepts and build the More Stamina app. The diverse skill sets within the team contributed to efficient prototype development. As DTx Co consists of a diverse and multidisciplinary team, creating a shared language and group dynamic was key in reaching joint goals.

The initial work was conducted as part of a collaborative project between researchers and collaborators from different institutions. Developing the concept took place in different stages and involved collaborators across Europe. The initial team was composed of a medical doctor, a human-computer interaction designer, a software developer, two researchers, and a physiotherapist. As funding was secured, the development phase started in collaboration between the founder and a hired senior full-stack software developer. They worked iteratively to go from design sketches to a working prototype, slowly increasing and refining the features. Having a proficient technical team is crucial in this process, as each team member plays a pivotal role in developing the prototype.

Currently, DTx Co is a relatively small multidisciplinary team composed of medical doctors, psychologists, software engineers, interaction designers, information systems specialists, UX designers, research assistants, and business developers. DTx Co also has a steering group board and a PPI acting as a strategic member who participates in strategic planning and decision-making. Recruiting individuals with experience in previous companies significantly influenced More Stamina, particularly in the design phase. A team composed of members with varied backgrounds, encompassing both business acumen and technical expertise, can enhance the prototype's features in diverse and comprehensive ways.

15.5 Recommendations and Implications

Lean Startup and Design Thinking The development approach used for the More Stamina app was designed to be iterative and flexible, meaning that it was tailored to suit the changing needs of the customer base. The team behind the app strongly emphasized customer feedback and agile development, enabling them to make quick adjustments and improvements [12]. This approach aligns with the lean startup methodology, which is focused on continuous learning, experimentation, and rapid iteration. The More Stamina app's case study can help provide an in-depth understanding of the practical application of lean principles in the health-tech sector. Furthermore, the team used design thinking principles to identify and define the unique problems that the app was designed to solve [10]. The team validated its ideas and concepts by involving patients and HCPs in the development process and using prototypes and demonstrations to gain feedback and make improvements. This process supports the use of design thinking in healthcare, which strongly emphasizes user-centered design and problem-solving.

Entrepreneurial Innovation in Healthcare The creation of More Stamina exemplifies the significance of entrepreneurial skills and technological innovation in tackling healthcare challenges. Such initiatives could motivate more HCPs to participate in technology-driven healthcare solutions and inspire similar ventures [6, 33]. However, the health tech is a challenging domain to survive in; even once considered promises in the field like Babylon Health, Woebot, and Akili Interactive Labs struggled, and some have shut down [1, 24, 28].

Multidisciplinary Team and Collaboration Having a diverse team in terms of skill set and expertise is crucial to achieving success in the health-tech field. A well-rounded team would benefit of HCPs who can provide clinical insights, software developers who can design and develop technology solutions, UX designers who can create user-friendly interfaces, and business strategists who can ensure that the product is commercially viable. Collaboration and communication between these team members are essential to creating products that can meet the needs of all stakeholders, including patients, healthcare providers, and investors. The end goal is to create products that are not only technologically sound but also clinically relevant and user-friendly, ultimately improving the quality of healthcare and patient outcomes.

A User-Centric Design and Evidence-Based Development It is vital to involve end users, such as patients and HCPs, from the early stages of development when creating a product for chronic disease management. This is particularly relevant for solutions that cater to chronic conditions with difficult progression assessment or that might affect people's motor and cognitive skills. This ensures that the final product is tailored to patients' specific needs and preferences, which can enhance the usability and adoption of the technology. Additionally, building solutions based on scientific evidence and research can increase the credibility and effectiveness of the product. Especially for startups in the health-tech industry, aligning their products with current medical research and practices is critical in establishing trust with potential users and ensuring the success of their products.

Leveraging Emerging Technology and Data The integration of cutting-edge technologies, such as artificial intelligence, machine learning, and wearable sensors, can significantly enhance the functionality and appeal of health-tech products. By deploying these advanced tools, HCPs can gain deeper insights into patients' health and conditions, leading to more accurate diagnoses and effective treatment plans. Furthermore, when data are collected responsibly and effectively, they can help identify patterns and trends, enabling HCPs to deliver more personalized care tailored to each patient's unique needs. This can result in better health outcomes and improved quality of life for those under medical care.

15.6 Conclusion

Health-tech startups face significant challenges in developing mHealth apps, as the success of these apps depends on a supportive ecosystem and the involvement of key stakeholders. Therefore, it is crucial to understand the dynamics of ecosystem interactions and the specific challenges of the targeted health condition. This study emphasizes the importance of evaluating mHealth app development from the startup ecosystem in a healthcare context. The research assesses the roles of different startup ecosystem elements and identifies key considerations in developing an mHealth app tailored for MS patients. This involves combining condition-specific knowledge with behavioral change models and utilizing advanced technologies, such as artificial intelligence.

References

1. Aguilar, M.: Akili interactive, maker of digital therapeutics, announces layoffs. STAT (2024). https://www.statnews.com/2024/04/30/akili-interactive-digital-therapeutics-firm-announce-layoffs-restructuring/
2. Ahmad, N., Tripathi, N.: Benefits, challenges, and implications of open-source software for health-tech startups: An empirical study. In: International Conference on Software Business, pp. 265–282. Springer (2023)

3. Bandera, C., Thomas, E.: The role of innovation ecosystems and social capital in startup survival. IEEE Trans. Eng. Manag. **66**, 542–551 (2019). https://doi.org/10.1109/TEM.2018.2859162
4. Beaulieu, M., Lehoux, P.: Emerging health technology firms' strategies and their impact on economic and healthcare system actors: a qualitative study. J. Innov. Entrepreneurship **7**(1), 1–27 (2018)
5. Cartes-Velásquez, J.: Cepis, a great opportunity for innovation in health. Int. J. Med. Surg. Sci. **5**(3), 91–92 (2018). https://doi.org/10.32457/ijmss.2018.022
6. Chakraborty, I., Ilavarasan, P.V., Edirippulige, S.: Health-tech startups in healthcare service delivery: a scoping review. Soc. Sci. Med. **278**, 113949 (2021)
7. Charles, W., Wulfovich, S., Meyers, A.: Digital Health Entrepreneurship. Convergence Mental Health: A Transdisciplinary Approach to Innovation, vol. 375. Springer, Cham (2021)
8. Day, S., Shah, V., Kaganoff, S., Powelson, S., Mathews, S.C.: Assessing the clinical robustness of digital health startups: cross-sectional observational analysis. J. Med. Int. Res. **24**(6), e37677 (2022)
9. Dighe, S., Joshi, A.: An autoethnographic study of hci effort estimation in outsourced software development. In: Human-Centered Software Engineering: 5th IFIP WG 13.2 International Conference, HCSE 2014, Paderborn, September 16–18, 2014. Proceedings 5, pp. 19–35. Springer (2014)
10. Eckman, M., Gorski, I., Mehta, K.: Leveraging design thinking to build sustainable mobile health systems. J. Med. Eng. Technol. **40**(7–8), 422–430 (2016)
11. Ellis, C., Adams, T.E., Bochner, A.P.: Autoethnography: an overview. Hist. Soc. Res./Historische sozialforschung **36**, 273–290 (2011)
12. Eppley, H.B, Zhou, W., Wilson, G.A., Toscani, M., York, J.M.: Using lean startup to discover customers in the mHealth industry: current landscape and challenges. J. Commer. Biotechnol. **26**(3) (2021)
13. Essén, A., Stern, A.D., Haase, C.B., Car, J., Greaves, F., Paparova, D., Vandeput, S., Wehrens, R., Bates, D.W.: Health app policy: international comparison of nine countries' approaches. npj Digital Med. **5**, 31 (2022). https://doi.org/10.1038/s41746-022-00573-1. https://www.nature.com/articles/s41746-022-00573-1
14. Fortune Business Insights: Digital health market size, share & trends | report, [2030]. Fortune Business Insights (2023). https://www.fortunebusinessinsights.com/industry-reports/digital-health-market-100227
15. Giunti, G.: Gamified design for health workshop. Stud. Health Technol. Inf. **225**, 605–6 (2016). https://doi.org/10.3233/978-1-61499-658-3-605. http://www.ncbi.nlm.nih.gov/pubmed/27332273
16. Giunti, G.: 3MD for chronic conditions, a model for motivational mhealth design: embedded case study. JMIR Serious Games **6**, e11631 (2018). https://doi.org/10.2196/11631. http://games.jmir.org/2018/3/e11631/
17. Giunti, G., Guisado-Fernandez, E., Caulfield, B.: Connected Health in Multiple Sclerosis: A Mobile Applications Review, pp. 660–665. IEEE, Piscataway (2017)
18. Giunti, G., Fernández, E.G., Zubiete, E.D., Romero, O.R.: Supply and demand in mhealth apps for persons with multiple sclerosis: systematic search in app stores and scoping literature review. JMIR mHealth uHealth **6**, e10512 (2018). https://doi.org/10.2196/10512. http://mhealth.jmir.org/2018/5/e10512/
19. Giunti, G., Kool, J., Romero, O.R., Zubiete, E.D., et al.: Exploring the specific needs of persons with multiple sclerosis for mhealth solutions for physical activity: mixed-methods study. JMIR mHealth uHealth **6**(2), e8996 (2018)
20. Giunti, G., Mylonopoulou, V., Romero, O.R., et al.: More stamina, a gamified mhealth solution for persons with multiple sclerosis: research through design. JMIR mHealth uHealth **6**(3), e9437 (2018)

21. Giunti, G., Haverinen, J., Reponen, J.: Informing the product development of an mhealth solution for people with multiple sclerosis through early health technology assessment. In: MEDINFO 2021: One World, One Health–Global Partnership for Digital Innovation, pp. 1042–1043. IOS Press, Amsterdam (2022)
22. Golinelli, D., Boetto, E., Carullo, G., Nuzzolese, A.G., Landini, M.P., Fantini, M.P.: Adoption of digital technologies in health care during the covid-19 pandemic: systematic review of early scientific literature. J. Med. Int. Res. **22**(11), e22280 (2020)
23. Grazier, K.L., Metzler, B.: Health care entrepreneurship: financing innovation. J. Health Human Serv. Adm. **28**, 485–503 (2006)
24. Hagen, J.: Woebot health is shutting down its app | mobihealthnews. MobiHealth News (2025). https://www.mobihealthnews.com/news/woebot-health-shutting-down-its-app
25. Jørgensen, M.T.N., Hovmøller, H., Nielsen, J., Tambo, T.: Improving offshoring of low-budget agile software development using the dual-shore approach: An autoethnographic study. In: Proceedings of 36th Information Systems Research in Scandinavia (IRIS) Seminar, pp. 2–17 (2015)
26. Kostkova, P.: Grand challenges in digital health. Front. Public Health **3**, 134 (2015). https://doi.org/10.3389/fpubh.2015.00134
27. Kulkov, I., Ivanova-Gongne, M., Bertello, A., Makkonen, H., Kulkova, J., Rohrbeck, R., Ferraris, A.: Technology entrepreneurship in healthcare: challenges and opportunities for value creation. J. Innov. Knowl. **8**(2), 100365 (2023)
28. Landi, H.: Babylon sells UK business to us firm as it winds down operations. FIERCE Healthcare (2023). https://www.fiercehealthcare.com/digital-health/babylon-closes-us-business-lays-employees-after-mindmaze-take-private-deal-collapses
29. Lee, M., Park, S., Lee, K.S.: What are the features of successful medical device start-ups? evidence from Korea. Sustainability **11**(7), 1948 (2019)
30. Manbachi, A., Kreamer-Tonin, K., Walch, P., Gamo, N.J., Khoshakhlagh, P., Zhang, Y.S., Montague, C., Acharya, S., Logsdon, E.A., Allen, R.H., et al.: Starting a medical technology venture as a young academic innovator or student entrepreneur. Ann. Biomed. Eng. **46**, 1–13 (2018)
31. Perez, S.: Nearly 1 in 4 people abandon mobile apps after only one use (2016). https://techcrunch.com/2016/05/31/nearly-1-in-4-people-abandon-mobile-apps-after-only-one-use/
32. Schulte-Althoff, M., Schewina, K., Lee, G., Fürstenau, D.: On the heterogeneity of digital infrastructure in entrepreneurial ecosystems. In: Proceedings of the 53rd Hawaii International Conference on System Sciences, pp. 1–10 (2020). https://doi.org/10.24251/hicss.2020.703
33. Shepherd, D.A., Patzelt, H.: The "heart" of entrepreneurship: the impact of entrepreneurial action on health and health on entrepreneurial action. J. Bus. Ventur. Insights **4**, 22–29 (2015)
34. Stahl, M., Zarco-Jasso, H., Miralles, F.: How can innovation intermediaries enable product innovativeness in startups? a configurational approach. J. Open Innov. Technol. Market Compl. **9**(1), 100007 (2023)
35. Tripathi, N., Klotins, E., Prikladnicki, R., Oivo, M., Pompermaier, L.B., Kudakacheril, A.S., Unterkalmsteiner, M., Liukkunen, K., Gorschek, T.: An anatomy of requirements engineering in software startups using multi-vocal literature and case survey. J. Syst. Softw. **146**, 130–151 (2018)
36. Tripathi, N., Oivo, M., Liukkunen, K., Markkula, J.: Startup ecosystem effect on minimum viable product development in software startups. Inf. Softw. Technol. **114**, 77–91 (2019)
37. Tripathi, N., Seppänen, P., Boominathan, G., Oivo, M., Liukkunen, K.: Insights into startup ecosystems through exploration of multi-vocal literature. Inf. Softw. Technol. **105**, 56–77 (2019)
38. World Health Organization: Global Strategy on Digital Health 2020-2025. World Health Organization, Geneva (2021)
39. Yrttiaho, T., Isomursu, M., Giunti, G.: Experiences using patient and public involvement in digital health research for multiple sclerosis. In: Challenges of Trustable AI and Added-Value on Health, pp. 735–739. IOS Press, Amsterdam (2022)

Chapter 16
Internal Organization of Software Startups During the Scale-Up Process

Sakari Sipola and Nirnaya Tripathi

Abstract A significant proportion of startups that reach a valuation of one billion dollars and attain unicorn status are either software startups or incorporate a software component in their offerings and have raised venture capital to finance the business. In contrast, among the startups established and financed by venture capitalists, only a small percentage successfully scale and achieve the positive exit required by the venture capital model.

To address the challenges software startups face during the scaling process, this chapter examines how successful software startups organize their human resources across key firm functions during the scale-up process. We identified three venture capital-financed software startup unicorns that (1) have successfully gone public through an initial public offering (IPO) in the US with an over $1 billion valuation as evidence of their scaling and (2) provide detailed statistics on employee numbers and resource allocation among key firm functions in the years of scaling up to their IPOs. We categorize the internal activities of these firms into four functions commonly used in financial reporting: research and development (R&D), marketing and sales (M&S), general and administrative (G&A), and cost of revenue (COR).

Our findings offer insights into how firms organize their human resources internally during the successful scaling process specific to software startups. We demonstrate that in this context, revenue can grow into hundreds of millions, and the number of employees, for example, in the R&D and M&S functions, can increase to several hundred within just a few years. Notably, the growth of the M&S function resourcing appears to play a crucial role in revenue growth during the scale-up phase.

S. Sipola (✉)
Marketing, Management and International Business Unit, University of Oulu, Oulu, Finland
e-mail: sakari.sipola@oulu.fi

N. Tripathi
M3S Research Unit, University of Oulu, Oulu, Finland
e-mail: Nirnaya.Tripathi@oulu.fi

N. Tripathi et al. (eds.), *Advances in Software Startups*,
https://doi.org/10.1007/978-3-032-04294-1_16

Keywords Lean startup · Scaling · Scale-up · Venture capital · Firm resources · Software startup

16.1 Introduction

Software startups attract a significant share of venture capital (VC) investment in the US [17], highlighting their importance as high-growth firms or scale-ups that introduce innovative products, renew industries, and contain the potential for significant business growth and job creation [15]. Indeed, a substantial share of the rare startups that have achieved a valuation of one billion dollar and, therefore, a unicorn status are either software startups or include a software component in their offering [25]. On the other hand, out of the globally increased pool of startups established and financed by venture capitalists, only a small share can successfully scale up and achieve a positive exit required by the venture capital model [13]. Hence, more knowledge of scaling in the software startup context is needed within academia, practitioners, and policymakers alike. This is evidenced by increased research on scaling [6, 8, 15] and, for example, by the fact that the European innovation and startup ecosystem has been lacking in its ability to scale out of a competitive number of promising startups to the unicorn level, especially compared to the USA and China [24]. The issue is not the number of potential startups in Europe but the weaker performance of their business scaling.

This book chapter approaches the issue of software startup scaling by relying on the Lean Startup framework that is widely diffused among practitioner-oriented entrepreneurship literature [23]. We define the development phases of software startup against the search and execution phases of the Lean Startup process [5] and identify the scaling to occur when the product-market fit, customer segments, and a predictable and repeatable sales process are achieved by the founding team and the strategic emphasis moves to execution. At this point, the founding team needs to professionalize job descriptions and structurally organize internally due to increased recruitment of new employees [10], including establishing key firm functions such as marketing and sales [2].

We explore how successfully scaled-up software startups organize their human resources internally between the key firm functions during the scale-up process. It is extremely difficult, even for the best venture capital partnerships, to know ex ante which software startup will eventually scale up successfully, especially to the unicorn scale. Therefore, we identified three venture capital-financed software startups that (1) have successfully listed on public markets via an IPO in the USA with over billion-dollar valuation, to evidence success in organizational and business scaling, and (2) provide detailed statistics of the number of employees and resource allocation between the key firm functions years before the IPO to illustrate their internal organization during the scale-up process.

Our findings first show how rapidly the rare outlier cases [9] can grow their revenue in relative and especially absolute terms annually. The case firms increase revenue from a few million to hundreds of millions of dollars only in a few years and year over year generate substantially more absolute revenue as they scale toward the IPO. We illustrate what types of organizational changes and annual increases in employment are connected with such revenue growth at the total and firm function levels. We show that the number of employees grows to several hundred and then to over 1,000 as a manifestation of the acknowledged new job creation associated with high-growth firms and scale-ups [15].

However, our most significant contribution is that the data enables us to illustrate how this job creation occurs between the key firm functions during the later years of the execution and scale-up process, when the firms aim to become IPO ready. Indeed, the M&S function and its employee growth seem to have an essential role in the scale-up success and revenue growth; all of the firms have the most employees in that function at IPO. This aligns with the basic premise of the Lean Startup framework [2, 5] and underlines the importance of M&S investment as a key strategic aspect for practitioners concerning scaling. More research is needed to understand how and why software firms differ in resource allocation to the key firm functions at the execution phase and how these strategic choices relate both to success and failure in scaling.

16.2 State of the Art

16.2.1 Lean Startup and Venture Capital

The Lean Startup is a practitioner-oriented theory that enables entrepreneurs to reduce the risks and common reasons for firm failure in launching new products and businesses. The central tenet is to help startups avoid building products that customers do not want [21]. The roots of the theory are in the work of Blank [3], Ries [21], and Blank and Dorf [4], with an important contribution of the business model canvas coming from Osterwalder and Pigneur [19].

Ries [21] defines a build-measure-learn feedback loop as the core of the Lean Startup process. It starts with building a minimum viable product (MVP) that enables the startup to get feedback from potential customers, measure the progress of product development, and learn about the needed potential changes and how to validate them [21, 26]. Blank [2] divides the Lean Startup process into two main phases: search and execution. The purpose of the search phase is to help the startup find a product-market fit, target customer segments, and create a predictable and repeatable sales process for product distribution [5]. The subsequent execution phase focuses on the activities needed to grow and scale the business. This includes the company-building step when sales and marketing functions are established in the organization structure and scaled in headcount and financial resourcing to the product distribution based on developed sales and marketing processes. Consequently, the number of customers and revenue begin to grow relative to the investment made, especially in sales and marketing. In this chapter, we approach the Lean Startup process via the search and execution phases.

Indeed, we define the development of software startups against the search and execution phases [5] and identify the scaling to occur when the product-market fit, customer segments, and a predictable and repeatable sales process are achieved by the founding team, and the strategic emphasis moves to the execution phase. At this point, the founding team that wears many hats needs to professionalize, create specific job descriptions, and design the internal organizational structure due to increased recruitment of new employees [10]. This includes establishing key firm functions such as marketing and sales [2].

The role of venture capital (VC) is closely connected to the Lean Startup process in the case of innovative startups that cannot raise capital from banks, need an initial capital investment to begin operations, and agree to build their venture based on the venture capital model, which requires an exit to take place against the equity investment[13]. Venture capitalists invest capital in selected startups in phases based on the success of the startup in achieving the set milestones and support them by board management, providing strategic and operational guidance and connecting entrepreneurs with potential customers, employees, and investors [17]. Startups that receive venture capital are more likely to be acquired and to experience growth, especially when they focus on innovative technologies [28]. This is the case with software startups that have high growth and scaling aspirations.

Figure 16.1 combines the Lean Startup process with the traditional development and venture capital investment phases of a startup. First, turning the idea into a minimum viable product to gain initial customer feedback is typically financed

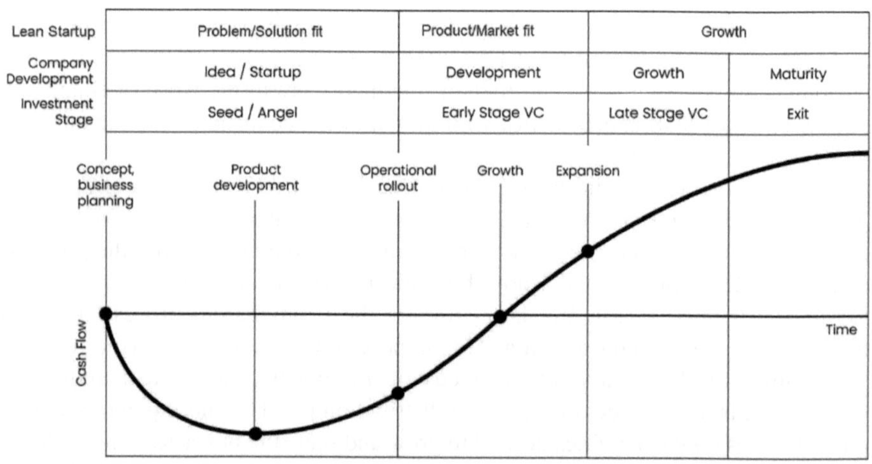

Fig. 16.1 Lean Startup and the venture capital-financed startup development process. Inspired by [18]

by seed or angel investment [1, 26]. As the startup moves closer toward achieving product-market fit and gets its first customers, more capital is raised from early-stage venture capitalists. During this time, cash flow can remain negative, forming the "Valley of Death," where many startups struggle to survive [22]. Upon achieving the repeatable and profitable sales process, the execution phase and company building begin. At this growth phase, the size of venture capital rounds increases, and later-stage investors with larger funds join former investors to make the investments. This allows rapid organizational scaling and revenue and valuation growth. The startup matures and becomes an established organization with performance that enables an exit via an IPO or trade sale.

16.2.2 The Context of Venture Capital–Financed Software Startups

A significant share of venture capital activity focuses on software startups at various stages of development. For example, in 2023, in the USA [17], 1,411 software startups raised venture capital for the first time, attracting $4.3 billion in total investment, making software the leading sector in both respects. Similarly, at the growth stage, software remained the top sector, with 174 software firms securing over $14 billion in total investments. Overall, the software sector accounted for 4,239 deals, representing 39% of all deals, and $59 billion in capital raised in the USA during 2023. The median time for the scale-up process, from initial venture capital investment to an IPO, ranged from 4.63 to 5.61 years for software startups between 2018 and 2023.

The significance of the software startup sector is equally evident in Europe. In 2023 [27], venture capitalists made nearly 3,400 investment deals with software startups, representing 34.8% of total investments in Europe, totaling over €16 billion (28.3% of all investments). Software startups also led in terms of exits, both in absolute numbers (364 exits, 44% of the total) and value (€6.2 billion, 52.6% of the total) across Europe. This trend has persisted over the longer term, as software remains the leading category in venture capital investments in Europe and the USA over the past decade [17, 27]. Notably, the volume of investment has consistently been higher in the USA than Europe—a trend that continues today. In summary, software startups represent a cornerstone of the startup ecosystems and play an important role in economic development. Their ability to scale up successfully—marked by substantial employee growth—contributes significantly to job creation, wealth generation, and industrial renewal [15].

However, as the recent *Draghi report* [11] indicates, European startups have not been as successful in business scaling compared to their US or Chinese counterparts when the number of unicorns is used as one success measure[24]. At the same time, research on scaling is at the emergent phase [6, 8, 15]. Therefore, there is a pressing need for research on scaling and insights regarding how successfully scaled-up firms operate throughout the execution phase after reaching the goals of the preceding search phase. Although the notion of company building is central to the execution phase of the Lean Startup framework[5] and includes the idea of establishing the key firm functions [5], neither prior studies on scaling nor the Lean Startup framework have examined how employment growth occurs across the firm functions during the scale-up process. We address this gap by studying how the venture capital-financed software startups organized internally while scaling to reach an IPO in the USA with unicorn-level valuations.

16.3 Method

It is extremely difficult to know ex ante which software startup will eventually scale up successfully, especially to the unicorn scale [9]. Even the best venture capital partnerships struggle with this, indicated, for example, by the anti-portfolio of Bessemer Venture Partners[1] that outlines how they choose not to invest in startups that later turned out to be highly successful.

Software Startup Scaling Case Study

- We studied three venture capital-financed software startups—Apex, Nimbus, and Orion—that have gone through the Lean Startup process and scaled up to reach an IPO in the USA with unicorn valuation.
- These firms were chosen because each of them provided more detailed information of their annual revenue growth and internal employee organization of the years before the IPO in their S-1 IPO filings than is officially required.
- Such company data is rarely accessible to researchers and practitioners, as it is kept private by firms or not reported in standard databases.

Based on the company data, we first constructed a timeline of annual revenue growth for each case firm using spreadsheet software. Second, we categorized the internal organization of each firm into four key functions: research and development (R&D), marketing and sales (M&S), general and administrative (G&A), and cost of revenue (COR).[2] These categories are used in standard financial reporting practices to improve clarity and comparability for investors and stakeholders [20]. We then

[1] https://www.bvp.com/anti-portfolio

[2] Cost of revenue refers to the total cost of manufacturing and delivering a product or service to customers. It represents the direct costs associated with the goods and services the company provides.

illustrated changes in the number of employees during the scale-up process at the firm function level.

In addition, we controlled for the impact of acquisitions [16] on the revenue and employment data. Only Nimbus had made acquisitions—two relatively small ones valued at under $1 million and $5 million, respectively—prior to its IPO. We estimate the impact of these acquisitions on both revenue and employment figures to be minimal.

All three case firms use the Software-as-a-Service (SaaS) model for distribution and do not produce any physical products. Nimbus develops a digital platform that connects individuals and companies and generates revenue by offering subscription-based solutions and selling advertising. It leveraged network effects and user-generated content to grow its user base. Apex offers cloud-based tools for automating enterprise operations and managing information technology (IT) services. Its revenue model is based on long-term contracts and deep integration with corporate clients. Orion provides software that transforms raw data into visual insights, enabling businesses to make data-driven decisions. It offers advanced analytics and intuitive dashboards, monetized via subscriptions.

We used within-case analysis to capture the scaling process at the individual firm level and cross-case analysis to identify divergences and commonalities across the cases [12, 29].

16.4 Findings

Our findings provide insight into the internal organization of human resources during the successful scale-up process to an IPO in the software startup context. First, we show the scaling and business performance achieved by each firm by analyzing their annual revenue growth in absolute and relative (%) terms, as well as their revenue per employee levels. Second, we discuss annual changes in the number of employees at the total firm level and within each firm function to illustrate how internal human resource allocation evolves during the scale-up phase.

On a general level, our results show how each software startup in the data achieved a "hockey stick" profile in revenue growth during the years leading up to the IPO (Fig. 16.2). The revenue of Nimbus grew from $1 million to over $522 million in six years, averaging 228% growth annually (see Table 16.1). In years 1 and IPO, it notably generated $123 and $279 million more revenue annually than the previous year.

The revenue growth of Apex similarly started low from the $2 million level and grew rapidly to reach $224 million at the time of the IPO, 5 years later, resulting in a 179% annual growth rate. At the absolute level, it increased revenue in a single

The service industry often favors using the cost of revenue metric because it comprehensively accounts for the various costs associated with selling a good or service.

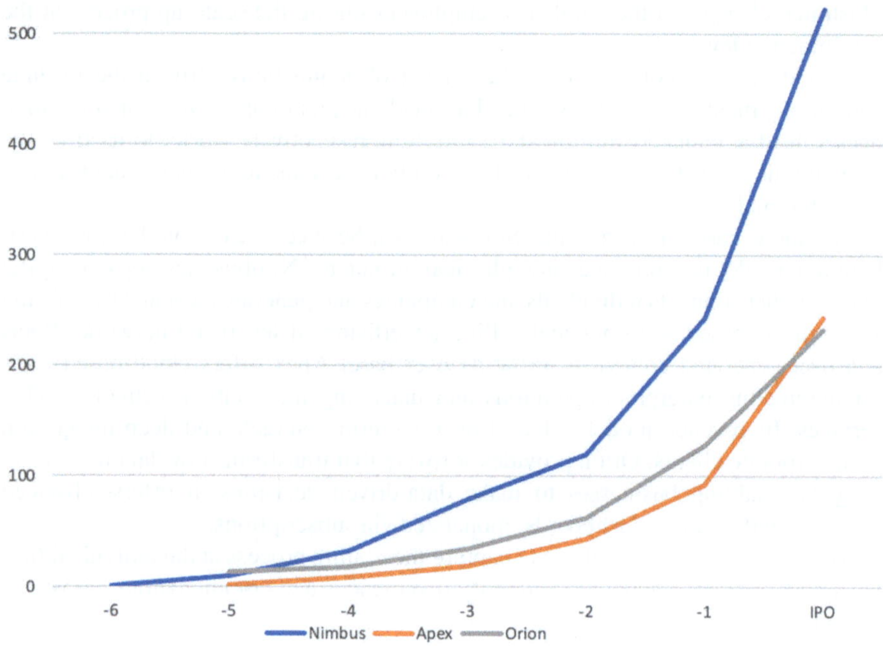

Fig. 16.2 Annual absolute revenue growth (in millions of dollars) of the analyzed software firms

year by $151 million from $93 (year 1) to 244$ million when ramping up toward the IPO.

The first revenue data point of Orion starts from a higher rate of $13 million 5 years before the IPO and grows an average of 79% annually to reach $232 million at the public listing. The highest single-year absolute revenue growth of $104 million occurred during the IPO year.

From the cross-case perspective, the low first-year revenue rates of Nimbus and Apex capture the transition from the search to the execution phase of the Lean Startup process early on. In the case of Orion, the execution phase appears to have progressed approximately 12–18 months forward, which has provided more time for revenue growth to reach $13 million. From the first-year revenue data onward, the cases evidence absolute revenue growth of tens or over 100 million dollars annually. Such high absolute revenue increases are extremely rare and illustrate how substantial the year-over-year revenue growth can be when IPO-enabling financial performance at the unicorn scale is achieved in a relatively short time period.

Second, we examine how the above-documented substantial revenue growth manifests at the organizational level. Concerning the changes in the number of employees (see Table 16.1) and internal organization of firms (see Table 16.2) during the scaling process, we capture 4 years of data for Nimbus and Orion and 3 years for Apex, all from the IPO backward. Temporally this is more than is common in previous research where 1-year or 3-year periods are typical for capturing growth

Table 16.1 Annual revenue and employee growth (absolute and relative) and revenue per employee (authors' own calculations)

	Year	-6	-5	-4	-3	-2	-1	IPO	Average
Nimbus	Revenue ($M)	1	10	32	79	120	243	522	
	Annual growth (%)		723%	230%	142%	52%	102%	115%	*228%*
	Absolute annual growth		9	22	47	41	123	279	
	Employees				338	480	990	2116	
	Annual growth (%)					42%	106%	114%	*87%*
	Absolute annual growth					142	510	1126	
	Revenue per employee ($M)				0,23	0,25	0,25	0,25	*0,24*
Apex	Revenue ($M)		2	9	19	43	93	244	
	Annual growth (%)			371%	120%	124%	114%	163%	*179%*
	Absolute annual growth			7	10	24	50	151	
	Employees					250	603	1077	
	Annual growth (%)						141%	79%	*110%*
	Absolute annual growth						353	474	
	Revenue per employee ($M)					0,17	0,15	0,23	*0,18*
Orion	Revenue ($M)		13	18	34	62	128	232	
	Annual growth (%)			37%	88%	83%	105%	82%	*79%*
	Absolute annual growth			5	16	28	66	104	
	Employees				165	306	661	1079	
	Annual growth (%)					85%	116%	63%	*88%*
	Absolute annual growth					141	355	418	
	Revenue per employee ($M)				0,21	0,20	0,19	0,22	*0,20*

Table 16.2 Annual firm function and total employee growth and relative share (%) of employees per firm function of total employees (authors' own calculations)

	Year	-3	-2	-1	IPO
Nimbus	R&D	155 (46%)	207 (43%)	383 (39%)	634 (30%)
	M&S	68 (20%)	125 (26%)	313 (32%)	844 (40%)
	G&A	42 (12%)	62 (13%)	153 (15%)	300 (14%)
	COR	73 (22%)	86 (18%)	141 (14%)	338 (16%)
	Total	338	480	990	2116
Apex	R&D		34 (14%)	83 (14%)	200 (19%)
	M&S		90 (36%)	242 (40%)	350 (32%)
	G&A		25 (10%)	61 (10%)	126 (12%)
	COR		101 (40%)	217 (36%)	401 (37%)
	Total		250	603	1077
Orion	R&D	61 (37%)	108 (35%)	205 (31%)	329 (30%)
	M&S	74 (45%)	137 (45%)	321 (49%)	534 (49%)
	G&A	19 (12%)	36 (12%)	59 (9%)	78 (7%)
	COR	11 (7%)	25 (8%)	76 (11%)	138 (13%)
	Total	165	306	661	1079

[7]. In the case of Nimbus, an annual revenue of $79 million was achieved by a 338-employee organization (year 3). From there onward, Nimbus increased its headcount by, on average, 87% annually, resulting in a 2,116-employee organization at the IPO. Notably, the organizational scaling of Nimbus accelerated annually and peaked during the IPO year when 1,126 new employees were hired, representing a 114% annual growth.

The number of employees at Apex grew more than fourfold in 3 years. Starting as a 250-employee organization generating $43 million in revenue (year 2), Apex reached the level of 1,077 employees by the time of its IPO. This represents an average annual employee growth of 110%, with the most significant increase occurring in the year before the IPO: a 141% rise, equivalent to 353 new employees. This was the highest single-year growth rate among the three cases studied. However, the distinction between absolute and relative growth becomes apparent in the IPO year. While 474 new employees were added—an absolute increase higher than the previous year—this represented a comparatively lower relative growth rate of 79%, resulting from the larger operational scale.

The data on employee changes in Orion illustrate that revenue of $34 million was achieved with 165 employees (year 3). From there, it scaled to a 1,079-employee organization at the IPO year, resulting in an 88% average annual growth. During the organizational scaling, Orion recruited increasingly more employees year over year, adding 355 and 418 new employees during the year 1 and IPO years.

At the cross-case level, the results show how the above-documented substantial revenue growth is connected to employee growth on a similar scale. The firms transitioned from startups and scale-ups into mature and credible public companies organizationally. Further, the results indicate that absolute annual employment growth may better capture the increased year-over-year growth from the unicorn-scale execution perspective than relative measures. Indeed, all firms recruited more employees each year than the previous one, while the relative percentage of growth fluctuated more due to the increasing absolute organizational size.

Regarding the revenue per employee, Nimbus generated an average of $0.24 million revenue per employee for 4 years and Orion $0.2 million on average during the same period. Apex achieved $0.18 million in average revenue per employee during the 3 years leading to the IPO. However, at the annual level, Apex evidenced the highest single-year increase of $0.08 million, with a growth from $0.15 million (year 1) to $0.23 million per employee at the IPO. Between the cases, the differences at the IPO were relatively small in this perspective, which indicates that although software startup SaaS models scale well, their ambitious execution is coupled with increasing organizational and operating costs.

Third, as a novelty, our data enables us to examine how the substantial organizational growth discussed above is distributed internally across firm functions during the execution phase of the scale-up process and in relation to revenue growth (see Table 16.2). In the case of Nimbus, R&D is the largest firm function by number of employees in each year, except for the IPO year. Moreover, its relative share of R&D employees gradually decreased from 46% (year 3) to 30% in the IPO year. In contrast, and parallel with the notable absolute annual revenue growth (see

Table 16.1), employee growth in the M&S function gradually accelerated from 68 employees (20% of total) in year -3 to 844 employees at the IPO—an increase of 776 employees over 3 years, making it the largest firm function with a 40% share of all employees. The number of employees in G&A and COR functions of Nimbus also grew-from 42 and 73 to 300 (14% of the total) and 338 (16% of the total) during the same period, respectively—creating substantial organizations in absolute headcount, though maintaining a relatively low share of total headcount.

In the case of Apex, COR is the largest firm function in terms of the number of employees 2 years before the IPO, with 101 employees (40% of the total) followed by the M&S organization with 90 employees (36% of the total). These two functions remain the largest relative to R&D and G&A when Apex begins its substantial annual absolute revenue growth toward the IPO. First, M&S expands with 152 new employees in year 1 and becomes the largest firm function (40% of total employees) in that year. However, in the year of public listing, COR increases even more—by 184 new employees—which gives it a 37% relative share of all employees and a 401-employee organization. Meanwhile, the M&S organization grows eventually to 350 employees in size at the IPO and is the second largest function, with a 32% relative share. The size of the R&D and G&A functions remains smaller, starting from 34 and 25 employees in year 2 and reaching 200 (19% of the total) and 126 (12% of the total) employees, respectively, out of the 1,077 total headcount of Apex at the IPO.

The organization of Orion is different as it has most employees working in the M&S function every 4 years up to the IPO; M&S starts with 74 employees (35% of the total) and ends up with 534 (49% of the total) employees at the IPO. This includes the 184 and 213 new M&S employee increases in year 1 and the IPO, parallel with the significant absolute revenue growth (see Table 16.1). R&D employee growth proceeds from 61 (37% of the total) to 329 (30% of the total) during the same period, but with a decrease of 7% of the overall share of employees at IPO. Orion also has the lowest combined share of G&A and COR employees among the three firms, ranging between 17 and 20% of all employees during the observation period.

A cross-case comparison suggests that the scaling to high absolute levels of revenue growth and unicorn valuation is, at the firm function level, connected to the important role of the M&S function and increasing resource allocation to its expansion. On one hand, this finding is not surprising, given that it is the function responsible for generating revenue through sales to new and existing customers. On the other hand, prior studies have not provided case-based evidence of this relationship in the software startup context.

Nimbus, with the most revenue ($522 million), had the largest M&S organization at the IPO, employing 844 employees. Apex ($244 million) and Orion ($232 million) were close in revenue, but Orion had significantly more M&S employees (534) compared to Apex (350) at the time of their IPOs. These differences in organizational size may relate to differing levels of investment in targeted post-IPO revenue growth, with Orion potentially seeking to invest more in this area. The logic for this argument is based on the observation that the increase of M&S employees in the previous year led to an increase in revenue in the following year. After the IPO, it is particularly important to show to the public investors that there is more room for growth and, hence, a positive outlook for the stock price increase.

Overall, the size of the R&D organizations—as can be expected with innovative growth-seeking software firms—was also significant for each case firm. When M&S is compared to R&D, Nimbus had 10%, Apex 13%, and Orion 19% more employees in M&S than R&D at the IPO. In addition, we observe the share of COR employees to vary as Nimbus and Orion have 16% and 13% of employees in this function at the IPO year. In contrast, Apex reaches a significantly higher share, with 37% of the total employee amount dedicated to COR.

The role of the COR function and its employee growth is likely connected to the number of customers/users in the SaaS offering of each firm, the type of customers (business, consumer or both) and the level of support required at increasing operational scale, and the growing computing power (such as cloud infrastructure) needed to ensure reliable service delivery.

16.5 Recommendations and Implications

Although the number of venture capital-financed software startups has increased globally, and methods such as the Lean Startup have emerged to support startup development, a significant share of firms still fail to reach their scaling targets or achieve the positive exit required by the venture capital model. Building and scaling startups is difficult, and the outcome of the process is ex ante uncertain. This highlights the need to understand what happens inside startups after they achieve product-market fit and transition from the search phase to execution and begin building the necessary organizational structure and recruiting new employees to scale the business in markets.

Our findings contribute new insights into the internal organization of software startups during the execution phase of their scaling process, an area that remains underexplored in current literature—particularly in the context of startups achieving unicorn-scale growth and a successful IPO in the USA.

First, we illustrate what unicorn-scale growth can look like inside a software startup and in terms of business performance at the transition from search to the execution phase [2]. We do this by illustrating "hockey stick" growth from a few million into hundreds of millions in revenue and over $1 billion valuation at IPO. This contribution is valuable not only within the software startup context but also in entrepreneurship research in general [9], as prior studies have typically analyzed firms with lower revenue growth levels.

Second, we shed light on the employee growth and organizational scaling required to achieve such a high absolute revenue growth level. Indeed, two of the case firms grew to over 1,000 employees in size and one to over 2,000 employees and a stock market listing in a few years. Again, such changes in size and scope are not commonly addressed in previous studies. However, our most significant finding concerns how these employees are allocated across key firm functions during the later phases of the execution and scale-up process.

Indeed, the primary contribution of our book chapter is the relationship between the M&S function resourcing and revenue growth. Each case firm evidenced a connection between high absolute revenue growth and a significant increase in M&S employees—pinnacled by an annual increase of 531 employees in the respective firm function by one of the cases. Our results suggests that when attention is turned into the different firm functions and their resourcing over time, M&S manifests as key strategic growth driver whose role should be accounted in relation to observed revenue growth. Or, conversely, if the firms are not achieving growth, it is worthwhile to analyze how much they allocate human resources to M&S compared to other functions over time.

We also found that the R&D function similarly had an important role in each firm, which can be expected given the competitive software startup landscape and operational scale the firms operate. Investment in R&D and innovation is required to remain competitive and to generate new functionalities that the M&S function can market to customers and use to increase revenue. The size of the COR function varied more and is likely related to differences in market segments and SaaS offerings and product characteristics between the case firms. The G&A functions were scaled into a size that each firm requires to run a credible and future scaling aiming public organization.

Curiously, the role of the M&S function—and other firm functions—is not well integrated into the existing scaling literature, as evidenced, for example, in the recent literature review by Coviello et al. [8] or in studies applying the Lean Startup framework [5]. Hence, we see the role and organization of the M&S function in relation to other firm functions during the execution phase of scaling as a promising area for future research. In such endeavors, studies that capture the related developments already in the early phase, or the search phase, in Lean Startup terminology, would be particularly valuable. This would help address a data limitation of this study, as we are not able to capture the internal organization of employees across firm functions from the early phase onward but only a few years after firms began generating revenue.

Moreover, additional case studies are needed to better understand how successful—and unsuccessful—firms allocate employees across key firm functions during the scale-up process. While our findings offer valuable insights, they are based on only three cases and cannot be generalized. In general, scholars must approach generalizations with caution in the context of scaling, as the dynamics between key firm functions are specific to the firm, its strategy, and the product market.

For practitioners and startups with growth ambitions similar to the cases studied in this book chapter, we recommend—while acknowledging the limitations above—that management teams carefully consider what type of organizational structure needs to be strategically developed over the coming years to achieve their targeted growth and successfully scale in their respective markets and competitive environments. Our findings suggest that management should be prepared to continuously invest in expanding the firm functions most critical to the specific strategic goals of the firm. This appears particularly relevant in the case of unicorn-scale growth, for which our results provide illustrative examples—especially regarding the absolute annual increases in employee headcount at the firm function level.

Furthermore, we underline that the role of the M&S function should be considered carefully in this connection. This relates not only to the quality of software development but also to the customer and market knowledge gathered during the search phase of the Lean Startup process, which forms the foundation for future execution and scaling. For example, firm management should ensure that the sales process is scalable, repeatable, and profitable before significantly increasing investment in the growth of M&S function headcount. Otherwise, recruitment into M&S may not necessarily translate into sales growth in the same proportion. This highlights the importance of careful recruitment and financial planning in the context of venture capital investment rounds, as these are key factors in realizing the strategic growth objectives of the firm. Experienced investors and board members can be particularly valuable to first-time founders by contributing scaling experience across key firm functions[14]. We recommend that practitioners take these aspects into account when planning their growth and scaling strategies and when selecting the right venture capitalists to partner with.

Key Lessons Learned for Practitioners

- Marketing and sales (M&S) function is a key driver of revenue growth for software startups that aim to reach over $100 million in revenue.
- Software startup founders aiming to reach unicorn-scale valuations need not only establish the M&S function within their organizational structure but also adequately resource it according to strategic revenue growth targets.
- Do not scale the M&S function resourcing before you have also validated a repeatable, profitable, and scalable sales process.

Finally, for policymakers aiming to foster more unicorn-scale success stories and exits in their respective regions [11], we recommend examining how startups, venture capital investors, and other stakeholders involved in scaling have historically invested resources in the M&S function after transitioning from the search to the execution and scaling phase. Perhaps due to the relatively younger startup culture of Europe, there is greater variation in how much investment is perceived as necessary in this firm function for scaling to occur at a pace that enables market leadership, unicorn valuation, and, ultimately, a successful exit via an IPO or trade sale. This is particularly important as the most promising European startups must compete in global scale, facing rivals from more mature startup ecosystems.

Therefore, ensuring sufficient resourcing and investment in the M&S function is essential for European scale-ups to remain competitive during the execution phase, particularly in comparison to their US and international counterparts. However, this recommendation should be considered preliminary and highlights the need for further research on the topic.

We hope that, despite its limitations, our study will inspire further research into the internal organization of software startups during the scale-up process.

References

1. Bauer, D., Junge, S., Reif, T.: May the resources be with you: a systematic review and framework of startup funding options. Manag. Rev. Quart. **74**(3), 1365–1396 (2024)
2. Blank, S.: Why the lean start-up changes everything. Harvard Busin. Rev. **91**(5), 63–72 (2013)
3. Blank, S.: The Four Steps to the Epiphany: Successful Strategies for Products that Win. Wiley, Hoboken (2020)
4. Blank, S., Dorf, B.: The Startup Owner's Manual: The Step-by-Step Guide for Building a Great Company. Wiley, Hoboken (2020)
5. Blank, S., Eckhardt, J.T.: The lean startup as an actionable theory of entrepreneurship. J. Manag. **50**, 01492063231168095 (2023)
6. Bohan, S., Tippmann, E., Levie, J., Igoe, J., Bowers, B.: What is scaling? J. Bus. Ventur. **39**(1), 106355 (2024)
7. Coad, A., Frankish, J.S., Storey, D.J.: Too fast to live? effects of growth on survival across the growth distribution. J. Small Bus. Manag. **58**(3), 544–571 (2020)
8. Coviello, N., Autio, E., Nambisan, S., Patzelt, H., Thomas, L.D.: Organizational scaling, scalability, and scale-up: definitional harmonization and a research agenda. J. Bus. Ventur. **39**(5), 106419 (2024)
9. Crawford, G.C., Aguinis, H., Lichtenstein, B., Davidsson, P., McKelvey, B.: Power law distributions in entrepreneurship: Implications for theory and research. J. Bus. Ventur. **30**(5), 696–713 (2015)
10. DeSantola, A., Gulati, R.: Scaling: Organizing and growth in entrepreneurial ventures. Acad. Manag. Ann. **11**(2), 640–668 (2017)
11. Draghi, M.: The Future of European Competitiveness Part A: A Competitiveness Strategy for Europe. Publications Office of the European Union, Luxembourg (2024)
12. Eisenhardt, K.M.: Building theories from case study research. Acad. Manag. Rev. **14**(4), 532–550 (1989)
13. Gompers, P.A., Lerner, J.: The Venture Capital Cycle. MIT Press, Cambridge (2004)
14. Hellmann, T., Puri, M.: Venture capital and the professionalization of start-up firms: empirical evidence. J. Finance **57**(1), 169–197 (2002)
15. Jansen, J.J., Heavey, C., Mom, T.J., Simsek, Z., Zahra, S.A.: Scaling-up: building, leading and sustaining rapid growth over time. J. Manag. Stud. **60**(3), 581–604 (2023)
16. McKelvie, A., Wiklund, J.: Advancing firm growth research: a focus on growth mode instead of growth rate. Entrep. Theory Pract. **34**(2), 261–288 (2010)
17. National venture capital association yearbook. https://nvca.org/document/nvca-2022-yearbook-final-2/wp-content/uploads/2024/05/2024-NVCA-Yearbook.pdf. Accessed: 30 Sep 2024
18. National venture capital association yearbook. https://nvca.org/document/nvca-2022-yearbook-final-2/ (2022). Accessed: 30 Sep 2024
19. Osterwalder, A., Pigneur, Y.: Business Model Generation: A Handbook for Visionaries, Game Changers, and Challengers. Wiley, Hoboken (2010)

20. Penman, S.H.: Financial Statement Analysis and Security Valuation. McGraw Hill, Columbus (2013)
21. Ries, E.: The Lean Startup, vol. 27, pp. 2016–2020. Crown Business, New York (2011)
22. Savaneviciene, A., Venckuviene, V., Girdauskiene, L.: Venture capital a catalyst for start-ups to overcome the "valley of death": Lithuanian case. Procedia Econ. Finance **26**, 1052–1059 (2015)
23. Shepherd, D.A., Gruber, M.: The lean startup framework: closing the academic–practitioner divide. Entrep. Theory Pract. **45**(5), 967–998 (2021)
24. Testa, G., Compañó, R., Correia, A., Rückert, E., et al.: In Search of EU Unicorns: What Do We Know about Them? Publications Office of the European Union, Brussels, Belgium (2022)
25. The complete list of unicorn companies. https://www.cbinsights.com/research-unicorn-companies. Accessed: 30 Sep 2024
26. Tripathi, N., Klotins, E., Prikladnicki, R., Oivo, M., Pompermaier, L.B., Kudakacheril, A.S., Unterkalmsteiner, M., Liukkunen, K., Gorschek, T.: An anatomy of requirements engineering in software startups using multi-vocal literature and case survey. J. Syst. Softw. **146**, 130–151 (2018)
27. Venture capital. https://pitchbook.com/news/venture-capital. Accessed: 30 Sep 2024
28. Wagner, M.: Acquisitions and growth of software startups: The dual role of venture capital as a success factor. In: Software Business: 8th International Conference, ICSOB 2017, Essen, June 12–13, 2017, Proceedings 8, pp. 18–31. Springer (2017)
29. Yin, R.K.: Case Study Research and Applications. SAGE, Thousand Oaks (2018)

Chapter 17
Shaping the Next Generation of Entrepreneurs: Educational Strategies for Startup Business Development

Aline de Campos, Rafael Chanin, Afonso Sales, and Nicolas Nascimento

Abstract This study examines the integration of startup-oriented teaching methods into higher education to foster entrepreneurial mindsets. It presents two case studies conducted over several years at Brazilian educational institutions, focusing on the use of active learning methodologies, particularly Project-Based Learning (PBL) and Challenge-Based Learning (CBL), along with agile frameworks and resources. Key findings from the research indicate enhancements in technical skills, improved socio-emotional competencies, and successful transitions of various student-developed Minimum Viable Products (MVP) into viable businesses. The study also addresses challenges related to team dynamics, resource allocation, and assessment integrity, offering practical recommendations for educators and practitioners. These recommendations emphasize the importance of iterative feedback cycles, promote partnerships with industry, and advocate for the broader adoption of startup education in academic settings.

Keywords Business development · Startup education · Entrepreneurial skills · Experiential learning · Educational practices

17.1 Introduction

In the current hyperconnected environment, the educational sector is increasingly emphasizing the need for practices that align more effectively with this dynamic landscape. Despite this productive environment, most learning practices still reinforce culturally passive and normalizing processes. These results become problematic due to a constant disparity between what is expected from current education and what is available, as they indicate that most areas of work in the

---

A. de Campos (✉) · R. Chanin · A. Sales · N. Nascimento
Pontifical Catholic University of Rio Grande do Sul (PUCRS), Porto Alegre, RS, Brazil
e-mail: aline.campos@pucrs.br; rafael.chanin@pucrs.br; afonso.sales@pucrs.br; nicolas.nascimento@pucrs.br

N. Tripathi et al. (eds.), *Advances in Software Startups*,
https://doi.org/10.1007/978-3-032-04294-1_17

future may not yet exist and will potentially focus on digital and socio-emotional skills rather than predetermined tasks [10].

Researchers and institutions have investigated the importance of education in a social context over the last decades. More recently, the concept of Education 4.0 (or even Education 5.0) has emerged as a vision for the future of learning [12, 26]. More than just a buzzword, it represents the idea that education is essential for fostering social, economic, and political change.

Global organizations such as the United Nations Educational, Scientific, and Cultural Organization (UNESCO) and the World Economic Forum (WEF) have discussed guidelines and proposed frameworks for shaping educational policies. For instance, the "Education 4.0 Framework" by the WEF [10] emphasizes the development of competencies. It highlights global citizenship skills, encompassing a broad understanding of the world, innovation, and advanced thinking abilities such as problem-solving and critical reasoning. It also mentions technological skills, including programming and digital responsibility, as well as interpersonal skills such as communication, leadership, empathy, and social awareness.

Regarding pedagogical strategies, the framework emphasizes personalized learning to address diverse learner needs and advocates for collaborative, problem-based practices using active learning methodologies. It prioritizes accessibility and inclusivity to broaden educational access and promotes lifelong learning, enhancing and cultivating skills based on identified needs [10].

This proposed framework offers helpful insights by emphasizing the development of competence over the specific subjects and focusing more on people and processes rather than final products. But despite the extensive debate about the role of innovation in teaching and learning methodologies, particularly in higher education, many academic contexts still need to align with the evolving training demands required for emerging career paths [34]. This lack of integration increases the need to enhance student motivation and adequately prepare them for professional challenges [19, 20].

In addition, the recent groundbreaking progress in artificial intelligence (AI) has been catalyzing a global transformation across all domains of knowledge, indicating the emergence of new roles and processes in the workforce dynamic and business models [26]. This presents significant challenges for future professionals responsible for business development and for educators tasked with fostering an entrepreneurial mindset in this generation.

Seeking ways to bridge the gap between the educational sector and the corporate environment, we have been integrating Active Learning Methodologies, with a focus on Project-Based Learning (PBL) and Challenge-Based Learning (CBL), alongside other methods commonly found in entrepreneurial environments, such as Agile and Lean Startup. This integration has been demonstrated to be a key factor in preparing students for business development.

This study highlights two experiences that foster a startup mindset within academic settings: the first within IT curricula in higher education and the second through an extracurricular learning program. We will present the key features of PBL and CBL, as well as related works that provide context and insights into the current state of the art in startup education. Additionally, we outline the methodological structure of our experiences in information technology education scenarios over several years. Finally, we share the results, lessons learned, and practical recommendations for educators, practitioners, and researchers seeking to implement business development learning models.

17.2 Active Learning Methodologies

Active Learning Methodologies have been a prominent topic in education. This approach shifts from traditional lectures to student-centered activities, promoting discussions, problem-solving, case studies, and hands-on experiences that enhance understanding and skill development [9].

Collaborative work and peer relationships are vital elements of active methodologies, as they empower groups of students to generate significance and deliver effective solutions to challenges. Students engage in tasks that promote analysis, synthesis, and evaluation, requiring them to participate and reflect on their actions [18].

Two of the most relevant methods in this approach are Project-Based Learning (PBL) and Challenge-Based Learning (CBL). Both methods strongly emphasize collaborative work and solution development, though they possess distinct characteristics and activities that will be introduced below.

17.2.1 Project-Based Learning (PBL)

Project-Based Learning (PBL) is an active methodology in which students engage in exploring real-world challenges through structured, extended projects, culminating in concrete outcomes or products [4].

This approach emphasizes student-centered inquiry, collaboration, and authentic application of knowledge, fostering deeper learning and increased motivation by connecting academic content to practical, meaningful tasks. These experiences can lead to the development of theoretical and technical knowledge, as well as the implicit growth of critical thinking, collaboration, and self-management skills. According to Buck Institute for Education [15], one of the leading research centers in this methodology, the following characteristics are essential in PBL (Fig. 17.1):

(a) **Challenging Problems**: meaningful questions with an appropriate degree of challenge aligned with educational objectives.
(b) **Sustained Inquiry**: prioritizing the search for necessary information by consulting instructors and a variety of available resources.
(c) **Authenticity**: real-world context where tasks, quality criteria, and impacts must align with participants' interests.
(d) **Student Voice and Choice**: students make decisions regarding various aspects of the project, including work approaches and outcomes.

Fig. 17.1 Project-Based Learning essential characteristics

(e) **Reflection**: students reflect on the learning process, evaluating activities' effectiveness, potential obstacles, and strategies for overcoming them.
(f) **Critique and Revision**: participants must provide, receive, and utilize feedback to improve both the process and the product.
(g) **Public Product**: students make their projects public by presenting them to an audience beyond their classroom.

These principles can introduce dynamism into classes and an authentic experience beyond theory. This involves adequately structuring all project processes, clearly defining quality criteria, continuously encouraging problem-solving and improvements, evaluating project stages, and providing constructive feedback that guides learning toward essential objectives.

In PBL, instructors must serve as facilitators and coordinators. Rather than prescribing information, the project itself ignites students' curiosity. It clarifies precisely what they need to learn to solve the challenge presented [18] and enhances their capacity to transfer and apply learned concepts effectively across diverse situations and disciplines.

17.2.2 Challenge-Based Learning (CBL)

Challenge-Based Learning (CBL) is an educational framework designed to engage students in realistic problems through experiential, collaborative, and inquiry-driven processes. Originating as a response to the limitations of traditional teaching methodologies, this method encourages active student participation by involving them in critical thinking, creativity, and innovation [22].

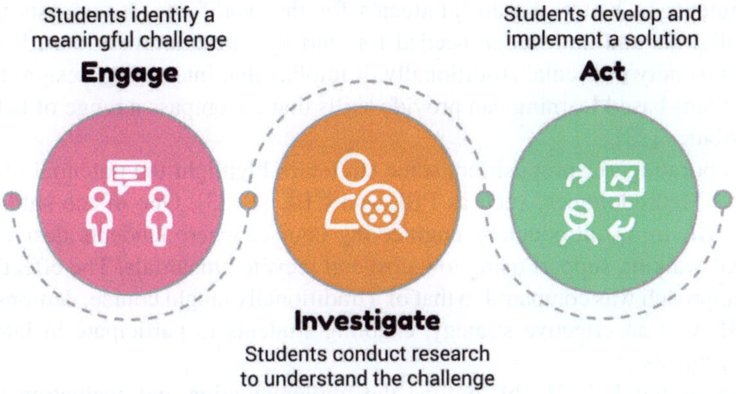

Fig. 17.2 Challenge-Based Learning stages

The approach is structured into three stages: ***Engage, Investigate, and Act***. In the ***Engage*** phase, students identify a relevant issue, fostering intrinsic motivation through their work's personal and societal relevance [22]. The idea is refined into an essential question and subsequently transformed into specific, actionable challenges [24]. During the ***Investigative*** phase, students collaborate in multidisciplinary teams, conduct extensive research, leverage technology, and engage with community stakeholders to develop solutions [22]. This broadens their understanding of the challenge and enhances their research skills in evaluating and synthesizing information. Finally, in the ***Act*** phase, they implement a solution, typically designing, developing, and testing [22]. This iterative process reflects the industry environment, providing students with meaningful learning and practical experience (Fig. 17.2).

This approach emphasizes the importance of student autonomy, delegating to learners the responsibility of taking ownership of their education while promoting intrinsic motivation, engagement, and lifelong learning practices. Successfully implementing CBL requires considerable changes in instructional practices. Educators must shift from providers to facilitators of learning. It demands thoughtful curriculum integration and design, clearly defined learning objectives, and continuous assessment practices to ensure that students receive the required guidance and resources throughout their challenge-based projects.

17.3 Related Work

This section presents a state-of-the-art review of recent studies, providing an overall showcase of innovative approaches to fostering entrepreneurial skills, particularly within Information Technology education.

Highlighting the significant gap between academia and industry, the study [11] emphasizes the importance of prioritizing practical skills alongside academic achievements to better prepare graduates for the workforce. It suggests that the essential skills and knowledge needed for start-ups are often overlooked in traditional university curricula. Additionally, it implies that integrating design thinking and problem-based learning can provide skills that encompass a range of behaviors and attributes [23].

Corroborating our proposition, some strategies highlight the potential of Active Learning Methodologies, such as PBL and CBL [1, 23]. One of the studies [17] adopts PBL in an introductory engineering course, where students designed and produced walking support using low-cost and recycled materials. The effectiveness of this approach was compared to that of a traditionally taught course, demonstrating that PBL was an effective strategy, enabling students to participate in interdisciplinary projects.

Other studies [14, 21, 29] outline the implementation and evaluation of PBL and CBL, designed to assist students in establishing startups through business development education, practical experience, and mentorship. In this context, students must apply their expertise in specific domains to develop business ideas.

The relationship between startup education and entrepreneurs' skills, including technical, business management, and personal entrepreneurial skills, is proposed to provide entrepreneurs with the skills needed to operate their businesses and overcome challenges [1]. Additionally, various tools, frameworks, and methodologies identified are indicated in recent research for teaching software startup concepts, emphasizing experiential and empirical learning [11, 16].

17.4 Research Methods and Scenarios

We will present two empirical case studies illustrating how startup scenarios have been integrated into undergraduate curricula and extracurricular activities as academic practices. The primary focus of the experiences was to transform traditional classes into hands-on experiences that built real-world products and fostered startup-like dynamics, immersing students in an entrepreneurial journey where they could apply theoretical knowledge to practical challenges.

The first case concerns a Development Project discipline in information technology undergraduate curricula. The second case presents a Mobile Development Program for undergraduate and postgraduate students across all knowledge areas. These case studies outline the models, stages, dynamics, and tools utilized to address the challenges of technological entrepreneurship.

17.4.1 Case 1: Bringing a Startup Mindset to the Classroom

This experience spanned seven years, involving students from the information technology course at a higher education institution in southern Brazil. As a

Table 17.1 Main structure of the experience

Class	Objective	Main activities
01	Understanding	Explanation of the dynamics, discussion on technical, human, and managerial skills
02	Exploring	Examining how technology can address various problems, generating ideas
03	Investigating	Identifying and analyzing similar projects to establish concrete differences
04	Defining	Engaging in thoughtful decision-making and defining the MVP
05	Planning	Creating a detailed plan that highlights the most important aspects of the project
06–11	Developing	Cycles of assigning tasks, implementing processes, reviewing tasks, and team feedback
12	Validating	Preliminary presentation of the project's progress and review by a guest professor
13	Analyzing	Perceptions of the presentation, feedback, and adjustments for the next stage
14–18	Developing	Cycles of assigning tasks, implementing processes, reviewing tasks, and team feedback
19	Presenting	Final showcase of projects with feedback from an external professional guest
20	Reflecting	Lessons learned, competencies developed, and new opportunities from the experience

mandatory final-year course, it aimed to simulate a software development project, building on students' prior knowledge and skills. Conducted in weekly meetings over 20 classes in one academic semester (72 hours), each session had defined objectives and a list of activities [6] (Table 17.1).

All activities were designed to align with contemporary practices in the software development industry, integrating best practices to offer experiences that reflect the scenarios students are likely to encounter in the job market. The experience's structure emphasized Project-Based Learning, allowing significant student autonomy, iterative development and review, and pitch-format presentations that mirrored typical startup scenarios. Unlike other disciplines that commonly use tests and exams for assessment, students in this experience were evaluated formatively with different instruments and artifacts.

Team Building

The initial action involves understanding the student's profile by collecting information about their preliminary experiences and interests in information technology. These details are gathered through a questionnaire containing key questions, which students must individually complete on the first day of class. Additionally, each

Fig. 17.3 T-shaped people

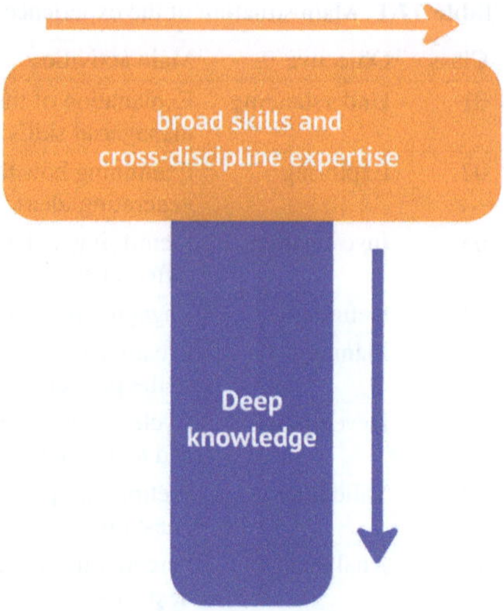

student is encouraged to develop a mapping of their knowledge and interests by creating a so-called T-Shaped Profile (Fig. 17.3).

This instrument is based on the T-shaped individuals concept from software engineering [13]. It combines deep, domain-specific expertise with broad cross-disciplinary skills. Students develop their profiles, with the vertical stroke of the "T" representing advanced skills and the horizontal stroke indicating general abilities and interests [3].

This visual tool helps identify each student's characteristics and their perception of competencies, aiding team formation. Typically, teams of four to five work on a project throughout the semester, but students cannot choose their teammates. This mirrors real-world situations where professionals rarely select their colleagues, allowing students to navigate diverse personalities and varying levels of expertise while fostering important interpersonal skills.

In this sense, with the collected data, it's possible to organize teams with members whose skills align with specific roles such as manager, analyst, developer, and tester. This approach ensures a diverse yet cohesive team focused on achieving the project's goals.

Brainstorming and Creative Process

In line with the PBL principle of giving students a voice and choice, they can select project themes, methodologies, and technologies. A brainstorming session encourages team members to propose innovative project ideas with practical market applications, such as new technologies or initiatives addressing social issues. An *Impact/Effort Matrix* (Fig. 17.4) is then used to evaluate the feasibility of these ideas and choose one for implementation over the semester.

Fig. 17.4 Impact/Effort Matrix

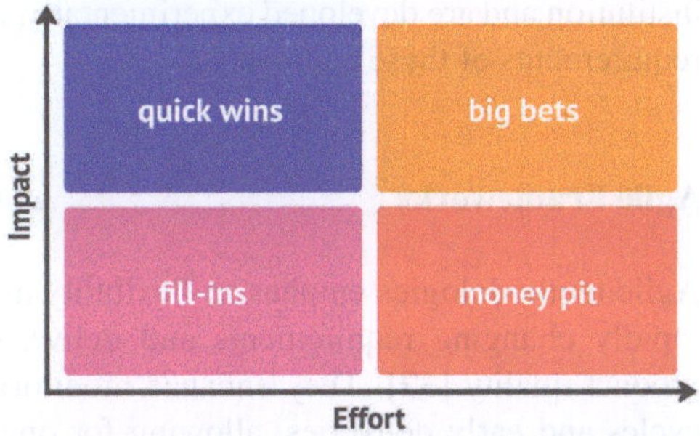

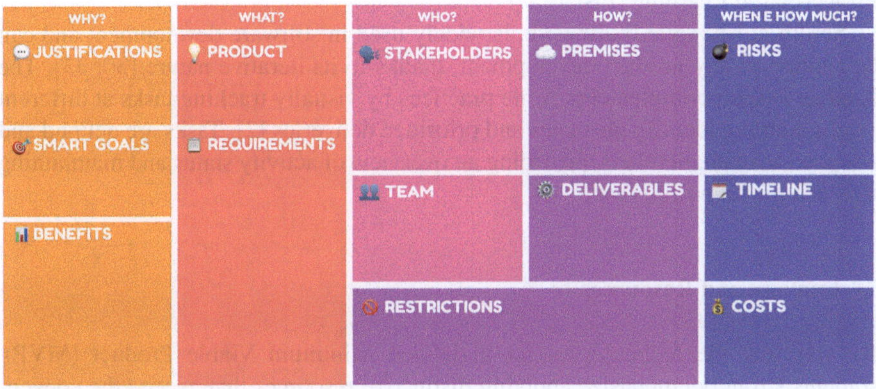

Fig. 17.5 Project Model Canvas

Analytical Thinking

After selecting the project idea, the team creates a Project Model Canvas (PMC), a visual tool designed to outline key aspects of the project, including justifications, objectives, benefits, risks, and processes [25]. Figure 17.5 illustrates the PMC structure.

A comparative table of related projects is also required to evaluate other projects in the same niche and clearly establish the differences between them and those available on the market. In didactic terms, this step helps in critically analyzing the project idea and considering the state of the art in a given area.

Students are introduced to the concept of a Minimum Viable Product (MVP), which is defined as the simplest version of a product that can be released to validate a set of hypotheses about a business idea or technical-related questions [28, 31]. Consequently, the MVP is a prototype that requires less effort and development time, intended primarily to initiate the learning process rather than fully complete the product.

Techniques like brainstorming and low-fidelity and high-fidelity prototyping [35] and tools including the Business Model Canvas and Empathy Map [16] are also explored. Frequently, these projects focus on real clients external to the educational institution and are developed experimentally, aligned with the recommendations and requirements of these end-users

Agile Frameworks

Agile methodologies emphasize flexibility and adaptability, making them ideal for rapidly changing requirements and delivering results quickly while prioritizing product quality [32]. They enhance monitoring and control through defined work cycles and early deliveries, allowing for ongoing project evaluation, especially in Project-based Learning (PBL).

Scrum, a key agile framework, is widely used in software development and can be applied to any product development, thanks to its iterative nature [30, 33]. The Kanban system complements Agile practices by visually tracking tasks at different stages, helping identify obstacles and prioritize deliveries [2]. Tasks are defined and assigned to team members, providing an overview of activity status and maintaining a record for future reference.

Technology and Resources

By selecting the technologies for a defined Minimum Viable Product (MVP), students strongly emphasize applying distinctive resources that exceed the conventional curriculum offered in the undergraduate course, stand out in their functionality and user experience, and meet initial market demand, reflecting an understanding of contemporary industry practices and customer needs. This approach enhances students' technical capabilities and supports their academic portfolios, positioning them for rapid industry innovations and emerging market dynamics.

Showcases and Feedback

Today's IT professionals need strong technical and communication skills. The curriculum features two key presentations: one mid-semester, where teams present their project's conception, choices, methodology, and progress, receiving feedback from a teacher, and a final presentation to showcase outcomes and the significance of development, with an external evaluator providing insights. At the end of the course, teams receive a report highlighting their strengths and areas for improvement, and students complete an online self-assessment to reflect on their performance and learning outcomes.

17.4.2 *Case 2: Providing Business Vision in an Extracurricular Experience*

Since 2013, a Mobile Development Program has cultivated emerging industry talent. This extracurricular program at an educational institution in southern Brazil is a 2-year course designed for undergraduate and postgraduate students, aiming to equip participants with diverse technical and socio-emotional skills essential for mobile development. Every 2 years, a cohort of 50 students is selected to participate in this initiative. Sessions are held from Monday to Friday, each lasting four hours a day, with students receiving scholarships and devices to support their development efforts [5, 7].

Integrated Methodologies

The program employs an *Agile Mobile Application Development* approach (Fig. 17.6) by integrating CBL, Scrum, and Lean Startup principles [27, 28]. Scrum enhances CBL by organizing work into short delivery cycles, called sprints, which allow students to collaborate in teams with clear roles and deliver regular software increments. This approach mirrors agile team dynamics in the industry, teaching continuous improvement, efficient task management, and adaptability to changes. The Lean Startup method focuses on value and efficiency, emphasizing the validation of ideas through Minimum Viable Products (MVP) and testing with real users.

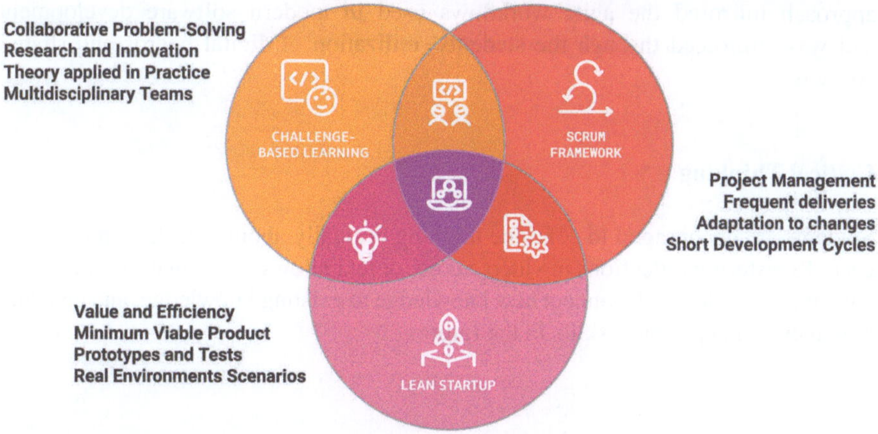

Fig. 17.6 Agile Mobile Application Development

Multidisciplinary Experience

Participants receive specialized training tailored to mobile development, gaining in-depth knowledge of development methodologies, design, user experience, and entrepreneurship. Although a background in technology is not a prerequisite, most applicants typically come from this field. The selection process assesses prior technical knowledge in programming logic, object-oriented concepts, and behavioral skills that align with the program's experiential and collaborative focus.

Macro Challenges

During the final six months of the program, students are required to develop a comprehensive application that addresses a recognized challenge. This project is to be executed in self-defined teams, ideally consisting of three to seven members. This experience allows students to apply the skills they have acquired in previous months and enhances their collaboration in projects.

Agile Workflow

The program incorporates Scrum practices, including daily standups, sprint planning, reviews, and retrospectives. These ceremonies created a consistent rhythm of continuous improvement, empowering students to form self-organizing teams. Daily checkpoints promoted short-cycle accountability, while sprint retrospectives encouraged metacognitive awareness of both the process and the outcomes. This approach mirrored the agile workflows used in modern software development and was reinforced through the students' utilization of digital boards and shared artifacts.

Critical Thinking

Students are encouraged to continue thinking critically about their learning experience. Registering reflections in video, audio, or text allows individuals to internalize what they have learned, connect new knowledge to existing knowledge, and consider how they can apply their skills in the future.

Comparison Between the Two Cases

Aspect	Case 1: classroom startup	Case 2: extracurricular experience
Pedagogical intent	Experience software and business development through a long-term project, adopting PBL and CBL methodologies to strengthen both technical and socio-emotional skills within the mandatory curriculum	Develop advanced business and mobile competencies by integrating CBL, Scrum, and Lean Startup in an extracurricular program focused on creating real products and incubating startups
Active methods	PBL and CBL, with emphasis on MVP development, Kanban, and Scrum, are adapted to the classroom context. Development of software and presentation to an external audience	CBL enhanced by Scrum rituals (daily standups, sprints, retrospectives) and Lean Startup, emphasizing continuous MVP validation in a real-market environment
Target audience	Final-year undergraduate IT students in the required course, working in teams of 4–5 formed by the instructor based on complementary criteria	Undergraduate and graduate students from any field (selected volunteers), in teams of 3–7, with intensive practical application and mentoring
Duration	One academic semester (72 h), over 20 weekly sessions of 3–4 h each	Two-year program, with in-person sessions Monday–Friday (4 h/day)
Cohorts	1 to 3 classes per semester, more than 500 participants in 7 years	Cohorts of 50 students every 2 years (over 300 participants between 2013 and 2024)
Assessment	Intermediate and final presentations with internal and external evaluators; reports and self-assessment via the LMS	Continuous delivery of software increments (sprints), real-user feedback, usage metrics from marketplaces, and market mentoring
Scale and resources	Integrated into the regular curriculum, using classrooms and labs, initial surveys, and institutional task-management tools	Scholarship-funded program providing mobile devices, labs, and advanced development platforms through industry partnerships

17.5 Key Findings

This section presents the main findings from our case studies. Additionally, it will highlight the outcomes and share some students' perspectives on how these experiences have helped them develop their technical, business, and soft skills.

17.5.1 Case 1: Outcomes from the Classroom Experience

Over 7 years, more than 500 students attended the course, resulting in 96 projects: 53 Web platforms, 21 Web applications, 4 desktop Arduino projects, 14 mobile applications, and 4 digital games. Nineteen projects were converted into course completion projects, and six evolved into further developed products.

Throughout the intervention, students demonstrated remarkable growth in their technical skills. The freedom to choose technologies and tools, and the necessity to articulate and justify those selections under the mentorship of a professor, cultivated analytical reasoning and enhanced problem-solving abilities.

Simultaneously, participants improved their interpersonal skills, gained organizational insight, and developed proper communication through structured teamwork exercises. Educators embraced the role of facilitators, fostering an engaging environment where decentralized task allocation empowered every member to participate actively in project management and decision-making processes.

Teams comprise members with varying experiences and knowledge to encourage the exchange of experiences among participants. Those with advanced programming knowledge often propose solutions, while others focusing on analysis contribute to the product's vision. Additionally, members with strong behavioral and management skills present strategies that benefit the team.

The introduction of task-management methods provided a more transparent structure and improved workflow, as communication breakdowns were among the central problems, and ambiguity surrounding individual roles and responsibilities within teams was also addressed.

Some challenges emerged as recurring issues throughout the projects. In some cases, unresolved interpersonal conflicts created tension among team members, while differing levels of commitment led to instabilities in motivation and productivity. These dynamics often drained the team's enthusiasm and effectiveness. This situation underscored the necessity for the professor's timely interventions, which guided and supported the team in overcoming these obstacles.

Feedback from students offered valuable insights about their experience. One student defined the discipline as an integrator of previously learned content and a space for exploring new knowledge: "I had the opportunity to remember some things and use the artifacts that I previously learned to build, reinforcing knowledge and evolving in the creation and development of projects."

Another perspective is that this discipline can be highly beneficial for individuals who have not yet entered the job market. One student remarked, "Even though I do not work directly in the field, this experience has brought me much closer to a real company scenario."

The technical learning and the development of management skills also emerge: "I gained a deeper understanding of new technologies and acquired a more architectural and managerial perspective on a project." Another student stated the importance of a cohesive team, saying, "One person out of sync can affect an entire project, which motivated me to be even more committed to my work."

Summary Results

- Simulation of real company scenarios actively integrating prior learning.
- More than 500 participants and 96 projects developed over 7 years.
- Mixed-experience teams for knowledge exchange and specialized contributions.
- Students learn to select and justify their choice of technologies under mentorship.
- Task management increases workflow transparency and clarifies individual roles.
- Interpersonal skills and communication improvement via teamwork exercises.
- Educators as facilitators, empowering students via decentralized task allocation.

17.5.2 Case 2: Outcomes from the Extracurricular Experience

Between 2013 and 2024, more than 300 students participated in the program, and over 200 mobile applications were published on the Apple App Store. Student engagement was notably high, with increased motivation closely tied to the practical relevance of the challenges presented. This strategy successfully bridges theoretical knowledge with practical application, creating a more invested learning environment centered on problem-solving and innovation.

The deliverables produced by the teams exhibited an elevated degree of technical sophistication, marked by extensive functionalities and streamlined development cycles. A critical component of the *Agile Mobile Development Process* is the requirement to submit to app marketplaces. This adds another level of quality assurance before they are accessed by users, which is particularly relevant for iOS applications, as one must adhere to a set of guidelines established by the App Store [8]. Additionally, this practice provides access to honest feedback on usage, which can be used to iteratively refine their projects by tracking app adoption, users' behaviors, and metrics offered by distribution platforms.

By learning agile methodologies and cross-functional team dynamics, students improved their ability to adapt to changing requirements based on feedback, which proved essential for success in fast-paced, tech-driven industries. Working in multidisciplinary teams simulating real-world conditions can make their transition to the industry easier.

Encouraging a culture of continuous improvement aligns with industry standards by utilizing widely recognized tools, including version control systems and task management tools. Feedback indicated a rise in confidence regarding the application of skills in a professional setting and an improvement in teamwork within interdisciplinary groups. This method enables students to comprehend the entire development cycle, from concept to product launch, thereby equipping them for environments that prioritize innovation.

Another notable outcome of the program is the emergence of startups from the experiences of student teams. A total of 29 startups were founded by graduates, often as direct continuations of the apps initially developed during the Macro Challenge. This highlights the effectiveness of the integrated pedagogical approach in aligning academic learning with industry needs, enhancing skills for innovation environments.

Summary Results

- Mobile development program combining CBL, Scrum, and Lean Startup.
- Over 300 students published more than 200 apps on the Apple App Store.
- Real-world cases promote student engagement and practical learning.
- Iterative app publishing enforced quality control and provided user feedback.
- Cross-functional teams prepare for complex workplace environments.
- Continuous improvement utilizing industry tools enhances collaboration skills.
- About 30 teams transformed their MVP into startups following the program.

17.6 Recommendations

After presenting the foundations, methodology, and outcomes of our case studies, we summarize the primary guidance for integrating active learning methodologies, agile frameworks, and innovation tools to enhance student engagement and foster an entrepreneurial mindset.

17.6.1 Educators and Instructors

For educators, instructors, and anyone responsible for conducting startup business development in educational contexts, whether inside or outside the classroom, we recommend paying special attention to the following aspects:

(a) Adopt active learning methodologies to engage students and contribute to developing technical and socio-emotional skills.
(b) Integrate Agile and Lean to bring the entrepreneurial mindset closer.
(c) Team diversity enhances knowledge sharing, but unresolved conflicts and a lack of commitment can hinder project success. It's necessary to incorporate team-building practices and conflict-resolution protocols.
(d) Provide structured and visual tools to guide the project's decision-making process and critical thinking.
(e) Self-assessment and structured reflection exercises encouraged students to critically analyze their learning processes and the effectiveness of their projects.
(f) To enforce quality standards and gather authentic user feedback, promote public access to projects.
(g) Create scenarios that allow students to understand how these experiences can impact their skills and abilities, ultimately enhancing their career opportunities.

17.6.2 Academic Administrators and Learning Program Managers

For administrators of academic institutions and managers of learning programs offering startup business development opportunities, we recommend focusing on the following aspects:

(a) The role of institutions in supporting these experiences is essential to foster a culture of innovation and entrepreneurship.
(b) Startup education can be effectively integrated into existing curricula without compromising academic standards, but it requires careful planning.
(c) Scale these initiatives across different contexts demands embedding ethical and societal impact for validating and refining this pedagogical approach.
(d) Create rubrics to assess both technical outputs and developed competencies, enabling instructors to provide targeted guidance during the project life cycle.
(e) Provide dynamic physical spaces that inspire creativity and encourage collaboration, equipped with flexible and adaptable resources.
(f) Offer guidance on transforming Minimum Viable Products into startups, through incubator programs, pitch workshops, and alumni networks.

17.7 Conclusion

Integrating startup projects as a fundamental teaching strategy in academic settings presents innovative opportunities to cultivate future professionals capable of addressing complex challenges and fostering positive change.

Through years of implementation, our experiences have shown that students not only acquire robust technical competencies but also develop vital socio-emotional skills, including teamwork, self-management, and adaptive problem-solving. Moreover, the iterative cycles of ideation, prototyping, and public showcases encourage a culture of continuous feedback and reflection, equipping learners with an entrepreneurial mindset.

One of the challenges in these experiences was our focus primarily on qualitative feedback, which left us with limited standardized metrics to formally compare outcomes against traditional lecture-based methods or other active-learning cohorts. Additionally, we acknowledge that a potential selection bias exists, as both cases involve self-enrolled students in required courses or participants selected based on their inherent motivation, which may skew the results toward individuals who are intrinsically motivated.

We consider that, while influenced by the Brazilian societal context, these approaches can be adapted or scaled to fit various cultural and institutional environments. We recommend starting by aligning the active-learning cycle with existing credit structures or exploring the possibility of offering extracurricular activities. Low-tech adaptations of Agile methods, such as physical boards and paper sticky notes, can be used in conjunction with free virtual tools. In other contexts, enhancements can be achieved through varied spaces and paid resources. Additionally, leveraging partnerships with local industries for mentorship and validation of the MVP can be beneficial. It is also essential to consider cultural norms. For instance, in collectivist cultures, emphasis is placed on group work and peer feedback practices, whereas in individualistic settings, greater flexibility is offered in team formation and individualized project pathways.

These experiences can also be applied in non-IT contexts. In addition to Active Learning Methodologies that are versatile across various fields, other components, such as the concept of MVP, iterative development of business ideas, and a focus on real-world issues, can be adapted to diverse areas of knowledge, including management, health sciences, communication, and social sciences.

Future research could investigate other experiential learning opportunities, such as hackathons, mentoring programs, and industry partnerships, to enhance the learning and development ecosystem. These initiatives enable students to collaborate with specialists, thereby improving their skills and expanding their professional networks. Additionally, there are opportunities to adopt learning analytics for early intervention, evaluate the long-term impacts of these experiences on students' careers, and establish faculty learning communities to sustain and amplify the transformative potential of startup education.

Advancing these strategies toward Education 4.0 promises to shape a generation of professionals who are technically proficient, resilient, socially aware, and poised to drive innovation in an increasingly dynamic global landscape.

Acknowledgments This study was partially supported by the Ministry of Science, Technology, and Innovation from Brazil, with resources from Law No. 8.248, dated October 23, 1991, within the scope of PPI-SOFTEX, coordinated by Softex.

References

1. Almahry, F., Sarea, A., Hamdan, A.: A review paper on entrepreneurship education and entrepreneurs' skills. J. Entrep. Educ. **21**, 1–7 (2018)
2. Anderson, D.J., Carmichael, A.: Essential Kanban. Blue Hole Press, Washington D.C. (2016)
3. Barile, S., Saviano, M.L., Simone, C.: Service economy, knowledge, and the need for t-shaped innovators. World Wide Web J. **18**(4), 1177–1197 (2014). https://doi.org/10.1007/s11280-014-0305-1
4. Bender, W.N.: Project-Based Learning: Differentiating Instruction for the 21st Century. Corwin, Newbury Park (2012)
5. Chanin, R., Sales, A., Santos, A., Pompermaier, L., Prikladnicki, R.: A collaborative approach to teaching software startups: Findings from a study using challenge based learning. In: Proceedings of the 11th International Workshop on Cooperative and Human Aspects of Software Engineering, pp. 9–12. Association for Computing Machinery (2018). https://doi.org/10.1145/3195836.3195844
6. de Campos, A., Machado, G.B., Rados, G.J.V., Todesco, J.L.: Aprendizagem baseada em projetos: uma experiência em sala de aula para compartilhamento e criação do conhecimento no processo de desenvolvimento de projetos de software. Int. J. Innov. Educ. Res. **9**, 17–35 (2016). https://doi.org/10.24936/2177-4986.v9n2.2016.405
7. Detoni, M., Sales, A., Chanin, R., Villwock, L.H., Santos, A.R.: Using challenge based learning to create an engaging classroom environment to teach software startups. In: Proceedings of the XXXIII Brazilian Symposium on Software Engineering, pp. 547–552. Association for Computing Machinery (2019). https://doi.org/10.1145/3350768.3353821
8. Developer, A.: App store review guidelines (2024). https://developer.apple.com/app-store/review/guidelines/
9. Doolittle, P., Wojdak, K., Walters, A.: Defining active learning: a restricted systemic review. Teach. Learn. Inq. **11** (2023). https://doi.org/10.20343/teachlearninqu.11.25
10. Elhussein, G., Leopold, T., Silva, A., Zahidi, S.: Defining Education 4.0: A Taxonomy for the Future of Learning (2023)
11. Fagerholm, F., Hellas, A., Luukkainen, M., Kyllönen, K., Yaman, S., Mäenpää, H.: Designing and implementing an environment for software start-up education: patterns and anti-patterns. J. Syst. Softw. **146**, 1–13 (2018). https://doi.org/10.1016/j.jss.2018.08.060
12. González-Pérez, L., Ramírez-Montoya, M.: Components of education 4.0 in 21st century skills frameworks: systematic review. J. Sustainab. **14**(3), 1493 (2022). https://doi.org/10.3390/su14031493
13. Hansen, M., von Oetinger, B.: Introducing t-shaped managers: knowledge management's next generation. Harvard Bus. Rev. **79**, 106–116 (2001)
14. Jimarkon, P., Shahverdi, M., Dikilitaş, K., Husebø, D.: Dimensions of multidisciplinary engagement beyond the classroom in challenge-based learning. In: Annual Conference of The European Society for Engineering Education. Uni. Politècnica de Catalunya (2022). https://doi.org/10.5821/conference-9788412322262.1318

15. Larmer, J., Mergendoller, J. R., Boss, S.: Setting the Standard for Project Based Learning: A Proven Approach to Rigorous Classroom Instruction. Association for Supervision & Curriculum Development, Arlington (2015)
16. Leal, G.L., Prikladnicki, R., Ebert, C., Balancieri, R., Pompermaier, L.: Practices and tools for software start-ups. IEEE Softw. **37**(1), 72–77 (2020). https://doi.org/10.1109/MS.2019.2946783
17. Lopera, H.A.C., Gutierrez-Velásquez, E., Ballesteros, N.: Bridging the gap between theory and active learning: a case study of project-based learning in introduction to materials science and engineering. IEEE Revista Iberoamericana de Tecnologias del Aprendizaje **17**, 160–169 (2022). https://doi.org/10.1109/rita.2022.3166862
18. Mattar, J.: Metodologias ativas: para a educação presencial, blended e a distância. Artesanato Educacional, São Paulo (2017)
19. Mendis, T.: Corporate index: bridging the academic–practitioner gap. J. Appl. Res. Higher Educ. **16**, 2091–2107 (2024). https://doi.org/10.1108/JARHE-08-2023-0357
20. Mukul, E., Büyüközkan, G.: Digital transformation in education: A systematic review of education 4.0. Technol. Forecast. Soc. Change **194**, 122664 (2023). https://doi.org/10.1016/j.techfore.2023.122664
21. Nascimento, N., Santos, A.R., Sales, A., Chanin, R.: An investigation of influencing factors when teaching on active learning environments. In: Proceedings of the XXXIII Brazilian Symposium on Software Engineering,SBES 2019, Salvador, September 23–27, 2019, pp. 517–522. ACM (2019). https://dl.acm.org/doi/10.1145/3350768.3353819
22. Nichols, M.H., Cator, K.: Challenge-Based Learning - White Paper (2008)
23. O'Brien, E., Hamburg, I.: A critical review of learning approaches for entrepreneurship education in a contemporary society. Eur. J. Educ. **54**, 525–537 (2019). https://doi.org/10.1111/ejed.12369
24. O'Mahony, T., Vye, N., Bransford, J., Sanders, E., Stevens, R., Stephens, R., Richey, M., Lin, K., Soleiman, M.: A comparison of lecture-based and challenge-based learning in a workplace setting: Course designs, patterns of interactivity, and learning outcomes. J. Learn. Sci. **21**(1), 182–206 (2012). https://doi.org/10.1080/10508406.2011.611775
25. Ozório, F.J.D.G., Cavalcante, P., Pitombeira, A.L.F., de Lima Junior, G.V., de Almeida, S.M.N., Almeida, E.R., da Costa Souza, A.M., Paim, I.D.M.: Project model canvas' contributions to the project-based learning method. Int. J. Innov. Educ. Res. **9**, (2021). https://scholarsjournal.net/index.php/ijier/article/view/2916
26. Rane, N.L., Choudhary, S.P., Rane, J.: Education 4.0 and 5.0: Integrating artificial intelligence (ai) for personalized and adaptive learning. Soc. Sci. Res. Netw. Electron. J. (2023). https://doi.org/10.2139/ssrn.4638365
27. Reis, L.P., Fernandes, J.M., Araujo, M., Beaulieu, M.: Lean startup practices: operationalizing the technological business planning process in an academic environment. In: European Conference on Innovation and Entrepreneurship (2022). https://doi.org/10.34190/ecie.17.1.544
28. Ries, E.: The Lean Startup: How Constant Innovation Creates Radically Successful Businesses. Crown Business, Broadway (2011)
29. Santoso, R.T.P.B., Priyanto, S.H., Junaedi, I.W.R., Santoso, D.S.S., Sunaryanto, L.T.: Project-based entrepreneurial learning (pbel): a blended model for startup creations at higher education institutions. J. Innov. Entrep. **12**(18) (2023). https://doi.org/10.1186/s13731-023-00276-1
30. Schwaber, K.: Scrum development process. In: Business Object Design and Implementation, pp. 117–134. Springer, London (1997)
31. Stevenson, R., Burnell, D., Fisher, G.: The minimum viable product (MVP): theory and practice. J. Manag. **50**(8) (2024), https://doi.org/10.1177/01492063241227154
32. Sutherland, J., Jacobson, I., Brian: Scrum essentials cards. Queue **18**, 83–106 (2020). https://doi.org/10.1145/3411757.3418775
33. Wallace, C., Mohan, S., Troy, D., Hoffman, M.E.: Scrum across the CS/SE curricula: a retrospective. In: Technical Symposium on Computer Science Education. Association for Computing Machinery, New York (2012). https://doi.org/10.1145/2157136.2157142

34. Wang, Y.: Research on the matching issue between higher education and employment demand. Int. J. New Develop. Educ. **6**(5) (2024). https://doi.org/10.25236/IJNDE.2024.060532
35. You, X.: Applying design thinking for business model innovation. J. Innov. Entrep. **11** (2022). https://doi.org/10.1186/s13731-022-00251-2

MIX
Papier aus verantwortungsvollen Quellen
Paper from responsible sources
FSC® C105338

If you have any concerns about our products,
you can contact us on
ProductSafety@springernature.com

In case Publisher is established outside the EU,
the EU authorized representative is:
Springer Nature Customer Service Center GmbH
Europaplatz 3, 69115 Heidelberg, Germany

Printed by Libri Plureos GmbH
in Hamburg, Germany